WOMAN AND SOCIETY IN THE
SPANISH DRAMA OF THE GOLDEN AGE

A STUDY OF THE *MUJER VARONIL*

WOMAN AND SOCIETY IN THE SPANISH DRAMA OF THE GOLDEN AGE

A STUDY OF THE *MUJER VARONIL*

MELVEENA McKENDRICK

*Fellow, Tutor and Lecturer in
Spanish, Girton College, Cambridge*

CAMBRIDGE UNIVERSITY PRESS

Published by the Syndics of the Cambridge University Press
Bentley House, 200 Euston Road, London NW1 2DB
American Branch: 32 East 57th Street, New York, N.Y. 10022

© Cambridge University Press 1974

Library of Congress Catalogue Card Number: 73–82457

ISBN: 0 521 20294 9

First published 1974

Printed in Great Britain
by W & J Mackay Limited, Chatham

FOR
MY MOTHER AND FATHER

La mujer casada y honrada, la pierna
quebrada y en casa, y la doncella, pierna
y media.
La mujer cuando sola piensa, mal piensa.
                                    Traditional

Contents

Acknowledgements

During the period of research which went into the writing of this book, I had the great fortune to receive the scholarly guidance of Professor E. M. Wilson of Emmanuel College, Cambridge. To him I am immensely grateful. My thanks are due, too, to Mrs Helen Grant of Girton College, Cambridge, for her kindness and encouragement; to Girton College itself, which first with a Research Scholarship and then with a Research Fellowship gave me the opportunity to undertake and complete this work; to my husband, Neil McKendrick of Gonville and Caius College, Cambridge, who, approaching my theme with the objective eye of a historian, was able to make many invaluable suggestions, and to Professor R. O. Jones of Downing College, Cambridge, who with enormous kindness gave me painstaking help with the typescript in its final stages. My debt to Professor A. A. Parker of the University of Texas cannot be measured. It was he who first drew my attention to the *mujer varonil* theme and hinted at its richness and complexity. More important, he taught me to love and appreciate the literature of the Golden Age, and his personal and scholarly example remains for me an unfailing source of inspiration.

Preface

The phrase *mujer varonil* almost defies translation. Certainly there is no translation with exactly the nuance of meaning which I wish to convey. 'Masculine women' or 'manly women' have too strong a flavour of sexual deviation, and although the women dealt with here are extraordinary in that they are deviations from the norm, they are not deviants in the specialized meaning of the word. But for a very few exceptions they are not even of the ambiguous nature of the characters in Gautier's *Mademoiselle de Maupin*, although many are, of theatrical necessity, transvestites. *Mujer varonil* is a term of praise, not of abuse, in the Golden-Age drama.

Other possibilities, such as 'career woman', 'exceptional woman', 'spirited woman' or 'tomboy', are all equally open to objection. As a description and as a judgment both particular and general on women, the Spanish phrase is at once richer and more comprehensive in meaning than any single English translation, and it is therefore retained as the only adequate label. But if it cannot be translated, it can at least be explained. For by *mujer varonil* is meant here the woman who departs in any significant way from the feminine norm of the sixteenth and seventeenth centuries. She can take the form of the *mujer esquiva* who shuns love and marriage, the learned woman, the career woman, the female bandit, the female leader and warrior, the usurper of man's social role, the woman who wears masculine dress or the woman who indulges in masculine pursuits. The cloak of *varonilidad* covers a wide range of behaviour and intention – from the recurrent *bella cazadora* type, who was often little more than an appealing dramatic device, to the more detailed portraits of characters of the stature of Calderón's Semíramis – but each variant marks a noticeable deviation from the contemporary Spanish norm.

ix

From the 1570s onwards, this motif of the *mujer varonil* became increasingly prominent in Spanish drama; she became one of the theatre's most popular character types. It is all the more surprising that a comprehensive study of her has never appeared. Certain aspects have been investigated. P. W. Bomli, in her book *La Femme dans l'Espagne du Siècle d'Or*,[1] mentions the *mujer varonil*, but her short treatment is both superficial and inadequate. Barbara Matulka has a short essay on the feminist theme in the Spanish drama, but this is not so much an exploration of the theatre's feminist sympathies as a description of the way in which the medieval debate of the controversy of the sexes was used by the playwrights as dramatic material.[2] Carmen Bravo-Villasante, in her *La mujer vestida de hombre en el teatro español (siglos XVI–XVII)*,[3] examines the use of masculine disguise made by the heroines of the Spanish drama, but this was only a conventional dramatic device and in itself comparatively unimportant. Other critics have noted the Spanish dramatists' fondness for heroines in male clothing and discussed the historical reality of such portrayals. M. Romera-Navarro[4] and J. Homero Arjona[5] have both written informative and well-balanced articles on the subject. B. B. Ashcom has a short essay expressing rather different views and also examining the origins of the *mujer heroica-guerrera*.[6] Indeed the use of masculine disguise has been almost the exclusive topic for research in this field, and no one has realized that it is but one aspect of a wider theme. For the *mujer varonil* – the woman who is 'masculine' not only in her dress but also in her acts, her speech or even her whole attitude of mind – is undoubtedly the best means of establishing the nature of that feminism which has been attributed to nearly every seventeenth-century Spanish dramatist at some time. For

[1] The Hague, 1950.
[2] 'The Feminist Theme in the Drama of the *Siglo de Oro*', *Comparative Literature Series, Publications of the Institute of French Studies Inc.*, Columbia University; a paper read at the Modern Language Association meeting at St Louis, December 1933.
[3] Madrid, 1955.
[4] 'Las disfrazadas de varón en la comedia', *HR*, II (1934), 269–86.
[5] 'El disfraz varonil en Lope de Vega', *BHi*, XXXIX (1937), 120–45.
[6] 'Concerning "La mujer en hábito de hombre" in the *comedia*', *HR*, XXVIII (1960), 43–62.

this reason, and because the possibilities for investigation of the use of *disfraz varonil* have been virtually exhausted, this book concentrates hardly at all on the *mujer vestida de hombre*, although she is referred to extensively.

Some explanation of my approach is necessary. In order to decide which dramatic heroines represented deviations from the norm, I have attempted to establish the norm itself. The stage appearances of female bandits waylaying travellers, or of heroines in masculine dress moving freely through society, usually in search of their lovers, have in the past led commentators to assert that such incidents were a regular feature of Spanish life. No such claims have been made for England on the basis of Julia, Rosalind, Portia and Viola; and there is no reason to suppose that Spanish plays with heroines of this kind should possess greater historical accuracy. The preliminary study of the social and historical background to the subject which forms the Introduction puts these assertions to the test. The study does not pretend to be exhaustive. Spanish social history is still in its infancy and much research will be needed before the gaps in our knowledge of sixteenth and seventeenth-century Spanish society are filled. The findings here are culled from a wide selection of printed sources – memoirs, letters, sermons, moral dissertations, contemporary travelogues, annals, Jesuit newsletters and legal codes, as well as contemporary imaginative literature and a host of secondary critical and historical sources. Much of the evidence was, of course, heavily duplicated; much was obviously too biased to use. One much-quoted account, Madame d'Aulnoy's *Relation du voyage d'Espagne* (1691), has to be almost entirely rejected. Entertaining as her comments are, they are often completely fictional.[1] Dr Bomli's sixty-two references to her show how seriously she has been taken as a source; they also give some indication of the limitations of Dr Bomli's book.

The feminine norm once established, the *mujeres varoniles* of the theatre themselves are considered. Although Lope popularized the *mujer varonil* type and although his influence in its development

[1] See R. Foulché-Delbosc, *Madame d'Aulnoy. Relation du voyage d'Espagne* (Paris, 1926). Also, El Duque de Maura and A. G. de Amezúa y Mayo, *Fantasías y Realidades del Viaje a Madrid de la Condesa d'Aulnoy* (Madrid, 1944).

is decisive, he did not invent it: the *mujer varonil* already existed
in many of her forms in the pre-Lope theatre. The pre-Lope drama
is thus discussed in chapter 2. Chapter 3 deals with Cervantes and
Lope's early contemporaries in Valencia, Tárrega, Aguilar and
Guillén de Castro. Since Cervantes' dramatic activities fall into
two periods – that immediately preceding the rise of Lope as Spain's
dramatic arbiter and that which coincided with the height of Lope's
career – he cannot be called a pre-Lopista. On the other hand,
although he eventually conceded victory to the *comedia nueva* and
allowed himself to be influenced by it, he was never a true follower
of Lope. He is therefore dealt with before Lope and his disciples,
partly for chronological and ideological reasons, and partly because this is where his views on women place him in the development of the feminist theme. Tárrega, Aguilar and Guillén de
Castro are also dealt with apart from the main body of the Golden-
Age theatre because, as Valencians, they fall outside the main stream
of development, and Tárrega and Aguilar, although writing at
the same time as Lope, produced most of the works that concern
me before 1600. Guillén de Castro is included in this chapter
because he was Valencian, and because his lack of interest in the
mujer varonil sets him apart from the school of Lope. This far, the
dramatists are dealt with chronologically and their plays examined
for precedents to the *mujer varonil* of the Golden-Age drama proper.
The need to trace the emergence and development of the *mujer
varonil* as a type made this necessary and the comparatively small
amount of relevant material made it possible. Because the number
of seventeenth-century dramatists and the relevant part of their
output are greater, making it impossible to discuss each dramatist
individually, the main body of the book is accordingly an analysis
of each category of *mujer varonil* taken in turn.

An attempt to trace and discuss any of the broad themes of the
Golden-Age drama involves certain difficulties. The sheer number
of plays concerned makes omission and oversight inevitable. One
hundred and twenty plays are dealt with under the various categories of the *mujer varonil*, and nearly thirty more are discussed in
the earlier chapters. Many more have been scoured for relevant
material. I hope that I have left out no play of any great significance

to my theme. The other problem is that of dating. In order to give some idea of the life-span of the type of the *mujer varonil*, I have given where possible the dates of composition. Failing this, I have given the dates of publication so that the plays may be placed within certain time-limits.

Abbreviations

Acad.   *Obras de Lope Félix de Vega Carpio*, ed. Real Academia
           Española (Madrid 1890–1913) 15 vols.
Acad.N.   *Obras de Lope Félix de Vega Carpio. Nueva Edición*, ed.
           Real Academia Española (Madrid 1916–30) 13 vols.
B.A.E.   Biblioteca de Autores Españoles.
BHi   *Bulletin Hispanique.*
BHS   *Bulletin of Hispanic Studies.*
BRAE   *Boletín de la Real Academia Española.*
C.C.   Clásicos Castellanos.
Esc.   *Comedias escogidas de los mejores ingenios de España*
           (Madrid 1652–1704) 48 vols.
FMLS   *Forum for Modern Language Studies.*
HR   *Hispanic Review.*
MLR   *Modern Language Review.*
N.B.A.E.   Nueva Biblioteca de Autores Españoles.
PMLA   *Publications of the Modern Language Association of
           America.*
RFE   *Revista de Filología Española.*
RFH   *Revista de Filología Hispánica.*
RHi   *Revue Hispanique.*

Abbreviations whose use is restricted to one chapter are explained
when they first occur.

Part I

Introduction

The position of women in Spain during the sixteenth and seventeenth centuries is not easy to ascertain. Modern historians and commentators – Altamira and Ballesteros in their Histories, Pfandl in his *El siglo de oro*, Valbuena Prat in his *La vida española en el siglo de oro* – rely heavily on information afforded by the literature of the time and tend to take as a faithful picture of reality the society which this literature portrays. The writings of the Golden Age provide a wealth of detail regarding contemporary customs, but imaginative literature is a dangerous basis for generalizations about real life. The wife-murder plays – a very small part of the dramatic output of seventeenth-century Spain – persuaded commentators until the twentieth century that domestic slaughter flourished there, but the testimony of contemporary observers shows that this was not true. History often makes nonsense of interpretations like this, based solely on literary evidence and divorced from historical reality.

The dangers of this kind of inference are obvious. The folly of relying upon Dickens alone for an accurate picture of Victorian society, or on Wordsworth for society's reaction to the arrival of industry, has damned much of the critical work on nineteenth-century English literature in the eyes of historians. In the same way, the view that the amorality of Restoration drama was a reflection of a high bastardy rate in English society reveals the danger of arguments based on historical causality which have neglected to verify the existence of the causes. Such views are now properly regarded as naïve, unhistorical, or even untrue. In reaction some have gone so far as to argue that literature is 'systematically deceptive'.[1] It is certainly arguable that within the literary hierarchy of historical reliability, 'high literature', that is the imaginative writings of major writers, is the least reliable of all.

[1] See Peter Laslett, *The World We Have Lost* (London, 1965), p. 82.

But to argue that the general preoccupations of contemporary dramatists have nothing to tell the historian of the society for which they wrote would be absurd. They may tell us something about a very restricted group, like the Court or the aristocracy, or about a theoretical intellectual controversy which barely touched society itself; they may be written in sharp reaction to the prevailing norm and therefore seem to offer us the opposite of the truth. But if the preoccupations are general they cannot be without historical interest; checked against a large enough literary sample they can tell us a great deal.

The problem is that instead of gathering the insights and rejecting the distortions offered by the Spanish theatre of the seventeenth century, too many commentators have simply swallowed the lot and regurgitated it as an accurate picture of the age. The 'mirror of society' found by the naïve and uncritical in the work of Lope, Tirso and Calderón will often be discovered to be a distorting mirror. The compensatory and contemplative elements in literature cannot be overlooked. Omissions may be as important as what is included. And omissions, distortions and exaggerations are commonplace in the drama of the Golden Age. The absence of the mother figure shows how the theatre distorted her role in real life. The information given by contemporary literature and its commentators can be accepted implicitly only when corroborated by documentary information from other sources.

While literary evidence must be approached with care if we are to establish the social *reality* of woman's life in any previous age, it is our most important source of information with regard to *attitudes towards* the concept of woman. And while these attitudes are often highly personal, they equally often reflect general trends which, however stylized, always have some psychological truth. For instance it is impossible to overlook the preoccupation with woman's role in society and marriage in the English drama of the 1890s. *Lady Windermers's Fan* in 1892, *A Woman of No Importance* and *The Second Mrs Tanqueray* in 1893, *The Case of Rebellious Susan* and *The Masqueraders* in 1894, *The Notorious Mrs Ebbsmith* and *The Benefit of a Doubt* in 1895, provide ample evidence. Many of these plays merely used the 'marriage question' to exploit 'that dullest of stock dramatic subjects, adultery'.[1] Some might express advanced ideas, some sympathy might be shown for female aspirations, but their conclusions were complacent and conservative: 'sin was punished, marriage was preserved, and the double standard was treated as a natural law'.[2] Nevertheless the plays are evidence of fixed attitudes being challenged, of contemporary interest in new ideas about woman's status, even if those ideas were a long time in being implemented.

The ideas about woman's role in society discussed by the dramatists of the Golden Age were far from becoming reality in seventeenth-century Spain, but they are revealing about contemporary Spanish attitudes to women. For in sixteenth-century Spain, woman, not as a social but as a moral entity, was still a subject of solemn concern. The question whether or not woman was fundamentally evil, had arisen out of the conflict between traditional Christian views of Eve and the glorification of womanhood purveyed by the troubadours. By the end of the Middle Ages, this debate had become a fashionable literary exercise heavily weighted in woman's favour.[3]

In the sixteenth century, literary attitudes to woman acquired new vigour and followed new paths. The secular Neo-Platonists of the Renaissance adopted and adapted the medieval traditions of courtly love. They spiritualized it, gave it coherence, rationalized it to a certain degree and thus freed it of some of its frustration. At the very least they gave it the spiritual sanction of a complete philosophy. The idealized lady of the Middle Ages reappeared in a pastoral setting, often dressed as a shepherdess, in the poetry of Garcilaso and Herrera, and in the pastoral novels. At the centre of the novels of chivalry, which enjoyed such a vogue in the first half of the sixteenth century, there likewise stands the idolized damsel, the dispenser of grace who instils virtue and courage. In other words, the secular humanists of the Renaissance produced in the

[1] Preface to Mrs Warren's Profession (dated January 1902), in G. B. Shaw, Prefaces (London, 1934), 223.

[2] Samuel Hynes, The Edwardian Turn of Mind (Oxford, 1968), 175.

[3] See Jacob Ornstein, 'La misoginia y el profeminismo en la literatura castellana', RFH, III (1941), 219–32.

chivalresque and the pastoral a literature of idealism which exalted woman to greater and more unrealistic heights than before. Their religious counterparts were equally concerned with her, but in a different way. Krantz[1] and Américo Castro[2] both hold that Erasmus was largely responsible for the change in attitude in the sixteenth century – what Castro calls 'un movimiento en favor de la dignificación del la mujer'. Ricardo del Arco y Garay[3] even claims that in Spain, as elsewhere, Erasmian literature played a large part in the formation of a more human ideal of woman. This does not mean that women were now regarded as men's equals. The Erasmian reformers did not themselves create or propagate a new image of woman, and in many respects their basic premises are still those of the medieval moralists. But many more thinking people than hitherto realized that there was no justification for keeping women in ignorance and subjection. Hence female education and upbringing became a subject for debate and reform.

This was not a peculiarly Spanish phenomenon; concern was shown for the education of women in enlightened circles all over Europe. At the centre of the movement was a Spanish woman: Catherine of Aragon, first wife of Henry VIII of England. Her mother, Isabel la Católica, had made sure that Catherine and her sisters received an advanced and enlightened education under two eminent Italian humanists, Antonio and Alessandro Geraldini, and Catherine herself was considered by Erasmus and Sir Thomas More to be a miracle of female learning. At her request, Juan Luis Vives between 1524 and 1528 wrote his *De institutione feminae christianae* for her daughter Mary, and he dedicated it to Catherine. Richard Hyrde, tutor to Sir Thomas More's children, likewise dedicated his translation of Vives's work to his Queen. Hyrde stands up stoutly for women's education in this dedication,

and moche I merveiled as I often do of the unreasonable oversight of men which never cease to complayne of women's conditions. And yet

[1] 'Les problèmes de la vie et de l'éducation dans le théâtre de Molière' in *La Revue des Cours et Conférences* (1898–9), 692–3.

[2] 'Algunas observaciones acerca del concepto del honor en los siglos XVI y XVII', *RFE*, III (1916), 382–4.

[3] *La sociedad española en las obras dramáticas de Lope de Vega* (Madrid, 1941), 405b.

havying the education and order of them in their own handes not only do litel diligence to theache them and bring them up better but also purposely withdrawe them from lernynge by whiche they mighte have occasyons to wax better by themselfe.[1]

One of Hyrde's pupils, Margaret More, translated Erasmus's *Precatio dominica in septum portiones distributa* at the age of nineteen. Hyrde wrote an introduction for it (it appeared in 1524) which Foster Watson calls 'apparently the first reasoned claim of the Renascence period, written in English, for the higher education of women'.[2] Watson also pays tribute to Catherine and Luis Vives,

if you wish to pursue inquiry into orgins in the particular direction of the education of women in England, attention must revert to the earlier picturesque and pathetic Spanish Princess, Catherine of Aragon. The chief directing and consultative force behind Catherine of Aragon was undoubtedly her compatriot, Juan Luis Vives of Valencia.[3]

As well as the *De institutione feminae christianae*, Vives dedicated to the Queen his plan of studies for girls, prepared in 1523 for Princess Mary and called *De ratione studii puerilis*. To the Princess herself he dedicated his *Satellitum* or *Symbola* (1524), composed of two hundred and thirty-nine maxims directed towards the instillation of wisdom, learning and virtue.

Because of Catherine's interest in female education, Luis Vives was probably one of the first reformers to turn his attention to this subject. He held the traditional moralist view that 'todo el bien y mal que en el mundo se hace se puede sin yerro decir ser por causa de las mujeres'.[4] He upholds the superiority of the male and sees chastity as a virtue demanded of a woman but not expected of a man, insisting that woman's preoccupations should be her home and her reputation. He subjects the outward tokens of female frailty – cosmetics, veils and finery of dress – to the bitter criticism which later became so familiar in Spanish literature. As a good Erasmian, however, he believed in the humanist ideal of

[1] Fol. Aij. v. in the copy of the 2nd edition at Sidney Sussex College, Cambridge.
[2] *Vives and the Renascence Education of Women* (London, 1912), 14.
[3] *Ibid.* 1.
[4] Chap. I, *Primavera y Flor* ed. (Madrid, 1936), 19.

enlightened good and this theory perforce applied to women as well as to men. He states firmly that without a correct upbringing and sufficient knowledge virtue is impossible. The key word is 'sufficient', and Vives's conception of what is sufficient education for a woman is more limited than that of Erasmus. Since the education of women could not be a proper or advisable end in itself, a sufficiency of female education was that necessary for the instillation of virtue. Nobody looks for eloquence, great intelligence or administrative gifts in a woman, said Vives: the ability to read and write, to sew and spin and to cook plain, wholesome food was enough. He advocated, in fact, just sufficient education to enable women to distinguish between good and evil and to avoid temptation. For him, the cultured noblewoman was as reprehensible as the illiterate serving girl. All this did not, of course, square with the scholarly upbringing and real learning of his patron Catherine; doubtless they agreed that those women called to the high destiny of monarchy needed the benefits of education in a way the ordinary woman, even the ordinary noblewoman, did not.

Vives's influence on thought in his own country was less than one might expect. He spent most of his life abroad and his treatise on female education was not translated into Spanish until 1539 (by Juan Justiniano). The explanation for any increased tolerance towards female education in Spain lies rather in the influence of Erasmus. Erasmus had been won for the cause of female education by Sir Thomas More,[1] with possibly some extra encouragement from Queen Catherine, at whose request Erasmus wrote his *De matrimonio christiano*.[2] Once convinced, Erasmus fought strenuously in defence of the educated woman. From 1527 until 1535, his works enjoyed enormous popularity in Spain and numerous translations made them available to a wide public. The *Colloquia familiaria*, which present a fair picture of Erasmus's views on women, were not banned until 1551, when they appeared on the Index of Toledo.

[1] See W. H. Wood, *Desiderius Erasmus concerning the Aim and Method of Education* (Cambridge, 1904), 148–9.
[2] Erasmus's MS dedication to the Queen can be seen in the copy of *De matrimonio christiano* in the Library of Emmanuel College, Cambridge.

In the *Colloquia*, Erasmus speaks always within the context of marriage. In one respect this was a retrogressive step, ruling out as it did, and as the Reformation was soon to do, the one career – the Church – which had formerly allowed women to pursue their intellectual, devotional and administrative gifts, and which had allowed them, up to a point, hierarchical advancement comparable with that open to men in the same sphere. In *Proci et puellae* Erasmus denounces spinsterhood as monstrous and acclaims marriage as the natural state for woman – and, indeed, the most complimentary and flattering to her. In *Virgo abhorrens a nuptiis* and *Virgo poenitens* he inveighs against convent life. Within the context of marriage, however, Erasmus's views are remarkably liberal. Marriage itself, discussed in *Coniugium*, he saw as a partnership in which the obedience owed by the wife to the husband was balanced by the respect and protection owed by the husband to the wife, and in which fault was never limited to one side. In *Puerpera*, a discussion about the superiority of men is neatly resolved by the conclusion that woman is not by nature inferior to man but has merely been given a role in life which of necessity makes her subject to him. And in *Coniugium impar* Erasmus denounces forced marriages and recommends that women as well as men be allowed to follow their inclinations.

With regard to female education, Erasmus is unequivocal. In *Abbatis et eruditae*, he categorically states that education and *learning* are as desirable in a woman as in a man. And although there is naturally no suggestion that the education and learning should be directed towards a career, there are no carping restrictions as to what the education should consist of or where the learning should end. A woman's business is to run her household and instruct her children. For this she needs wisdom, and where is wisdom to be acquired if not from books? If a woman may learn French, it was illogical to deny her Latin and Greek. Erasmus's remarks point to a virtually unlimited secular home education for girls of the upper classes. He goes on to end his *Colloquia* with what is implicitly the most feminist discussion of all, *Senatulus*. Here, a group of women tired of the lack of regard men have for them, decide to form a council to defend their interests. Furthermore, they are revealed as

capable of self-organization and of rational argument, traditionally male qualities.

The evidence available indicates that as the century advanced
there was a considerable intensification and expansion of the
secular education allowed girls whose fathers could afford tutors
and books. That the impetus came from the teachings of Erasmus
seems almost certain. But influential as Erasmus's ideas were, they
naturally did not sweep away more conventional attitudes to
women, and churchmen and moralists still thundered from their
pulpits and their desks about female wickedness. No doubt
Erasmus's eventual fall from respectability in Spain added vehemence to their denunciation of the feminist views he stood for.
And even apparent champions of the opposite sex sometimes
turned out to be saboteurs: Juan de Espinosa, for example, who
after devoting three quarters of his *Diálogo en laude de las mujeres*[1]
to a theoretical defence of women illustrated by classical examples,
has to admit in the last part, where he gets down to practicalities,
that women are weak, easily led astray, and ultimately fit only for
their womanly duties.

It is interesting, therefore, that one of the most noble defences
of woman in sixteenth-century Spain was written by an orthodox
theologian, Fray Luis de León. *La perfecta casada*, written in 1583,
is remarkable in that for the first time a churchman joined the
ranks of poets and novelists in praising women; hitherto churchmen had been their most violent critics. For Fray Luis, however,
woman was not the idealized, unattainable creation of the imaginations of courtly lovers and Neo-Platonic theorists. She was a
real person with a valuable social function; a person presented in
terms of material and social reality. Up to this point, Spanish
literature had in general either idealized woman or grotesquely
misrepresented her, often to the point of caricature. The 'dios' of
the *cancioneros* and the sentimental novels is offset by the bawd and
the predatory *serrana*; the misogynists' 'female incarnation of evil'
is balanced by the superwomen of classical antiquity and church
history so lionized by the *profeministas*. Fray Luis did woman the
inestimable service of seeing her as she was and yet seeing merit

---

[1] Earliest extant edition is 1580.

in what she was. Her sphere is still restricted to the home, but she is endowed with a nobility and a dignity absent from Luis Vives's picture of woman as an inferior appendage to man. Woman, says Fray Luis, is physically and emotionally weaker than man but not inferior to him: indeed her weakness gives her a moral superiority over man, for since it is less easy for her to be good, goodness in her is superlative. Furthermore, unlike that of man, woman's goodness is creative because it is communicated to others, and the love she inspires in man should stem from a realization of her unique worth in everyday life. The whole tone of Fray Luis's appraisal is different from anything written in Spain before.

The realism of his attitude is significant. It heralded a general move at the end of the sixteenth century towards realism in the depiction of women. Lope's heroines, for all their extravagant features, are more often than not recognizable human beings, and the love intrigues in which they are involved depict passion in conflict with social and moral issues. Poetry continued to be written in the courtly love/pastoral tradition, but there was among poets a growing dissatisfaction with the expression of merely platonic relationships. Poetic love becomes more active and more sensual, a love conditioned by the realities of human nature. The change did not stop here. After centuries of emotional continuity in love literature, the move away from idealism towards realism almost immediately degenerated into cynicism. Within a comparatively short time, woman the object of servile adoration became for many the object of scorn, ridicule and bitter disillusion. And in seventeenth-century Spain, when moralist and creative literature became so often indistinguishable, poets and other writers surpassed churchmen in pouring upon woman a stream of invective never before equalled, even by the misogynists of the feminist debate. Her beauty was a lie, her virtue a sham, truth and trust were incomprehensible to her. The vilification, both in serious and burlesque writings, was as unrealistic[1] and often as stylized as

[1] It is perhaps significant that many of the *costumbrista* works of the time are remarkable for their lack of criticism of women. Liñán y Verdugo in his *Guía y avisos de forasteros que vienen a la corte* (1620) and Francisco Santos in his *Día y*

the idealization against which it was reacting. At certain moments it was as sincere, and as deeply felt. It reached its height in Quevedo, whose tormented obsession with women produced some of the finest love poetry of his age and occasionally views which would now qualify him for psychiatric care. His warning 'De la mujer, como de las otras coass, usa; pero no te fíes'[1] is, for Quevedo, only mildly cynical.

The theatre remained outside the new fashion. *Graciosos* made jokes at woman's expense and sometimes inveighed against their fashionable extravagances. But the jokes were mild and the criticisms standard. The theatre by its nature needed heroines, and heroines it usually got. And its anti-heroines answered the demands of plots and themes which were, if anything, feminist in implication. The dramatic portrayal of women was of course based on premises which, like those of Fray Luis de León's *La perfecta casada*, now seem less valid, but these apart, it is probably true to say that in the seventeenth century the dramatist succeeded the courtly lover, albeit in a different way, as the champion of women and the upholder of the feminist cause.

Woman's critics, covering every shade of opinion on the misogynist scale from mild mockery to extreme aversion, shared for the most part a common feminine ideal, which in many respects differed from the heroines created by seventeenth-century playwrights and admired from the safe distance of their seats by seventeenth-century audiences. The qualities they looked for in a woman differed little from those advocated by reformers of the previous century and by moralists for centuries before and after. Virtue, humility, modesty, tenderness, silence, diligence and prudence were still the most desirable attributes in a daughter and a wife. In *El passagero*, Suárez de Figueroa's Isidro with self-righteous nostalgia recalls:

noche de Madrid (1663) both voice the age-old complaints about women but nothing more. Verdugo's quarrel anyway is with the *mujer de mala vida* while Santos is sufficiently far-sighted to realize that when a wife goes astray the blame often lies with her husband.

[1] *La cuna y la sepultura. Obras completas de Don Francisco de Quevedo Villegas. Obras en prosa* (Madrid, 1941), 1093a.

Acuérdome, y no soy muy viejo, se solían criar muchachas, que cualquiera podía ser gloria de su patria y honor del mundo; cuerdas, temerosas, humildes, teniendo siempre al recato y mesura por guardas de su honestidad. Muchos frenos puso la naturaleza a las mujeres, entre quien el más principal fue la vergüenza.[1]

As for female education, seventeenth-century writers seem to have retreated from enlightened opinion in the sixteenth century. And here the theatre falls in line with literary opinion in general. Few would have denied woman basic instruction in reading and writing but few would have advocated much more. Had these men had their way, the unlimited intellectual horizons hinted at by Erasmus would have been denied woman. As it was, the brave, pathetic attempts of the Spanish court's bluestockings and *précieuses* were cruelly ridiculed – by Lope in *El desprecio agradecido*, by Tirso in *La celosa de sí misma* and by Calderón in *No hay burlas con el amor* and *¿Cuál es mayor perfección?*, as well as by Quevedo in *La culta latiniparla*. Quevedo professed admiration for the *mujeres varoniles* of antiquity who 'siempre fueron milagrosa aclamación de los siglos'[2] and as far as he was concerned, the fewer feminine qualities a woman possessed the better. Logically, he should have approved of woman's aspiring to a *masculine* level of learning. His attitude was strictly anti-intellectual, however, and in one of his *romances* he makes it clear that faced with a choice he would opt for the 'dumb blonde':

> Muy docta lujuria tiene,
> muy sabios pecados hace;
> gran cosa sería de ver
> cuando a Platón requebrare . . .
> ¿Qué gracia puede tener
> mujer con fondos en fraile
> que de sermones y chismes
> sus razonamientos hace?
> Quien deja lindas por necias
> y busca feas que hablen,
> por sabias coma las zorras
> por simples deje las aves . . .

[1] Alivio V (Madrid, 1913), 179.   [2] *Vida de Marco Bruto*, 729b–30a.

Que yo, para mi traer,
en tanto que argumentaren
los cultos con sus arpías
algo buscaré que palpe.[1]

In a letter to the Countess of Olivares, who was eager to marry him off, he stipulated,

La virtud, que sea de mujer casada, y no de ermitaño, ni de beata, ni religiosa: su coro y su oratorio ha de ser su obligación y su marido. Y si hubiese de ser entendida con resabios de catedrático, más la quiero necia.[2]

Amédée Mas pointed out that Quevedo did not much approve of *discreción* in woman and that he rarely separated the idea of *discreta* from that of *fea*.[3] For him the legitimate opposite of *necia* was not *discreta* but *entendida*, by which he meant natural wit. His ideal woman, in short, was far removed from Catherine of Aragon and the daughters of Sir Thomas More.

These were, in brief, the literary and moralist attitudes towards women, the personal and shared ideals of womanhood: but what were the realities of woman's life? The reality is more elusive, more complex than any combination of attitudes and ideals. Eileen Power succinctly stated the problem:

The position of women has been called the test point by which the civilization of a country or of an age may be judged, and although this is in many respects true, the test remains one which it is extraordinarily difficult to apply, because of the difficulty of determining what it is that constitutes the position of women. Their position in theory and law is one thing, their practical position in everyday life another. These react upon one another, but they never entirely coincide, and the true position of women at any particular moment is an insidious blend of both.[4]

[1] *Obras completas, Obras en verso* (Madrid, 1952), 345a.
[2] *Epistolario completo de D. Francisco de Quevedo Villegas,* ed. L. Astrana Marín, *Carta* CXXXVI (Madrid, 1946), 264.
[3] *La Caricature de la Femme, du Mariage et de l'Amour dans l'Oeuvre de Quevedo* (Paris, 1957), 76.
[4] 'The Position of Women', *Legacy of the Middle Ages* (Oxford, 1926), 401.

But while the law is not an entirely reliable guide, it gives the most solid foundation for an account of woman's position. The Spanish laws in force at the time were contained in the *Recopilación de las leyes destos reynos hecha por mandado de la Magestad Catholica Del Rey Don Philippe segundo nuestro Señor*, first printed in Alcalá de Henares in 1569 and usually called the *Nueva recopilación*. This compilation formed Spain's legal code until the publication of the *Novísima Recopilación* in 1803, and was, for the most part, an emended restatement of the legal codes already in existence. Where the new code differed from these, the new code prevailed, but in matters not touched upon by the *Nueva recopilación*, the relevant existing code held good.

The *Nueva recopilación* was quite firm about sexual offences. If a married woman was discovered in the act of adultery, the husband could dispose of the culprits as he wished; he could not, however, spare one without the other.[1] If the husband turned both over to the law and adultery was subsequently proven, the couple were handed back to him to be punished as he thought fit. He could even execute them himself in public if he so desired.[2] Similarly, a prospective husband, officially engaged to a woman over the age of twelve, had the right to kill her, and her lover, should he catch them *in flagrante delicto*.[3]

Whereas the legal code protected the husband, no provision was made for the *wife* who was a victim of adultery. Adultery, in other words, was a one-sided offence which only the wife could commit in law. She was not even allowed to counter her husband's accusation with a similar one against him.[4] A wronged

---

[1] *Nueva recopilación* [referred to hereafter as *N.R.*], Libro octavo, Título 20, Ley 1:

Que pone la pena de los adulteros

Si muger (*a*) casada ficiere adulterio, ella, i el adulterador ambos sean en poder de el marido, i faga (*b*) dellos lo que quisiere, i de quanto han, assi que no pueda matar (*c*) al uno, i dexar (*d*) al otro.

[2] *N.R.*, Libro octavo, Título 20, Leyes III and V. These laws were not merely a dead letter. Cf. 'Las leyes no mandan sino que se entregue y ponga en poder del marido, para que se haga della a su voluntad. El cual si quisiere matarla, usando oficio de verdugo puede hacerlo' – *Colloquios satíricos de A. de Torquemada*, no. V.

[3] *N.R.*, Libro octavo, Título 20, Ley III.

[4] *N.R.*, Libro octavo, Título 20, Ley III.

husband acquired both his wife's dowry and the possessions of her lover, provided he put them to death with the express permission of the law.[1] A wronged wife, however, had no redress against an adulterous husband although she could seek legal redress from the other woman concerned. This was one of the provisions laid down by the *Fuero juzgo* which were still in force.[2] Also still in force were those laws in the *Fuero juzgo* which referred to daughters. The father who discovered his daughter and her lover misbehaving under his own roof was entitled to kill both.[3]

The behaviour of widows did not escape the law. The *Fuero juzgo* had ruled that the widow who remarried within a year of her husband's death, or who committed adultery, forfeited half her possessions to the children of her first marriage or, if there were none, to her relations-in-law.[4] The *Nueva recopilación* reaffirmed the *Fuero juzgo*'s ruling in the case of adultery but granted widows the right to remarry whenever they wished.

If women were at a legal disadvantage with regard to adultery they were given some protection against violence. Rape was punishable by lashes and by servitude to the offended woman;[5] even the seduction of that traditional victim of the libertine master, the serving girl, could entail a lashing,[6] and nobody had the right to force any woman in his service to marry against her will or persuade her parents to do so.[7] Male behaviour was also restricted in another direction – husbands guilty of consenting to their wives' prostitution were publicly shamed and given ten years in the galleys for a first offence; the punishment for a second offence was one hundred lashes and the galleys for life.[8]

Outside the realm of sexual relations women were well protected by the law. The married woman, it is true, lacked individual rights to any large extent and almost invariably needed her husband's permission before taking action of any sort. She could accept, but not reject, any inheritance *ex testamento* and *ab intestato*

---

[1] *N.R.*, Libro octavo, Título 20, Ley v.
[2] *Fuero juzgo* [referred to hereafter as *F.J.*], Libro III, Título IV (IX).
[3] *F.J.*, Libro III, Título IV (v).   [4] *F.J.*, Libro III, Título II (I).
[5] *F.J.*, Libro III, Título IV (XIV).   [6] *F.J.*, Libro III, Título IV (XVI).
[7] *N.R.*, Libro quinto, Título I, Ley XI.
[8] *N.R.*, Libro octavo, Título XX, Ley IX.

without the permission of her husband;[1] she could not enter or break a contract; she could not go to court either to prosecute or to defend.[2] On the other hand, she had the right of appeal in these cases and a judge in a court of law could compel the husband to give his permission.[3] And the wife, unlike her husband, could not be held responsible for her partner's contracts or debts.[4] A married couple's wealth and possessions belonged equally to both, except for those proved to have belonged to one or the other before the marriage.[5] The proceeds of a couple's wealth likewise belonged equally to both even when one owned more of the capital than the other.[6] The *Nueva recopilación* in the section on wills,[7] does not mention whether women were entitled to witness them or not, but from many contemporary reports, such as some of those compiled by Pérez y Pastor,[8] it seems that women often did. Finally, when her husband died, a woman became the legal head of her family, controlling its affairs and arranging the marriages of her sons and daughters.[9]

Given that, as in most countries until recently, the man was the undisputed ruler of his family, it is clear that the interests of women in seventeenth-century Spain were comparatively well cared for by the law. Its rigorous attitude towards their sexual misdemeanours seems one-sided and unjust. But the punishments allowed by the law were by no means inevitably inflicted. Human nature does not change, and then as now husbands often preferred to forgive their wives, to turn a blind eye to their misconduct or to exact some lesser punishment. Similarly, fathers often discovered they loved their daughters more than their honour. The very existence of penalties might have been expected

---

[1] *N.R.*, Libro quinto, Título III, Ley I.   [2] *N.R.*, Libro quinto, Título III, Ley II.

[3] *N.R.*, Libro quinto, Título III, Ley IV.

[4] *N.R.*, Libro quinto, Título III, Leyes VII and VIII.

[5] *N.R.*, Libro quinto, Título IX, Leyes I and II. At the time of writing the English Parliament is debating a proposed 'revolutionary' Bill to introduce similar legislation in Great Britain.

[6] *N.R.*, Libro quinto, Título IX, Ley IV.

[7] *N.R.*, Libro quinto, Título IV.

[8] *Noticias y documentos relativos a la historia y literatura españolas, Memorias de la Real Academia Española* (Madrid, 1910–26).

[9] *F.J.*, Libro III, Título I (VIII).

to have exerted a restraining influence on women's behaviour. But there is little evidence to show that they constituted a real enough threat to do so. They existed rather as a rarely invoked threat, rarely invoked doubtless because of the question of proof.

Her legal status established, a composite picture of woman's practical position has to be pieced together. Contemporary eye-witnesses often seem to contradict one another. Several factors are involved here. A traveller's view of a foreign country is coloured by his personal prejudices, by the standards of behaviour current in his own country, and by the part of society with which he comes most into contact. Allowance must also be made for exaggeration, due in this case to the highly romanticized vision of Spain held by foreigners even in the sixteenth and seventeenth centuries and embellished then by Spain's aura of wealth and power. And of course, the *kind* of woman being referred to is all important. Commentators seem misleadingly to talk of Spanish women in general when they are discussing women of a particular social class. A woman's way of life obviously varied according to her social position, her morals and whether she lived in town or country. The problems of sociological generalization are enormous.

The best point of departure is that topic which, more than any other, was for some time a subject of serious concern – female education. In Spain, as elsewhere, education for girls was no more compulsory than it was for boys. The daughters of wealthy families were usually taught in their own homes. The usual subjects were on the one hand reading, writing, elementary arithmetic and religious knowledge, taught by an ecclesiastic or a lay tutor, seldom by a governess; and, on the other hand, feminine duties like house-keeping, sewing, spinning and embroidery, together with some music and a little dancing, under the supervision of a *dueña*. Feminine education was not wholly private, however, even among the upper classes. Many convents ran schools for girls attended by both rich and poor – the poor being taught apart, free of charge and probably less extensively. Schools for girls were also founded by the Crown as well as, by ecclesiastical and lay benefactors. In the middle of the seventeenth century, the nuns of the French order of the Company of Mary began to found schools. The teachers in all these schools were invariably nuns or male tutors; there is no evidence that lay women taught in them. Instruction was limited to reading, writing, elementary arithmetic, religious knowledge and needlework.

There is no evidence that girls, with one notable exception, ever went to university and certainly no women lectured there as Doña Francisca de Nebrija and Doña Lucía de Medrano were supposed to have done at Alcalá and Salamanca at the end of the fifteenth century, in the first flush of Spanish enthusiasm for Renaissance learning. The one exception was the noblewoman Doña Feliciana Enríquez de Guzmán, born in Seville at the end of the sixteenth century, who fell in love with a gallant studying at Salamanca and is supposed to have followed him there disguised as a man. She was there three years, won literary prizes, and then returned to Seville, where she dedicated herself to literature, writing poetry which won considerable applause, and two plays – one based on her own life – with which she tried to win support for the classical dramatic precepts. She eventually married Don Francisco de León Garavito, a Sevillian lawyer. Lope in his *Laurel de Apolo* mentions a Feliciana who, disguised as a man, studied philosophy and astrology at Salamanca, then quarrelled with the man she had been in love with there and went off to the Sierra de Guadarrama to write poetry.[1] La Barrera identifies one Feliciana with the other.[2] It is hard not to be sceptical, although Lope and others evidently believed in the adventure. Doña Feliciana probably embroidered her story to heighten its glamour. Even if her university career was a fact she must be looked upon as an exception. J. Deleito y Piñuela is wrong in using her to prove that such events were common.[3]

Clearly, the general level of formal education amongst women was low, although it increased somewhat in spread as the years went by. A minority of girls, however, and, in the sixteenth

[1] *Silva tercera.*
[2] *Catálogo bibliográfico y biográfico del teatro antiguo español* . . . (Madrid, 1860), 142.
[3] *La mujer, la casa y la moda* (Madrid, 1946), 42.

century particularly, a much larger minority than ever before, were fortunate in having parents who encouraged, or at least tolerated, further instruction. These girls learned the rudiments of history and geography, acquired the fashionable modern languages, French and Italian, studied Greek and Latin, and on occasion even approached the fringes of philosophy, science and astrology. A case in point is that of Doña Catalina de Mendoza (1542–1602), who devoted herself to her studies in her youth and whose father developed such a high opinion of her capabilities that when he became viceroy of Naples in 1575 he left the administration of his estates in her hands, though she was his natural daughter and he had five legitimate sons.[1] Another is Doña Ana Girón, wife of Juan Boscán, a woman of great culture who used to join her husband in his study of Homer, Virgil and Catullus. For upper-class girls, of course, formal education was not all-important. Those who were intelligent and curious no doubt read considerably and not always scholarly books. The repeated complaints of the moralists show that in many a maiden's pocket was hidden a pastoral or chivalresque novel, or a volume of verse.

The existence of a pool of comparatively advanced female education, whether formal or informal, is testified by the considerable number of learned and literary women that Spain produced during these years. Several of these are well-known, many are minor figures; many more must have been lost to posterity altogether. We know that women sometimes took part in the literary competitions held to celebrate important events, and that they also attended the literary *academias*. In 1608 two ladies of Zaragoza founded an *academia* called *Pítima contra la ociosidad*. A lady of Huesca sponsored one called *Los humildes*, while the daughters of Philip II, Catalina and Isabel Clara Eugenia, are said to have presided over *academias* in the palace.[2]

Xavier Lampillas[3] provides a detailed list of 'mujeres ilustres

---

[1] See A. Morel-Fatio, *Etudes sur l'Espagne*, 4ième série (Paris, 1925), 295–372.

[2] See R. Altamira y Crevea, *Historia de España y de la civilización española* III (Barcelona, 1906), 596–7.

[3] *Ensayo histórico-apologético de la literatura española contra las opiniones preocupadas de algunos escritores modernos italianos, traducido al español por Dª Josefa Amar y Borbón* II (Zaragoza, 1783).

españolas' of the sixteenth century, mentioning amongst others: the Toledan Luisa Siega who wrote poems and various other pieces, including a letter to the Pope in five languages – Latin, Greek, Hebrew, Syriac and Arabic – and who went to the Portuguese court as tutor to King Don Manuel's daughter, the Princess María; Cecilia Morillas of Salamanca, a gifted musician, who taught Latin, Greek, Italian, French, philosophy and theology to her nine children, turning down in order to do so the unusual offer of a post as governess to Philip II's daughters; Oliva de Sabuco whose treatises on natural philosophy and medicine were published in Madrid in 1588; Juana Morella from Barcelona, who at the age of twelve was offering learned philosophical observations in public debate, and by the age of seventeen was versed in theology, jurisprudence, languages, music and drawing; and Isabel de Joya from Lérida, who gained renown in Rome by converting several Jews with her eloquence and discoursed on philosophy and theology before a large gathering of cardinals. Pérez y Pastor[1] gives a more modest list of women writing in the first half of the seventeenth century. This includes Doña Ana Caro Mallén de Soto who wrote plays, only one of which survives,[2] and three long poems;[3] and Doña Catalina Zamudio, whose poetry appears in the *Cancionero de López Maldonado*. A longer but less reliable list is provided by Deleito y Piñuela in *La mujer, la casa y la moda*, while La Barrera in his *Catálogo* mentions several female dramatists.

The most extraordinary of these now virtually forgotten women was Doña Luisa de Carvajal y Mendoza, born in 1566 in Jaraicejo in the province of Cáceres, who in 1605 went to England as a Catholic missionary. There she lived for nine years until her death in 1614, visiting imprisoned Catholics and in her spare time acquiring an impressive knowledge of theology and polemics. She was twice sent to prison but freed both times through the representations of the Spanish Ambassador. Philip III advised the

---

[1] *Noticias y documentos*, I.
[2] *El conde Partinuplés*, printed in *Dramáticos posteriores a Lope de Vega* II, B.A.E. XLIX.
[3] Edited by Antonio Pérez y Gómez (Valencia, 1951).

Ambassador to send her to Flanders out of harm's way, but before the order could be carried out she died in Highgate. During her lifetime she wrote a considerable amount of verse and several religious works in prose.[1]

Of all the Spanish women striving for intellectual and creative fulfilment during this priod, however, only four names still live. Of the only outstanding woman writer of the Golden Age, Santa Teresa de Jesús, little need be said here. Her works rank with the greatest of her religious contemporaries. More muted renown was acquired by another churchwoman, Sor María de Agreda, through her close but exemplary relationship with her king, Philip IV. Her letters reveal extensive biblical and theological knowledge, and an acquaintance with classical thinkers such as Seneca, as well as a remarkable grasp of current affairs and a lively interest in the welfare of her country: in short, a woman of intelligence, learning and discernment. Her writings were impressively varied and included a compendium of geography and cosmology entitled *Mapa de los orbes celestiales y elementales desde el cielo empíreo hasta el centro de la tierra*. Francisco Silvela comments:

no tienen los diversos tratados que en la obrita se exponen sobre la redondez de la tierra, su profundidad, razas que la pueblan en Europa, Asia, Africa y América, animales de varios climas, constitución física del globo y de los astros, distancias, astronómicas y movimientos de los planetas, valor científico, pero sí ofrecen especial interés por revelar en Sor María concocimientos nada comunes sobre el estado de tales ciencias, entonces poco cultivadas como estudios generales y menos por los que dedicaban su espíritu a meditaciones teológicas y místicas.[2]

The other two women were first and foremost story-writers, although they both wrote plays which have not survived, and one of them was in addition the most famous poetess of her time. Doña

[1] See Luis Muñoz, *Vida y virtudes de la venerable virgen Doña Luisa de Carvajal y Mendoça, su jornada a Inglaterra y sucessos en aquel reyno* (Madrid, 1632). Also *Poesías espirituales de la venerable Doña Luisa de Carvajal y Mendoza, muestras de su ingenio y de su espíritu* (Seville, 1885); and *Luisa de Carvajal y Mendoza (poetisa y mártir), apuntes bibliográficos, seguidos de tres cartas inéditas de la venerable madre,* by Antonio R. Rodríguez-Moñino and María Brey Moñino (Madrid, 1933).

[2] *Cartas de la venerable madre Sor María de Agreda y del señor rey Don Felipe IV* (Madrid, 1885), II, 79 note.

Mariana Carvajal y Saavedra, with her *Navidades en Madrid y noches entretenidas*, published in 1663, only just managed to slip into the list of those who survived in the wake of the great; that she survived at all was partly due to the fact that she cultivated a literary genre where competition was not strong. Doña María de Zayas, on the other hand, was widely applauded in her day for both her short stories and her poetry – Lope praises her in his *Laurel de Apolo* – and her success in what was still a period of high-powered literary production ensured a lasting, albeit more modest, renown. Her *Novelas amorosas y ejemplares*, the first ten published in 1637, and the second ten – *Parte segunda del sarao y entreteni-miento honestos* – in 1647, are interesting on account of their overt feminism; particularly since this quality is absent from the work of Doña Mariana Carvajal and from the extant works of other women writers of the time. Doña María reacted strongly to the verbal disapproval meted out to women in the seventeenth century and sets out in these tales to rebut it. For her, the root of the problem lay in the fact that girls were still largely excluded from intellec-tual pursuits and compelled to remain helpless and weak. Her work is a plea for the recognition of women as individuals, instead of as creatures both inferior and dangerous to man. The plea is im-passioned, but it goes no further than this. Melodramatic as her stories are, her views are balanced. She does not denounce men and she offers no practical suggestions for the improvement of woman's lot. She merely asks for recognition of the fact that virtue is not the prerogative of the male and that female wicked-ness may have its reasons.

Doña María's complaints reveal that for all these women who succeeded in overcoming the limits imposed by society upon their sex, female education was still limited in Spain towards the middle of the seventeenth century. Then, as in the preceding century, it was designed to equip women for the life they were expected to lead and no more, certainly not for scholarly and literary activi-ties. The lives of the vast majority of Spanish women followed the familiar pattern of the age.

What was this pattern? The information available refers almost entirely to women of the middle and upper classes. The life of peasant women in the country and of lower-class women in the towns can have differed little from that of their counterparts anywhere. Many would have had to do some kind of work outside their housewifely duties, and this must have been an emancipating influence, making their lives not all that dissimilar from that of their men. As elsewhere, female villagers would have been subject to more rigid standards of behaviour than those who lived in towns. To the remainder of Spanish women, four main courses were open. They could join the ranks of the *mujeres de mala vida* somewhere in the hierarchy from courtesan to common prostitute.[1] They could enter a convent. They could enter into service as a *dueña* or a lady-in-waiting. Or they could remain with their families, marrying or not as inclination or opportunity decided. Those who embarked on this last course concern us most, for the life of the prostitute and the nun, by the nature of their calling, ran along fixed and predictable lines; that of the superior servant was also circumscribed and fairly stereotyped, although at the highest level – at the Court – service for the daughters of the nobility was a form of finishing school prior to marriage. Marriages were usually arranged – whether the wishes of the girl were considered depended upon her relationship with her parents – but they normally brought greater freedom. The married woman enjoyed a dignity denied to her hitherto. She was second-in-command in her own household and was not nearly as tied to the hearth as she had been as a single girl.

As for the freedom of movement enjoyed by women in Spain in the sixteenth and seventeenth centuries, foreign observers seem at first sight to differ. In the eighteenth century, Mrs Western, discovering that her niece Sophie has been locked in her room, can say to her brother Squire Western,

. . . English women, brother, I thank heaven, are no slaves. We are not to be locked up like Spanish and Italian wives.[2]

---

[1] Although in 1632 brothels were forbidden, by the middle of the century there were eight hundred all-night brothels in Madrid alone. In 1661 the King decreed that all prostitutes should be removed to *casas galeras* (correctionals for women) but the order was not put into effect. See A. Ballesteros y Beretta, *Historia de España y su influencia en la historia universal*, IV, II (Barcelona, 1927), 586–8.

[2] *The History of Tom Jones, a Foundling*, I, Book VI, Chap. XIV (Oxford, 1926), 64.

and the conventional image of the life led by Spanish women in the past is one of strict seclusion. This is partly borne out by a contemporary French account of a journey to Spain in 1655,

Au reste, les Maris, qui veulent, que leurs Femmes vivent bien, s'en rendent d'abord si absolus, qu'ils les traitent presque en Esclaves, de peur qu'ils ont, qu'une honneste liberté, ne les fasse emanciper au delà des loix de la pudicité, qui sont fort peu connues et mal observées parmy elles. On m'a asseuré, qu'en Andalousie, où les Maris sont encore plus violents, ils les gouvernent comme des Enfants, ou comme des Servantes.[1]

But the curious feature about this remark is that the author, Frans Van Aarsens, obviously disapproved as much of some Spanish women as he did of some Spanish husbands. The qualification 'qui veulent' implies that not all husbands exacted the same standard of behaviour of their wives. And the hint that the author had seen evidence of immodesty amongst Spanish women indicates that by no means all of them were kept in purdah by tyrannical husbands. Juan Álvarez de Colmenar, who visited the peninsula at the end of the seventeenth century, likewise mentions this dual pattern of behaviour, 'les femmes étant renfermées plus étroitement que des Religieuses, cherchent à se dédommager'![2] A longer and more charitable explanation is given by Bertaut, who visited Spain in the same decade as Van Aarsens,

Ce n'est pas que les Dames ne soient de la meilleure volonté du monde, et que bien souvent elles n'aillent chercher les hommes sans faire connoistre qui elles sont, croyant toutes que c'est une chose dont on ne se sçauroit passer que de se divertir, à cause de quoy les hommes les enferment, ne pouvant comprendre comment nos Dames en France sont avec eux dans la liberté dont ils entendent parler, sans faire du mal, au lieu que je leur disois que c'estait cette liberté-là qui les rendoit sages et qui faisoit qu'elles ne s'abandonnoient pas au premier venu mais qu'elles vouloient connoistre si les gens meritoient d'etre aymez; mais que bien souvent elles trouvoient que non, et n'avoient point d'empressement pour un plaisir qu'elles estoient en estat de prendre quand elles voudroient.[3]

---

[1] Frans Van Aarsens, *Voyage d'espagne*, IX (Cologne, 1666), 57.
[2] *Les délices de l'Espagne et du Portugal*, VI (Leyden, 1715), 840.
[3] *Journal du voyage d'Espagne* [1659] (Paris, 1669), 293–4.

These three commentators refer indiscriminately to Spanish women in general, but apart from a handful of incidents they probably heard about on their travels, they must be referring to two different groups of women – the secluded and the not-so-secluded – and their generalized deductions are an attempt to explain the existence of this dichotomy. The contrast between the two groups served to emphasize both, and the Frenchmen were no doubt right in judging that each affected the other.

That the more emancipated woman was not uncommon in Spain is borne out by the Portuguese traveller, Tomé Pinheiro da Veiga, who seems to have met virtually only women of this type. The date of his visit, 1605, rules out the possibility that these women were solely a feature of a later, decadent Spain.[1] At the same time, we must remember that the Portuguese were regarded in Spain as being stricter with their women than the Spaniards themselves. Throughout his account,[2] Pinheiro expresses astonishment at the uninhibited behaviour of Spanish women of all classes, at their readiness, for example, to accept and reply to the gallantries paid them, but he sees it as a mere desire to amuse themselves and constantly insists on their virtue:

Y aunque muchas señoras castellanas tengan esta facilidad en las visitas y conversación no dejan muchas de ser muy honradas y honestas, y que ninguna cosa las obligará a hacer lo que no deben.[3]

For Pinheiro this open behaviour contrasted favourably with the hypocrisy that characterized attitudes to women in his own country. Spanish women, he says, are treated as people and as Christians, and not as 'bichos que vuelan y saben hablar'.[4] He speaks of the mutual confidence of husbands and wives and of the harmony typical of marriage in Spain. Extremely interesting is his claim that as a result of these equable relations, wife-murder rarely happened: 'Y así no hay muertes de mujeres sino raremente'.[5] Pinheiro also noted the courtesy accorded to women in Spain.

[1] As Martin Hume suggests in *The Court of Philip IV* (London, 1907), 55 note.
[2] *La Fastiginia o fastos generales,* translated by Narciso Alonso Cortés (Valladolid, 1916).
[3] *Ibid., Primera parte,* el 30 de mayo, 51.
[4] *Ibid., Primera parte,* el 13 de junio, 85.   [5] *Ibid., Pincigrafía,* 209.

Eventually, however, his ingrained prejudices rose to the surface. The immorality he met with he attributes towards the end of his diary to the freedom enjoyed by men and women in their social relations, and it was with relief that he finally turned his back on 'permissive' Spain: 'Llegué, finalmente, a besar la dulce tierra de mi amada patria, libre del cautiverio de tanta libertad.'[1]

Given that Pinheiro's impressions were coloured by the social standards of his own country, the freedom he describes is surprising. Probably two factors are at work. First, Pinheiro's narrative suggests that many of the women he met were not entirely respectable. He seems to have had a propensity, natural in a foot-loose stranger, to meet with the female froth on the social ocean; not necessarily prostitutes, but adventuresses and women of the world. Second, Pinheiro (unlike the French travellers quoted) spent nearly all his time in anonymous and cosmopolitan Madrid, where standards of behaviour were more elastic than elsewhere. The capital naturally attracted women of easy virtue, and in 1611, when there arose in Madrid a scandal about homosexual practices, Lope de Vega could slyly report to the Duke of Sessa, 'Dizenme que estan en Madrid mui quexosas las mugeres de que, siendo tan fáciles, aya onbres presos por traydores a la naturaleza.'[2] All the same, there is an abundance of evidence from ambassadors, diplomats and other visitors that the respectable women of the nobility and often of the wealthy bourgeoisie in Madrid (and to some extent other large cities like Barcelona and Seville) had a reputation for liveliness and wit, and that social intercourse with members of the opposite sex was relatively relaxed. The life of bourgeois women in small towns and villages was inevitably much more restricted. Here was the true home of the female ideal beloved of the moralists; the secluded woman who spent her life in housework and prayer. These country *mores* sometimes imposed themselves on the great. When Bertaut visited Écija, he attended a play at the house of the Duke of Osuna; the Duchess entered when the play was about to begin and after it was over retired immediately,

[1] *Ibid., Segunda parte,* el 26 de julio, 186.
[2] From Madrid on 6 August 1611: *Epistolario de Lope de Vega Carpio,* ed. A. G. de Amezúa (Madrid, 1935–43), III, letter 44, p. 50.

merely bowing to the visitors and without exchanging a single word with her husband. Even the freedom of women in the capital was not freedom in modern terms. However gay and bold, those who wished to retain if only the outward vestiges of respectability were still subject to certain tacit but unbreakable rules.

Marriage was the passport to what freedom was available. Unmarried girls were treated with the care due to a valuable commodity and their movements were limited. They could usually attend Mass accompanied by a chaperone but most other non-domestic pastimes were denied them. They told their beads, learned their lessons, sewed a fine seam and dreamed. The married woman on the other hand could visit her woman friends and receive visits from them. She could go to the theatre, to bull-fights and to cane-tourneys as well as to church. She could take walks, ride in her carriage, and even go hunting, fishing and hawking. Card-playing and other forms of gambling were not unknown to her.[1] All, of course, had to be done with propriety. She would never venture out alone. If she were wealthy she went by carriage and accompanied by a female relation or servant; if on foot, she went accompanied by a female companion and usually preceded by an *escudero* of advanced years. She rarely went out with her husband. Indeed segregation of the sexes, in private and in public, was fairly general. The *estrado* where the mistress of the house received her friends was reserved for women, and for female visitors contact with the men of the house would be brief. In a house of mourning, visitors sympathized with the bereaved of their own sex. Amongst the nobility, however, it became increasingly common for husband and wife to receive together, particularly in the case of official embassies, and a noblewoman would even receive her husband's guests alone if their arrival anticipated his own. The general segregation extended even to meals. It was usual for men and women, even of the same household, to eat separately, and if they did eat together, the men sat at table, the women on cushions on the floor. Again, some of the nobility gradually abandoned this method of eating, according to the testimony of Sir Richard

[1] See J. Fitzmaurice-Kelly, 'Woman in Sixteenth-century Spain', *RHi*, LXX (1927), 577.

Fanshawe who visited Spain in the late 1660s and wrote in a letter home,

> At supper he (the Governor of Cadiz) and his Lady would bear me and my Wife company, which I accepting as a great favour, told him my Wife should eat with her Ladyship, retired from the Men after the Spanish fashion . . . But by no means That he would not suffer; and to keep us the more in Countenance alleged this manner of eating to be now the custom of many of the greatest Families in Spain, and had been from all antiquity to this day of the Majestical House of Alva . . .[1]

In public, too, segregation was less strict for the aristocracy than for the bourgeoisie, presumably because a reputation supported by rank and power was less vulnerable than one supported by wealth or good name alone. In the public theatres, the *cazuela*, where the mass of the women sat, was strictly segregated, with its own separate entrance; and no respectable woman entered it unmasked. From 1630 on, an *alcalde* even cleared the street round the women's exit so that they could set off for home unmolested.[2] In the better *aposentos* (boxes), however, men and women often sat together, and noblewomen sometimes even had them reserved in their own names.[3] Similarly, while windows were usually reserved for the use of women at bull-fights, jousts, *autos-da-fé* and other public celebrations, here too noblewomen mingled a little more freely with the men. At the bull-fighting and jousting held to celebrate the birth of Philip IV on 10 June 1605, the English Ambassador and Lord Howard, Earl of Nottingham, sat amongst the court ladies on the left of the King and Queen.[4] A trivial but interesting incident three days later upsets the common image of the Spanish lady as a prisoner of her jealous husband's honour. Six of these same ladies of the court thought up the innocent prank of bursting in upon the English entourage at dinner. Their husbands accompanied them to the door of the dining room but then remained outside while the women went in alone. After the amused

---

[1] *Original Letters of Sir Richard Fanshawe* (London, 1701), 33.
[2] See N. D. Shergold, *A History of the Spanish Stage from Medieval Times until the End of the Seventeenth Century* (Oxford, 1967), 391.
[3] *Ibid.* 535.
[4] See Pinheiro, *Fastiginia, Primera parte,* el 10 de junio, 72.

Englishmen had toasted the intruders, these returned to their doubtless bored but indulgent husbands.[1]

That Spanish women were not starved of social contact is revealed by their reputation for liveliness and wit and for being excellent company. Ruth Kelso[2] refers to a letter written by Annibal Guasco to his daughter, Lavinia, on the eve of her departure to the court of Savoy[3] and parapharases him thus,

Above all she will need to consider well how she talks with the men of the court that she is allowed to meet, to do it according to the custom of the court, because to women and, especially, girls care and modesty are more necessary than to men, men being generally praised for more understanding. Her models in these matters as well as in others should be the Spanish ladies with which that court is filled, for they surpass all others in the pleasing gravity, and grave pleasantness shown not only in their speech but in all their actions, so natural and suited to this nation.

Also in another matter they excel, the wit and readiness at jesting with which they carry on discussions. These she should seek to imitate.

A hundred years later, Lady Fanshawe said much the same thing,

They (Spaniards) are generally pleasant and facetious company; but in this their women exceed, who seldom laugh, and never loud; but the most witty in repartees, and stories, and notions in the world![4]

These relationships occurred within a formal social context. Men did not hesitate to address women in the street, but the virtuous woman would not by the flicker of an eyelid acknowledge the stranger's presence. If she was accompanied by a man who was not a servant, he regarded such an overture in his presence as a direct insult and scuffles often arose for this reason. The sound of serenading was familiar at night, but no woman of virtue would allow herself to be seen listening. Conversation at the *reja* where women, withdrawn a discreet distance, watched the world go by,

---

[1] *Ibid.* et 13 de junio, 83–4.

[2] *Doctrine for the Lady of the Renaissance* (Urbana, 1956), 225.

[3] *Ragionamento del Sig. Annibal Guasco ad Lavinia sua figlivola, della maniera del governarsi ella in corte; andando, per dama alla Serenissima Infante D. Caterina, Duchessa di Savoia*, Turino, l'herede del Bevilacqua, 1586.

[4] *Memoirs of Lady Fanshawe* (London, 1905), 193.

was permissible only between a formally engaged couple. The use of church-going to meet an admirer was a ploy few respectable women would readily adopt. Love-letters could be openly received by a girl only from her official fiancé, although it was by no means unusual, particularly amongst the nobility, for women to receive ordinary communications from a number of acquaintances. Amongst the letters Lope de Vega penned for the Duke of Sessa, for example, are many addressed to ladies – letters of condolence, of congratulations and of thanks, business letters and purely friendly, informative letters.[1]

The tenour of life at the highest level of society, within the royal family's entourage, depended a great deal on the mood established by the sovereign himself. All witnesses testify to the general air of gravity and even drabness exuded by the court of the austere Philip II. And although the ladies of the court were by no means strictly secluded, their behaviour was undoubtedly more decorous and restrained than it was later to become. In the reign of Philip III, and even more markedly in that of his son, Philip IV, court life acquired a marked frivolity and extravagance. Outwardly, the life of the Queen's ladies-in-waiting continued to be governed by elaborate protocol. The only married man who actually slept in the palace was the King himself, and most of the ladies-in-waiting seem to have been widows or girls. The single women were officially only seen by their admirers in public. Hence, whenever the Queen, surrounded by her attendants, gave audience, the crowded chamber throbbed with aspiring lovers. On these days there took place a procedure called *dar lugar*, by which each of the Queen's ladies was allowed to have two gallants in attendance. These gallants were granted the grandee's privilege of keeping their hats on in the Queen's presence, the frenzy of their love being supposed to make them indifferent to normal procedure: 'les Dames ayant sur ceux qui se donnent à elles, le mesme droit que le Roy sur ses sujets, qui est de les faire couvrir'.[2] In time the gallants, growing bolder, took to following their ladies on horseback when these rode out in carriages with the Queen, and

[1] *Minutas de Lope de Vega para cartas del Duque de Sessa, Epistolario*, IV, Section II.
[2] Bertaut, *Journal*, 291.

gradually gallantry of this and more extravagant sorts increased until it reached a pitch which amazed visitors from other countries. As early as the 1560s a native Spaniard, Eugenio Salazar, could complain in a letter to a friend, Juan de Castejón,

Quien podrá explicar el trabajo de los pobres maridos cortesanos con las galas, con los arreos, con los afeites, con las devociones, estaciones, visitas, juntas, fiestas, meriendas y colaciones de sus mujeres?[1]

but the gallantries spread to other relationships and even into the palace itself. Hume quotes the following passage from the report of the Venetian ambassador in Spain at the time of Olivares' fall:

In the royal palace the gentlemen are permitted to carry on with the ladies of the Queen the relations they call 'gallanting', in which lavishness, ostentation and expenditure are carried to such an extraordinary excess as to be beyond belief, although here it is considered the most ordinary thing in the world, for rivalry and competition do away with all moderation. Those who go to the greatest lengths are held in the highest esteem, not only by the courtiers in general, but also by the royal personages, who make quite a recreation of hearing the accounts of the presents given and attentions paid to them, that the ladies narrate daily to their Majesties[2]

In 1641, the attention of some of these admirers had taken an alarmingly acute turn: according to Rodríguez Villa, three of the principal grandees of Spain were banished in that year for scaling the walls of the Retiro at night and making love to some maids of honour.[3] By the 1670s this situation had become a commonplace, according to the Memoirs of the Marquis of Villars,[4] who commented with disapproval on the illicit relations between the majority of the young women who attended the Queen and married gallants who showered them with gifts and money.

There seems little doubt that the decline in standards of behaviour at court percolated through into those social spheres immediately adjacent and in Madrid to other levels of society. The

[1] Cartas (Madrid, 1866), 9.   [2] The Court of Philip IV, 55–6, n.1.
[3] Ibid. 356 note.
[4] Mémoires de la cour d'Espagne de 1679 à 1681, pub. by M. A. Morel-Fatio (Paris, 1893).

frivolity and extravagance even acquired its sombre side as it became fashionable for women to dabble in white magic. Lope commented on this in one of his letters to the Duke of Sessa giving news of life in the capital:

y no ay muger en él, por prinçipal que sea, como trate en esta mercaderia de tomar dineros a cambio sobre prendas de los gustos, que no trayga sus abas en la manga, y sepa qué es vn sigilo, y cómo se pone un clabo en el fuego para que se abrasse un ombre[1]

More significant than this murky undertow of amateur witchcraft were the scandals of 1633, when the surface of social respectability was agitated by a series of violent waves. An affaire between the young Countess of Seville, niece of Cardinal Zapata, and Joseph Cabra, the Cardinal's favourite servant, came to light and sparked off revelations of similar liaisons, one involving the Duchess of Peñaranda and her steward Avellanada, another the Dowager Duchess of Pastrana.[2] With the mask of respectability slipping to this extent, virtuous women had to look to the niceties of their behaviour. Paradoxically, they were increasingly forced into greater seclusion, not so much by jealous husbands as by those members of their own sex who grasped at a freedom not only social but moral. As the seventeenth century advanced, Madrid's hordes of what are appropriately called 'public women' invaded public life, and the respectable had to shun those pursuits which their less virtuous sisters usurped. In 1610, the Duke of Lerma, in a half-hearted attempt to improve public morality, ordered that only ladies should travel in coaches (which were curtained), indicating that already women of ill repute were encroaching upon the prerogatives of the respectable upper classes. He even tried to ensure virtue amongst the noble and the wealthy by adding that the ladies themselves should leave their faces uncovered while riding in their vehicles and that for masculine company they should have only fathers, sons or husbands.[3] These

[1] Madrid, May 1617 (?), *Epistolario*, III, Letter 309. The Inquisition would seem to have looked on these dabblings with the leniency with which they regarded witchcraft as a whole

[2] See Hume, *The Court of Philip IV*, 268ff.

[3] See M. Lafuente, *Historia General de España* (Barcelona, 1888), XI, 157.

orders had so little effect that the coach became the haunt of the prostitute and the courtesan, and fewer and fewer respectable women could afford to be seen in them.

The fashionable public places – the Calle Mayor, the Prado, the Plaza Mayor and the Puerta del Sol – teemed with women of varying degrees of availability. And when the Italian Count, Fulvio Testi, made the following remark about the river Manzanares in a letter to a friend in Modena in 1635, it is fairly safe to assume that the women he was referring to would not have qualified as highly respectable,

Es pobre de agua pero riquísimo de mujeres, porque en la estación más cálida van allí a lavarse casi todas las mujeres de Madrid, que allí se exponen a la vista de cualquiera, del menos curioso expectador'[1]

Lope refers to the same custom in 1611 in a letter to the Duke of Sessa, 'Ya refresca en Madrid, Senor excm.º, con que amayna la furia de nadar las mugeres en el cuitado Manzanares.'[2] Travellers were astonished that few men seemed to be without mistresses whom they showered with gifts and money, many being prepared to reduce their wives and children to penury. Frans Van Aarsens was one of many when he said,

tous ceux, qui ont vécu a Madrid asseurent, que ce sont les Femmes qui perdent la plûpart des Maisons. Il n'y a personne qui n'entretienne sa Dame et qui ne donne dans l'Amour de quelque Courtesane.[3]

Repeated attempts were made by the government to impose reform. On 12 April 1639, a law with moral as well as sumptuary aims was proclaimed, forbidding all women from wearing veils (which, like coaches, were thought to encourage, because they helped conceal, disreputable behaviour), and restricting the wearing of the capacious *guardainfante* (for the same reason) to prostitutes.[4] The decree was virtually ignored. One of Isabel of Bourbon's last actions before she died in 1644 was to issue another reforming decree. By this, no unmarried woman or widow was allowed to appear on stage, and no gentleman was permitted to

---

[1] See J. García Mercadal, *España vista por los extranjeros*, III (Madrid, 1921), 96–7.
[2] Dated Madrid, 6 August 1611: *Epistolario*, III, Letter 44.
[3] *Voyage d'Espagne*, 53–4.   [4] Ballesteros, IV, II, 562–3.

visit an actress more than twice.[1] Similar legislation had been passed before, and was to be re-enacted later, to little effect. Equally unsuccessful were the numerous attempts made, first to prevent actresses wearing masculine dress at all and then to restrict it to above waist level.

In this atmosphere of growing licence, it is not difficult to believe that parents were somewhat stricter with their daughters and wives with themselves than hitherto; particularly amongst gentlefolk and the bourgeoisie, where extravagant behaviour was less likely to be labelled mere eccentricity than it was amongst the nobility. To foreigners, the gap between the respectable and the worldly must have seemed a yawning one at times. But both existed, and it is an over-simplification to see woman's life in seventeenth-century Spain, even seventeenth-century Madrid, as one of extraordinary liberty contrasting completely with the conventual strictness of the sixteenth century. In the first place, the strictness had not been as claustrophobic as has been made out. In the second, the increased liberty was licence rather than freedom, and was for the most part restricted to those women who could afford to indulge in it; the adventuress, who had no reputation to lose, and the noblewoman, whose reputation was largely impervious to assault. The great mass of respectable women if anything led a *more* restricted life than hitherto. Undoubtedly there was the odd rebellion against what seemed the over-anxious strictures of reactionary parents or husbands, and indoubtedly there were jealous husbands and tyrannical fathers. But in the main, these restrictions were not imposed upon women by the brute force of male egoism. They were accepted, or at least tolerated, by her as the natural result of social circumstances and social habit.

The practical position of women before the honour-vengeance code is as delicate a problem as that of the code itself. The concept of honour was certainly outwardly and theoretically recognized as the principal arbiter of social and personal behaviour, but it did not have the sanction of the law. Duelling was a punishable offence, while the one instance of legitimate vengeance (conceived

[1] J. de Pellicer y Tobar, *Avisos históricos,* ed. A. Valladares de Sotomayor, *Semanario erudito,* (Madrid 1788), xxxiii, newsletter for March 1644.

of as instant private justice) was subject to the burden of proof –
the husband who killed his wife or daughter and her lover in
flagrante delicto was well advised to leave their bodies where he
found them until he could find a witness. Convicted wife-
murderers were subjected to harsh penalties, as Lope shows in a
melodramatically-phrased remark in a letter to the Duke of Sessa,
'No hazen sino encubar honbres porque matan a sus mujeres;
tanto, que en dos dias, que xamas se ha visto, han sacado dos, a
cuya fiesta ha salido al Rio toda la corte en coches, en caballos y
en mula de alquiler.'[1] (*Encubar* was a peculiarly nasty punishment
reserved for heinous crimes like patricide and wife-murder which,
fully elaborated, involved placing the criminal in a barrel with a
cockerel, a monkey, a dog and a snake and then throwing the lot
into the water.) Certainly there is little contemporary evidence
that women lived in constant fear of bloodthirsty husbands,
brothers and fathers. Most foreigners make no mention of this
point at all, while Pinheiro asserted the very opposite,

De suerte que imagino que de esta gente, los más no hacen caso de los
cuernos y a lo que la honra alcanza es a no querer averiguarlos . . . en
Castilla no pesan tanto los cuernos y en Portugal sólo de la sombra
andan los hombres espantados.[2]

It is significant that the actions of the three famous wife-murder
plays of Calderón, which have been largely responsible for the
wife-murder legend, do not for the most part take place in
seventeenth-century Spain. *El médico de su honra* takes place in
Seville in the fourteenth centruy, *A secreto agravio secreta venganza*
in Lisbon, and much of *El pintor de su deshonra*, including the
murder, in Italy. In each case the plot is subjected to a distancing
process.

The consenting cuckold is, of course, a constant victim of
Quevedo's satire, while Covarrubias in his *Tesoro de la lengua
castellana y española*,[3] published in 1611, affirms that many hus-
hands preferred to profit from rather than punish their wives'
infidelities. Naturally wife-murder, as in other countries and in

---

[1] Letter from Madrid in the middle of February 1612, *Epistolario*, III, Letter 80.
[2] *Fastiginia, Segunda parte*, el 25 de junio, 112; and *Tercera parte*, 209.
[3] Under *cornudo*, (Barcelona, 1943), 360–1.

modern times, was not unknown. The Jesuit newsletters and Pellicer's *Avisos* contain several examples which must be regarded as authentic, but their newsworthiness shows they were unusual. When a husband did take action, murder was less common than confiscation of the wife's goods, or prosecution of her and her supposed lover. Even then a man sometimes decided to withdraw the charge and have recourse to what was known as the *perdón de cuernos*. The violent compromise, of course, was to kill the rival, as occasionally happened.

That stories of violent vengeance are unreliable is evident from the bully's boasts of two seventeenth-century soldiers. Diego Duque de Estrada claimed to have murdered his fiancée and the man he suspected of being her lover on 25 October 1607. His tale was that arriving at her house without warning, he found his best friend at the top of a rope ladder attached to Isabel's balcony. Duque de Estrada killed him, entered Isabel's bedroom and stabbed her in her sleep. The girl's father approved the motive if not the rigour of the deed and prevented Isabel's brother killing Duque de Estrada in his turn. He then urged the murderer to escape with the warning 'aunque yo te perdono, no lo hará la madre del muerto ni la justicia'. Duque de Estrada concludes the tale by stating with no trace of regret that Isabel was found after her death to have been still a virgin.[1] Alonso de Contreras also claimed to have killed both his wife and her lover at about the same time.[2] The memoirs of these men are so full of obvious and absurd exaggeration that it seems likely that these claims of theirs were in reality just two more ego-flattering flights of fancy. Duque de Estrada's story, in particular is too perfect and the details too pat – the best friend to exalt even further his over-riding concern for his honour, the unheeded protestations of innocence to emphasize his ferocity and extreme sensibility, the understanding father to condone and therefore minimize the severity of his action, and the virginity to prove after all that he was a successful, because revered, lover. It has all the flavour of a campfire tale of the most transparent sort.

---

[1] *Memorias de Don Diego Duque de Estrada, Autobiografías de soldados (siglo XVII), Biblioteca de autores españoles*, XC, 266–8.

[2] *Vida del Capitán Alonso de Contreras, Ibid.* 107.

When wife-murders did occur – the murder of daughters and sisters seems to have been virtually unknown – public sympathy almost invariably lay with the victims, particularly when it was obvious that through influence and wealth the husband would not be brought to justice, or where it was felt that a timely concern for his honour was not the true motive. There were two sensational affairs of this sort in the reign of Philip IV, one in Madrid, the other in the Philippines. A Jesuit newsletter from one Sebastián González to P. Rafael Pereyra, written on 24 Nobember 1643, tells of a man who, being 'melancólico y de edad', suspected his wife of betraying him with a dwarf. He killed her and would have killed the dwarf had not the latter been warned. González ends his dispatch,

La mujer tenía muy buen crédito en todo el barrio, y muy buena opinión con todos los que la conocían. Ha causado gran lástima, y cargan mucho al marido de melancólico, y que este disparate ha sido efecto de su condición y no de causa que la mujer le hubiese dado. Con todo eso él tiene dineros y en breve con ellos saldrá por ventura bien, que así suceden otras muchas cosas.[1]

The earlier murder was perpetrated on 11 May 1621, by Alonso Fajardo de Tenza, Governor of the Philippines,[2] who killed his wife in confused and suspicious circumstances while she was on a visit in male disguise to the house of a clerk the Governor apparently suspected of being her lover. There was no suggestion of secret vengeance. The Governor seems rather to have deliberately focused attention on the affair by warning the guards and soldiers of his intentions and taking along with him a band of supporters. He referred to her murder almost casually in a letter to the King on 10 December 1621, not even bothering to use his honour as an excuse. Public feeling against Fajardo ran very high, for it was strongly suspected that the murder was an elaborate plot, and that he had attempted to kill his wife several times before. His

[1] *Cartas de algunos PP. de la Compañía de Jesús*, v, *Memorial histórico español*, xvii (Madrid, 1863), 375–7.
[2] See E. H. Blair and J. A. Robertson, *The Philippine Islands* (Cleveland, 1903–9), xx (1621–4), 35–43. Also a letter to the King from an opponent of Fajardo's, the Licentiate Don Álvaro Messa y Lugo, 195–8.

position and influence alone prevented a thorough investigation of the affair.

However seriously the honour code was taken in the sixteenth and seventeenth centuries, there is no possible doubt that social pressure was against wife-murder. That this pressure could be effective is revealed by another letter to P. Rafael Pereyra from Francisco de Vilches on 23 August 1634,

Ya sabrá V.R. como en Jaén mató un escribano a su mujer con menos causa; levantóse el género femenino de manera que para sosegarle fue menester con presteza ahorcar al malhechor, sin que le concedieran mula y luto[1]

The average Spanish woman was not, in other words, the sacrificial lamb she has been painted. And if she was a slave, it was to the conventions of the patriarchal society in which she lived, conventions which she, as a product of that society, believed in and upheld. She was a woman of limited education who led a life centred round her home; a life of seclusion as a girl and, as a married woman, of modest freedom within the limits set by virtue and propriety. She imposed upon her daughters the restrictions she had at times found irksome as a girl, in the mature conviction that they were necessary and wise; but she was content to leave the affairs of men in their own hands, confident that she did not lack influence. She emerges from Lady Fanshawe's blanket description of Spanish women thus,

They sing, but not well, their way being between Italian and Spanish; they play on all kinds of instruments likewise, and dance with castañuelas very well. They work but little, but very well, especially in monasteries. They all paint white and red, from the Queen to the cobbler's wife, old and young, widows excepted, who never go out of close mourning, nor wear gloves, nor show their hair after their husbands' death and seldom marry. They are the finest-shaped women in the world, not tall, their hair and teeth are most delicate; they seldom have many children; there are none love cleanliness in diet, clothes and houses more than they do . . . They delight much in the feasts of bulls and stage plays, and take great pleasure to see their little children

[1] *Cartas de algunos PP* . . . I, *Mem. hist. esp.* XIII (Madrid, 1861), 88.

act before them in their own houses, which they will do to perfection; but the children of the greatest are kept at great distance from conversing with their relations and friends, never eating with their parents but at their birth . . . Until their daughters marry, they never stir so much as downstairs, nor marry for any consideration under their own quality, which to prevent, if their fortunes will not procure husbands, they make them nuns . . . Their women seldom drink wine, their maids never.[1]

Naturally this norm was occasionally surpassed, and not only in the realm of literary and intellectual pursuits. The Infanta Margarita, made regent of the Netherlands by her brother Philip II; Philip's daughter, Isabel Clara Eugenia,[2] who continued to govern Flanders on the death of her husband the Archduke Albert; Princess Margaret of Savoy, made governor and viceroy of Portugal in 1633; all undertook masculine tasks. The Duchess of Braganza, a formidable woman of enormous ambition, was the emotional force behind her hesitant husband's revolt against the Spanish Crown. Catalina de Erauso served in the Spanish army in America for eighteen years before her sex was discovered.[3] Lope in his *Laurel de Apolo* asserts that Catalina, Lope de Rueda's actress wife, served the Duke of Medinaceli dressed as a page.[4] The Duchess of Lorena fled from Spain with her husband, dressed as a charcoal-burner.[5] Occasionally a girl escaped from a convent, occasionally one became a bandit,

Hoy se vió una causa en Chancillería por vía de apelación, de Medina del Campo. Uno y una mataron en un camino cerca de allí a un hombre

---

[1] *Memoirs of Lady Fanshawe*, 193–5.

[2] An example of female leadership that Doña María de Zayas is careful not to overlook in her disquisition on woman's abilities in the *Desengaño quinto* of her *Novelas amorosas y ejemplares*, II.

[3] See *La historia de la Monja Alférez escrita por ella misma, e ilustrada con notas y documentos por J. M. de Ferrer* (Madrid, 1918); also, James Fitzmaurice-Kelly's translation, *The Nun Ensign* (London, 1908).

[4] See Narciso Alonso Cortés, *Un pleito de Lope de Rueda* (Madrid y Valladolid, 1903).

[5] *Cartas de algunos PP* . . . I, *Mem. hist. esp.* XIII, 65. The Duchess of Chevreuse, on the other hand, fled *to* Spain dressed as a man: see, J. Homero-Arjona, 'El disfraz varonil en Lope de Vega', *BHi* XXXIX (1937), 143.

por quitarle 150rs y la mujer fue la que sacando una navaja le degolló.[1]

and occasionally a woman returned force with force,

Salió una mujer de Salsas para Perpiñán y en camino encontró con un soldado de a caballo que la quiso forzar. Ella, lidiando con él le sacó el puñal del cinto y le dió con él tres heridas, de las cuales cayó muerto; quitóle las armas y púsoselas, y subiendo en el caballo se encaminó a Perpiñán donde entró en la forma dicha[2]

The actress Bárbara Coronel took to wearing nothing but masculine dress, for which she had obviously conceived a liking after wearing it so often on stage; while the Marchioness of Leganés was obviously a woman to be reckoned with if ever there was one,

Este miércoles pasado fue la marquesa de Leganés a la casa de Campo a tirar, como suelen otras veces, a los conejos. Iban con ella sus dos hijas y su sobrina, la condesa de Mona. Acertó a ir también el Almirante, en su coche, las cortinas corridas, y dos damas con él, vestido como de campo. Iba el coche del Almirante siguiendo al de la marquesa, porque las damas que el Almirante llevaba, tuvieron gusto de verla tirar. La marquesa envió un recado al cochero diciéndo fuese por otra parte; su amo le dijo caminase. Volvió con segundo recado un criado de la marquesa, y dijo que la marquesa de Leganés iba allí con sus dos hijas y su sobrina, y que le pedían echase por otra parte. No se dió por entendido, y prosiguió ; salió del coche la marquesa y pidió una escopeta que cargó con sólo pólvora y taco, y apuntó al cochero para espantarle y obligarle fuese por otro camino; disparó y no hizo caso el cochero. Viendo esto la marquesa, cargó segunda vez con perdigones y apuntándole dio con él en tierra. Las damas que iban con el Almirante se desmayaron; el Almirante no estaba con vestido decente para darse a conocer.[3]

Women were not totally absent even from the business world. Widows sometimes continued to run shops after their husbands died, and occasionally a widow carried on her husband's publishing business. Francisca Verdugo continued to run her husband's theatre company after his death, while Mariana Vaca de Morales,

[1] *Cartas de algunos PP* . . . III, *Mem. hist. esp.* XV (1862), 113.
[2] *Ibid.* 293.
[3] *Cartas de algunos PP* . . . VII, *Mem. hist. esp.* XIX (Madrid, 1865), 118.

the daughter of Jusepa Vaca, actually formed a company of her own in 1652. H. A. Rennert points out that in 1660 the two companies of players in Seville were managed by women – Francisca López and Juana de Cisneros.[1] Even more notably, women were by no means unknown in the highly competitive world of the military orders. Although technically administrators and not *comendadores*, women frequently held *encomiendas*. They were allowed to continue to hold an *encomienda* after their husbands' death and were granted *encomiendas* in the name of a son. A woman, the Princess Doria, was amongst the 23 candidates for the *encomienda* of Moratalla in 1612 and by 1712 more than one-fifth of the *encomiendas* of the Order of Calatrava in Castille and Aragon were in the hands of women.[2]

Spain's territories in the New World seem to have provided a congenial atmosphere for the blossoming of the female spirit. The pioneering enthusiasm of the Anglo-Saxon women who settled North America is matched by that of the Spanish women who sailed west with their fathers and husbands, or in batches under the care of some lady of rank to provide the colonizing Spaniards with wives.[3] Their exploits range from the brutally physical to the purely administrative. At the siege of Santiago de Chile, a group of women beheaded five captured chiefs and, throwing the heads over the wall, succeeded in frightening off the attackers. María de Estrada, the wife of Pero Sánchez Farfán, a soldier of Cortés, 'en la salida de México hizo maravillas con espada y rodela, y . . . en la batalla de Otumba peleó a caballo'.[4] The wife of the *alférez real* Peñalosa in Juan de Oñate's expedition, 'viendo desbandarse a la hueste la contuvo y rehizo con sólo gritar que de vergüenza de verlos así se le caían las tocas'.[5] The wives of Nueva Imperial in Chile scaled ladders to enter the house of the Governor, Don García Hurtado de Mendoza, to plead for mercy for two men, Alonso de Ercilla and Juan de Pineda, whom he had condemned to death for duelling during the coronation

---

[1] *The Spanish Stage in the Time of Lope de Vega* (New York, 1909), 60.
[2] See L. P. Wright, 'The Military Orders in Sixteenth and Seventeenth Century Spanish Society', *Past and Present* 43 (May 1969), 34–70.
[3] See Cesáreo Fernández Duro, *La mujer española en Indias* (Madrid, 1902).
[4] *Ibid.* 23.   [5] *Ibid.* 23.

celebrations of Philip II. Doña María de Toledo governed the West Indies as vicereine. Doña Juana de Zarate was named Adelantado of Chile by Charles V. Doña Isabel Manrique and Doña Aldonza de Villalobos were governors of the Venezuelan island of Margarita. Doña Beatriz de la Cueva governed Guatemala. Doña Catalina Montejo succeeded her father as Adelantado of Yucatán. The wife of Hernando de Soto governed Cuba during her husband's absence, while Doña Isabel Barreto even captained a fleet that sailed from Spain to the Philippines. Obviously, in a land where Europeans of either sex were scarce and where the distance of supreme authority encouraged rivalry and revolt amongst the men, women, especially wives, came into their own.

These Spanish women of the eastern and western hemispheres were the real-life examples of the *mujer varonil* of the Spanish drama. They were the women who, through inclination or through circumstance, departed from the feminine norm of the society in which they lived, or which had, at least, nurtured them. Compared with the vast anonymous ranks of unexceptional femininity, they were a mere handful. The interest, sometimes scandalous, they aroused might have made them the source of the literary phenomenon. It would certainly have indicated to dramatists and theatre managers that such characters would have very great audience appeal. But such cases, spread out as they are over two centuries, were rare. It is impossible to conclude that the dramatists were merely holding up their mirrors to nature in their depiction of the *mujer varonil*. Indeed, art may have influenced reality. Most of the incidents involving women in masculine dress, for example, belong to the period when their dramatic counterparts were already well-established stage characters. It is not impossible that the theatre inspired some real-life *mujeres varoniles* to action or at least suggested to them the form that action might take.

More precise definitions of the role of women in Spanish society at that time must await further research. All that is possible at present is an impressionistic picture of the variety of experience that was open to women, against the drabber backcloth of the norm. Historical reality does not seem to have matched very exactly the literary and moralist attitudes, though inevitably the two interacted upon each other. Indeed the dangers involved in straightforward assumptions about art as a mirror to society and the pitfalls involved in the use of literary evidence as a key to historical reality are dramatically revealed in this case. Golden-Age drama may not accurately reflect the reality of woman's position in society, but it may very well reflect contemporary concern about the wisdom of allowing changes in that position. The reality of woman's actual place in society is in any case very complex. All that one can usefully conclude at the moment is that while it would be absurd to regard the theatre as an accurate mirror of society, it would be equally absurd to conclude that the theatre was immune to the new ideas on female education, unaware of the possibilities of female freedom, and uninterested in the feminist debate. The very contrast between the permissiveness of the minority and the comparative seclusion of the majority would heighten interest in the whole feminist question.

The ideas of Erasmus, the theological debate on woman as a 'moral entity', the very existence of exceptionally educated and emancipated women, and the new demands of a seaborne Empire, could all have acted as catalysts towards greater female freedom and expression – however uncharacteristic they were of female society as a whole – and it would have been odd if a popular theatre like that of the Golden Age had not reacted to, and exploited, the novel implications of these developments. The whole debate about women's position was, after all, full of titillating dramatic possibilities, as the popularity of the *mujer varonil* theme will amply illustrate.

2

The pre-Lopistas

I

Of the early pre-Lopista dramatists only one is of any interest in the context of the *mujer varonil* – Gil Vicente. The feminist debate, regarding the relative virtues and imperfections of women, was adopted early on in the drama by Juan del Encina in his *Égloga de tres pastores*, and subsequently taken up by other dramatists, including Sánchez de Badajoz in his *Farsa del matrimonio* and Per Álvarez de Ayllón in his *Comedia Tibalda*. But in these plays women are merely the passive object of intellectual discussion (usually between men) in a conventional mould; we see nothing in them of feminism in action.

Gil Vicente's contribution to the *mujer varonil* theme is limited to his *Auto de la sibila Casandra* (*c.* 1513), one of the most interesting of the early Spanish plays and the first in which the theme of active feminism appears. The figures of the unrequited or importunate lover and the unyielding maiden are common in the early drama but the rejection of man by maid is born not of principle but of personal preference. Vicente's *Auto* offers us the first, and for many years the only, example of the heroine who denounces the very concept of marriage and all it entails in words of sublime arrogance,

> ¿Quién mete ninguno andar
> ni porfiar
> en casamientos comigo?
> Pues séame Dios testigo
> que yo digo
> que no me quiero casar.
> ¿Quál será pastor nacido
> tan polido
> ahotas que me meresca?
> ¿Alguno hay que me paresca

45

en cuerpo, vista y sentido?
¿Quál es la dama polida
que su vida
juega, pues pierde casando,
su libertad cautivando,
otorgando
que sea siempre vencida,
desterrada en mano agena,
siempre en pena,
abatida y sujuzgada?
¡Y piensan que ser casada
que es alguna buena estrena!

(C.C. pp. 43–4, lines 1–22)[1]

In similar diatribes she inveighs against the tribulations of marriage, childbirth and parenthood. Interpretations of her abuse of marriage have ranged from the historically literal to the symbolic. A. F. G. Bell saw in her descriptions of marriage an accurate picture of 'the sad life of married women in Portugal'.[2] Thomas R. Hart[3] thinks that Casandra's words denouncing marriage as slavery have a deep significance of which Casandra herself is unaware. In rejecting marriage with Salomón, the *figura Christi* of medieval literature, Casandra is rejecting the union of the soul with Christ; the slavery she dreads is already hers and the only means of escape is acceptance of the marriage she rejects. Both critics go too far. The 'joys of marriage' are an old joke, here placed by the demands of character and action in the mouth of a woman. We do not need to look beyond the play to explain Casandra's complaints. Hart's interpretation is unsatisfactory because there is no reason inherent in the action why maidenhood should be slavery, and marriage an escape from it. One might argue that the analogy reflects contemporary social reality in that the sixteenth-century girl led a more restricted life than the sixteenth-century wife, but Casandra does not lead the life of a sixteenth-century girl: this kind of strained reasoning makes the

---

[1] Quotations are from Clásicos castellanos vol. 156 (Madrid, 1962).
[2] *Portuguese Literature* (Oxford, 1922), 114.
[3] Introduction to the C.C. edition and also 'Gil Vicente's "Auto de la Sibila Casandra"', *HR*, XXVI (1958), 35–51.

metaphor far-fetched and unsuccessful. Casandra can certainly be regarded as representative of the pagan world converted on the birth of Christ, but any closer analogy violates the text. As I. S. Révah remarked:

Nous ne ferons qu'une objection à l'interprétation subtile de Thomas R. Hart Jr: si Gil Vicente avait voulu parler du mariage spirituel de l'âme chrétienne et du Christ à ses spectateurs, il aurait sans doute pris la peine de les avertir de son intention[1]

Most commentators have been preoccupied with the outer and wider significance of Casandra's role within the religious framework of the *Auto*. But it seems to me that the psychological interest offered by Casandra is as great as the theological, and perhaps, given the early date of the piece and the rudimentary characterization usual in so much of the drama of the sixteenth century, even greater. Now that characterization and the study of character are once again respectable in literary studies, perhaps I shall be forgiven for suggesting that the inner, personal significance of Casandra merits attention. The general assumptions about Casandra have been that she has arrogantly interpreted the prophecy in her own favour and has accordingly feigned an aversion to marriage in order to preserve the virginity upon which fulfilment of the prophecy depends. Seen thus, her aversion to marriage is, if not a conscious effort to deceive, a rationalisation of her ambitions. These assumptions do Vicente less than justice. They relate Casandra's words strictly to the bare development and outcome of the plot, but do not account for the enormous *impact* which Casandra undoubtedly has. This has been widely felt. As Leo Spitzer has said, 'It is as if the whole final scene of the Adoration were staged especially for her conversion, for her entrance into the fold of believers.'[2] Various critics have tried to isolate the effectiveness of the central character. Spitzer, seeing Casandra as aspiring towards superhuman perfection, states, 'I believe that the visionary, otherworldly seriousness of the lonely figure of the

---

[1] 'L'*Auto* de la Sibylle Cassandre de Gil Vicente', *HR*, xxvii (1959), 174.
[2] 'The Artistic Unity of Gil Vicente's *Auto da Sibila Casandra*', *HR*, xxvii (1959), 58.

maiden, surrounded as she is by suitor and advisers speaking only in mundane terms and calling her "insane" from their point of view, must be deeply moving in a stage performance.'[1] Révah thinks the secret lies in 'la jonction du thème transformé de la Sibylle Orgueilleuse et de celui des "Joies de Mariage", mais des "Joies de Mariage" vues du côté féminin.'[2]

Révah's 'jonction' is not in itself, I think, 'le trait de génie' he claims. Vicente's Casandra, as Révah himself pointed out,[3] is in outline an amalgam of details given about all ten sybils in Andrea di Iacopo di Tieri's chivalresque novel *Guerino il Meschino*. Casandra's presumptuous interpretation of the prophecy was that ascribed by legend to the tenth sybil. Having chosen his theme, Gil Vicente had to create out of it some form of dramatic interplay. From the idea of virgin birth, to refusal to marry, to pressure to marry, to rationalization of refusal to marry, seems a natural progression, particularly in view of the 'joys of marriage' theme and the inborn humorous appeal of all grouses against established institutions such as marriage. The 'trait de génie' is a subsequent step. It lies in Vicente's ability to make a complex and fascinating character of the presumptuous prophetess who refuses to marry and makes obvious objections to marriage and men. And he does this by endowing his portrait of Casandra, consciously or unconsciously, with what might be called motivational depth. It has not only a psychological richness unusual for its time but also an enigmatic, open-ended quality not usually found in Spanish drama.

The surface development of the plot and the surface meaning of Casandra's words halt our awareness of Casandra, at the furthest point back in time, at the prophecy and its interpretation (which happen before the action begins). Casandra thought *she* was to be the virgin mother of God and hence refuses to marry. Gil Vicente gave enough 'dimension' to Casandra to allow, even encourage, our awareness to go back a step further and ask, 'But why did she interpret the prophecy in this way?' And there is enough in the text, in the development of the action and in the scope of Cas-

[1] *Ibid.* 65.
[2] 'L'*Auto* de la Sibylle Cassandre . . .', 193.   [3] *Ibid.* 183–8.

andra's words, to suggest an answer. Casandra has what today would be called a neurotic obsession about marriage. There is no evidence that her denunciations of wedlock are anything but sincerely and deeply felt. They certainly do not have the ring of firm, secret commitment *masquerading* as headstrong antipathy. Her diatribes on the married state and the character of husbands are not solely a means of concealing her conviction that she has been chosen to become the virgin mother of God. Rather this very conviction can be seen as the outcome of a real fear of marriage. Casandra is arrogant – to this Isaías bears witness,

> Tú eres de ella al revés
> si bien ves,
> porque tú eres humosa,
> sobervia, y presumptuosa,
> que es la cosa
> que más desviada es.

(p. 60, lines 538–43)

But at the same time she is afraid of life and of what it entails in the way of compromise, emotion, passion,

> No quiero verme perdida,
> entristecida
> de celosa o ser celada . . .
> Y ser celosa es lo peor,
> que es dolor
> que no se puede escusar . . .
> No quiero entrar en passiones
> pues que bien puedo escusarlas.

(pp. 48–9, lines 163–78)

Underneath her confident assertion that no man is worthy of her lies this fear of entering into a contract which might turn out to her disadvantage, of finding herself tied to a hateful partner in a captivity from which there is no escape. Salomón himself has nothing to do with it: she expressly tells him so. Her disinclination to commit herself is generalized, and part of her very make-up, as she implies in a double-edged remark,

49

> mas nació quando nací
> comigo esta opinión,
> y nunca más la perdí.
>
> (p. 46, lines III-13)

It extends not only to marriage, but also to the obvious alternatives – religion or the life of a hermit. And she therefore prefers the *status quo*, the freedom of her single state. Casandra, however, is a prophet and realizes that a virgin is to give birth to the incarnate God. Immediately her conceit together with her fixation on maidenhood make her interpret the prophecy in her own favour. She has found the ideal solution: without commitment or sacrifice, without losing her purity, she can become a mother, the mother of God.

Casandra, then, rejects marriage and makes her absurd but pathetic presumption out of pride born of fear. She lacks confidence in her ability to cope with life and comes to see herself as the passive object of glory. These implications are all present in the text and Casandra's dramatic stature sets the imagination questing in their direction. They do not interfere in any way with Casandra's role as a symbol of pride which must abase itself in the presence of humility before attaining to true worth. They merely add a new dimension to it. Similarly, they add to, not detract from, Casandra's surface role as a *mujer esquiva* who hates men and prizes her liberty – a figure which will become familiar in the secular drama in the seventeenth century.

The dramatist's attitude to Casandra and her views on marriage is inseparably linked with the religious message of the *auto*. The sybil-aunts disapprove of her on the materialistic grounds demanded at that moment by the action with its overt humorous appeal. The mood changes suddenly with the appearance of the uncles, however: Moisés denounces her attitude as blasphemy, since marriage is a sacrament. As Spitzer perceptively remarked,

the gemütlich details of family life found in our play are dogmatically justified by a basic character of the Christian religion: the God revealed by Christ is not only the World-Ruler or Heavenly King of other religions, but the Loving Father and the atmosphere of the human family pervades the Christian heaven even as the heavenly family is reflected in any human family: Casandra has denied first the human, then the divine family.[1]

In view of the particular religious context of the play and the provenance of the characters, the action of the play cannot lead to the marriage of Casandra and Salomón. This is the kind of inconsistency inevitable in religious drama. Like later heroines who reject marriage, Casandra is humbled and made to see the error of her ways, but there the analogy necessarily ends.

Apart from this one fascinating example, the theme of the *mujer varonil* does not appear in the early Spanish theatre. Casandra is at once too defined (in conception, as a sybil with a specific religious role) and too ambiguous (in presentation, as a richly and evocatively-drawn character) – in other words too individual – to have been an effective precedent in the creation of a type. It is possible that the absence of the feminist theme before the 1570s means simply that interest in woman and her place in society had not yet become significantly widespread; but perhaps more probable (since Erasmus was widely read in Spain from the 1530s on) is that there was no dramatist sufficiently interested. Dramatic themes, after all, are created or selected by dramatists. From the 1570s the picture changes considerably,[2] not only because interest in woman and her position had had time to gather momentum, but because at least two dramatists, Juan de la Cueva and Cristóbal de Virués, saw in strong female characters dramatic possibilities to be explored. Their plays are worth attention because they reveal the growth of a dramatic convention, and also the precedents available for Lope to draw on.

II

Out of the fourteen plays published under the title *Comedias y*

[1] 'The Artistic Unity . . .', 76.
[2] Leonardo de Argensola's Isabel, in the play of that name written for presentation about 1585, and Jerónimo Bermúdez's Nise, the heroine of *Nise lastimosa* and *Nise laureada*, first published in 1587, while not *mujeres varoniles*, serve to reveal the growing fashion for female protagonists.

tragedias de Juan de la Cueva in Seville in 1588, no less than nine are of some interest in the emergence of the *mujer varonil*. Within these nine the span of female 'abnormality' is a wide one. Included at the lower end is an early example of a dramatic device which later becomes a convention monotonous in the regularity of its appearance – the heroine's use of masculine disguise.[1]

The part of Celia in the *Comedia del degollado*,[2] first presented in Seville in 1579, is one of the largest female parts in Juan de la Cueva and without doubt one of the most attractive. Celia's motives throughout are love and honour. Love impels her to dress as a man at the start, and love prompts her to admit to murder in the hope of absolving Arnaldo; honour causes her to fight in her own defence. And these motives are traditionally feminine ones – her concern for her honour is the respectable concern of woman for her virtue which has led to the concept of the 'fate worse than death'. For all her strength of character Celia is, indeed, essentially feminine, in her aims and even ultimately in her behaviour: when her love seems thwarted she bursts into tears. With her warm, passionate nature, her temperamental weight and mesomorphic desire for action she is first cousin to a host of Golden-Age heroines who don male garb for the sake of love and honour. She is only a leavening of egoism, shrewdness and wit away from Tirso's 'Don Gil' and Doña Violante.

The important point about Celia is that in spite of being wholly feminine, her behaviour *is* regarded by the other characters as far beyond what is normally expected of a woman. The highest praise they can give her is therefore to assert that her qualities are masculine in their excellence. Her maid, describing Celia's abduction, remarks

> La bella Celia, no medrosa en esto,
> Con *varonil* esfuerço resistia
> El barbaro, que le era tan molesto,

[1] The device is used as early as 1559 by Juan de Timoneda in his *Comedia llamada Cornelia*.

[2] For the probable source of this play, which has points of similarity with *Measure for Measure*, see J. P. Wickersham Crawford, *Spanish Drama before Lope de Vega* (Philadelphia, 1937), 169.

Que su querer con fuerça le impedia.

(Act I, *C. y T.* I, 228)[1]

and the Prince eulogizes her in similar terms,

¡O constancia *varonil*,
Animo jamas movido,
Valor de muger no oydo,
Esfuerço no feminil!

(Act IV, 266 [the italics in both cases are mine])

This use of the adjective *varonil* as a standard of excellence becomes widespread in the seventeenth century[2] but although its implications as a value judgment are clear, the very frequency with which it is later used of women reflects a greater tendency than is shown here to take for granted – on the stage at least – woman's capacity for resolute action. As the type of the *mujer varonil* flourished and spread, familiarity bred acceptance and even expectancy.

The *Comedia del degollado* contains the one example in Juan de la Cueva of a woman who acts in a manner not normally expected of her sex, while dressed as a man. There is a group of four plays, however, in which the heroines adopt a masculine rather than a feminine pattern of behaviour while retaining their female identity. These are the *Tragedia de la muerte de Ayax Telamón sobre las armas de Aquiles* and the *Comedia de la constancia de Arcelina*, first presented in Seville in 1579; and the *Tragedia del príncipe tirano* and the *Comedia del viejo enamorado*, presented in the same city in 1580.

The *mujer varonil* of *Ayax Telamón* is the classical heroine Andromeca, Hector's wife. Cueva added little to the traditional *persona*. Proud and fearless, Andromeca acts in the best tradition of the fallen warrior who deliberately provokes his enemy into killing him. Doriclea and Teodosia in *El príncipe tirano* are women of the same formidable stock. Threatened with rape by the tyrant Lycimaco who has ordered that their father and husband be buried alive, they kill the Prince and then murder his henchman, Liguro.

---

[1] Quotations are taken from *Comedias y tragedias de Juan de la Cueva,* Sociedad de bibliófilos españoles (Madrid, 1917), referred to as *C. y T.*

[2] Like 'virago' in sixteenth-century Italy it was rarely used in a derogatory sense. Some other word, like *marimacho* or *marihombre*, is used to indicate disapproval.

And although in both cases, they act in self-defence, the capacity for unhesitating, cold-blooded action is by any standards remarkable:

> *Doriclea* ¿Que te agrada, Teodosia, que hagamos
> En vn riesgo de muerte tan notable?
> *Teodosia* Libremos nuestras prendas y muramos,
> Pues será vida muerte tan loable;
> Y assi no cumple dilatar momento
> Si avemos de salir con nuestro intento.
>
> *Liguro* ¡O traydoras, que al rey le distes muerte
> La qual os dare aqui con fiera mano!
> *Teodosia* Yo te hare que passes por la suerte
> Que passó dignamente el rey tirano.
> ¡Muere con el!
> *Liguro*   ¡O brazo duro y fuerte
> Quel fin m'á dado con su golpe insano!
>   (Act IV, *C. y T.* II, 267–8)

Now whether this somewhat comic woodenness is merely the result of hurried characterization or of some vision of heroic womanhood is a moot point. One would incline to the former view if the lack of femininity in Doriclea and Teodosia were not so extreme – even to the 'brazo duro y fuerte' – that it seems unlikely to have been accidental.

Olimpia in *El viejo enamorado* – an extravagant mixture of the supernatural and the commonplace – while no less capable of determined, even ruthless, action, is a much more credible and sympathetic figure. Like Celia in *El degollado*, if she acts with masculine determination, it is love which enables her to do so. For love she brings about directly or indirectly the death of two people. When she sets out to free Arcelo, undaunted by the supernatural powers at large or by the hazards of her journey, love drives her on: when she is lost and dispirited, love and faith are her guiding lights:

> Quiero seguir esta senda;
> No, que no se donde voy;
> Si, se, que voy donde estoy
> Aunque Fortuna me ofenda.

Pues por aqui tengo de ir
Aunque mas fragoso esté,
Que amor me guia y mi fe
Y no me pueden mentir.

(Act iv, 348)

There is in this intrepid quest more than an echo of the chivalresque, and of the Byzantine novel, an echo which continues to
sound through the innumerable love-chase plots of the seventeenth-century drama, albeit more faintly. Here we have the
fairy-tale formula in reverse. Instead of knight freeing lady from
tyrant, monster or spell, we have lover helpless and captive and
heroine killing his enemies to set him free. It is interesting that
Cueva did not put his wandering heroine into masculine dress; he
had after all made use of the device not long before in *El degollado*.
During the first decades of the following century a maiden errant
in her own clothes would be almost inconceivable, but as yet the
device is not firmly established.

Olimpia, then, is a woman who in pursuit of normal feminine
aims – love and happiness – reveals remarkable qualities of courage
and perseverance. Events force her to usurp what is traditionally
the role of the male in such adventures, but whether, in Cueva's
conception of the character, love imbues her with the qualities she
needs in this crisis, or whether it merely brings to light qualities
which are innate, it is impossible to say. The action takes a turn
which suggests the second, for Olimpia is not entirely a woman
compelled to masculine acts. Her reasons for killing Liboso are
two-fold. She wishes to remove every obstacle from her path in
her attempt to find Arcelo, and Liboso is such an obstacle. In addition, she explicitly states that by killing Liboso she is avenging
Arcelo (who, after all, is not dead),

Muere agora por mi mano
Con que doy vengança a Arcelo.

(Act iii, 334)

Even if the avenging impulse merely accompanies rather than
promotes the deed, the impulse is there, and since at the time
vengeance, like the related concept of honour, was a masculine

affair, by this impulse Olimpia can be seen as once again, if more obliquely, usurping man's social role. The vengeance motif is tossed in casually by Cueva, who does not in any way question Olimpias' right to avenge her lover, and it acquires significance only in the context of Olimpia's character and actions as a whole. Nevertheless it is a feature of the play worth bearing in mind. Later on, when the social conventions of the drama emerge with greater clarity and authority, the subject is dealt with seriously by dramatists who make their views more explicit.

Andromeca, Doriclea, Teodosia and Olimpia are women of strong character who under stress react in a way not normally associated with women, and are driven by force of circumstances to violent modes of action traditionally associated with men. Yet all four seem to have the approval of their creator, and the great majority of Cueva's female characters are strong, resolute and daring, in the tradition of many of the heroines of classical anti-quity and of Biblical characters like Jael and Judith.[1] And while he never explicitly says 'This is how all women should be', he presents them as worthy of admiration and even of imitation, in spirit at least. Even more remarkable: he is saying, or at least im-plying, 'This is what many women are capable of being' or even 'This is how some women are.'

The fourth play of this group, the *Comedia de la constancia de Arcelina*, is Cueva's most fascinating. It must surely be unique in Spanish drama in that here the usual roles of girl and lover(s) are reversed. Crisea and Arcelina, sisters, are both in love with Menalcio and quarrel violently over him. The language and imagery they use to describe their passion will become the peculiar property of male lovers on the seventeenth-century stage,

> *Arcelina* ¡Amor a ti me encomiendo!
> Y en el fuego en que esto ardiendo
> Las suertes voy a escrevir.
>
> (Act I, *C. y T.* II, 12)

and,

---

[1] See *Judges*, Chap. IV, verses 17–21, and *Judith*, 4th book of the Apocrypha.

Crisea   Arcelina, tu me sigues,
             Dexame gozar mi amor

(Act i, 19)

Further, to rid herself of competition Arcelina resorts to murder –
the solution attempted in later plays by the disappointed lover. If
Crisea and Arcelina take over the active role in love usually played
by the male, Menalcio's role is correspondingly reversed. The
girls' passion reduces him to fear and trembling. Afraid to offend
either with a refusal, he weeps and starts at everything he sees. His
soliloquy in Act I would be entirely convincing in the mouth of a
woman,

> Las venas siento de vn temor heladas,
> La voz al respirar no halla via,
> Tremo y no se de que . . .
> Cubrome todo de vn sudor elado
> Y derramo de lagrimas gran vena,
> El espiritu siento conturbado
> Y dentro en el vna excesiva pena;

(Act i, 21)

This reversal of roles is so marked and so extraordinary that it is
difficult to discover Cueva's motive. The sisters' aggressiveness
paves the way for the murder and to some extent for Arcelina's
subsequent self-sacrifice, but there seems no obvious justification
for Menalcio's timorousness. The contrast lends emphasis certainly, but the strength of the contrast remains, in terms of the
plot, inexplicable. The reversal was probably a piece of conscious
experimentation on Cueva's part, to carry the idea of the *mujer
varonil* to its logical conclusion by offsetting it with an *hombre
femenil.*

Arcelina, of course, is *varonil* in a peculiar way. Her *varonilidad*
lies not so much in masculine traits of character as in the fact that
she 'plays the man' in the first half of the play. She is the passionate
lover who presses his suit and kills his rival. Cueva's conception of
the character, however, is inconsistent. At this point Arcelina
undergoes a metamorphosis and sloughs her strange *varonilidad*
like an outgrown skin. Once she has fled into the hills, far from

feeding her aggressiveness with a life of crime she suddenly becomes all woman, weeping and bewailing her deeds. In other words, instead of driving her to desperation, the murder and enforced flight serve to restore her to 'normality'. Cueva does not stop here. Towards the end of the play Arcelina's character enters yet a third stage. After the abnormal adoption of the male role and the subsequent reduction to feminine tears, she becomes the woman lent courage and resolution by love but with a strong element of active feminism. In confessing to the murder of her sister, love for Menalcio is not Arcelina's only motive. She wishes to show that woman is capable of constancy and she wishes to win praise and glory for it. And while love cannot be considered a masculine motivation, the desire for glory and renown probably can.

The *persona* of Arcelina, it is obvious, is not of a piece. Since the inconsistencies of character could scarcely be accidental, it looks as if Cueva was aiming at a certain complexity of character which he was unable to bring off convincingly. We can, however, without difficulty salvage some diamonds of intention from this patchwork of personality. In the first part of the action Cueva, it seems clear, is showing that feminism taken to its furthest extreme makes woman a repellent monster. The rest of the play, on the other hand, seems intended to show that, with this proviso, woman is not the inferior being she is so often made out to be. The very title of the play seems to suggest that the theme is that constancy is not an exclusively masculine attitude; though one might be forgiven for not realizing this, since the theme is conjured out of nowhere in the third act, instead of being woven into the whole fabric of the play.

The last four of Cueva's plays relevant here contribute to the emerging picture of his attitude to women in a rather different way. Their heroines are *varoniles* in a much more conventional mould. Their roles are for the most part smaller and their circumstances and reactions are all less extreme. Doña Urraca in the *Comedia del rey don Sancho y reto de Zamora*, presented in Seville in 1579, is one of the earliest examples on the Spanish stage of royal authority in a woman. With her Cueva was much more successful

at conveying temperamental complexity than he was in the case
of Arcelina. She is presented as a courageous leader who defends
her city of Zamora in defiance of her brother Sancho who himself bears witness to her fighting spirit,

> ¿Qué puedo, si el poder de vna donzella
> Y hermana mia es bastante
> Que no passe adelante
> Con mi desseo? Tal valor veo en ella,
> Que pierdo con infamia mi renombre,
> Y de rey no posseo más que el nombre.
>
> (Act I, *C. y T.*, I, 14)

For all her qualities of leadership, however, Urraca is essentially
feminine. Weeping, she begs Arias Gonzalo not to leave her, an
orphan with no one to turn to, and within the brave sovereign
doing what her position demands of her, we glimpse a defence-
less woman. The combination is not Cueva's own – he faithfully
reproduced here the Urraca of ballad tradition.[1] But he blended
these qualities into a satisfactory dramatic whole and made it to
some extent his own by emphasizing those attributes which set
Urraca apart from the common run of women rather than those
which join her to them.

The women of strong character in the other three plays – the
*Comedia del saco de Roma y muerte de Borbón y coronación de nuestro
invicto emperador Carlos Quinto*, the *Comedia de la libertad de España
por Bernardo del Carpio*, both presented in Seville in 1579, and the
Comedia de la libertad de Roma por Mucio Cevola, presented there in
1581 – are all in the tradition of the Roman matron. Camila, Julia
and Cornelia in *El saco de Roma* are literally three *matronas romanas*
(albeit of the sixteenth century) captured during the sack of the
city by Charles V's army, who decide to die in defence of their
honour but are rewarded for their courage with liberty. In *La
libertad de España* Urraca Sánchez and María Meléndez risk the
King's displeasure by revealing Bernardo del Carpio's true identity to him, and, although they are nuns, urge him to revolt.
Finally, in *La libertad de Roma*, which dramatizes the siege of Rome

---

[1] See A. Durán's *Romancero general* I, B.A.E. x, nos. 795 and 796.

by the Etruscans, Emilia and Tiberia urge their men to battle instead of surrender. Theirs is a limited part in the play and they in no way affect the action. The impression given is that for Cueva the depiction of a slice of Roman history would be incomplete without a couple of Roman women uttering defiance and encouragement.

While the examples of *varonilidad* in these four plays may individually seem trivial, as a group they are important because they represent the sum total of the female roles contained in the plays. In depicting women Cueva was evidently drawn to those of energy and character; evidently too his opinion of women was higher than was usual. Taken together, his plays suggest that he was a champion of the opposite sex. He does not believe in woman's abandoning her essentially feminine role in life (Arcelina), but he does see her as capable of possessing and revealing admirable qualities.

It is arguable that Cueva depicted such women for practical reasons. In his *Ejemplar poético*, where he gives rules for dramatic portraits, he advises,

> Al siervo sin lealtad, y cauteloso,
> a la dama amorosa o desabrida,
> ya con semblante alegre, ya espantoso.[1]

But the definitive version in autograph manuscript of the *Ejemplar poético* bears the date 1609, thirty years after his first plays were performed, and a little less than twenty-eight years after the last were performed. So although it is not inconceivable that Juan de la Cueva portrayed strong female characters merely because of their audience-appeal, it seems more likely that, looking back and realizing how successful his women of this type had been, he was advocating feminine types he himself had depicted largely from preference. The practical consideration of what would or would not please naturally played a part. By 1609, of course, he had the authority of Lope's *comedia nueva* behind him. But even thirty years earlier, since he must have wanted success, we may assume that in depicting women of this type he had sized up his public.

---

[1] *Epístola* III, Clásicos castellanos LX (Madrid, 1924), 242, lines 628–30.

The initiative seems to have been his own, and must to some extent have helped *create* public taste; at the same time the climate was right for the dramatic presentation of the 'woman of spirit' and Cueva, through his own interest in the type, sensed this and exploited it.

III

That the climate was indeed favourable is indicated by the fact that Cueva's tendency to portray strong female characters was equalled, even surpassed, by that of his contemporary Cristóbal de Virués. Virués seems to have known Cueva's work and possibly was influenced by it. His strong attraction to the type of woman Cueva depicted led him to produce what W. C. Atkinson has called 'a predominantly feminine series of plays',[1] indicating that he too expected a receptive audience (in his case in Valencia or Madrid, not in Seville). Each of his five plays – written probably between 1580 and 1585 – contains a remarkable woman and four out of the five even have a woman's name in the title.

The fifth is interesting for its peculiarities. Virués, like Juan de la Cueva, experimented with the idea of putting his heroine into masculine disguise – in the fantastic *Atila furioso*, a play in which through a series of chain reactions with a single source in the 'heroine' herself, all the characters die violent deaths. Flaminia differs however from the usual *mujer vestida de hombre* in that she has been compelled to don her 'traje profano', as she calls it, by her captor the King, who wishes to have her near him without her presence becoming known. Almost inevitably, a *Twelfth Night* situation develops in which the Queen falls in love with the 'page', who pretends to reciprocate. Virués was patently bolder in his treatment of masculine disguise and its implications than Cueva, and *Atila furioso* was one of the earliest Spanish plays with a titillating complication of this sort. It was a complication which became popular – more usual in the seventeenth century than the disturbing attraction felt by the *hero* towards the disguised heroine. The reason is not difficult to see for the situation was at least

[1] 'Seneca, Virués, Lope de Vega', in *Homenatge a Antonio Rubió i Lluch*, I (Barcelona, 1936), 121.

visually normal and implications of female homosexuality would have been less readily detected than those of male homosexuality.

Her masculine disguise apart, Flaminia's claim to *varonilidad* is equivocal. Statistically, serious crime is a male pastime, so does Flaminia's propensity for it make her *varonil*? If we answer 'no' we are tacitly subscribing to the value judgment implied in the use of *varonil* as a term of praise bestowed by men upon women: women who depart from the norm in an admirable, positive or at least forgivable way, are *varoniles*; those who do so in a totally reprehensible way are just wicked women. Flaminia *is* a remarkable woman, yet falls into no convenient category of *varonilidad*. She is ambitious, but her ambition is directed towards becoming a consort queen. She is totally ruthless, yet although four murders in the space of a day might seem excessive, they are in the sound tradition of the fury of the woman scorned. The one time she commits murder directly she uses that traditionally female weapon, poison. One might say that rather than possessing unfeminine qualities she epitomizes the worst feminine ones of tradition – cunning, spite, a gift for intrigue and ruthless ambition. All the same, Flaminia does strike one as having a generous helping of male hormones in her temperamental chemistry. This impression of *varonilidad* arises from her *esfuerzo*, from the energy which distinguishes women like Flaminia and Lady Macbeth from the average woman of convention. Unaccompanied as this is in Flaminia by more attractively feminine qualities, she is not a character who would have appealed to Lope and his *comedia nueva*.

Felina in *La infelice Marcela* is a much clearer case. Although she has a minor role she is important in that she is the first known example of a female bandit in the Spanish drama. In comparison with what Lope and others made of the theme later on, Felina's banditry is a very sketchy affair. Although she refers to a past of violence and outlawry,

> No seré yo Felina, la que suele
> rebolver un linaje, un Reino, un mundo . . .
> ¿No soi Felina yo, la que en Galicia
> tuvo en bandos partida i alterada
> contra el alto poder de la justicia

la gente más florida i más grande . . .

(Act II, *PDV* I, 127b)[1]

and although she lives with bandits, we are not told why she has become a bandit and she seems not to play an active part in the criminal life of the gang. Conceivably these details were left out because Felina was known to the audience, either through a previous play or as a legendary/historical figure; the specific mention of Galicia might well be an indication of this. In the present play the extraneous references seem to have been introduced only to lend a rather naïve ferocity to her character. She is essentially a bandit's moll – she even retains her feminine skirts – and her claims to infamy in her own right merely lend a little superfluous surface drama.

No less formidable than Flaminia and Felina is the protagonist of *La cruel Casandra*, who like Flaminia brings about the destruction of all the main characters in the play. Like Felina she is a rebel but one of a much more significant sort. She is a rebel against masculine authority and against the social convention which decrees that she is subject to this authority even in that matter which concerns herself most closely – marriage. In this case the masculine authority is embodied in her brothers Fabio and Tancredo, whose disapproval of the man their sister wishes to marry is so intense that they are prepared to resort to murder. Casandra is as forceful and aggressive as her brothers, and swears to them that she will allow nothing to stand in her way,

> es escusado
> pensar que [h]avéis los dos de tener fuerça
> que mi amor i mi fe i palabra tuerça.
> I con un rayo me confunda el cielo
> en el profundo centro del infierno
> si dañáis a Leandro en sólo un pelo
> i usáis comigo desse mal govierno,
> si no remedio el daño i desconsuelo
> que me causéis, con un exemplo eterno

---

[1] Edition used is *Poetas dramáticos valencianos*, referred to as *PDV*, edited by E. Juliá Martínez and published in the Real Academia Española's Biblioteca selecta de clásicos españoles, 2ª serie, 2 vols (Madrid, 1929).

que a ningún otro deve ser segundo,
i atemorize i ponga grima al mundo.

(Act II, *PDV* I, 81a)

In pursuing the course of her fateful love she causes the deaths of five people and her own. Does this mean that Virués is pointing out the dangers of allowing women to follow their inclinations in such matters? Cecilia Vennard Sargent says

One wonders if Virués is approaching, back in the sixteenth century, the rising peril of the feministic movement. For Casandra was obviously a rebel to the existing order for feminine society, and Tancredo a martyr to conservatism. One cannot, however, be exactly sure of Virués's own attitude. For he himself had endowed Casandra with brains. Or are they too one – perhaps chief – of her vices?[1]

Miss Sargent is right to be equivocal. After all, Virués might equally well be condemning (as later dramatists did) the social conventions that drive Casandra to such lengths in her very natural desire to marry the man she loves. Nearer the truth, perhaps, is the possibility that Virués was unconcerned by the feminist or social implications of this part of his plot. His explicit theme was the evils of court life and certainly the crossed-love motif is smothered under a veritable dung heap of intrigue, treachery and rape; there is no hint of a serious examination of the conflict between love and social convention of the sort that preoccupied Lope.

The remaining two of Virués's five plays may be grouped together in that both have as protagonist a superwoman on a heroic scale. Here the similarity ends, for whereas Queen Dido in *Elisa Dido* is a paragon of womanly and queenly virtue – the epitome of female *varonilidad* in its most flattering sense – Semíramis in *La gran Semíramis* is a woman of tragic faults. (Inevitably Semíramis is the more fascinating of the two.)

Since Virués chose the version of Dido's story found in Justin's *Historiae Philippicae* and not Virgil's more familiar story of Dido and Aeneas,[2] his Dido is the perfect monarch – noble, virtuous,

---

[1] *A Study of the Dramatic Works of Cristóbal de Virués* (New York, 1930), 85.
[2] For a comprehensive study of the Dido story in Spain, see María Rosa Lida's article 'Dido y su defensa en la literatura española', *RFH* IV (1942), 209–52 and 313–82.

adored by all. Even the discovery that the men they love are emotionally committed to the Queen cannot stop her slave girl and
her confidante loving her, and it is the latter's account of her
mistress that reveals those qualities of courage and resolution,
prudence and shrewdness, which are not fully discovered by the
action. Virués has allowed nothing to detract from Dido's perfection as wife and leader. She gives Virgil the lie by being faithful
to the memory of her husband and by placing the welfare of her
people above all else; she remains true to both through self-
sacrifice. Love, in other words, can ennoble, just as in the case of
her general and her governor, who out of jealousy break the
peace treaty, it can render ignoble. Virués's attitude to his Dido
is unequivocal. His choice of Dido – the idealized Queen instead
of the passionate woman – was probably largely determined, as
María Rosa Lida suggested, by aesthetic considerations, by his
conception of tragedy:

De que Virués, clasicista, prefiriera la Dido de Justino a la de Virgilio no
sólo se infiere la difusión extraordinaria de la defensa de Dido, sino
también la austeridad de su sentido de la tragedia antigua; a la tragedia
de sólo amor de la Eneida, al conflicto pasional del arte alejandrino,
Virués prefiere, y acierte a preferirlo, el conflicto moral del arte
ateniente.

But there is little doubt that for the Dido he chose he entertained
the greatest admiration. For him she obviously epitomized the
heights of nobility and virtue that the human soul can reach. The
fact that she is a woman is an unconscious acknowledgement that
greatness of soul is a human, not a sexual, quality.[1]

Virués reveals in his plays not merely an interest in female
characters but a fascination with extremes of female character. Dido is perfect, Felina apparently infamous, Flaminia and

---

[1] The tragic Queen had been dealt with several years before by Alonso de Ercilla:
see *La Araucana*, III, XXXII–XXXIII (published 1589). A contemporary of Virués's,
Gabriel Lobo Lasso de la Vega, also wrote a play in defence of the chaste Dido,
called *La honra de Dido, restaurada*. The action here is much fuller than that of
Elisa Dido, tracing the story back beyond the death of Dido's husband. Amongst
others to write plays about Dido were Don Antonio Folch de Cardona, marqués
de Castelnovo, Alonso de las Cuevas and Álvaro Cubillo.

Casandra evil. And if we cannot so easily attach one single adjective to Virués's outstanding heroine, Semíramis, her larger-than-life personality, her temperamental stature, are if anything more apparent. She is the perfect foil to Dido: a superwoman for whom love and power represent things radically different from the chaste fidelity and self-sacrificing devotion of the Carthaginian queen. The pleasing symmetry and moral significance of the contrast may indeed have influenced Virués in his choice of Dido. Certainly Virués's aim in *La gran Semíramis* seems to have been didactic, and much less ambiguously so than Calderón's subtler and more complex treatment of Semíramis in *La hija del aire*.[1]

Semíramis, 'King' of Syria, is an early and supreme example of the *mujer guerrera*. Her instinct for war is established early in the play and thereafter never lets her down. At Menón's request Semíramis turns up outside the besieged city of Bactra, dressed as a man, in order to be at his side – the tender, loving wife. She immediately perceives the weak spot in the city's defences to which everybody else has been blind. At this stage her ambition is only beginning to unfold and she has the grace to ascribe her military acumen to her love for Menón.

> Tengo [vuest] ra alma en mí i por esso acierto.
>
> (Act I, *PDV* I, 27b)

In Act I we see no formal evidence of ambition in Semíramis, but the signs are unmistakable. In such a woman the half-hearted protests at Nino's proposals and the transparently feeble complaints when she is taken from her husband – 'O[h], injusto apartamiento!' (Act I, 33a) are eloquent indications that a calculating ambition is flowering. She has glimpsed power and glory. With the help of fate she has risen from being the foster daughter

---

[1] Virués's plot differs considerably from Calderón's. A description of the Virués plot is to be found in Miss Sargent's book. G. Edwards in his London University doctoral thesis on *La hija del aire* states that the changes Virués introduced into his source material were designed 'to carry out the moral purpose suggested in the Prologue, and within this context to deal particularly with the evils of ambition on the one hand and of erotic love on the other'. (Chap. 4, 54). See also, 'Calderon's *La hija del aire* in the Light of his Sources'. *BHS* XLIII (1966), 177–96; and his critical edition of *La hija del aire* in Colección Támesis (London, 1970).

of a shepherd, through marriage to the King's general, to marriage with the King himself.

As a woman this is as far as Semíramis can go, but it is not enough. After sixteen years as the power behind her husband's throne her insatiable appetite for power breaks its bounds and she seizes absolute control. She poisons the King, and, since the presence of a natural male heir prevents her ruling in her own name, she sends Ninias to the temple in her place and, dressed in his clothes, reigns in his stead. Her sexual insatiability is already making itself shown, but ambition comes first. She lusts for power more than men,

> Pero, mis pensamientos amorosos,
> dexadme aora en paz, mientras la guerra
> de mis altos desseos valerosos
> haze temblar i estremecer la tierra;
> los filos azerados, rigurosos,
> que en la baina mil anos [h]a que encierra
> mi coraçon, dexad que aora corten,
> que tiempo [h]avrá después que se reporten.
>
> (Act II, 38b)

She has a need, a compulsion, to dominate, to conquer and to legislate, and there is presumably much of this compulsive desire to conquer in her subsequent sexual behaviour. Semíramis, in short, was by conventional standards born into the wrong sex: she has the character, the ambitions, the physical urges, the abilities, the soul of a man. She is lacking even in maternal love and, as Miss Sargent points out, is feminine only in her instinctive knowledge of how to handle men. But she *is* a woman, she is Semíramis; and such is her egotism that she wishes to be recognized as Semíramis the woman, and applauded as Semíramis the woman. Disguised, she is merely creating glory for her son and she wants immortality for herself. Totally successful as she is, her ambition carries within itself the seeds of its own defeat. She is driven to admit to the impersonation although it means the end of her career, and appropriately, at the point of decision, the supreme egoism of this superwoman who has not been able to rule *qua* woman manifests itself as supreme feminism,

> Ya llegó al punto mi desseo ardiente
> de que el mundo por mí en su punto viesse
> una muger [h]eroica i ecelente;
> una muger que en guerra i paz rigiesse
> fuertes legiones, pueblos ordenados,
> i que en todo a mil Reyes ecediesse
>
> (Act III, 47a)

In spite of the play's didacticism there is much of the tragic hero in Semíramis. Her faults are pride, ambition and latent promiscuity (the last Calderón discreetly omits), and Fate in the person of the King's general intervenes and places her in a position where these faults can flourish. As indisputable as her faults are her great qualities, to which Diarco the porter bears touching testimony at the end (Act III, 54a–55a). And we, and Virués too, share Diarco's awed pity,

> ¡Qué diré . . .
> de esta fuerte muger, que inútil peso
> haze en la tierra fría, fría tierra!
>
> (Act III, 55b)

It is pity, not for the death of a person sympathetic to us, but for the sight of greatness wasted and destroyed, of greatness betrayed by human frailty. It is the pity properly inspired by all victims, for Semíramis is the victim of Fate – her tragedy is that she was not born a man.

If Virués's approach to Dido is essentially asexual, in the case of Semíramis we are conscious all the time of his acute awareness of her as a woman. Her superhuman qualities, which he makes much more of than Calderón was to do, are made to seem more impressive for being the property of a member of the 'weaker' sex. Her promiscuity is for the same reason made to seem more shameful. Much is made of her protracted rule disguised as a man and of the problem this represents for her ego. Her greatness and her weakness alike gain emphasis from her sex. And we need not be surprised in view of all this that Virués plays down the most feminine quality of the legendary Semíramis – her irresistibility; none of Virués's heroines is notable for her charm, and in this case charm was superfluous to Virués's purpose. Yet in spite of the close integration of Semíramis's sex into the development of plot and theme, and in spite of Virués's obvious condemnation of Semíramis's lust for power and her praying-mantis sexual excesses, there is no question, I think, of his drawing conclusions from her example about women in general. Semíramis is treated as an individual woman and not as a representative one. Zelabo may grumble about her,

> esta infelice i grande Monarquía
> que estar en mano varonil devría.

and,

> quien es de una muger avassallado
> ¿de qué miseria no podrán dolerse?

> (Act III, 50a)

but who is he to pass judgment or to speak for his creator? These are the grudges of a disappointed man who was prepared to plot with Semíramis to kill Nino and cheat Ninias of his inheritance. Semíramis is a tyrant and a murderer, but she is preceded on the throne by a weak and tyrannical king and is succeeded by a son who shows every sign of being as false and ruthless as she was. Indeed far from condemning women in power, Virués shows that men and women alike are capable of its abuse. Ironically, by making Semíramis's sex of paramount importance, Virués illustrates that the barrier of sex is surmountable, that woman can be as great and as weak, as able and as evil, prey to the same desires and as capable of realizing them, as any man.

Semíramis is a fitting person with whom to end an examination of Virués's 'predominantly feminine' series of plays, rising as she does to a crescendo of *varonilidad*. Given the characters we have been looking at, Atkinson's phrase 'predominantly feminine' becomes peculiarly inapt. It is hard to conceive of women less conventionally or traditionally 'feminine' than Virués's heroines, whether one thinks in terms of the destructive aggression of Flaminia, Casandra and above all Semíramis, or in terms of the supreme courage and integrity of Dido. 'Predominantly female' would be a more accurate phrase in that it is less open to ambiguity, but there is no reason why one should not reach beyond such pusillanimous labelling and call the plays predominantly feminist. For if feminism means the depiction of women in a way which emphasizes their common humanity with men at the cost of conventional sexual distinctions, then Virués is a feminist playwright. Indeed he is more completely feminist than those subsequent dramatists whose apprehension of the problem was more complex and involved. Whether Virués ever thought about the matter in the deliberate and exhaustive way that Lope patently did, it is impossible to say from five plays. Probably not, for it has to be done, if it is to have any bearing on reality, in the context of normal womanhood and Virués was interested only in extremes. The extreme was a dramatic device to which Lope also resorted – the *bandolera* – but only in order consciously to examine social attitudes of supreme importance to all women living in a society where the double standard of morality operates. Virués's thematic interests lay elsewhere; he illustrated them with extremes of female personality because such extremes obviously held for him a compulsive fascination. These were the women he knew how to portray: Marcela – gentle, faithful and loving – is a colourless wraith in comparison. We cannot guess at the reasons for this fascination, though no doubt a psychoanalyst could construct a pretty edifice of conjecture on the basis of Virués's man-destroying harpies. On the evidence of his plays Virués's feminism was not so much an intellectual or emotional conviction as an intuitive response. Whether or not he approved of women of assertive character is unimportant. What is important is that he seems to have accepted their existence, and this makes him, in effect if not necessarily in intention, a champion of women within the context of his age; and a true champion, since he did not destroy one false image of womanhood only to replace it with an equally false but more flattering one, as the sentimental and chivalresque novels had done. Like Fray Luis de León Virués did woman the invaluable service of treating her like a human being; not, however, in the context of every-day life but in the more rarified atmosphere of exceptional circumstances. He took it for granted that women, no less than men, have both plumbed the depths and scaled the heights of morality.

Virués completes the pattern traced by the emergence of the *mujer varonil* theme in the Spanish drama which can properly be called *pre-Lopista*. This pattern is well-defined. Until the last third, even the last quarter, of the sixteenth century, unusual female characters *brillan por su ausencia*. The one exception is Gil Vicente's Casandra. With Juan de la Cueva and Cristóbal Virués such women come to dominate the stage. Their heroines of strong and independent character habitually play a large and important part in the development of plot and theme. And the importance of these two dramatists is not limited to this fact alone, for in their various portrayals of this type of woman they introduced into the Spanish theatre many of the variations on the *mujer varonil* theme subsequently adopted, perhaps in slightly altered form, by other dramatists. As far as one can tell the Roman-matron type,[1] the bandit,[2] the rebel against social convention[3] (at this stage these last two are separate), the leader and warrior,[4] were originally their contribution. These cannot all have been mere by-products of a predilection for Spanish historical and classical themes or for Senecan gore; *a fortiori*, the many other heroines in their plays who have less easily pigeon-holed masculine qualities[5] are even less likely to be directly traceable to such sources.

Since there seem to be no other extant examples of these types before Lope and his contemporaries, we have to look upon Cueva and Virués as being to a large degree responsible for the introduction of the theme of feminism into the Spanish theatre. It cannot be shown that they influenced Lope directly although Lope almost certainly knew Virués and his work in Valencia, and it is impossible to establish whether the female characters of Cueva and Virués were to any degree copied from or by other playwrights, and whether their dramatic feminism was part of a wider movement. The process of influence from the inception of the theme to Lope's

[1] Cueva, *La libertad de España, La libertad de Roma, El saco de Roma.*
[2] Virués, *La infelice Marcela.*
[3] Virués, *La cruel Casandra.*
[4] Cueva, *La muerte del rey don Sancho*; Virués: *La gran Semíramis, Elisa Dido.*
[5] Virués, *Atila furioso*; Cueva, *El príncipe tirano, La muerte de Ayax Telamón, La constancia de Arcelina, El viejo enamorado, El degollado.*

71

exploitation of it can be anything one cares to make it. In the case of Juan de la Cueva, Marcel Bataillon has suggested that in all probability Cueva's works were for the most part forgotten by the time Lope dominated the theatrical scene. The fact that he is rarely mentioned by later dramatists would seem to confirm this, argues Bataillon, and Cueva's historical importance today is great simply because he was one of the few dramatists of his time canny enough to have his works published, whereas it is very likely that a great number of plays by more influential writers just do not survive.[1] The possible truth of this conjecture is evident, though it is by no means inconceivable that Lope omitted Cueva's name from his *Arte nuevo* for other reasons. But literary influence is an elusive and dangerous game to play at this level of hypothesis. Who is to say that Cueva did not influence or at least reflect the influence of this shadowy host of writers and their missing plays? Why should Cueva's far-sightedness in the midst of creative fecklessness serve to banish him in our eyes to some outer limb of the tree of dramatic influence when, in his day, he might equally well have enjoyed a position close to the trunk? We can only work with the plays which for better or worse are extant. The extant plays of both Cueva and Virués mark a sudden dramatic efflorescence of the *mujer varonil* and it is difficult to believe that this was pure coincidence or that it was a completely isolated phenomenon. The commitment of these two dramatists to women of this type is a strong indication that they were probably influential in the establishment and the propagation of the new vogue, but it is equally feasible that they reflected a growing fashion for the type amongst other dramatists. Their *mujeres varoniles*, after all, must have been to some degree, like their historical and classical themes, a response to what they considered to be the public pleasure, the public mood, and it is hardly likely that Cueva and Virués were alone in their willingness to court applause and success.

[1] 'Unas reflexiones sobre Juan de la Cueva', *Varia lección de clásicos españoles* (Madrid, 1964), 206–13.

3

Cervantes and the Valencians

Slightly outside the mainstream of the Spanish theatre of the Golden Age stand four figures who are, for varying reasons, of interest in the growth and spread of the *mujer varonil* theme. They are Cervantes, Tárrega, Aguilar and Guillén de Castro.

Cervantes's position is unique: he had a foot in each of two distinct eras of dramatic creativity, and he is therefore the most obvious writer to look to for evidence of Lope's impact on the feminist tendencies of the Spanish stage. Tárrega, Aguilar and Guillén de Castro were in many respects transitional figues but their interest is geographical not merely chronological. That they worked in Valencia may be significant, since Cristóbal de Virués too was Valencian. Did Lope first meet the *mujer varonil* in the theatres of Madrid, her appearance there signifying a *generalized* popularity to which Cueva in Seville and Virués in Valencia also testify? Or was it a more localized affair? Did Virués perhaps take his *mujer varonil* to Madrid from Valencia? Or did Lope perhaps meet her in Valencia during his exile there and, finding her to his taste, take her back with him to the capital? In Valencia itself the possibilities are even more complex. Is the influence on Tárrega, Aguilar and Castro indigenous to Valencia or was there some cross fertilization, with Lope – particularly in the case of the last two – directly or indirectly exerting upon the Valencians an influence whose source was Valencia itself? All that is certain is that in the space of six years or so stage heroines who departed markedly from the social female norm appeared in Seville and Valencia and that within another ten years this type of female protagonist was well on the way to becoming an established convention of the Madrid stage. While it is possible that simultaneous spontaneous genera-tion explains the Seville/Valencia coincidence, it would be wrong to underestimate the extent of theatrical contacts, and the effect of travelling theatrical companies. As for Lope, his visit to Valencia and the staging of some of Virués's plays in Madrid probably drew his attention to the dramatic possibilities of the 'abnormal' heroine and her intriguing anomalies.

I

Cervantes's curious position in the history of Golden-Age drama is not the only reason for approaching his plays with expectancy. His views on love and marriage, on female virtue and integrity, are prominent in the *Novelas ejemplares*. Furthermore, his sympathy with that famous *mujer esquiva* of Spanish letters, Grisóstomo's Marcela,[1] indicates acute awareness of the injustice of the accepted attitudes that governed relations between the sexes. The expectations his prose works create, however, are not fulfilled in his drama. Only two of the plays he wrote before 1588 survive, and only one gives any indication of a pre-Lope approach to the *mujer varonil*. The eight plays published in 1615 add little to our knowledge of Cervantes's views, although they certainly corroborate them. But as a whole, his relevant works are not without interest.

The early play, *El cerco de Numancia*, which was probably presented not long after his return from captivity in Algiers in September 1580, is Cervantes's dramatization of the siege of Numancia by the Romans under Scipio. Cervantes confines himself to the last hours of resistance and the famous finale of the mass suicide. Within this context the inclusion of a clutch of women in what I have called the Roman matron tradition is virtually inevitable. They reprimand their menfolk for suggesting that the Romans be fought outside the city walls and declare their wish to die by their husbands' sides. Lira, one of the city's maidens, refuses to eat the bread her lover has found her at the cost of his life, preferring to follow him into death. These women at no time break through the stylization of their characters and might have been taken straight from Juan de la Cueva. They represent the female citizens of heroic Numancia and they are for the most part formally presented as such: 'Mujer primera', 'Mujer segunda', or just 'Mujer'. They

---

[1] *Don Quijote*, I, Chaps. XIII–XIV.

are Numantians first and women second, and their sex is important only in so far as it demonstrates the city's total unity in civic and national pride.

Limited as the evidence offered by these early women of Cervantes is, they belong very definitely to the period in which he was then writing. In conception their characters were obviously dictated by the plot and they are types who reappear in the Spanish drama later. But in presentation they are cast in a mould of marked rigidity, a rigidity common in the depiction of women in pre-Lope drama: they call to mind Juan de la Cueva. This woodenness, although present in some of Lope's early plays, largely disappeared from the Spanish theatre after Lope had started showing the way towards a finer, subtler and more complex presentation of feminine psychology.

Cervantes's later plays certainly show Lope's influence in this respect. Cervantes's most obvious *mujer varonil*, Marfisa in *La casa de los celos y selvas de Ardenia* – a play based on chivalresque romance with elements from classical mythology and medieval moralities – is an exception, but even she has more in common with the Amazons and warrior queens produced by Lope in considerable numbers in the 1590s and 1600s than with the superwomen of Cueva and Virués. The direct sources of this self-proclaimed *mujer guerrera* who is female only in that she has the name and body of a woman, are Italian, as Schevill and Bonilla pointed out.[1] Cervantes allows her to introduce herself:

> Soy mas varon en las obras
> que muger en el semblante;
> ciño espada y traygo escudo,
> huygo a Venus, sigo a Marte;
> poco me curo de Christo;
> de Mahoma no ay hablarme;
> es mi Dios mi braço solo,
> y mis obras, mis penates,
> Fama quiero y honra busco . . . ,
>
> (Act III, *C. y E.* I, p. 215, lines 3-11)

[1] In the introduction to *Comedias y entremeses* (Madrid, 1915–22), VI, 107. References are to this edition.

He took her unchanged from Boiardo and Ariosto. Ariosto's description of the Indian Queen runs,

> La vergine Marfisa si nomava,
> Di tal valor, che con la spada in mano
> Fece più volte al gran Signor di Brava
> Sudar la fronte, e a quel di Montalbano:
> E'l dì e la notte armata sempre andava
> Di qua di là cercando in monte e in piano
> Con cavallieri erranti riscontrarsi
> Et immortale e glorïosa farsi.
>
> (*Canto* XVIII, stanza XCIX)

Cervantes's inclusion of this ferocious figure is quite arbitrary. She has a small part and, like most of the play's characters, is unnecessary to the action. Her presence can only be the outcome of the fashion for this type of militant female character created by Lope, and considerably bolstered up by the already well-established appeal of the *mujer vestida de hombre*. Cervantes presumably intended some of Marfisa's visible female attributes to show beneath the weight of her armour.

The two heroines of *El laberinto de amor*,[1] Julia and Porcia, are very different – shrewd and resourceful but entirely feminine, after the manner of so many of Lope's women. Their disguises as shepherds and their changes of female identity, with the complications to which these understandably give rise, are amusing, ultimately effective but altogether unremarkable. But, underneath the bland humour, lies a note of stridency. Cervantes leaves us in no doubt that the girls' antics are desperate measures to which they have been driven in order to marry the men they love, in order even to *meet* them. Anastasio has never seen his cousin Porcia and Manfredo was not allowed to meet Julia at her father's house; this unnatural separation of the sexes drives the girls to the bizarre solution of wandering the countryside dressed as men in search of two lovers who have never set eyes on them.[2] Both Julia and Porcia

---

[1] Schevill and Bonilla think that this plot too was probably taken from Ariosto, canto v. See their Introduction, 112.

[2] See Casalduero's remarks on Cervantes' views about feminine seclusion and parental authority in *Sentido y forma del teatro de Cervantes* (Madrid, 1951), 151–63.

mention the seclusion in which Julia's father has kept them, Julia
with eloquent poignancy,

> Teniame mi padre
> encerrada do el sol entraua apenas;
> era muerta mi madre,
> y eran mi compania las almenas
> de torres leuantadas,
> sobre vanos temores fabricadas.
>
> (Act II, *C. y E.* II, p. 279, lines 17–22)

Julia's world was peopled only by the castellated towers built by
her father's unfounded fantasies and fears, the brutally concrete
solution of a mind which, like that of Carrizales, puts its faith in
externals. Yet deprivation gives rise to curiosity and desire, as
Julia remarks,

> Auiuóme el desseo
> la priuacion de lo que no tenia
> – que crece, a lo que creo,
> la hambre que imagina carestia –;

and if frustrated curiosity alone cannot overcome an ingrained
sense of social decorum, true love when thwarted can. In taking
the initiative in running their lovers to earth Julia and Porcia contravene the laws of social and sexual decorum. The fault, Cervantes
makes clear, is not theirs but that of Society, which with its con-
straints on relations between the sexes prevents Nature from fulfilling itself. The very conflict between Nature and Society makes
Society's rules counterproductive. The precautions taken to protect the girls' virtue drive them to a course which exposes them to
greater perils than they would encounter in normal social intercourse. The situation here, like that of *El celoso extremeño*, is the
reverse of that in *La ilustre fregona* and *La gitanilla*, but the thesis
is the same: freedom is the natural habitat – the only habitat – of
virtue.

The tension between Nature and Society, between man's
impulses and the effort of the established order to protect itself
by restraining them, became a recurring theme in seventeenth-
century drama. Within the context of love and marriage Lope, a

man of strong impulses himself, was particularly absorbed by the conflict and its tragic possibilities. In Cervantes's play, although the tragic potential in the girl's situation does not pass unnoticed, it is never realized. The girls ignore Society and Nature triumphs; once Nature has taken its course, order is re-established with the marriage of the couples. Personal desires and social demands are both ultimately gratified – but only after authority has been flouted. The pattern is that of a hundred seventeenth-century plays. In one respect, though, Nature's case is put more strongly and explicitly than usual. Anastasio receives the news that Porcia might have left home in search of him with a complacency based on the intellectual conviction that women are as affected by sexual attraction as men:

> Di: no puede acontecer,
> sin admiracion que assombre
> que vna muger busque a vn hombre
> como vn hombre a vna muger?
> Como a su centro camina,
> esté cerca o apartado,
> lo leue o lo que es pesado,
> ya a procuralle se inclina,
> tal la hembra y el varon
> el vno al otro apetece
> y a vezes más se parece
> en ella esta inclinacion;
> y si la naturaleza
> quitasse a su calidad
> el freno de la honestidad,
> que tiempla su ligereza,
> correria a rienda suelta
> por do mas se le antojasse,
> sin que la razon bastasse
> a hazerla dar la buelta;
> y ansi, cuando el freno toma
> entre los dientes del gusto,
> ni la detiene lo justo
> ni algun respeto la doma.
>
> (Act II, p. 262, lines 3-7, 12-31)

The second half of the quotation seems to echo the theological view of woman as essentially wanton and lascivious, but there is in the first half a remarkable acceptance of sexual attraction in ordinary respectable women as part of the natural order. The complementary function of woman is of course a commonplace of the theatre based on Aristotle's theory that the relationship of woman to man is that of matter to form. Equality in the very nature of the process, however, is something different and at odds with the premises on which many societies, including seventeenth-century Spain, have based their attitudes to marriage and sexual morality.

The conflict between Nature and Society is repeated in Cervantes's *El gallardo español* in the person of Margarita. Like Julia and Porcia she represents thwarted femininity. Her brother refuses to allow her to marry, and Cervantes again resorts to the same device, this time in reverse: Margarita has never met the young man she loves and who once asked for her hand. The tension is resolved in the usual way. Margarita escapes from her convent, disguises herself as a man and follows Fernando to Italy and Africa where she willingly enters captivity for his sake. The seriousness of Margarita's remedy is again not overlooked. Fernando calls her attire 'indecente', while her brother Juan puts Society's attitude to her in the strongest terms,

> en perdiendose el respeto
> al mundo, se pierde a Dios.
>
> (Act III, *C. y E.* I, p. 113, lines 25–6)

And this view is not merely the 'que dirán' mentality given ultimate sanction. It is the philosophical stance which sees mirrored in Society's order the order of the universe as conceived by God. Margarita in defying her brother's authority, delegated by Society, has defied that delegated to Society through the monarch by God. The contention of Cervantes, Lope and others was that, in love and marriage, Society often misinterpreted its authority in its attempt to achieve the impossible: to rationalize the irrational and thwart man's nature, equally God-given. The outcome is potential disaster which, with more realistic and humane social attitudes working within the moral law on which social order is based, could easily have been avoided. Margarita's aim – marriage – is both natural and respectable, socially and theologically, and, by denying it, her brother is to blame for what follows. Eventually it is Juan, who has driven her out of society, who with his forgiveness allows her re-entry. The authority is still his, Society is placated, and Margarita marries the man she loves.

The familiar figure of Margarita is offset in the play by a much odder character – the mooress Arlaxa. The contrast between them has been dealt with by Casalduero who sees Margarita as a symbol of Christian fortitude, constancy and marriage and Arlaxa as a symbol of heathen shallowness, sensuality and caprice.[1] That the women were conceived as contrasting figures is clear, and it is equally clear that Cervantes intended to illustrate the true nature of *varonilidad* in women. Arlaxa claims to have 'vn alma bizarra/y varonil' (Act I, p. 41, lines 23–4), and her obsession with physical prowess and courage attracts her to Fernando. Her desire to see his virility prostrate at her feet reveals a lust for sexual dominance which is more than sensual caprice. Yet Arlaxa proves to be merely a spectator of the qualities she claims to admire and her 'alma bizarra and varonil' dissolves like a cloud of smoke at the first adverse puff of wind,

> Christiano [a Spanish soldier], yo me rindo; no ensangrientes
> tu espada en mugeril sangre mezquina.
> Lleuame do quisieres.
>
> (Act II, p. 77, line 29 to p. 78, line 1)

She is content in danger to hide behind her sex. Margarita, in contrast, who wants only love and marriage in the form of Fernando, actually seeks danger out in her determination to let nothing stand in the way of fulfilment of her normal feminine desires. And it is Margarita who has to defend Arlaxa. True *varonilidad* in a woman, in other words, has nothing to do with superficial whims; rather it is consonant with inner resources of mental and moral strength – which in Margarita's case Casalduero sees as the outcome of a Christian upbringing.

Ironically, Arlaxa, the *mujer varonil* who turns out otherwise

---

[1] *Sentido y forma* . . . , 42.

is the only extraordinary creation in the group. Marfisa, Julia, Porcia, Margarita and the women of Numancia are all stock characters. And it is not easy to deduce from them the full extent of Cervantes's feminist sympathies. Marfisa is a mere sop to the audience; the others indicate only that he admired courage and resolution in women and confirm that he was staunch in defence of their right to fall in love and marry where they pleased. So perhaps it is Arlaxa who through her oddity tells us most. Perhaps the deflation of her self-proclaimed *varonilidad* and the eloquent comparison with Margarita show what Cervantes thought of the swaggering viragos of the Spanish stage – the bandits, the Amazons and the warriors. While prepared to urge freedom and respect for women, was he perhaps reluctant to let them forsake their own feminine mystique by trying to acquire, in their efforts to assert themselves, the traditional mystique of the male?

Certainly Cervantes does not like Cueva and Virués conceive of women almost exclusively as individuals; he is always aware of their essential femininity: that he protests on their behalf in itself implies this. This protest is limited to the world of love and marriage – he preaches recognition of woman's natural inclinations and her need to be allowed that acquaintance with the opposite sex which will teach her to choose with discrimination. Cervantes's stress on the femininity of his later women characters marks a close approximation to the point of view of Lope, who had been writing for some thirty years when the *Ocho comedias* appeared. This point of view is more complex and profound than that of Cueva and Virués and has greater dramatic possibilities. Lope was conscious that for the seventeenth century woman *was* different; aware of the qualities she has in common with man, he was also alive to the conflict between woman as she is and woman as her society envisages her. Thus far Cervantes keeps pace with Lope. But Lope goes further, leaving Cervantes at a half-way point in the development of feminist attitudes in the drama. Virués and Cueva present woman as Nature created her. Cervantes depicts the conflict in woman between Nature and Society. Lope too depicts this conflict, but unlike Cervantes he conceives of Nature's demands on woman as being no less dictatorial than the demands of seventeenth-

81

century society. It seems strange that the creator of Marcela did not write a *mujer esquiva* play. Was it because Lope's dramatic format for the character, which became *the* format, was in some way distasteful to him? Certainly the stand taken by Marcela – that she is free to marry or not as she pleased – is one that no subsequent *mujer esquiva* of the theatre is allowed to maintain for long.

II

Some years before Cervantes produced his second batch of plays, Francisco Agustín Tárrega, who died in 1602, included in his contributions to the Valencian stage several examples of the *mujer varonil*. That these were merely the result of the dramatist's sensitivity to a growing public taste is shown by their sketchiness or superficiality. There is nothing to indicate that Tárrega found the idea of the unconventional woman particularly interesting or fertile and in this respect he acts largely as a gauge: his works reflect the increasing popularity of the type, and the need felt by dramatists to follow the trend, in however casual a way. Just how easily the demand for a little feminine bravado could be met is clear from three of Tárrega's plays: in each the heroine appears entirely normal until the last act, when she is compelled by circumstances of varying degrees of probability to act like a man.

In *El cerco de Rodas*[1] the mooress Lidora, in order to save the man she loves, has improbably to meet the Great Turk in single combat. The body of the play contains no indication that she is either capable of, or inclined towards, such feats; in hasty anticipation of our incredulity, Tárrega merely describes her as having the courage of a man shortly before she enters laden with armour. Doña Lambra in *La sangre leal de los montañeses de Navarra* is similarly shown in the last act to have reserves of aggression not usually associated with women. In the absence of her father, her brother and the King – admittedly a fairly conclusive situation – she mounts guard on the battlements of Roncesvalles, kills the traitor Manfredo, and remains there determined to kill as many

---

[1] This play and the following three mentioned were published in 1608 in the collection *Doze comedias famosas de quatro poetas naturales de la insigne y coronada ciudad de Valencia*.

Frenchmen as possible. Up to this point she has been portrayed as a woman of integrity, nothing more. Tárrega's propensity for last minute *varonilidad* seems even less justified in *Las suertes trocadas y torneo venturoso*, where the heroine's motives are entirely hidden. Sabina, thinking her lover the Count is dead, puts on armour and enters the lists in a joust. The prize is to be Sabina or her sister, and the situation gives rise to a predictable little piece of dramatic irony. The Count too enters the lists, fights Sabina, and on winning claims as reward the girl he has been unwittingly battling with. What is never made clear is why Sabina entered the joust in the first place. Tárrega either forgot or could not be bothered to work into the plot some plausible motive for Sabina's actions which would make the dénouement a structurally integrated one.

Only one of Tárrega's plays gives the kind of attention to a *mujer varonil* which we find in subsequent plays, where the heroine's *varonilidad* is the focus of attention. And even here, in *La perseguida Amaltea*, the *varonilidad* of the heroine is not intrinsic to the development of the action as it normally is in the case of the *mujer esquiva* or the *bandolera*. None the less, as a dramatic type Amaltea has a certain importance. For although she has much in common with some of the female bandits of the Spanish theatre – Gila, for example, in Luis Vélez's *La serrana de la Vera* – she is the earliest example of a kindred female character type that was to achieve wide currency, the *bella cazadora* or beautiful huntress. Although in no way profound, the characterization of Amaltea is at least consistent and sustained. The energies which have made her a *cazadora* are translated into many of her subsequent actions and make them seem plausible. Amaltea is a shepherd's daughter who has been raised in the forest, so riding and hunting are second nature to her. She is strong-willed and quick tempered, but beyond her freedom and mobility she claims to have no unconventional ambitions. She has fallen in love with Polidoro and when one of the huntsmen who come across her in the forest asks,

> ¿Es Marfisa la francesa
> que con Orlando pelea?[1]

[1] Another example of the strong impression made by Ariosto's warrior queen.

she replies,

> Aunque soy de menos presa,
> villanos, soy Amaltea,
> la gallarda montañesa;
> puntos menos que esa dama,
> porque aventuras no sigo.
>
> (Act I, *P.D.V.* I, 305a)[1]

None the less, ferocity and impetuousness are central to her personality. In the course of the action, in which she is repeatedly the victim of intrigue and misunderstanding, the solutions she naturally turns to are violent ones. Her portrayal in other words, is of a piece, which is by no means true of many of the *bellas cazadoras* who succeed her, whose taste for hunting never survives the first scene. This first treatment of the *bella cazadora* type is dramatically perfectly adequate, and she may therefore be Tárrega's creation.

Tárrega's attitude to his fiery heroine does not seem on the evidence to have been very favourable. Although Amaltea does not reject her femininity in any serious way, the only explicit comment on her behaviour is one of disapproval. This takes the form of an interchange between Artemisa and her maid, who tells her mistress of the Count's impending marriage with Amaltea:

> Artemisa   ¡Ay, calla, no me la nombres,
> que igualmente dan enfados
> ver hombres afeminados,
> y mujeres marihombres.[2]
>
> Criada   Dices bien, por vida mía.
> Artemisa ¿No ha de ser cosa imperfeta
> ver hombres con cadeneta
> y damas en montería?
> Cace quien ha de cazar,
> cosa quien ha de coser;
> que si es hombre la mujer,
> el marido [h]abrá de hilar.

---

[1] The edition used of Tárrega's and Aguilar's plays is E. Juliá Martínez's *Poetas dramáticos valencianos*, 2 vols (Madrid, 1929).

[2] Note the use of the word *marihombre*, always derogatory in the seventeenth century.

> Yo lo tengo por muy malo
> que unas destas regaladas
> os dará una cuchillada
> por deciros un regalo.
>
> *Criada*   Artemisa, mi señora,
> tienes sobrada razón.
>
> (Act I, 312a–b)

Artemisa is the villain of the piece and singularly anti-pathetic; furthermore she is a woman, talking about a possible rival, so she is naturally prejudiced. On the other hand, these opinions antedate her meeting with Amaltea and her decision to get rid of her, and they are also echoed by her maid. So her words on the proper difference of function and behaviour between man and women can either be seen as pure spite, or as a reflection of the opinion of dramatist, or an attempt on his part, conscious or not, to engage the sympathy of the audience by mouthing contemporary platitudes.

If Tárrega *was* speaking from personal conviction, his view would be compatible with the brief glimpse of liberalism that we get in *El cerco de Pavia y prisión del rey de Francia*. This play is a straightforward example of the conventional use of masculine disguise; Casandra and her maid dress as *villanos* in order to follow Casandra's lover and she subsequently saves his life by carrying his unconscious body to safety during the siege. Her behaviour (which, as she points out in a seeming paradox is entirely normal – 'me he convertido en hombre/ para ser buena mujer'[1]) elicits two interesting remarks. One is a testimony to the extreme behaviour of which woman in certain circumstances is capable, a testimony which in itself becomes a platitude of seventeenth-century dramatic dialogue,

> mas ¿qué no ha de hacer
> por su honra la mujer
> que tiene mezcla de gusto?
> Todo la mujer lo iguala.
>
> (Act III, *P.D.V.* I, 483b)

---

[1] Act I, *P.D.V.* I, 458.

The other is a realistic, Cervantes-type condemnation of the mentality which tries to ensure virtue in women by denying them exposure to life:

> Túvola en mucha clausura
> su padre, que no debiera,
> que mujer muy encerrada
> corre mucho si se suelta.

(Act III, 482b)

These are mere glimpses of an attitude, nothing more. For the most part Tárrega's plays mirror only the popular demand for heroines of spirit, and Tárrega himself was not interested enough to use the opportunity to express a coherent standpoint.

III

Gaspar de Aguilar, on the other hand, did use the *mujer varonil* to express his views on the feminist question. Like the other dramatists of the age he used the adjective *varonil* in a very catholic way as an expression of male admiration for woman. In *El mercader amante* Labinia responds to the rich Astolfo's offer of marriage by walking away because she is in love with Belisario who is poor, and Astolfo generously exclaims,

> ¡O[h], qué corazón tan firme!
> ¡O[h], qué varonil mujer!

(Act III, *P.D.V.* II, 152b)

Much more interesting, however, is that when he personified *varonilidad* in a consistent and easily recognizable way, Aguilar chose distinct types of *mujer varonil*. And these types which appear in his extremely popular plays written towards the end of the sixteenth century, figure amongst the most constantly recurring manifestations of the *mujer varonil* on the seventeenth-century stage. At the time when he was writing, in other words, the taste for heroines of strong character was being channelled by some force in definite directions. The evidence points, as one might expect, to Lope's being this force. Three out of Aguilar's four relevant plays contain in turn a *bandolera*, a *mujer guerrera* and a *mujer esquiva*. It can hardly be a coincidence that Lope's production in these years was as follows:

Bandolera: La serrana de la Vera 1595–8; *Las dos bandoleras* 1597–1603.

Mujer guerrera: La infanta desesperada 1588–95; *El grao de Valencia* 1589–95, probably 1589–90; *La serrana de Tormes* 1590?–95; *El alcaide de Madrid*, performed 1599; *La fe rompida* 1599–1603.

Mujer esquiva: El soldado amante 1590–1600, probably 1593–5; *La varona castellana* 1597–1603; *La fe rompida* 1599–1603; *Los milagros del desprecio* (?) 1599–1603.[1]

And this, given the possibilities of oversight and disappearance, is probably a conservative list. In the case of the *mujer esquiva* Lope's influence is likely to have been particularly decisive because, apart from Casandra, there are no extant precedents for this type.

The fourth play too – *La suerte sin esperanza* – contains a potential *mujer guerrera*, but in the casual, last-act manner favoured by Tárrega. Leonarda, who has shown no signs of unfeminine behaviour throughout the body of the play and is thought to be dead, intervenes disguised in armour in single combat between her brother and her supposed murderer. The similarity with Tárrega's *Las suertes trocadas y torneo venturoso* is evident but, unlike Sabina, Leonarda does not actually fight. Her identity revealed, she challenges anybody who questions her honour, and when nobody does so a suitable ending is contrived. The only interesting point in the play is this very question of Leonarda's honour, for much is made of the fact that although married she is still a maiden. Her continued virginity strikes a false note. Leonarda after all loves Lamberto, he is strongly attracted to her and is a fairly unscrupulous man. That he was already married did not prevent his courting her so his scruples at consummating his second, bigamous 'marriage' do not convince. Aguilar, clearly, is avoiding the issue here and it is not difficult to see why. Had Leonarda been enjoyed by the man she took to be her husband, she would

---

[1] The dates are from S. G. Morley and C. Bruerton's *The chronology of Lope de Vega's 'Comedias', with a Discussion of Doubtful Attributions, the Whole Based on a Study of His Strophic Versification* (New York, 1940).

at the end of the play have been unacceptable to any other man. The situation where a man marries a woman who has lost or given her virginity to someone else is uncommon in the Spanish drama; we remember Pedro Crespo's news of his daughter – 'un convento tiene ya / elegido' – and Rosaura's marriage, not to Segismundo who loves her, but for her honour's sake, with Astolfo, her former lover. When Rojas Zorrilla dealt with the theme later, his play was booed off the stage at its first presentation. Few dramatists had the courage to deal with such a sensitive subject. As it is, by keeping Leonarda's virginity a secret for an act and a half, Aguilar managed to squeeze the maximum drama and titillation out of the situation while still playing safe.

If Aguilar was influenced by Lope's female bandit plays he did his models less than justice, for with his *bandolera* he merely paid lip service to the idea which Lope explored so powerfully and presented so dramatically. Leonora in *El gran patriarca Don Juan de Ribera* is merely a cypher in a series of incidents designed to reveal the saintliness of Don Juan, the Archbishop of Valencia. Convinced that her love for him is, for that reason, hopeless, Leonara sets off for Valencia with a suitor to get married. When they next appear they have become bandits, and except that Roberto has killed a rival in a duel, there is no obvious reason for this. It seems clear that their criminality is only an artificial and dramatically inorganic device to bring them once more into contact with Don Juan, who, as patriarch of Valencia, has undertaken a programme to stamp out crime and prostitution. Leonora sees the errors of her ways and returns home, not to be heard of again, and Roberto repents and in the 'santos y bandoleros' pattern becomes a hermit. Aguilar's theatrical excursion into female banditry has the total superficiality of its precedents, at the very time when Lope was giving the theme new significance.

Aguilar's female warrior, on the other hand, is the subject of a complex and sustained presentation. She is not just a *mujer guerrera* of the straightforward chivalresque type, for Aguilar has woven two separate strands into the *persona* of Aber in *La gitana melancólica*. The first strand is taken from the Biblical account of Judith and Holofernes. Aber is chosen by lot to save Jerusalem from the Romans by seducing the Emperor Tito and then killing him, in explicit imitation of the famous widow. Although he patterned Aber on Judith, Aguilar went to considerable lengths to give her individuality, and her motivation throughout the play is so laden and involved that as a coherent dramatic personality she is at times in danger of disappearing under the weight of it. The complexity is carefully prepared for by the basic variations introduced into the original story. First, the idea is not Aber's own and she quells her repulsion out of obedience to her father. Second, the plan misfires and she kills the wrong man. Within this slightly different frame Aguilar then embroiders upon the idea of the female executioner. Once she is committed to the deed, Aber begins to savour the glory that will be hers. And this glory becomes for her contingent either upon victory or upon death. When she discovers she has murdered the wrong man, she begs Tito to kill her,

> dadme con presteza mucha
> la muerte, que he menester
> para mi vitoria.
>
> (Act II, *P.D.V.* II, 25b)

and when he refuses, she resolves to do the deed herself. But victory is obviously preferable and she humbly accepts Tito's offer of peace, content in the knowledge that she has helped to achieve it.

The character of Aber's *amour-propre*, her concern for glory, reveal her as a woman acutely aware of her image in the eyes of the world. When the peace is revoked, her temperamental assertiveness and eagerness to excel are translated into a desire for action – she decides to return to her beleaguered city and to fight. Her rationalization of this urge is interesting because it is so patently bogus – she will fight in order to avenge her lover who will surely die in the battle. Aber, in other words, feels the need to justify the unfeminine compulsion she is about to convert into unfeminine action, by relating it to the feminine part of her that is involved in love and marriage. Still present in her, too, is the wish for death after failing her people in her bid to secure peace, but this motive is now less important. The focus of her personality has changed; the appointed female executioner has become

the voluntary *mujer guerrera*. The dangerous task she was chosen
for has released unsuspected feelings. That the dramatist quite
consciously built this progression into the character is obvious
from Unías's expressions of dismay when he sees the woman he
loves engaged in the slaughter of battle,

> Tú mueres, Aber, por dar
> a nuestros contrarios muerte,
> y yo mucho más por verte
> tan inclinado a matar;
> que el matar es del varón
> por ganar eterno nombre:
> La mujer basta que al hombre
> mate con la condición.

> (Act III, 32b)

The implications are clear: killing and the pursuit of glory are
masculine pastimes. And Aber has indulged in both.

Aber, then, is a character of considerable complexity. The
achievement should not be underestimated. Aguilar's treatment of
the *mujer guerrera* – in general a highly stereotyped figure – is unusual, and elaborated with a care rarely bestowed upon this particular variation of the *mujer varonil*. This unconventional approach
is his peculiar contribution to the *mujer varonil* theme, for it is
present also in his one depiction of a *mujer esquiva*, which is significantly different from Lope's conception of the type. In the first
place the aversion to love of his *mujer esquiva* does not necessarily
extend to marriage, and in the second, this aversion is conquered
in the first instance by greed. The values she is used to propound,
however, are identical.

While Emilia in *La fuerza del interés* regards marriage as a social
necessity, she does not believe that love and marriage are synony-
mous. She does not even regard marriage as the natural outcome
of love; for her love, or an appearance of it, is a tedious though
inevitable preliminary to marriage. Such views on the independence of marriage from love are more normally associated with
the vested interests of establishment materialism than with young
women of marriageable age. They are the views which support
the property marriage and the marriage of convenience and the

reduction of girls to mere pawns in a fairly sordid game. But Emilia's cynicism goes even further: she regards love as a game women play in order to get married, a conviction which arises from her inability to believe that a woman could involve herself with love for any other reason.

This position makes Emilia eminently vulnerable to attack. Aguilar soon makes it clear that Emilia's views are the outcome of a fear of personal commitment that is similar to that of Gil Vicente's Casandra. In her eyes love and honour are incompatible because a woman in love loses dignity and commands less respect. The element of truth in her argument convinces her father, Mauricio; but, cunningly, Aguilar tenders approval only to withdraw it unequivocally soon afterwards. For if her father sees her attitude as revealing her 'valor', her *dueña* speaks her mind in less flattering terms; and since Mauricio is influenced by guilt at allowing himself to be bought into touting for one of Emilia's suitors, and the *dueña* on the other hand puts the objective case for Love, it is not difficult to detect which of the two speaks for the dramatist:

                    que si es deshonra el querer,
                    todo el mundo es deshonrado,
                        pues todos en general
                    rinden al amor el cuello,
                    desde el animal más bello
                    hasta el más feo animal.
    Emilia   Yo, de mi naturaleza
                    tengo fuerte el corazón.
    Dueña   ¿No ves que es obstinación,
                    lo que llaman fortaleza,
                        y que, cuando seas fuerte,
                    monstruosidad viene a ser,
                        pues una fuerte mujer
                    el orden común pervierte?
                        Que ella en vez de combatir
                    sólo ha de ser amorosa;
                    que Dios crió cada cosa
                    para lo que ha de servir,
                        y así, pues tal fortaleza

> las Amazons tuvieron,
> sin duda alguna que fueron
> monstruos de naturaleza.
>
> (Act I, *P.D.V.* II, 175a)

How familiar these words become in the seventeenth century! By rejecting love, Emilia is denying her God-ordained identity as a human being and as a woman.

Dramatic action naturally requires that Emilia remain unconvinced by these admonitions and that she be forced to come to terms with herself through events. From now on Aguilar becomes implacable in the task of humbling Emilia's pride, and it is done mercilessly. No sooner has she dismissed with impatience the *dueña*'s words than a jeweller enters with the contents of his entire shop. The sight of these riches laid at her feet by an unknown admirer awakens in the 'woman of principle' feelings she has never before experienced. At this point the action loses conviction, for hitherto the great wealth of Emilia's suitor, Ludovico, has made no impression upon her resolution. None the less Aguilar's intention is clear: the sight of the baubles is supposed to stir the latent femininity in Emilia, the appeal to her acquisitive instinct to rouse at least her curiosity. Her succumbing to material riches is followed by subjection to love itself, and she falls in love with Grisanto, the supposed donor of the gift. Emilia now undergoes all the traditional emotions of the woman in love: disdain, anger, jealousy. Even the discovery of Grisanto's deception and threatened imprisonment cannot change her. At this stage Lope would forgive his wayward heroine and allow her to live happily ever after. Not so Aguilar, who moves in for the kill. Final humiliation comes to Emilia when Grisanto gives her to his master, Ludovico, in exchange for a large sum of money. She has not merely given her love to a servant, but has to suffer the indignity of being passed on by him to the suitor she has always despised and rejected. Her *esquivez* and her greed have been punished in kind and at one blow – she has been sold to the man she disdained. Nature has been avenged.

It is clear that, like Tárrega, Aguilar felt the need to be in the dramatic swim by depicting *mujeres varoniles* in a few of his plays.

Aguilar's choice of heroines, however, is a more significant indication of the direction in which theatrical taste was growing. Significant too is the serious treatment he gives two of these characters and his obviously interested awareness of their unusualness as women. In the first instance his approach differs from the essentially casual one of Tárrega; in the second from the to-a-large degree asexual one of Juan de la Cueva and particularly Virués. It bears, in other words, a marked similarity to that of Lope. And like Lope, Aguilar seems to have had determined views on woman's place in the order of things. These views were standard ones. Where love and marriage in general and the double standard in particular, were concerned, he was entirely conventional. As Emilia learns, love and marriage are woman's lot and her role in life is essentially passive. Aber's assertiveness, her desire for glory, are unfeminine.

IV

As a moderately prolific dramatist contemporary with Lope, Guillén de Castro might well be expected to have produced a fair sprinkling of *mujeres varoniles*. Although he did not move to Madrid until 1619, he appears to have been quite close to Lope, for he dedicated the first part of his plays, published in Valencia in 1618, to Lope's daughter Marcela, and Lope in his turn dedicated his *Las almenas de Toro* to Castro. From such contact one might expect considerable influence. But out of the forty-two of Guillén de Castro's plays published by Juliá Martínez,[1] four alone are directly relevant and of these only two make a significant contribution to the *mujer varonil* theme. Two further plays are worth looking at, not for what they contain, but rather for what they lack. In view of Castro's reputation for being rabidly anti-marriage and anti-woman, this at first sight seems doubly strange. The feminist theme seems ideal for the dramatic presentation of such prejudices. Possibly the answer is that for all his supposed prejudices Castro remained a believer in love. Juliá Martínez,

[1] *Obras de Guillén de Castro y Bellvís*, 3 vols (Madrid, 1925-7), published by the Real Academia Española in Biblioteca selecta de clásicos españoles, series 2. The plays were originally published in two parts in 1618 and 1625.

agreeing with the anti-marriage bias, rightly thinks that Castro in spite of his bitter criticisms of women, paints some of the most favourable pictures of them in the whole of the seventeenth-century drama,

Tiene acres censuras Guillén de Castro para las mujeres; pero es difícil encontrar entre nuestros clásicos quien las interprete tan como signos de firmeza, de amor, de sacrificio.[1]

He rightly considers love, not honour, to be the prime mover in Castro's works and the basis of his feminine psychology. If Castro saw women as exclusively creatures of love – and this need not have detracted from his misogyny – then it would follow that he did not conceive of them in terms of feministic assertion.

Certainly the plays concerned here contain no message other than that of love. The first part of *Las mocedades del Cid*[2] tells the story of Jimena, wife of Rodrigo Díaz de Vivar. Here is a woman who, on the death of her father, feels it is her filial duty to put the claims of honour before those of love. Were she a man, no Spaniard of the seventeenth century would quarrel with these priorities, but in a woman, Castro shows, such a notion could not be taken seriously. His Jimena battles with her feelings for Rodrigo and insists with great emphasis but little conviction on vengeance. The King and his court, while admiring her fortitude and tenacity, gradually weary of her insistent cry for justice. A little deception finally reveals that Jimena still loves Rodrigo, and they do their utmost to persuade her to forget her grudge and marry him. For a son their advice would have been 'Forget your love and avenge your father'; for a daughter it is 'Forget the wrong and accept your female destiny'. Honour and vengeance are men's business, a woman's concern is love.[3] We are left in no doubt that these were Castro's views. They were views, moreover, that he

[1] 'Observaciones preliminares', vol. I, xxxix.
[2] Published, probably for the first time, in 1618 in the *Primera parte*. Juliá Martínez thinks the play belongs to Castro's middle period.
[3] That Castro thought vengeance was a masculine affair is obvious from *Las canas en el papel,* where Elvira, vowing vengeance on her apparently faithless lover, says to her servant 'Ven y verás / que no en todo soy mujer'. (Act III, *Obras* II, 401b.)

had not inherited with the Jimena tradition. The *romances* merely relate how Jimena insisted on justice,

> Cada día que amanece – veo quien mató a mi padre,
> y me pasa por la puerta – por me dar mayor pesar,
> con un falcón en la mano – que trae para cazar;
> mátame mis palomillas – que están en mi palomar,
> Rey que no face justicia – non debía de reinar,
> ni cabalgar en caballo – ni con la reina folgar.[1]

and how she was eventually persuaded to marry the Cid. There is no hint in them that by capitulating she is taking the only action appropriate to a woman. Some solution is necessary to the King,

> Si yo prendo o mato al Cid – mis Cortes revolverse han.

but he does not try to persuade her into marriage with the argument that her behaviour is unseemly. And none of the *romances* suggests that the King and his court finally lost patience with Jimena. The stress on the appropriateness as well as on the expediency of a capitulation is Castro's own. Castro's sanction for making Jimena secretly in love with Rodrigo seems to have been the version of the *romance* in the 1550 *Cancionero de romances* where Jimena herself, to the exasperated amazement of the King, suggests that she should marry the Cid,

> – Tente las tus Cortes, rey – no te las revuelva nadie,
> al Cid que mató a mi padre – dámelo tú por igual,
> que quien tanto mal me hizo – sé que algún bien me hará –.
> Entonces dijera el rey – bien oiréis lo que dirá:
> – Siempre lo oí decir, – y agora veo que es verdad,
> que el seso de las mujeres – que no era natural:
> hasta aquí pidió justicia, – ya quiere con él casar.[2]

---

[1] *Romance de Jimena Gómez*, version found in the *Cancionero de romances*, Amberes, s.a.; in the *Silva* of Zarogoza 1550; and in the *Cancionero de romances*, Medina, 1570. It was reprinted by Wolf and Hofmann in their *Primavera y flor de romances* I: see Menéndez Pelayo's *Antología de poetas líricos castellanos* VIII, 58. Wolf and Hofmann reprint two other very similar versions, one from Escobar's *Romancero del Cid* and Timoneda's *Rosa española*, the other from the *Cancionero de romances* 1550,

[2] Wolf and Hofman I, 61.

But Castro elaborated the love motif into a double conflict: that between what Jimena feels she ought to do and what she really wants to do, and that between what she feels she ought to do and what the court thinks she ought to do. What the court thinks she ought to do is at one with her own secret feelings. In other words, in Castro's eyes her social duty and her natural inclinations are identical and their common identity lies in love and marriage. Her concern for vengeance is a mistaken conception of duty which must be overcome.

In *Las mocedades del Cid* Castro adopted a ready-made case of female honour and proceeded to demolish the very concept of it by bringing it into conflict with the far more powerful force of love. It is illuminating in the circumstances to see how his attention focuses on love in two other borrowed plots, each of which is treated very differently elsewhere. He rejected the idea of the chaste Dido in favour of the impassioned lover in his *Dido y Eneas*, which, as the title indicates, is the story of the Carthaginian queen's love affair with Aeneas. Given the obviously greater dramatic appeal of this version of Dido's history the choice is perhaps not so surprising. More interesting is his treatment of the gruesome Procne and Philomela legend, particularly in the light of Rojas Zorrilla's play on this theme years later. In spite of first act similarities, the plays are very different. Rojas's belongs to the 'high' seventeenth century in that essentially it deals with the theme of honour/vengeance. The distinction is that the honour and the vengeance are both female, not male. His play is quite deliberately preoccupied with the concept of female honour, in both its wide and its narrow sense, and Ovid's gory vengeance (where Tereus unwittingly eats his own son's flesh) is modified in order not to alienate the spectator's sympathy from the two sisters. Castro's *Progne y Filomena*,[1] on the other hand, is primarily a tale of love and of straightforward vengeance, of the primitive urge for revenge with no rationalizations in terms of an honour code. Neither Progne nor Filomena once mentions her 'honor' and only on one occasion is the matter even referred to indirectly, by Progne,

[1] Written according to the evidence before 1600. See Juliá Martínez *Observaciones preliminares* to vol. II, lxi.

> ¡Oh traidor, oh falso amigo,
> vil esposo, infame arpía,
> que en mi mesa y en mi cama
> ensucias mi sangre limpia;
>
> (Act II, *Obras* I, 148a)

The vengeance aspect of the plot is in other words a more or less faithful rendering of the legend with no seventeenth-century Spanish 'shaping'. The early date of the play may well be partly responsible for this.

Castro's eagerness to stress the love element can be deduced from the fact that, incredibly, although his Progne does serve their son to Tereo for dinner, he contrives to give the play a happy ending. This is made possible by the fact that Tereo never manages to rape Filomena. Since it is the idea of rape rather than the cut tongue (which later heals) which angers both Progne and Teosindo, the discovery that it never occurred allows Progne to forgive her husband and Teosindo to marry Filomena without losing face. Here, however, it must in fairness to Teosindo and to Castro be said that Teosindo, faced with the apparent rape of Filomena emerges out of his dilemma with an explicit rejection of the double standard. At the time this takes the form of a rather uncertain decision to succour the maimed creature he loves rather than attend to his honour, but separation and the intervening years effect, when they meet again, a firm and moving declaration of priorities,

> Vuelve a mí los ojos bellos
> sin vergüenza que en tu abono
> mis agravios te perdono
> pues que no culpaste en ellos.
>   Quédese el mundo en las leyes
> que atropello y que maldigo,
> y esté yo, estando contigo,
> entre cabras y entre bueyes.
>
> (Act III, *Obras* I, 160b)

For Castro love seems indeed to have been man's strongest motivation. And his interpretation of one of the most famous of all female vengeance stories clearly reveals not only the play's separation from the seventeenth-century dramatic ethos in general, and from Lope's introduction of the female honour theme in particular, but also his love-orientated approach to women and life.

While *Las mocedades del Cid* at least makes a distinctive contribution to the theme of female vengeance in the theatre, the same cannot be said of Castro's two presentations of another type of *mujer varonil* – the *bella cazadora*. In the late 1590s Lope produced, apart from his two famous female-bandit plays, several portrayals of the strong, intrepid, rather wild woman accustomed to life in the open air. This is an argument in favour of Juliá Martínez's attribution of *El renegado arrepentido* to the period 1595–1600 partly on the basis of its heroine.[1] Even so, the play might equally well belong to the next decade. The progress of influence is not always speedy, and indeed Castro's other *bella cazadora* is probably later. Both Catalina in *El renegado arrepentido* and Briseida in *Los enemigos hermanos*[2] are in any case merely unexplored dramatic devices. Catalina is a one-dimensional character and there is no justification other than theatrical sensationalism for presenting the former Duchess of Milan as a huntress. After a spectacular, breathless entry on stage, this aspect fades into insignificance. Similarly, although Briseida has apparently been brought up to ride, hunt and fish on the usual pattern, there is no prior nor subsequent justification for presenting her upbringing as anything other than a conventional one. The motif of *varonilidad* is not integrated into the play and is in both cases a concession to public taste.[3]

The fourth play of specific relevance is an extraordinary one and its heroine fits into no stereotyped pattern. It is also one of the most charming comedies the *siglo de oro* produced. The very great value of *La fuerza de la costumbre*[4] is that it presents us with the

---

[1] *Obras*, I, 217. The play was not published in either of the *partes*. The earliest known edition is a volume of plays discovered by Schaeffer with its cover and identifying pages missing. See Juliá Martínez, lxxi.

[2] Published in the *Segunda parte* in 1625. Juliá Martínez thinks it is a fairly late play.

[3] The Judith story crops up again in this play. Judith appears to Florentina, the other heroine, and urges her to cut off the Moorish King's head.

[4] Published in the *Segunda parte* in 1625. The play was *refundida* later on by Francisco Villegas under the title *Lo que puede la crianza*, published in *Esc.* xxv (1666).

deliberate and conscious transformation of a masculine woman into the feminine norm of the age. The plot can be simply outlined. After twenty years in Flanders, Don Pedro returns to his wife, now that her hostile father is dead, bringing with him their daughter Hipólita. She has been reared by him and has lived at his side as a fellow soldier. Doña Costanza for her part has brought up as a girl the son she was left with twenty years before. She has kept him firmly tied to her apron strings and his world is that of his mother's *estrado*. The central action involves Don Pedro's efforts to make his son Félix a worthy man, but this procedure has its comic parallel in the conversion of Hipólita into a woman. And the manner and nature of this conversion reveal exactly what femininity implied for Guillén de Castro and for the seventeenth century.

When the play opens, Hipólita is a being unacceptable to the society into which she is precipitated at the age of twenty. Brought up as a boy, she has always worn breeches, has learnt to talk and walk, to fight and swear, to act and react like a man. On returning home she is expected to occupy immediately her true place in society and in her family as a woman, to become at will something which girls normally grow into with years of conditioning and practice. Don Pedro tells his wife,

> Y a Hipólita le poned
> largo vestido y tocado,
> y en aposento y estrado
> para consuelo tened.

(Act I, Obras III, 43a)

After fulfilling one parent's need for a son, she has to supply the other's for a daughter. But Don Pedro reckons without two things: *la fuerza de la costumbre* and Hipólita's disinclination to betray what she has come to regard as her true self. She neither wants to be a woman, neither can she easily become one. She hates the constriction of her long skirts, cannot cope with her awkward, thick-soled *chapines*. Only with the greatest reluctance does she part with the sword her brother is loath to acquire, while the sudden need for modesty is irksome in the extreme. And while these scenes where she struggles with her female accoutrements and her masculine gait, with her ignorance of what is expected of a woman – she unthinkingly reveals an outstretched leg while trying to put on her shoes – are full of humour, they have their pathos too. Hipólita is revealed as the puppet of convention which most of us are; having learnt to dance to one tune, she has to unlearn it and be taught to keep time with another. For Castro, of course, the question is not so much one of social conditioning, although there is a strong element of awareness of this, as that of the reconstruction by means of social superficialities of Hipólita's true identity.

External reconstruction is not enough, however; the transformation, if it is to be real and complete, must also come from within. Slowly but inevitably the transformation is effected through Don Luis, to whom she becomes increasingly attached: love alone, in other words, will be the touchstone. The change is portrayed with subtlety. Her very lack of the usual feminine inhibitions facilitates the process. She is attracted first to Don Luis's manly bearing and physical courage and although made somewhat uneasy by his attentions,

> ¿Qué me buscan, qué me quieren
> ojos que tanto me miran?
>
> (Act I, 50a)

has no scruples about gazing at him in frank admiration. Her mother has to warn her about excessive use of the eyes, and although Hipólita protests that her stares are prompted by masculine appreciation, and not feminine interest, the damage is done. If the eyes are love's gateway to the soul, then Hipólita's masculinity has been betrayed by her masculine directness. Gradually she finds in Don Luis's valour compensation for her own frustration. But although she is slipping into femininity she has not yet capitulated, as the combination of encroaching sensitivity and masculine imprecation in these words to her brother rather nicely shows,

> Eso sí, cuerpo de Dios,
> comenzad a tener bríos,
> pues los voy perdiendo yo. (Act II, 63a)

When we meet Hipólita in Act III the process has accelerated. Love has brought with it its attendant emotions – in Hipólita's own words, 'ternuras', 'temores' and 'cuidado' – all alien to the Hipólita that was. But Guillén de Castro does not remain content with love alone: a hardened case like Hipólita requires more thorough treatment. When Hipólita with characteristic forthrightness eventually declares her love, she still lacks the total commitment necessary in a woman, reminding Don Luis, should he ever think of betraying her, that she has been raised to battle. Her total capitulation is brought about in two ways. The conventional medicine of jealousy has to be administered – she is told that Don Luis is going to marry someone else, and reacts in a predictably violent way. But she also has to experience, and here Castro *is* unconventional, sexual subjection to the male. When she insists on fighting Don Luis, he cunningly takes her to a spot where the grass is covered in dew, she slips and falls and he makes love to her saying,

> Para que vea
> pues es mujer, que lo es.
>
> (Act III, 74a)

And, as she says to her mother when she throws herself into her arms to confess,

> y en efecto, madre mía
> desde entonces soy mujer.
>
> (Act III, 74a)

The admission in both senses is meant to be true.

This is the real Hipólita, her essential femininity revealed. The masculine ways inculcated by her unorthodox upbringing have with a certain amount of help yielded to the inner compulsion of her true nature. And the new Hipólita represents the proper and accepted pattern for woman's behaviour. Woman, whatever she is capable of being, is expected to appear tender and timorous, and her place is on the *estrado*. Hipólita's voice is that of the seventeenth century,

> Ya olvido, como mujer,
> el ser valiente en la guerra

> desde que la paz probé.
> Ya me espanta un arcabuz,
> y para mi no ha de haber
> tratar en cosas de acero,
> si no es que opilada esté;
> ya me duele, si me pica
> la punta en un alfiler,
> y si hay sangre, será cierto
> el desmayarme después.
> Todo en mi pecho es ternura
> y todo en mi boca es miel.
> Enfermo tengo la voz,
> y aun el corazón también;
> ya tengo palpitaciones,
> remedios he menester.

(Act III, 73a)

Love effects this transformation and it cannot be deterred or deceived by upbringing. In his concept of love as the essence of femininity and his belief in its unstoppable force, Guillén de Castro differs from other seventeenth-century dramatists only in his realistic inclusion of the precipitating power of sex.

Castro's general aloofness from one of the prominent dramatic trends of his day indicates a laudable streak of inspirational independence.[1] Whether this independence was strongly coloured by disapproval of the self-assertive woman it is impossible to say for certain. But his views on what being a woman involved certainly point to an explanation of this sort. Even when he did present unorthodox heroines, however, his approach, although rooted in conventional attitudes, was novel. His two *bellas cazadoras* of course are something apart. They represent an automatic and short-lived response of the most superficial kind to current fashion, and this in itself indicates that these two plays are earlier than *Las mocedades del Cid* and *La fuerza de la costumbre*. On turning his serious attention to the *mujer varonil*, on the other hand, Castro tackled

---

[1] He made use on several occasions, of course, of *disfraz varonil* and in *Pagar en propia moneda* his *mujer vestida de hombre* even hovers momentarily on the edge of becoming a *bandolera* by joining forces for a scene with some highwaymen. The situation does not develop, however, and no crimes are committed.

two central feminist questions without making his women conform to any of the outstanding feministic theatrical types. In *Las
mocedades del Cid* he explored in Jimena a tension which conventionally found expression within a masculine context – the tension
between intellect and emotion, between reason and instinct, between honour/duty and love, a tension which manifests itself in
part as a desire for vengeance, essentially a masculine concern.
Castro was one of the first dramatists to deal in a detailed and
overt way (overt as compared with the implicit approach of Lope
in *La moza de cántaro*) with the theme of female vengeance, though
his attempt to depict the anguished waverings of a torn mind is
undermined by the obviously partisan attitude which shapes his
conception of the nature of Jimena's motives. The opinions that
emerge from this historical drama are restated even more explicitly in the comedy where Castro deals in close-up with an
extreme version of the common theme of the 'reduction' to
femininity of the *mujer varonil*. These two plays, although unconventional, are each in its own way an important contribution to a conventional theme. They are the eccentric offerings of a
dramatist with unexceptional views who was affected only
marginally by the theatre's concern with the feminist question and
then only in so far as it prompted him to a reaffirmation of established attitudes. The double standard may yield in Castro but it
yields to love, not to intellectual conviction.

The common element in Cervantes, Tárrega, Aguilar and
Guillén de Castro is the very way in which their *mujeres varoniles*
are conceived and presented. Individually they are significant in
different ways and to various degrees. Cervantes consistently
explored the problem of female happiness and fulfilment and its
dependence on freedom. Tárrega illustrates the growing vogue for
the unorthodox heroine and the way in which it 'imposed itself'
even on dramatists not interested in exploring her full dramatic
possibilities. More positively, he produced what was conceivably
the first example of the *bella cazadora*. Aguilar's importance lies in
the evidence his plays provide of the crystallization of the hitherto
rather amorphous treatment of the *mujer varonil* into specific types,

and in the seriousness with which he approaches them, probably under the influence of Lope. His views on love and marriage are illuminating, for themselves and for their similarity with those of Lope. This is equally true of Guillén de Castro, who, paying lip-service to the dramatic stereotypes with his *bellas cazadoras*, otherwise went his own way in respect of formal characterization.

But whether the treatment is superficial or in depth, whether the attitudes are by the standards of the time liberal or conventional or a blend of both, the four dramatists bear witness to the change the *mujer varonil* of the Spanish drama has undergone. She is no longer, at least not when treated at any length, the statuesque heroine of classical antiquity, the wicked ruthless schemer of Italian tradition, or the accident-prone damsel of chivalresque romance. She is consistently – as we have glimpsed in Juan de la Cueva – a recognizable woman. Even the *mujer varonil*, in other words, was now accorded her identity as a woman. And this was increasingly the consequence of an awareness of her sex and the questions it gave rise to. Dramatists were beginning to be interested in her *qua* woman and in the specific problems that faced her. Naturally some of the *mujeres varoniles* at this time, like many throughout the following century, were merely spawned in the wake of this concerned interest, on account of their innate dramatic appeal, but even these betray the influence of the new approach. Superficial and interesting alike, these are seventeenth-century women; they are Lope women, far removed from most of the heroines of Cueva and Virués. Brave and daring, often arrogant, often erring, they are all essentially feminine and are made to conform finally to the feminine norm.

The part played by Lope himself in this transition from the automatic and firmly implicit feminism of Cueva and Virués to the questioning and exploratory attitudes of a few decades later is not capable of clear definition. It must, however, have been vital. Lope held strongly-felt and clearly expressed views on woman and her relationship with Nature and Society and his contribution to the theme of the *mujer varonil* was, as the following chapters will show, of prime importance from the 1590s on. (It is possibly significant that Tárrega, who barely survived to see the transformation by

Lope of the *mujer varonil* into a device for the serious examination of woman's position in society,[1] was, of the four, the one dramatist who remained on the whole oblivious to its potential.) Furthermore Lope's formative influence was not solely a specific one exercised by his views on woman. It can be seen as part of the overall changes he wrought upon the Spanish drama. The 'recognizable', more feminine *mujer varonil* and her exploitation as a source of thematic material is one aspect of a more general tendency amongst dramatists from Lope's time to seek inspiration within their own society, to draw for their themes upon the very ideological stuff of which their society was made. Even when there are temporal or spatial discrepancies, the issues involved are seventeenth-century Spanish ones. Plots taken from legend or history are given actuality with seventeenth-century concerns – love, honour, vengeance, family and social duty; wherever the action supposedly takes place, it is the preoccupations of seventeenth-century Spain which are really at issue. Similarly, the drama of the seventeenth century is usually not interested in unorthodox women for their own sakes, as heroic or wicked individuals, but as unorthodox women in a highly orthodox society, as the objects of social attitudes and pressures.

The feminism inspired by the writings of Erasmus and his followers and by the Renaissance in general, and consciously or unconsciously absorbed by Cueva and Virués, is, with the advent of the *comedia nueva*, subjected to the social and moral realities of contemporary life to which seventeenth-century drama and seventeenth-century literature as a whole were committed. The outcome is a feminism of a different and more limited sort: liberal in important respects, but ultimately conservative. The paradox is that this more restrained feminism, although perhaps in its reservations more irritating, is, in the final analysis, more honest and potentially more effective because it is intentional and aware. Lope and many of his followers were conscious of the anomalies and injustices of woman's situation and prepared to devote their talents and a part of their drama to grappling with these. This explicit, concerned approach is more helpful than an all-embracing

[1] He died on 7 February 1602.

feminism that remains passive, that does not face up to the moral and ideological 'realities' of the particular society, that does not try to achieve a realistic compromise. The underprivileged need specific concessions, not blanket goodwill.

Part 2

4

The *bandolera*[1]

Oigame aquel que se llamare a engaño:
los hombres hacen las mujeres buenas
y sólo por su culpa viene el daño.

                                        Lope de Vega

I

One of the most interesting manifestations of the *mujer varonil*
type, and certainly the most violent, is the female bandit, the
woman driven by internal and external pressures to open rebellion against authority. Cristóbal de Virués in *La infelice Marcela*
had presented such a character in outline, but it was Lope de Vega
who saw the figure's thematic and dramatic possibilities and was
first able to give her substance and motivational depth some years
later in his *La serrana de la Vera*.[2] Compared with Virués's Felina,
a shallow and absurdly melodramatic presentation, Leonarda is an
inspired creation and mother of an extensive female-bandit
progeny.

While *La serrana de la Vera* is the prototype of the seventeenth-
century *bandolera* play, in several respects it differs from all the
others. In fact, Lope's second dramatization of the *bandolera* theme
written soon afterward, *Las dos bandoleras y fundación de la Santa
Hermandad de Toledo*,[3] should probably be regarded as co-parent
of the plays subsequently produced in this tradition. A. A. Parker
has dealt with male and, briefly, female bandits in the Spanish

---

[1] An earlier version of this chapter has been published in the *Bulletin of Hispanic
Studies*, XLVI (1969) Vol. I, pp. 1–20.

[2] Written 1595–8. See Morley and Bruerton, 129–30.

[3] Morley and Bruerton's dating of *Las dos bandoleras* (1597–1603, pp. 278–9), if
correct, invalidates the assumption made by Menéndez Pidal and María Goyri in
their edition of Luis Vélez de Guevara's *La serrana de la Vera* (Teatro antiguo
espanol, I, Madrid, 1916), that *Las dos bandoleras* is an imitation of Luis Vélez's
play. This assumption is presumably based on the difference between Lope's
La serrana de la Vera and the other plays, but of course Lope might well have
written two rather different plays on the same pattern. Attribution of *Las dos
bandoleras* to Lope, it must be said, is not entirely beyond doubt.

Golden-Age theatre.[1] The importance of banditry as a dramatic theme was that it provided a means not so much to right social wrongs as to avenge personal hurt, to avoid loss of consciousness of personal dignity after humiliation. Professor Parker points out the peculiar significance of this connection in Spanish literature between criminality and personal honour, social revenge and personal injury. The female bandit has been dishonoured; she resorts to banditry to avenge herself on society which has ostracized her. She will not submit to the indignity of society's *desprecio* and affirms her dignity as a woman by her anti-social behaviour. This sums up the situation in nearly all the well-known female bandit plays. Lope's *La serrana de la Vera,* is the exception. Unlike Luis Vélez's play, it lies outside the dishonoured-woman-turns-bandit group. There is nothing in the play to indicate that Leonarda has been dishonoured in the technical sense. Her provocation to crime is not nearly so great.

To explain her subsequent actions, two aspects of Leonarda's character must be considered. First, she is an arrogant, self-assertive and extremely mannish woman.[2] Secondly, until she falls in love she has always disliked and despised men. Her reaction when she is rejected by Carlos is therefore proportionately violent. There is no blot on her honour. Of this even her brother Luis is sure:

> Bien la [Estela] pudo pretender
> Don Carlos sin mi deshonra;
> que yo entiendo que mi honra
> no la ha podido ofender.
> Que es mi hermana hermana mía
> y por sí misma tan buena,
> que quita al alma la pena
> y al honor la fantasía.
>
> (Act I, Acad. xii, 12b)

But she has lost her dignity in her own eyes and, she feels, in the

---

[1] In his article 'Santos y bandoleros en el teatro del Siglo de Oro', *Arbor* xiii (1949), 395–416. Doña Blanca de los Ríos includes a description of some of the better-known female bandit plays in her introduction to Tirso's *La ninfa del cielo, Obras* (Aguilar) I, 911ff. This chapter, I hope, explores the theme a little further.

[2] She herself admits she is 'medio hombre' (Act ii, Acad. xii, 27b), while Galindo warns his master: 'Haz cuenta que te desposas/con Hércules' (Act i, 13b).

eyes of the world. It is essentially her pride, and not the censure of her family and of society, which sets her on the road to crime. Her progress towards banditry, however, falls into two stages. Carlos's desertion and Luis's betrayal of the promise he made not to harm Carlos fill Leonarda with disgust for men, and she escapes to the hills to hunt. At this point there is no question of any anti-social feelings. This gradual build-up of psychological pressure in the female bandit is peculiar to Lope and Moreto. The other dramatists reject the accumulation of motivating circumstances in favour of the sudden crisis which immediately drives the heroine out of society. The decisive factor now occurs in the shape of an attempt by Luis to force Leonarda into marriage with Rodrigo, whom he wants to compensate for an uncertain insult. As head of his family Luis has the right to do this. This final insult to her pride drives Leonarda to a revolt which takes what is to become the familiar form – a determination to kill as many men as possible. Unlike that of her sisters in crime, however, her fury is directed, not at the man she loves, but at the brother who has disobeyed her wishes with regard to Carlos, and now wishes to dispose of her against her will.

The responsibility for her crimes is therefore not entirely Leonarda's. She cannot return home and she has lost the only man she ever loved. She is as much the victim of intrigue and social convention as of her own pride. This mitigation of responsibility is common to all the dramatists who use the female bandit theme, except Luis Vélez de Guevera. Lope, Mira de Amescua, Tirso, and Calderón were all aware that the impulse to anti-social behaviour is devious and complex, and that the hatred and desperation which drive the individual to destroy are the outcome of deep-seated conflicts often created by external elements. At the end of the section of *romances vulgares de valentías, guapezas y desafueros* in his *Romancero general*, II, Durán deprecates the popularity enjoyed by these ballads in the eighteenth century but consoles himself thus: 'Pero en desquite, si hemos celebrado los hechos de tales facinerosos, fuera de aquí es donde han nacido los sistemas que tratan de erigir como principio doctrinal, que la sociedad en masa, y no los hombres, es culpable de semejantes excesos. Nosotros los hemos admirado, y nunca justificado.'[1] Judging from the female bandit plays alone, what Durán claims is patently untrue. Certainly the Spanish dramatists do not absolve the individual of responsibility, but neither do they absolve society. If Luis Vélez errs on the side of harshness, Lope errs on the side of generosity. He alone overlooks the serious implications of the anti-social behaviour of his female bandits.[2] With a gesture of sentimental generosity more characteristic of Romanticism than of the seventeenth century, he dismisses their crimes as *yerros de amor*. *La serrana de la Vera* contains not one word of censure for Leonarda's behaviour and she is finally pardoned by the King.

For Lope repentance is enough because it marks Leonarda's willing acceptance of her femininity. When the enormity of her actions strikes home, she immediately blames her jealousy and the violence of her character,

> Esto mis celos han hecho;
> esto mis fuerzas y brío.

> (Act III, 38b)

In these words Lope conveys an implicit condemnation of the type of woman she is. Pride makes her revel in her strength, pride makes her *esquiva*, and pride helps to make her a bandit. Only when this pride is broken and shame robs her of speech does she earn the full approval of her creator.

With Leonarda Lope established the type of the *bandolera*. Her successors may differ from her in character, motives and ultimate fate, but the pattern of their case histories is the same. After *La serrana de la Vera*, Lope became interested in the problem of the individual who has a more real and understandable grudge against society. This, as A. A. Parker points out,[3] is essentially the problem of anarchy, with its positive quality from the standpoint of the aggrieved individual and its negative and destructive quality from the point of view of society. Here obviously is a subject of greater

---

[1] B.A.E. XXVI, 390a.
[2] I am referring here, of course, to the important female bandit plays. The *yerros de amor* argument reoccurs in some of the minor ones.
[3] 'Santos y bandoleros . . .'

intrinsic interest than that of *La serrana de la Vera*. It is the theme of *Las dos bandoleras* and the one subsequently adopted by other dramatists.

The ways in which *Las dos bandoleras* differs from Lope's first bandit play reveal why it must be considered as having almost as great an influence on succeeding versions. In the first place, Inés and Teresa are neither unfeminine nor *esquivas*. More than half the later women bandits resemble them in this. But even more important, they actually lose their virginity. Nearly every female bandit after them will lose hers, whether by rape, seduction or deceit. But here again, Lope uses the technique of a gradual alienation from society. Because of the promise of marriage that Alvar and Lope made, dishonour for Inés and Teresa does not follow immediately upon the loss of their virginity. Only when, after leaving home, they fail to persuade the men to admit their obligations, does the weight of their shame fall upon them. They cannot return to their family and, as the shepherd's song shows, they have been condemned by public opinion,

> Por ser en su amor livianas,
> se dejaron engañar;
> y aunque nobles cortesanas,
> los vinieron a buscar
> en hábito de villanas.
>
> (Act III, Acad. IX, 34a)

Their grudge, like Leonor's, now becomes a grudge against men in general.

The sisters are completely unbalanced by their dishonour and humiliation. By the time the King falls into their hands they have murdered twenty-nine men. Successive female bandits will take a similar delight in enumerating their victims. Their plan of action, however, is unique. Other women merely ambush their victims; Teresa and Inés work on the principle of a distorted poetic justice. Since their beauty caused their downfall, they now use it to destroy the enemy, luring men into a false sense of security with their pretty faces and kind words, then killing them. Neither has any false illusion that they are recovering their honour with their crimes. Vengeance alone is their conscious aim. Subconsciously they are attempting to re-establish their self-esteem.

It is characteristic of nearly every *bandolera* that at some time she shows mercy. Leonarda sets the example by sparing both Carlos and Don Juan. Inés follows it by sparing the king and Téllez and allowing Orgaz to escape. These glimpses of surviving compassion are obviously intended, by Lope at least, to reveal the girls as still worthy of forgiveness. In *Las dos bandoleras* the compassion is Inés's alone, however, for Lope has succeeded in giving his sisters personalities which are entirely distinct. Inés is more cautious and restrained than Teresa, yet at the same time more enterprising. She is also the more merciful and the more prudent. Teresa is emotional, fiery and impulsive. Only with difficulty is she restrained from killing the king, and only by force from killing her father. Even when she has regained her sanity she cannot bring herself to relate the story of their dishonour. Lope's idea of bandit sisters was not, for some reason, adopted by any other dramatist. *Las dos bandoleras* itself, however, was *refundida* years later by Matos Fragoso and Sebastián de Villaviciosa under the title *A lo que obliga un agravio y las hermanas bandoleras*.

These two plays of Lope establish firmly those features of plot which are to become typical of the female bandit plays. The girl, sometimes *esquiva*, who loses her honour, the flight from the *desprecio* of society into a life of crime, the series of outrages, the occasional act of compassion, the dishonoured father who helps track his daughter down, and the eventual repentance, all reappear time and again. None the less, the genre does not remain static and new features are gradually introduced. The vogue for the *mujer vestida de hombre* puts the *bandolera* into doublet and hose. She often acquires a male partner in crime. She usually becomes a member, even the leader, of a robber band. Most important, however, Lope's romantic dénouement is supplanted. In *Las dos bandoleras* a serious problem is posed, then neatly side-stepped. The sisters are pardoned and their former lovers compelled to marry them. Yet, like Leonarda, they have transgressed against all laws, human and divine. Are they, then, to be forgiven provided they show verbal repentance? Mira, Tirso, Luis Vélez and Calderón all answer no, and in the standard dramatization of the bandit theme the heroine has to pay for her crimes. Except in the case of Luis Vélez's *La serrana de la Vera*, payment comes in the form of complete repentance and surrender to the divine will. The tragic ending of Luis Vélez's play sets it slightly apart from the others, and for this reason it is dealt with at this point instead of in correct chronological order.[1]

Although based on Lope's play of the same name, there are considerable differences in detail and in mood. Luis Vélez gives the tale an atmosphere of savagery and violence of its own, and his heroine, Gila, is a caricature of her dramatic prototype. She wrestles, shouts and swears; she even overcomes a bull with her bare hands. The type of hoydenish girl here found in extreme form does not occur in the other female bandit plays, which take Lope's *Las dos bandoleras* as their model instead of his *serrana*. This is the case too with Gila's *esquivez*. Leonarda sets the example and Gila follows it, but the only other *bandolera esquiva* is the heroine of Tirso's *La ninfa del cielo*. She, like them, loves to ride and hunt, but she lacks their violence. Leonarda, Gila and Ninfa are each, in fact, a combination of three distinct types of the *mujer varonil* – the *bandolera*, the *mujer esquiva* and the *bella cazadora*. These last two are often found in combination but nowhere else do we find the combination of all three. The intensity of *varonilidad* in these cases is not aimed merely at increased dramatic impact. It is an attempt, somewhat unsubtle perhaps, to render the girls' subsequent actions more psychologically plausible. The woman who resents her sex or who despises men, and is their physical equal, even superior, will react more violently than the normal woman when she is sexually victimized and has no means of real retaliation.

Gila's behaviour is certainly consistent. She does not despise men; rather, she would like to be one and she agrees with Magdalena that

---

[1] The play was assumed by Menéndez Pidal and María Goyri to have been written after 1613 (*La serrana de la Vera*, 'Observaciones y notas', 125–7). Their arguments are convincing but were not accepted by Milton A. Buchanan in his review of the edition in *MLN*, XXXII (1917), 423–6. However, the fact that a play called *La serrana de la Vera* was performed on 14 June 1623, and paid for a month later, might lend support to the Pidal dating. See N. D. Shergold and J. E. Varey, 'Some Palace Performances of Seventeenth-Century Plays', *BHS* XL (1963), 238.

> Erró la Naturaleza,
> Gila, en no herte varón.
>
> (Act II, T.A.E. I, 26)[1]

leaving the housework to Magadalena while she goes off to play dice with the men. Her objections to marriage are based on the loss of independence it entails for a woman, and her roughness is her way of revolting against the femininity she considers so degrading. Her feminine ideal is Queen Isabel, the woman who rules successfully in a world of men,

> Madalena, en viendo yo
> mugeres dêsta manera
> me buelbo de gusto loca.
>
> (Act II, 26)

She forgets that Isabel rules *jointly* with her husband, and that, as well as an active sovereign, she is also a wife and mother. The trouble with Gila's feminism – and it is significant that Vélez should thus see it – is that it is based not on a reasoned dissatisfaction with woman's lot but on personal pride, flanked by vanity and self-esteem born of her immense strength. She accepts the Captain's offer of marriage not out of love but because, promising as it does freedom and fame,

> que abéys de ser al lado de don Lucas
> si merezco esa mano, otra Semíramis,
> otra Evadnes y Palas española.
>
> (Act II, 60)

it satisfies both her vanity and her desire for self-assertion. The blow, when it falls, strikes not so much at her ambitions or her honour as at the core of her egoism. She, Gila, has been used like the lowest prostitute and deceived like the most credulous fool. The course of revenge upon which she now embarks is monstrous, yet Gila is the only female bandit whose excesses seem plausible, such is the nature of her personality. Her main aim, unlike that of Leonarda, Inés and Teresa, is vengeance on her betrayer. At the same time she rationalizes her behaviour by posing as a champion

---

[1] The edition used is Menéndez Pidal's in Teatro Antiguo Español, I, (Madrid, 1916).

of her sex, intent on avenging what is essentially an *agravio de mujer*. Before she catches up with the Captain she kills two thousand men.

The position of Gila's father in the play is an interesting one. Gila blames her fate on his past indulgence of her headstrong whims, an indulgence based on excessive paternal pride. When Gila suddenly bites his ear saying,

> que esto mereze quien pasa
> por las libertades todas
> de los hijos. Si tú usaras
> rigor conmigo al principio
> de mi inclinación gallarda
> yo no llegara a este estremo.

(Act III, 120)

her father admits his responsibility.[1] This would seem to be an explicit condemnation of the father for not bringing up his daughter in the way becoming to a woman. That Luis Vélez disapproves of Gila there can be no doubt. The mitigating circumstances are not enough to save her from execution. Furthermore the significance of the little girl, Pascuala, is plain. She pronounces judgment upon Gila with precocious cynicism,

> La que engañan, se lo quiso . . .
> porque no ay onbre tan malo
> que cuando da la muger
> cozes, la pueda ensillar.

(Act III, 99)

and although Gila has not been raped, the statement reveals the public disfavour she has provoked. Of greater importance, however, is Pascuala's physical presence at Gila's capture and at her execution. Here is a female child witnessing the consequences of

---

[1] Buchanan (*MLN* XXXII, 425) points out that this incident is Luis Vélez's adaptation of an old folk-tale in which a son bites his father's nose on the gallows. For the spread of the tale see Stith Thompson's *Motif Index of Folk Literature* (Copenhagen, 1955–8), V (L–Z), 265, Q 586. Spanish versions of the tale occur in Climente Sánchez de Vercial's *El libro de los enxemplos* CCLXXIII, B.A.E. LI, 513b; *Castigo e documentos del Rey D. Sancho*, Chap. I, *ibid.* 90b; and *El Libro del cauallero Zifar*, ed. C. P. Wagner (Ann Arbor, 1929), 283–9.

woman's refusal to submit to the natural order of things. Gila's death is obviously meant as a warning to the girl and to woman in general. She is the most overtly masculine woman in the Spanish theatre, and she does not even redeem herself by falling in love. In condemning her to death, Luis Vélez is condemning the arrogant feminism which brings about her downfall.[1]

If Luis Vélez saw Gila as a rebel against her sex, his fellow playwrights preferred to depict her as a rebel against society. The first dramatist to make a serious approach to the problem of anarchy was Mira de Amescua in *El esclavo del demonio*.[2] Into his play he introduces details absent in Lope which he then hands down to his successors: the lover's mistaken identity, the domineering father, the *disfraz varonil*, the robber boy-friend, the bandit gang and, ultimately, spiritual salvation. The *bandolera* herself no longer occupies the centre of the stage. Mira's Lisarda has to share the limelight with Don Gil, the holy man who, in desperation after yielding to temptation, also resorts to crime.

The train of events in the play is set in motion by Lisarda, who writes to her lover Don Diego suggesting that they elope. But the moral responsibility for the events is not hers alone. She is driven to her action by her father's attempt to force her into a loveless match, and by his fury at the news that she is in love with Don Diego,

> Plega a Dios, inobediente,
> que casada no te veas,
> que vivas infamamente,
> que mueras pobre, y que seas
> aborrecible a la gente.
> Plega a Dios que destruída
> como una mujer perdida,
> te llamen facinerosa;

---

[1] The manuscript of the play is dedicated at the beginning and end 'Para la Señora Jusepa Vaca', and in Act I there is the stage direction 'Éntrase el capitán retirando, y Gila poniendole la escopeta a la vista, que lo hará muy bien la señora Jusepa'. The part of Gila, in other words, was created with Jusepa Vaca's talents in mind and the heroine's acts of bravado introduced accordingly. This does not invalidate the moral Luis Vélez uses her to point.

[2] Printed in 1612 in the *Tercera parte de las comecias de Lope de Vega y otros autores*.

> y en el mundo no hay[a] cosa
> tan mala como tu vida.
> (Act I, C.C. LXX, p. 84, lines 121–30)[1]

His curses come true because through his displeasure he has the power to make them come true. Lisarda's life on earth follows the pattern decreed by him. Over her soul, though, he has no control. And what Marcelo foretells is unimportant compared with what he does not foretell – her ultimate salvation. This is directly related to the share of blame which Marcelo must shoulder, and also to the responsibility which is Don Gil's. He not only takes Diego's place in Lisarda's bed but deliberately lies to her in an attempt to drag Lisarda down to infamy with him. Cursed by her father, deceived and dishonoured (so she thinks) by the man she loves, and violated by the Canon of Coimbra, she understandably decides she has no more to lose.

Lisarda enters with gusto upon her life of crime, swearing to kill every man she encounters.[2] But in her ferocity there is much bravado and when put to the test her basically noble nature triumphs. She spares her father and sister. The humility with which she kneels before her father and asks his blessing marks the first stage in her moral regeneration, although the contrition proves only momentary. The essential difference between Lisarda and Don Gil is that he considers himself beyond salvation, while she fully intends someday to repent and reform, and in preparation for that day refuses to renounce the Virgin Mary. Don Gil's desperate fatalism is far removed from her simple hopeful approach to good and evil. Her awareness of her sins does not diminish her confidence in divine grace. So that by the time she meets Don Diego she is well on the way to reform:

> Pues ¿cómo una mujer, siendo cristiana,
> se opone contra Dios y se condena
> por el gusto que da vida tan corta?
> (Act II, p. 173, lines 1991–3)

---

[1] References are to A. Valbuena Prat's edition in Clásicos castellanos LXX, *Teatro* I (Madrid, 1926).

[2] Mira justifies the ease with which she adapts herself to her new life by remarking that she has always been a keen huntress and is familiar with the mountains and forests: by making her, in other words, a *bella cazadora*.

When she fails to fire her gun at him the reform is complete. The form her penance takes is important in that it is determined by the nature of her original crime – disobedience. She stresses her disobedience twice:

> que en esto paran las hijas
> que a sus padras no obedecen
>
> (Act I, p. 110, lines 630–1)

and

> Perdida soy, y es razón
> que tengan tal desventura
> las que inobedientes son.
>
> (Act I, p. 113, lines 712–14)

and now thinks slavery the most important form of penance because

> Perdíme no obedeciendo
> y he de ganarme obediente.
>
> (Act II, p. 179, lines 2134–45)

Lisarda revolted against paternal authority and therefore (this is the seventeenth century) against society. Her slavery, which Ruth L. Kennedy included amongst the 'extraneous material' which Matos, Cáncer and Moreto omit in their version of *El esclavo del demonio*,[1] is a symbol of her deliberate submission to that authority and to society. The proper order of life is restored.

If Lisarda epitomizes revolt, her sister Leonor represents submission. Her temperamental make-up is not meant to be the same as Lisarda's. She represents the submission to authority necessary for the harmonious working of family and society. Lisarda's disobedience is, after all, catastrophic; she brings grief and suffering to her family and heartbreak to Don Diego; she enables Don Gil to be tempted and is therefore responsible for the deaths of their victims. Leonor does not lack the nobility and generosity which help to save Lisarda. She restrains her father's anger and gives him sound and prudent advice. She offers her life for her father's, she takes pity on the 'slave'. As a girl destined for the

[1] In her monograph *The Dramatic Art of Moreto*, *Smith College Studies in Modern Languages*, XIII (October 1931–July 1932), Appendix, 155ff.

convent and cut off from normal social intercourse (nobody before Don Sancho has praised her beauty) Leonor may be allowed a little coquetry. She is nonetheless a positive force for good, a life-giving force, whereas Lisarda's rebellion is a negative force for evil and destruction. Appropriately, Leonor's meekness brings her happiness as Queen of Portugal. A more powerful statement of woman's role in life could not be made, yet it would be a mistake to overemphasize the play's importance as an anti-feminist document. Mira is dealing with the conflict between the individual and society within a given setting. That he chooses for his purposes to accept that social setting does not mean he thinks it entirely just.

With *El esclavo del demonio*, Mira established a tradition of penance and spiritual salvation in the female bandit, which Tirso was to take to its logical conclusion by sanctifying his heroine. Mira's play itself gave rise later on to two very similar plays. Matos, Cáncer and Moreto based their *Caer para levantar*[1] on it and Moreto, probably later, wrote *San Franco de Sena*[2] which resembles *Caer para levantar* very closely. Like Lisarda, Violante (*Caer para levantar*) and Lucrecia (*San Franco de Sena*) rebel against the authority of their families and arrange to elope. They are seduced by and flee with the wrong men, then embark upon a life of crime. Eventually they repent and ascend to heaven. In detail the two plots sometimes differ from each other and from Mira's prototype: Violante, for example, is converted by her original lover, who has become a hermit, while Lucrecia is converted by her seducer, Franco, when he has forsaken his irresponsible life in order to dedicate himself to God. But in essence they are the same. Moreto and his collaborators, however, take a somewhat less

---

[1] Written according to Ruth L. Kennedy before 1655. See her Appendix 154–5, for an examination of the relationship between the two plays. Miss Kennedy judges that the play could be entirely Moreto's and that the first and part of the third acts are certainly his.

[2] First printed in *Esc*. I, 1652. A play called *San Francisco de Sena* was probably performed on 7 December 1631; see Shergold and Varey, 'Some Palace Performances . . .', *BHS* XL (1963), 237. It is later than *Caer para levantar*, I think, because its debt to this play is much greater than any debt it might owe *El esclavo del demonio*. As Miss Kennedy pointed out, *San Franco de Sena* is clearly much closer to *Caer para levantar* than to either Tirso's *El condenado por desconfiado* or Lope's *La mal casada*, sources which have been suggested in the past.

severe attitude to the sin of disobedience than Mira and subject their heroines to no harsh atonement. At the same time, their attribution of a large proportion of blame to the girls' families is as unequivocal as his. Violante elopes because her father, Don Vasco, refuses to allow her to marry Don Diego: he cannot forgive Diego for killing his son in a duel. His lack of mercy and forgiveness make her a criminal; God's mercy and forgiveness redeem her. The inference is obvious.[1] Lucrecia's case is more extreme, for in order to avoid a distasteful marriage she decides to elope with the nearest suitor to hand. What else is this but a warning of the dangers of encroaching upon another's right to self-determination?

The plays differ markedly from *El esclavo del demonio*, and from each other, in the personalities of their heroines. Violante, like Lisarda, is a spirited girl of strong will, who feigns indifference to her father's curses only to be deeply affected later by his blessing (this blessing counteracts the curses not for any supernatural reasons but for sound psychological ones; the kindness and acceptance signified by the blessing – although not really directed at her at all – soothe the girl's thirst, mitigate her grudge against authority and set her reconsidering her position). But she is nothing like as ferocious. We see little of her in her role as co-chief of the gang, and by far the greater part of her stage appearance takes place when she is already on the road to conversion. Her desire to avenge herself on society is largely a subconscious one. This has about it an air of psychological truth missing in other plays; most criminals, after all, cannot formulate their motives or relate their social rebellion to its cause. Violante, in short, is the type of female bandit we might have expected of Moreto, and an argument for the suggestion that he wrote most of the play. His *bandolera* is less aggressively virile, her criminal activites are not allowed to obtrude more than absolutely necessary, and her emotions are neither violent nor extreme. As a result, she is more believable than, but not nearly as effective as, Mira's heroine, and

[1] Don Vasco lives to regret his crime but his egoism prevents him from recognizing where the true responsibility lies: '¿Tuve yo culpa de su injusta estrella?/Si estaba contra ella/vuestra justicia airada,/¿no pudiera sin mí ser desdichada,/pues yo en nada os ofendo?' (Act III, B.A.E. xxxix, 594a).

the points the play is making do not come across as dramatically or as powerfully as in Mira's melodramatic maze of plot and subplot.[1]

Lucrecia in *San Franco de Sena* differs from Violante and Lisarda in that even *before* the elopement she is no model of conventional feminine virtue; rather, she is a strange mixture of frivolity and hardness. Her resistance to her brother is tinged with an entirely novel note of scorn and sarcasm,

> ¡Quisiera usted (¿quién lo duda?)
> con el milanés empleo
> gastir, lucir y triunfar
> a costa de mi tormento!
> ¡Yo en penas, usted en glorias!
> pues no, Señor; que es muy cierto
> que con penitencia agena
> no puede ganarse el cielo.
> (Act I, B.A.E., xxxix, 124c–5a)

She is obviously in the habit of roaming the streets and on one occasion meets Franco himself. Lucrecia is the only bandit who feels attracted to her deceiver before the seduction takes place. Finding herself seduced by the wrong man she wastes no time on tears and self-pity, but fatalistically decides to cut her losses and throw in her lot with Franco. Lucrecia is, again, the only girl who on her way to banditry passes through the stage of the conventional 'fallen woman' by living openly with Franco. This resolute renunciation of social position and reputation betrays a hardness of character unusual in Moreto's women. It is, of course, her pride and self-respect that drive her to scorn the world and its opinions, a desperate pride which can only thus preserve itself. When Franco abandons her, her situation becomes intolerable and she resorts to crime. The object of her vengeance is Frederico her

---

[1] Miss Kennedy sees the plays leading characters as being Violante, Gil and Leonor. But Leonor plays little part in the plot (she merely represents earthly values for Gil) and, unlike Leonor in *El esclavo del demonio*, she plays no part in the theme. The key figures are Violante, Gil and Diego. Diego compensates for his thoughtlessness towards Violante by helping her repent and he repays Gil by aiding in his conversion. He is the play's earthly representative of mercy and forgiveness.

brother ('causa . . . de toda mi ruina,' Act v, 135), not out of choice but necessity, since if she does not kill him, he will kill her. This inevitable choice (peculiar to this play) is translated by her self-assertiveness into a vow for vengeance which enables her to pretend that the initiative is hers.

Caer para levantar and *San Franco de Sena* are interesting as variations on the theme explored first by Mira de Amescua in *El esclavo del demonio*, the theme of guilt and responsibility. A much more complex and profound treatment of this same theme is found in Calderón's *La devoción de la cruz*, written *c.* 1633. Its heroine, Julia, is a bandit in the most violent tradition and has proved the most controversial *bandolera* that the Golden Age produced. Many critics have found her, a nun turned bandit, guilty of unconsummated incest and ruthless murder, hard to take. Gerald Brenan considers her crimes to be merely one of the absurdities in a 'religious melodrama of the most romantic and extravagant kind'.[1] Romera-Navarro dismisses Julia as 'absurda sencillamente'.[2] Valbuena Prat in a desperate effort to explain her, makes the absurd assertion that 'Respecto a los excesos de Julia, en el acto III, debemos darnos cuenta de que el tipo tan marcadamente neurótico, estaba predispuesto para el sadismo, del mismo modo que había tendido, subconscientemente, al incesto.'[3] But we do not need to resort to a diagnosis of neurotic sadism in order to explain Julia's excesses. They are no greater than those of many another female bandit. Calderón is merely following here what, by the 1630s, had become a well-established theatrical convention. The overtones of incest have shocked the commentators into a state of moral indignation over something to which they do not normally take exception. A. A. Parker has shown how Calderón used the bandit theme to say something valuable about human nature and the human predicament.[4] He puts the question: Eusebio has com-

---

[1] *The Literature of the Spanish People* (Cambridge, 1953 [2nd ed.]), 287.

[2] *Historia de la literatura española* (Boston, 1949 [2nd ed.]), 387.

[3] *Historia de la literatura española*, II (Barcelona, 1950 [3rd ed.]), 526 note.

[4] See 'Santos y bandoleros . . .', 403–10; *Approach to the Spanish Drama of the Golden Age* (Diamante VI, London, 1957), 17–22; 'Towards a definition of Calderonian tragedy', *BHS* XXXIX (1962), 227–28; also, 'The father-son conflict in the drama of Calderon', *FMLS* II (1966), 99–113.

mitted many crimes, but is the guilt for these crimes wholly his? The question is equally applicable to Eusebio's sister, Julia; the chain of causality in both cases leads back to the same man – their father Curcio. Curcio is responsible twice over for what happens to Julia. Had he not behaved so abominably to his wife, Eusebio would have been brought up as Julia's twin and they would not have interpreted the feeling they have for each other as sexual attraction. But given the existing state of affairs Curcio is still responsible because, blinded by selfish pride, he tramples upon Julia's right to freedom and self-determination. Julia differs from the normal woman bandit in that she is only emotionally committed to Eusebio. His responsibility for her fate is therefore minimal. Her downfall is precipitated not by a deceitful seduction but first, by the impulse which sends her after him and then by the removal of her escape ladder, which she interprets as a sign of divine disapproval. Her repentance, it seems, is ignored; mercy and salvation are denied her. She is the victim of an unjust father and an unjust God. In her desperation she defies Divine Providence, swearing

> mis hechos
> de mujer *desesperada*
> darán asombros al cielo
> darán espantos al mundo,
> (Act II, B.A.E. VII, 64a [The italics are mine])

Like Don Gil in *El esclavo del demonio* and Paulo in *El condenado por desconfiado*, she turns to a life of crime out of despair in its full theological sense. This marks a departure from the normal female bandit tradition, where the heroine never loses hope of forgiveness. W. J. Entwistle deals with the theme of despair in his article 'Calderón's "La devoción de la cruz"'.[1] In response to Menéndez y Pelayo's statement[2] that Julia's crimes are 'todos sin necesidad, ocasión ni motivo', Entwistle holds that her criminal behaviour is entirely consistent with the tenets of theological psychology. Since theological despair is the Devil's sin, he maintains, Julia by

---

[1] In *BHi* L (1948), 472–82.
[2] See *Calderón y su teatro* (Madrid 1881), IV, 'Dramas religiosas', 56.

despairing has become a devil. The murders she commits are supposed to indicate this. But like other critics he is over-concerned with the extravagant form that Julia's criminality takes. The murders are a conventional symbol of revolt. Calderón's attitude to Julia is at once less naïve and more humane than Entwistle implied.

Yet Entwistle is right to maintain that Julia is not an unnessesary melodramatic device. She is necessary to the plot because her social disgrace and her criminal life form one of the three stages of Curcio's punishment.[1] She is necessary to the theme because with Eusebio she exemplifies Calderón's conception of the collective responsibility for human suffering. In so far as she is immediately responsible for her victims' deaths, she has to atone by spending the rest of her life in the convent she initially refused to enter. But she is given the opportunity of atonement precisely because the responsibility is not ultimately hers.[2] Julia's story is rather different from that of other *bandoleras*. She is not merely a tyrannized daughter or the victim of a man's lust. The tragedy that befalls her was initiated before she was born. Her sex, therefore, is not as important as it is where an attempt to force marriage upon a girl is the direct cause of all subsequent events. Calderón's disapproval of such marriages is patent but, except on one insignificant occasion,[3] Julia is presented as an individual like her brother. For Calderón she is as much a representative of mankind as he is, as capable of evil and as worthy of salvation. Calderón realized that at this level of inquiry into the human condition, sex no longer has any meaning.

[1] See Parker, *Approach* . . ., 22.

[2] How ironical that while Curcio greets his long-lost son, a bandit, with open arms, he goes to attack Julia when she reveals herself, although as far as he knows her only sin is that she has fled from the convent! Such is his egoism that he can welcome the robber-son whose appearance absolves him of responsibility for the child's supposed death at birth, yet leap hysterically at the daughter who has defied him. Curcio is to the last ignorant of the weight of guilt he bears. In the midst of his grief and dishonour, his pride humbled, his life shattered, he is as foolishly self-centred as ever. The play's final comment on human nature is not an optimistic one.

[3] 'Eusebio: ¿Tú con profano vestido/dos veces violento en ti?' (Act III, B.A.E. VII, 65a). Julia is not merely a woman in man's clothes but a nun in lay dress.

So far, the female bandit theme has been given three different *dénouements*: Lope's romantic happy ending, Luis Vélez's execution and, the most popular, Mira de Amescua's religious penance. The third *dénouement* Tirso chose for his *La dama del olivar*.[1] In this play although he leans heavily on Lope, Tirso, makes one important departure: the heroine is not seduced or deceived but abducted and raped. She is therefore the most seriously wronged of all the *bandoleras*, degraded to the extent that the *gracioso* Gallardo assumes, when his master has finished with Laurencia, that he too can enjoy her,

> Estaos, Laurencia, quedita;
> los zapatos que se quita
> mi señor son siempre míos;
> y así por mía os acoto;
> pues después que os ha calzado
> venís a ser del criado,
> porque sois zapato roto.
>
> (Act II, N.B.A.E. IX, 222a)

Similarly, her grudge against society is a real one, since the society to which she belongs – her village – refuses to help her. The significance of this is made obvious by J. Caro Baroja's remark that 'until the beginning of this century such events [i.e. rape] provoked memorable collective reactions' in Spanish villages.[2] *La dama del olivar* has not the interest of the plays already discussed, but it is noteworthy for Tirso's implicit assertion of woman's rights as a human being. Laurencia is a woman of the lower classes; her fate at Don Guillén's hands implies that for him she is without integrity, dignity, feelings, a mind even; she is there to be used and discarded at will. But a person treated as an animal will react like one. Laurencia by her beast-like behaviour is paradoxically reaffirming her worth as a human being, and Tirso, by granting her repentance, is approving, if not the means of her self-assertion, then certainly the aim.

---

[1] First published in 1636 in the *Quinta parte de comedias del maestro de Molina*.
[2] See his essay 'Honour and Shame: A Historical Account of Several Conflicts' published in *Honour and Shame. The Values of Mediterranean Society*, ed. J. G. Peristiany (London, 1965), 79–137.

In *La condesa bandolera o La ninfa del cielo*[1] Tirso takes forgiveness even further by making his bandit a saint, so introducing a fourth *dénouement* into the female bandit framework and integrating the *bandolera* fully into the *santos y bandoleros* theme. Here, Tirso obviously looked to Lope's *serrana* in his choice of a heroine; for Ninfa is both *esquiva* and *hombruna*. Everything she does, however, is on a vaster scale: she joins a robber gang fifteen hundred strong and kills ninety men in the space of a single day. For the most part, Tirso's plot is a dreary imitation of Lope's until Ninfa's reconciliation with Carlos. Then after a dream of death, she is saved from suicide by an angel, is converted and is afterwards killed by Carlos's wife in mistake for the wild beast she is hunting. Christ descends from heaven to receive her as his bride. The theme is clearly that of the doctrine of repentance and forgiveness, and Tirso's interests here are predominantly theological. Perhaps as a result, his treatment of the female bandit is disappointing – it is conventional, melodramatic and completely lacking in psychological or social interest.[2] The play was *refundida* at the end of the seventeenth century under the title *La bandolera de Italia*. This version, in which the religious element is more exaggerated, is equally unrewarding.

A much better play is *El prodigio de Etiopía*, attributed to Lope but almost certainly not by him.[3] It combines two elements of the female bandit theme found separately elsewhere: the tyrannical father who drives his daughter to elope, and the sanctification of the heroine. Its new details are on the whole unimportant; they are merely variations on a common theme. The one important innovation is the way in which Teodora's father, pretending to be the hermit Isidore, gives her the advice she needs, thereby atoning for the wrong he has done her,

[1]First performed in 1613. E. Cotarelo y Mori, *Tirso de Molina: Investigaciones bio-bibliográficas* (Madrid, 1893), 137, thinks the authorship is doubtful, but Doña Blanca de los Ríos, *Tirso de Molina. Obras dramáticas completas* (Aguilar) I (Madrid, 1946), 911ff, is convinced the play is Tirso's.

[2] K. Vossler, *Lecciones sobre Tirso de Molina* (Madrid, 1965), 67–73, claims that this is a play of considerable psychological profundity but I do not feel he succeeds in proving his point. Certainly I cannot agree with him.

[3] See Morley and Bruerton, 331. Menendez Pelayo, Acad. IV, lxx, thought the play was *refundida*.

¿Cómo podré cobrar hija que adoro?
Tu padre ha perdonado tus errores,
vuelve a tu casa ya.

(Act III, Acad. IV, 149)

As the family representative of society, he forgives her for her crimes; as head of his family he forgives her for the dishonour she has brought upon it. He is the only father to do so.

The preceding plays have been dealt with in some detail either because they illustrate the major variations on the female bandit theme or because they contain some noteworthy minor variation. There are, of course, many others. The heroines of *El catalán Serrallonga y bandos de Barcelona*[1] by Luis Vélez, Antonio Coello and Rojas Zorrilla, and the anonymous *Antonio Roca*,[2] both help their lovers rule a bandit gang. Neither is a victim of social convention or family prejudice and both end their days in a convent. The heroine of *El negro del mejor amo*[3] also flees with her lover to a life of crime but in this case their career never gets under way. The *bandolerismo* is just a way of introducing conventional dramatic colour and proves the popularity of the bandit theme. The same is true of Luis Vélez's *La montañesa de Asturias*,[4] named after its sub-plot, which deals with a mountain maid who regrets having yielded to the Prince of León and wages war on all men (her brother, out of disgust, wages war on all women, but this attempt at psychological symmetry is even more unrealistic and unconvincing than the usual mass-murder revenge of the female). In Lope's (?) *El loco por fuerza*[5] there is a rather contrived bandit

[1] First performed in 1635. To be found in B.A.E. LIV.
[2] Formerly ascribed to Lope. The third act is Lanini Sagredo's but the authorship of the first two is unknown. Lope wrote a play of this name of which this is probably a late *refundición*. See Morley and Bruerton, 258. Published as Lope's in Acad. N. I. Dr V. A. Dixon discusses Lope's authentic play, to be found in manuscript in the Hollond Collection, in his essay 'El auténtico *Antonio Roca* de Lope' in *Homenaje al Profesor William L. Fichter* (ed. A. D. Kossoff and J. Amor y Vázquez, Madrid, 1971), which he very kindly allowed me to read before publication.
[3] Ascribed to Mira de Amescua but according to Cotarelo y Mori ('Mira de Amescua y su teatro', *BRAE* CVIII [1931], 84) probably not his. The play was published as Mira's in *Esc.* IV, 1653, and possibly in a collection of his own before this.
[4] Published in *Esc.* XXX, 1668.
[5] If Lope's, written 1597–1608. See Morley and Bruerton, 301–2.

episode in Act III, which serves to bring together the characters in preparation for the *dénouement*. Yet another cursory appearance of the woman-turned-bandit in Mira's (?) *El santo sin nacer y mártir sin morir*,[1] shows how this figure had become almost an obligatory feature of the *comedia de santos*. A refreshing variation on the theme is found in Matos Fragoso's *La corsaria catalana*,[2] where the abandoned heroine joins the Moorish pirate who rescues her, and renounces Christianity. The crime here is her renunciation of her faith, and there is no judgment, implicit or explicit, on her revolt against society. Lastly, the female bandit's progression from sin to repentance even proved suitable material for at least three *autos sacramentales*: Lope's *La venta de la zarzuela*, Tirso's *La ninfa del cielo* and Valdivielso's *La serrana de Plasencia*.

The female bandit is a rebel against an essentially masculine society, and her quarrel is with those unjust social conventions imposed upon her sex by men: the convention that in the choice of her husband a woman must yield to the wishes of her father (or other head of family) and the convention that upon the seduced woman must fall the *desprecio* of an outraged world. The concern in all these plays with the deceived woman is natural in a society preoccupied with honour, and with chastity – on which honour often depended. More interesting is their common concern with the abnormal reactions of unusual women who defy the rules of society in which they live. The extent of this defiance should not be underestimated. Whatever the initial cause of shame and dishonour, the subsequent recourse to a life of banditry entails even greater shame and dishonour; not merely because laws are broken and commandments ignored, but because as Julian Pitt-Rivers has said, 'a woman who takes to physical violence or attempts to usurp the male prerogative of authority . . . forfeits her shame'.[3] The one is an automatic outcome of the other. Yet the ambiguous complexity of woman's position here presents an almost insuper-

[1] The play is attributed to Mira but it was first printed anonymously in *Doce comedias de varios autores*, 1638. See Cotarelo y Mori, 'Mira de Amescua y su teatro', 60.
[2] Published in *Esc.* XXXIX, 1673.
[3] 'Honour and Social Status', *Honour and Shame* . . ., 42.

able problem. The same ethico-social structure which forbids a woman to be violent or to take upon herself the task of vengeance that falls to her father or brother, also decrees that acceptance of humiliation and failure to defend reputation constitute shamelessness, and shamelessness is obviously an ethical stance inappropriate to either sex.[1] In other words, according to the code the wronged woman cannot really win. The resort to crime is, paradoxically, an attempt to assert honour and a sense of shame by means of a process of increased dishonour and shamelessness. It is an attempt to meet contradiction with contradiction, unreason with unreason and somehow find a way out of the moral maze. Generally speaking, the dramatists sympathize with the female rebel, in so far as they let her repent at the end of the play. Luis Vélez's *La serrana de la Vera* is a solitary exception. But the dramatists would not have been men of their age had they failed finally to insist on an ending in which social authority subdued individual anarchy. So Lisarda's slavery, the marriages of Leonarda, Teresa and Inés, and the acts of penance of the others, are all used as symbols of the restoration of social order. The revolts are condemned; but the need to revolt is understood and sympathized with. The very readiness to portray female rebellion shows a more questioning and less rigid attitude to woman's place in society than is hitherto found in Spanish literature. In short, the playwright's investigation of woman's response to injustice reveals his lack of confidence in the justice of the prevailing attitudes towards her.

For these women are not only trying to revenge themselves on the fathers, brother or lovers who wronged them. Their revenge is general, not particular. They murder all and sundry; they even boast of the number they have killed. Vengeance and murder, of course, appealed to the blood-lust of the mob. But the wanton, indiscriminate character of the murders also emphasizes that these women are rebelling against *all* men, against the prevailing male social attitudes and against the masculine authority that imposes them. Their feminist rebellion (in the period in question it necessarily takes a

[1] See this same essay, 44. Professor Pitt-Rivers gives a diagrammatical breakdown of the complex relationship between honour, dishonour, and shame in its two diametrically opposed senses.

masculine form) stresses their right to marry the man they love. It is also a rejection of responsibility for the dishonour inflicted on them by an individual man's treachery, and a refusal to accept the social conventions (the expression of male dominance in general), which, because of society's views on female chastity, allow them no escape from their dishonour. It is above all their attempt, pathetic in its very desperation, to become arbiters of their own destiny, and as such it may be regarded as a significant move towards the personal and social maturation of women.

Their behaviour is an illustration of the alienation principle. They feel alienated from the whole of society and therefore free of all society's rules. Often, it is true, they were, like Gila, already chafing at the restrictive attitude to woman and rebelling against the obvious domestic limitations on her freedom, but it usually requires the trauma of dishonour to trigger their dissatisfaction into revolt.

That this should be a criminal revolt, and that they should wish to revenge themselves on society as bandits, is not so very surprising. The parallel with male revolutionaries – alienated from society by lack of social rights in a feudal environment or by lack of political rights in an industrial one – is obvious. And it is an accepted generalization of historians that 'the social brigand appears only before the poor have reached political consciousness or acquired more effective methods of social agitation'.[1] The bandit is 'a prepolitical phenomenon',[2] evidence of the first stirrings of active revolt against the conventions and rules of society. As Dr Hobsbawm says, 'banditry is a rather primitive form of organized social protest, perhaps the most primitive we know',[3] and it is not

---

[1] E. J. Hobsbawm, *Primitive Rebels. Studies in Archaic Forms of Social Movement in the 19th and 20th Centuries* (Manchester, 1959), 23. Also Chap. II, 'The Social Bandit', *passim*. Unfortunately little work has as yet been done on the sociology of crime in Spain. The lack of criminal records at a national and even a regional level constitutes a major hindrance. An article by I. A. A. Thompson, 'A Map of Crime in Sixteenth-Century Spain', *Economic History Review* XXI 2 (1968), 244–67, only serves to reveal the sad stage of infancy in which investigations still lie. Since Mr Thompson's findings are based on the galley-slave population of Spain between 1586 and 1589 there is no information with regard to female offenders.

[2] Hobsbawm, *Primitive Rebels*, 23.   [3] *Ibid.* 13.

unfair to see the female bandit of the Golden-Age theatre as an early literary expression of feminism, of whose fullest implications the dramatists themselves almost certainly were not aware.

II

The female bandit, then, is a rebel against a predominantly male-orientated society and her quarrel is with the unjust social conventions imposed upon her sex by men. Her rebellion is taken to the extremes of violence. But of course, in seventeenth-century drama, rebellion is not restricted to the *bandolera*. The *mujer varonil* in all her guises is a rebel in so far as she is defying the expectations of society. The distinction is that the *bandolera* is an aggrieved woman and her resistance is precipitated into action by active prejudice or persecution. Even so, crime is not the only recourse of heroines who find themselves in this position.

By far the commonest method of coping with rejection or parental tyranny is flight. This allowed lavish use of disguise, particularly masculine disguise, and could land the heroine in a wide range of dramatically appealing situations, from battle to the sort of labyrinthine comic intrigues favoured by Tirso and Calderón. The plays with a maiden errant in search of a recalcitrant lover are too numerous to mention. The intention is to make the gallant consent to marry her and this, by dint of courage or cunning, she almost invariably manages to do. The grievance is normally slight, because the affair has rarely progressed beyond the *reja*; the heroine is presented as a woman in love determined to get her man. Where the grievance is more real, the mood can become more serious: in *La vida es sueño* Rosaura's grievance against Astolfo becomes identified with the play's themes of free-will and moral reality. On the whole, however, the theme of the jilted girl is treated light-heartedly outside those bandit plays where the potentially desperate predicament of such women is feelingly explored. More consistently, serious treatment is usually given to the case of the girl threatened with a marriage distasteful to her, or prevented from marrying the man she loves. Even where the play is a comedy, the far-reaching implications of such repression are rarely overlooked and the playwrights are normally as vehement as Cervantes in their condemnation. Only occasionally is this approach modified by other thematic considerations.

Lope's *La serrana de Tormes* and Tiros's *La gallega Mari-Hernández* will serve as examples. The *serrana* of Lope's play[1] is not a *serrana bandolera* and the plot is the conventional one of the wandering girl. For all its conventionality, there comes across very strongly the folly of trying to hinder the course of true love. Disregarding the wishes of the young people concerned, Diana's uncle and Alejandro's father decide it is best the lovers separate and together arrange to marry Diana off to somebody else. Their motives are more honourable than those of many a tyrannical father, for they believe they have the best interests of their children at heart – best interests, however, as *they* see them. Their unconsidered behaviour has predictably the reverse effect, for it drives Diana to expose herself to greater danger in her natural pursuit of love. She leaves the security of her home, living first as a rough soldier, then as a peasant girl, and in the course of her adventures is almost raped. The humour of the play and its happy ending do not obscure Lope's conviction about the dangers of trying to impose artificial restraints and taboos upon man's natural inclinations. This was a conviction he always held and one which possibly accounted for his loathing for the rich merchant Roque Hernández, to whom Lope's *Amarilis*, his *Marcia Leonarda* – Marta de Nevares Santoyo – had been sacrificed on the altar of worldy wealth at the age of thirteen.

Beatriz in *La gallega Mari-Hernández*[2] is subjected to even greater pressure, for the order to marry comes from the King himself, the very source of social authority. Her protests lead to her imprisonment; but she escapes with the aid of a rope made of sheets, and brandishing her sword and pistol and avoiding the bullets that come flying after her, she races her unwelcome suitor to Galicia. Beatriz is making a courageous stand for freedom,

---

[1] Dated by Morley and Bruerton (p. 152) as 1590 (?)–1595.

[2] Cotarelo y Mori thinks the play was written around 1625 when it was performed (See N.B.A.E. IX, *Catálogo razonado* xxii) but Blanca de los Ríos in her introduction to the Aguilar edition (p. xix) puts the date of composition at 1611 or 1612. The play's two *mujeres varoniles* do not help with the dating.

which is of as paramount importance to her as his honour is to Pedro Crespo in *El alcalde de Zalamea*:

> Yo que por no ver cautiva
> la prenda mejor del alma
> menospreciaré la vida.
>
> (Act II, B.A.E. v, 116c)

The emphasis in this play, however is markedly different. Whereas Lope's *La serrana de Tormes* hinges on the theme of parental tyranny and its effects, of the tension between love and authority, in Tirso's drama this is a subsidiary issue in a complex action that involves Beatriz but centres on the scorned Mari-Hernández. Consequently approval of Beatriz's spirited defense of her integrity and the accompanying disapproval of forced marriages, although unequivocal, are not developed with Lope's singleness of purpose. A comparison of Lope's plays with those of his fellow playwrights does suggest that none of the others, except possibly Cervantes, was as preoccupied with the concept of freedom in love. Illuminating in this respect is the end of Tirso's play. Lope would have enforced the principle of poetic justice and ensured that the brave and resolute Beatriz be allowed for her pains to marry the man she loves and who loves her. Tirso's attentions, however, are otherwise occupied – not only with Beatriz but with the promises made by her lover Don Alvaro to Mari-Hernández. And Tirso's belief in woman's right to free choice in marriage falls victim here temporarily to a different vision of the jungle of human feeling. Since both women cannot have Don Álvaro, poor Beatriz is rather spitefully married off by the jealous king to someone completely extraneous to the plot,

> Beatriz, con él de Olivanza
> os habéis de casar;
> pues ya que yo no os merezca
> no será razón que os goce
> mi competidor.
>
> (Act III, 127a–b)

The competitor is Don Álvaro, whom the king has arbitrarily promised, along with a title, to Mari-Hernández. This bland 'tidying-up' procedure at the end of the play, although typical of seventeenth-century dramatic practice, should not be taken at its face value. Mari-Hernández alone is finally satisfied in love. Beatriz, Don Álvaro and the king himself all fail to marry the object of their affections and the first two are forcibly married off elsewhere. The ending belies our expectations of a satisfactorily romantic happy-ever-after dénouement. For the play is, more than anything else, a deft dissection of the comic absurdities of life and love, of the sad ironies of fickleness, of the network of passion and counter-passion so vulnerable to the manipulations of envy and resourcefulness. In the seventeenth-century theatre the fantasy-world of love is rarely depicted with the romantic ingenuousness with which a first superficial reading might be satisfied.

Diana and Beatriz illustrate in their distinctive ways the sort of treatment of which the rebellion-by-flight motif was susceptible. The plays which incorporate this motif are essentially adventure plays. The crisis caused by the threat of a forced marriage is also solved in the drama in a more devious manner, within a framework of domestic intrigue, and this solution constitutes rebellion-by-deceit, arguably less morally attractive but probably more true to life. There are a number of such intrigues in the Spanish drama at this time – Lope's *La discreta enamorada* amongst them – but Tirso's *Marta la piadosa*[1] is one of the most powerful. It is certainly representative.

Marta, faced with marriage to an old man she does not love, decides to rely for her salvation on her wits and her histrionic abilities, and pretends to her father that she has taken a vow of chastity. Inés in Lope's *El caballero de Olmedo*,[2] it will be remembered, likewise takes refuge behind an assumed religious vocation. Her case, though, is very different. Ines's father is very much her friend, and her rashness in the face of life's realities leads to tragedy. Tirso's play on the other hand is very firmly a comedy, although a comedy of the most astringent sort. Its heroine is typical of Tirso's

1 Written in late 1614 or early 1615. See Ruth L. Kennedy, 'On the dates of five plays by Tiros', HR x (1942), 214, n. 85; and G. E. Wade, 'Notes on Tirso de Molina', HR VII (1939), 69–70.
2 Written according to Morley and Bruerton (177–8) between 1615 and 1626, probably between 1620 and 1625.

female offspring – strong-willed, clever and scheming – and she plays her role of prospective *beata* with the convincing unction of a Tartuffe. Marta is not a Tartuffe, however, because she is not a hypocrite. She merely uses hypocrisy to achieve her rightful ends. Her characterization has its caustic side for she uses in her schemes not only hypocrisy but her less agile-minded sister who is also in love with Felipe, imitating in this a host of Golden-Age protagonists who victimize other people in the relentless pursuit of their amatory aims. But, for all this streak of ruthlessness, our sympathies, and Tirso's, are entirely with her and the play presents what is surely one of the most persuasive cases against forced marriage in the Spanish theatre. Neither its charm nor its gentle mockery succeeds in hiding its more serious undercurrent. For if Martha victimizes others, it is because she too is a victim of a selfish, materialist father who, when she first protests at the proposed marriage, threatens to kill her as he sees his dreams of extra riches fading. She resorts to deceit only when honesty is shown to be useless and any blame must be imputed, not to her, but to her father and thence to a society which, still living in the past, condones forced marriages. Every society is modern in its own eyes, and 'modern' society in Tirso's cannot uphold such a practice,

> No es en eso prudente, aunque atrevido,
> que en este tiempo no parece justo
> casar las hijas contra el proprio gusto.
>
> (Act I, B.A.E. v, 447b–c)

A forced marriage of its very nature is motivated by vested interests of the more materialistic sort. And in addition to making a stand for woman's right to self-determination *Marta la piadosa* also lays bare the materialism inherent in society's restrictive attitude towards young girls. As Marta scathingly observes,

> Linda sangre y humor cría,
> pastrana, la hipocresía.
> Nunca tuve libertad,
> mientras viví a lo damo,
> como agora; si intentaba
> salir fuera, me costaba

una riña: ya no llamo
a la dueña, al escudero,
ni aguardo la silla y coche,
ni me riñen si a la noche
vuelvo: voy a donde quiero.

(Act II, B.A.E. v, 451b)

For seventeenth-century Spain, as for many societies,[1] marriageable women were valuable property who represented for their 'owners' considerable bargaining power. Logically, value and bargaining power depended on the state of the goods and every effort was made to prevent their becoming shop-soiled. But once let an item be withdrawn from the sale and its condition was no longer of prime concern. Marta soon learns that the woman who claims to have been called to a life of chastity and devotion is allowed total freedom, not so much because her religious vocation puts her above suspicion or out of danger but because she is no longer a marketable commodity. A *beata*'s robes are no guarantee against molestation, after all. And she realizes that hypocrisy breeds hypocrisy. The hypocrisy of enforced propriety will tolerate that of hidden impropriety because its interests are no longer involved, and a vow of chastity can thus become a more effective means of social emancipation than marriage itself. Whatever the realities of seventeenth-century *beata* life – and it is by no means inconceivable that it became a cloak for behaviour of a far more unorthodox kind than Marta's – the principles at issue here are vital ones and the play is a serious, though ironic, exposé of wrong thinking.

These examples of plots where female rebellion within the context of a strongly patriarchal society assumes a less violent form, together with the bandit plays, reveal their authors as men sensitive to the anomalies and injustices of certain aspects of female life. The dramatic arbiters by example, and to some extent their followers by imitation, show in their exploration of the situations to which

---

[1] For a literary-historical study of the property marriage in England, see Christopher Hill, 'Clarissa Harlowe and her times', *Puritanism and Revolution* (London, 1958).

these anomalies and injustices could give rise – theatrical over-statement being a vehicle, not a substitution, for psychological realism – that they sympathize with woman's rejection of the stigma imposed upon her by the double standard of morality, that they abhor the idea of the unwilling bride and that they understand and very often approve of the act of rebellion to which women in these circumstances might be driven. In terms of the conventional attitudes of their own day, and indeed of those of innumerable generations to come, their attitude towards women was in this respect remarkably liberal. It would be wrong to read into this, however, any impulse towards female emancipation in twentieth-century terms. Succeeding chapters will show how their feminism was circumscribed by traditional views about woman's role, and a look now at one last rebel should prove both a salutory footnote to the rebellion theme and an anticipatory glimpse into the treatment of other *varonilidad* themes to come.

Whether Calderón's *Guárdate del agua mansa*[1] is a comment on embryonic real-life moves towards emancipation or upon the theatre's concern with and exploitation of the theme in both its serious and frivolous aspects, a comment it certainly is and a fairly barbed one at that. In it the germ of female emancipation present in all plays with a *mujer varonil* or merely a *mujer vestida de hombre* amongst the *dramatis personae* is subjected to the full bright light of day. Eugenia, the younger sister, is the only example in the Golden Age theatre of the woman who deliberately defies all social conventions and aims at complete emancipation. She tries to claim for herself the total freedom from restriction of the male. She reads and writes poetry and does not hesitate to send or receive the odd sonnet. She insists on going wherever she wants and on talking to whomsoever she wishes. She will not wear a veil when out, and can see no harm in addressing men from her balcony. For appearances she cares nothing, nor for the *qué dirán* attitude by which women's behaviour is usually governed. Honour she regards as an outmoded restriction, and she has no patience with her elder sister's conviction that a pretence of non-existent virtue is infinitely

---

[1] Internal evidence shows the play to have been written in 1649. Its title was originally *El agua mansa*.

preferable to a virtue which is real but not readily apparent. The entirely admirable views, one might now think, of an intelligent and clear-sighted girl. Not so: Calderón makes it clear that this wilful flouting of convention is not based on rational convictions about the freedom and integrity of the individual, whether male or female, but on a spoilt child determination to have her own way and indulge her every whim. The portrayal of Eugenia, which could have been that of a mature, thoughtful and courageous person is shaped into an altogether different image – that of a pleasure-loving, impressionable, headstrong, materialistic and totally 'giddy' young woman, who rejects the restrictions of her sex as hindrances to her enjoyment. This shaping is not merely the outcome of Calderón's particular dramatic vision, conceived in conjunction with a specific plot, although of course it is this too. It is also the result of an unwillingness, general throughout the theatre, to allow the woman who *without provocation* revolts against social convention any motives other than those that are the projection of some defect of personality. The conviction that such revolt was not only unnecessary but improper is amply illustrated by the *mujer esquiva* plays.

Because Eugenia's unconventional behaviour has no rational basis, it is easily jeopardized. No sooner do two of her former suitors, both of whose advances she has received, appear on the scene together, than she is overcome with alarm that her father might find out about her past. This serious threat to her reputation reveals her bravery to have been bravado and her conviction mere whim: she orders them to leave her in peace, explaining hastily to her reproachful sister

> las mujeres
> como yo, puestas en salvo,
> si se esparcen y divierten
> es para aquesto no más;
> que amor bachiller no tiene
> más fondo que solo el ruido.
>
> (Act II, B.A.E. IX, 392a)

Her relief at surviving the danger unscathed is so great that she humbly *begs* her father to give her in marriage to the boorish country cousin she swore she would never marry. Her retreat from revolt is thankful and complete, identifying, as she does, safety with orthodoxy, even unwelcome orthodoxy. Her request is a symbol, perhaps overstated, of her grateful submission to the normal standards of behaviour expected in a woman and an acceptance of her proper place in society. The unwelcome marriage is, characteristically, avoided and Eugenia is lucky enough to be married off by her prudent father to one of her two gallants; but happy as this solution is, the comedy remains an unequivocal reminder that for all their liberalness the Spanish playwrights' views on women and feminine behaviour were not the same as our own, and that sympathy for the female rebel had well-defined limits.

5

The *mujer esquiva*[1]

There is no adequate English translation of the phrase *mujer esquiva*.
Disdainful, elusive, distant, shy, cold – *esquiva* contains something
of them all. But if the phrase cannot be translated, it can be explained: the *mujer esquiva* is the woman who, for some reason, is
averse to the idea of love and marriage. As a natural outcome, she
is usually, but not invariably, averse to men as well. The *esquiva* is by
far the most popular of the many variations on the *mujer varonil* theme
used by the Spanish dramatists of the Golden Age, largely because
hers is an abnormality which is not out of place in women who
belong primarily to another variant group. About half the female
bandits in the drama of this period are *esquivas* when they first
appear on the scene. The Amazon, of course, is traditionally
esquiva. *Esquivas*, too, are many of her seventeenth-century counterparts, those women who, having been brought up in an atmosphere
of physical freedom, resent the threat to their independence that
love and marriage represent. However, this chapter does not include those female characters whose *esquivez* is, within context,
subordinate to or less interesting than their other unfeminine traits.
These are discussed under the appropriate headings. The heroines
dealt with here are those whose primary importance to plot and/or
theme lies, or seems to lie, in their reluctance to marry.

The *mujer esquiva* is the most important manifestation of the
mujer varonil as well as the most popular. She is in fact central to
the whole theme of feminism in the Golden-Age theatre, because
she, more than any other female type, illustrates the exact nature
of the seventeenth-century attitude to women. Her central position
is determined by the nature and seriousness of her revolt. Other
woman may revolt against what they consider the unjust laws and

[1] An earlier version of this chapter was published in the *Hispanic Review*,
XL (1972), No. 2, pp. 162–97.

conventions of the masculine society in which they live, and their grievances are often found by their creators to be justified. Here, too, it must be pointed out by way of warning, in terms of the dramatic action men are largely to blame. The *esquiva's* revolt against Nature, as it is presented to us, is not a revolt in absolute terms: it is not prompted by homosexual impulses. It is not prompted by a desire to reject the essential nature of her sexual being, but by the way in which the concept of Nature is invoked by men to justify their delegation of woman to an inactive, inferior role in life. Yet Nature *is* involved. Love and marriage are the realm where the essential difference between the sexes is most pointed. In the eyes of the dramatist the *mujer esquiva* is not, ultimately, rebelling against man-made rules which, given the weakness of human nature, may well be misguided ones. *Her* defiance, whatever the motive, whatever the incitement, is directed against the natural order of things as decreed by God.[1]

This natural order may be briefly explained thus: woman was created out of man in the Garden of Eden to be his help-meet; on the temporal level he is therefore her first cause and final end; love and marriage are her birthright; towards them her entire nature is directed, and in them she finds her fulfilment. To this natural law no woman, unless she has a religious vocation, is an exception, and the misguided woman who considers herself immune to love, who claims to dislike men or who prefers to avoid matrimony, must therefore be led, or driven, back to the path of sanity, reason – and true happiness. Such sentiments are repeated time and again throughout the body of plays which have *mujeres esquivas* as their heroines, and the unanimity of opinion amongst the dramatists can be judged from the fact that not one of these women finally remains *voluntarily* single. These ideas about the natural role of woman, whether explicitly expressed by the play's *dramatis personae* or implicitly conveyed by the development of the action, are not dramatic platitudes. They were seriously held by the men of the

---

[1] Explained in the following way by St Thomas Aquinas: '. . . to the natural law belongs everything to which a man is inclined according to his Nature. Now each thing is inclined naturally to an operation that is suitable to it according to its form . . .' *Summa Theologica* II, 1, Q 94, Art. III (translated by the Fathers of the English Dominican Province, London, 1915).

age. Of this, Lope, in his dedication of *La vengadora de las mujeres*, to 'la Señora Fenisa Camila', gives impressively adequate proof,

Desde que supe que querían imprimir *La vengadora de las mujeres*, que por ventura por este intento andaba perdida por la corte, previene dirigirla a v.m., como a persona a quien más justamente tocaba el título, pues ha vencido más mujeres con su hermosura que hombres han engañado con palabras de casamiento, lazo en que tan fácilmente caen. Y aunque yo estaba en sagrado, así por el oficio como porque en las ventanas de los años no alcanza el toro, quise hacer este gusto a v.m. por si pudiese persuadir su imaginación que fue el dueño de esta fábula. *Vanidad es en una mujer despreciar los hombres, pues cuando Aristóteles dijo que la mujer le apetecía como la materia a la forma no pensó que era pequeño el encarecimiento.* Mas responderá v.m. que Dios, habiéndole criado, le halló solo, y que le dio la mujer por compañía; de donde querría inferir que él debe apetecerla y que ella puede huirle. El argumento es falso, *porque saliendo del mismo, ha de volver a su primera causa, como a la mar los ríos. El solo, dijo el filósofo que era Dios o bestia; v.m. no puede ser lo primero: mire al peligro en que se pone con lo segundo;* y si le ha de suceder lo que a Laura, que con todas sus letras, sus estudios, cuidados y melindres vino a querer sujeto, donde si la mentira del disfraz fuera verdad de la persona, más que de las mujeres, había sido la vengadora de los hombres, no intente por vanidad cosas que, *no teniendo por fundamento la virtud, se oponen a la naturaleza.* No ame v.m., pero no aborrezca; no diga bien de los hombres, pero no los infame; siquiera porque sus padres desearon que lo fuese, y les pesó de que naciese mujer: y aun a la misma naturaleza, *que por su falta la hizo hombre imperfecto,* título que dieron a la mujer tantos filósofos. Mas porque no parezca que, habiendo de ser esta carta dirección de esta comedia y, como en los libros se usa, primera en las licencias de las lisonjas, aseguro a v.m. que la tengo por hermosa y que la tendré por discreta si la veo de la opinión de Laura, con algún dichoso Lisardo que la merezca, *porque la más pintada mariposa, sin que la busque la llama, se abrasa en ella*; y nos han enseñado los ejemplos de las historias, así antiguas como modernas, notables castigos de semejantes libertades; por lo menos entran aquí los avisos de los poetas, y el de Horacio con Garcilaso cuando dijo:

En tanto que de rosa y azucena

Porque v.m. podría aguardar a tiempo que los mismos de quien ahora se burla se burlasen de ella. Dios guarde a v.m. Capellán de v.m., Lope de Vega Carpio. [The italics are mine,]

This age-old conception of woman forms the very basis of the plays discussed here. The thesis is almost invariably dramatized in the manner established by Lope: the heroine's aversion to love and marriage; her gradual yielding to love, a process helped along by the pretended *desprecio* of the man and by the jealousy he succeeds in creating in her; the crisis which precipitates the transformation; and finally, the willing subjection to the *yugo blando* of matrimony. But obviously the theme of the woman who scorns love in asserting her independence is susceptible of a variety of treatments, and while differences in plot detail are usually unimportant, the differences in the *nature* of the heroine's *esquivez* and in the motives behind it *are* important because they determine the degree of the dramatist's disapproval and hence the whole tone of the play.

The *mujer esquiva* plays can, for the most part, be divided into two groups according to the motive ascribed by the dramatist to the woman concerned. These two motives are (a) vanity and (b) arrogant pride.[1] Their continual recurrence reveals the dramatists' inability to conceive of any assertion of female independence other than that based on some reprehensible character trait; none of the playwrights of the Golden Age sympathizes with his *esquivas* in the way that Cervantes sympathizes with his Marcela. Where vanity is the underlying cause of the heroine's *esquivez,* the treatment is light-hearted, but where the *mujer esquiva* is guilty of arrogant pride, the theme is sometimes dealt with more seriously and the play then leaves the plane of light comedy.

I

The woman who glories in being surrounded by despairing suitors appears in *Las milagros del desprecio*, which for lack of convincing

[1] Theologically, vanity is the more venial sin. St Thomas Aquinas calls pride the most grievous of sins (*Summa* II, 2, Q 162). Of vanity he says: 'If, however, the love of human glory, though it be vain, be not inconsistent with charity, neither as regards the matter glorified in, nor as to the intention of him that seeks glory, it is not a mortal but a venial sin' (*Ibid.* II, 2, Q 132, Art. 3). Pride is more serious because the proud man 'raises himself above that which is appointed to him according to the Divine rule or measure' (*Ibid.* II, 2, Q 162, Art. 5).

evidence to the contrary I assume to be Lope's[1] and which, if it is, must have been one of the earliest plays to deal in depth with the *mujer esquiva*. Hers is the soon-to-be-familiar story of the girl who is caught on her own hook. Doña Juana's confessed hatred of men is such that she explodes into hysteria whenever they are mentioned. When she thinks her views are being questioned she even resorts to physical violence, and any signs of a change of heart in her maid, Leonor, she meets with the threats of punishment typical of her emotional, unstable character:

> que en empezando a tener
> mudable la condición
> y que estés a devoción
> de los hombres, te he de hacer
> pedazos la voluntad
> a desabrimientos míos,
> a pesares y desvíos.
>
> (Act II, Acad. N. XIII, 10a–b)

Her denunciation of men has not the authority of personal experience – since she has never allowed a man within conversation distance – nor even of vicarious experience, for she proffers none of the usual classical examples of man's worthlessness. Why, then, the vehement scorn, the displays of violence and bad temper? Lope leaves us in no doubt that the answer is vanity. Juana delights in the fruitless efforts of her suitors; she glories in the power she has over them; she revels in her own haughtiness and untouchability.

> Viendo a un hombre padecer
> me considero gloriosa.
>   Con tanto imperio me veo
> en mi libre condición,
> que ni siento inclinación
> ni se me altera el deseo.
>
> (Act II, 13a)

---

[1] If the play is Lope's the dates are 1599–1603. See Morley and Bruerton, 314–15. Payment was made for a play called *Los milagros del desprecio* on 24 December 1632. See Shergold and Varey, 'Some Palace Performances . . .', *BHS* XL (1963), 230. But of course composition could have taken place much earlier, or alternatively the 1632 play could have been a *refundición* or even a substantially different piece with the same title.

Equally flattering to her vanity is the public respect and esteem her aura of aloofness and unquestionable virtue has earned her, and it is through this regard for her public image that Nature accomplishes its revenge. Consistent with her vanity, too, is her self-appointment as an instrument of *venzanza universal* upon men, and her desire to impose her views on all women. Yet again, it is vanity which makes Juana so unkind to her cousin Beatriz, and leads her to betray Beatriz to her father, Juana's uncle; she wishes to conform to his high opinion of her virtue.

Lope is illustrating the premise that hatred of men is neither natural nor plausible in a woman, and that beneath apparent antagonism there is a fault of character which makes her behave in this way. Appropriately, therefore, after being subjected to the scorn and neglect with which she has hitherto treated her suitors, Juana is finally punished and made to see the error of her ways through this very fault. Self-deception gives way to self-knowledge. Since vanity is what Juana is accused of, the public pricking of this vanity is her punishment and she is caught on a wet night, dishevelled and covered in mud, in actual pursuit of a man. Juana does make an attempt to justify herself,

> Yo soy. ¿De qué os admiráis?
> Si pensáis que me ha sacado
> de mi casa algún cuidado
> amoroso, os engañáis.
>   Las mujeres que nacemos,
> señor don Pedro Girón,
> con sangre y estimación,
> más que las otras sentimos.
>   ¡Vive Dios que he de saber
> quien es esta vuestra dama
> por quien mi opinión y fama
> se ha echado tanto a perder!
>   que eso solo me ha sacado
> de mi casa.
>
> (Act III, 26a–b)

and to an extent she is correct. For Nature in her wisdom, and aided by the wily Hernando, has used Juana's self-esteem to put her in a position where she has to yield to love. The news that Don Pedro had another lady and had been ridiculing Juana, first affected her vanity and only afterwards led to jealousy. The general process of reform is the same in all the *mujeres esquivas*, but in the best plays it is always adapted to the individual character of the particular heroine. The punishment is suggested by the weakness and is therefore the most effective antidote for it.

If Juana personifies an attitude alien to woman's true nature, her cousin Beatriz, on the other hand, is all that a woman should be for Lope: warm, appealing, in love and interested in the love affairs of others. This two-sided portrayal of womanhood is characteristic of many of the *esquiva* plays, the two standing respectively for warning and example. Here Lope prudently strengthens his case by using Beatriz, and not any of the male characters, as mouthpiece for the claims of love and marriage,

> ¿No somos también mujeres,
> y en las mujeres también
> natural el querer bien?
>
> (Act II, 14a)

and,

> Dios obra en el casamiento
>
> (Act II, 16a)

Lope with his *Los milagros del desprecio* created a genre; some fifty years later the genre culminated in Moreto's polished and utterly delightful play *El desdén con el desdén*.[1] Again the situation is that of the disdainful heroine won over to love by feigned scorn and betrayed by her own vanity. Diana's quarrel, however, is essentially with love, which she considers to be responsible for all the world's tragedies and troubles, and unlike Juana she bases her views on the knowledge and wisdom she has culled from her books. Her reaction to them is one of cold indifference born, so she

---

[1] Published in 1654. Probably written between the date of publication and April 1652. Ruth L. Kennedy, *The Dramatic Art of Moreto*, Appendix, 161-2, note 65. For the sources of the play see Miss Kennedy's Appendix, 160-9, and M. M. Harlan, *The Relationship of Moreto's 'El desdén con el desdén' to Suggested Sources*, Indiana University Studies (June 1924).

claims, of disillusionment. The siege that her disdain now undergoes is altogether a much subtler campaign than the barrage of scorn, neglect and ridicule to which Juana is subjected. To begin with, the efficacy of disdain has already been proved to his chagrin by Carlos, who has fallen in love with Diana in spite of her 'hermosura modesta / con muchas señas de tibia' (Act I, B.A.E. xxxix, 1) because for the first time in his life he is unable to take what he wants just for the asking. He is not slow to realize that only the challenge which the unattainable represents for his own egoism will succeed in shaking Diana's, and he therefore poses as an *hombre esquivo*, daring Diana to try to reduce him to the same state of abject submission as her other suitors. Diana swallows the bait,

> he de hacer empeño
> de rendir su vanidad.
>
> (Act I, B.A.E. xxxix, 6c)

little realizing that with these words she is passing judgment, not on Carlos's motives, but her own. Slowly but surely the vanity wounded by Carlos's immunity gives way to a desire not only to impress but to possess, and when Carlos plays his ace card by pretending interest in one of Diana's ladies in-waiting, she is irretrievably lost. As befits the play's subtlety of plot and character, there is no public humiliation of the vain, misguided woman here as there is in *Los milagros del desprecio*. An official declaration of obedience to Diana's wishes on the part of Carlos allows her to grant him her hand with the dignity appropriate to her situation.

Moreto is no less convinced than Lope of the importance of the part which love must inevitably play in woman's make-up, and he likewise stresses that any evasion or denial of love is a revolt against Nature itself. Carlos with graphic eloquence states that the result of Diana's studies is

> un común desprecio
> de los hombres, unas iras
> *contra el orden natural*
> *del amor* con quien fabrica
> el mundo a su duración
> alcázares en que viva.
>
> (Act I, 2a [The italics are mine])

and this conviction that Diana is behaving unnaturally is shared by Cintia who exclaims in amazement,

> ¡Que por error su agudeza
> quiera el amor condenar;
> y si lo es, *quiera enmendar*
> *lo que erró naturaleza!*
>
> (Act I, 4a [The italics are mine])

Bruce W. Wardropper[1] has interpreted the theme of the play as a secularized form of free-will which is radically different from theological free-will. Moreto, he says, is asking to what extent woman is free to choose whether she will marry or not. The evidence provided by the *esquiva* plays necessarily qualifies the truth of these assertions. Although Professor Wardropper's interpretation of the play and his discussion of the tension in Diana between Reason and Will correspond exactly to the ideas the play suggests to the reader and are therefore in one respect entirely valid, it seems unlikely that Moreto is *actively* speculating about this problem of free-will. He is writing after all within a well-worn tradition, with ready-made situations and ideas, and a ready-made phraseology to draw upon. His play thus appears to be rather a testimony of faith in an ingrained pattern of belief. To choose *El desdén con el desdén* to illustrate a secularization of the Spanish theatre in Moreto's drama is a mistake. The ideology of self-determination in all the *esquiva* plays is perhaps as far removed from 'consciously Christian ethics' as that of the play in question. Each one poses the question (consciously or not) of the extent of woman's self-determination and each one plumps for the concept of a limited degree of free-will which Professor Wardropper finds in *El desdén con el desdén* alone. At the same time, in every case the love-force is directed towards the harmony produced by marriage. In other words the dramatists uphold a secularized free-will within the framework of what is essentially, even in Moreto, a Christian social and natural order. Furthermore, the Love–Reason debate in Moreto's play is even more conventional than the

[1] 'Moreto's "El desdén con el desdén": the *Comedia* Secularized', BHS XXXIV (1957), 1–9.

heroine's *esquivez*[1] and it must not therefore be granted too much importance in an assessment of the dramatist's intentions. Finally Professor Wardropper, by dint of omission, gives the impression that this lack of true freedom was woman's alone. And, of course, it was not. For the Golden Age the natural forces in man were as powerful as those in woman and he was as subject to love as she. The *hombres esquivos* of the theatre discover they are no more free to choose to remain single than the *esquivas* themselves.

The position that Calderon takes in his *No hay burlas con el amor*[2] is slightly less unambiguous than Moreto's. His heroine, Beatriz, is a vain, conceited and silly girl who makes a show of her learning and speaks in an affected manner. The praise she receives from the undiscriminating flatters her conceit and creates in her a self-congratulatory disdain for her suitors.[3] The play also contains one of the several examples in the Golden-Age theatre of the *hombre esquivo*[4] – Don Alonso, a young rake who hates the idea of love and marriage because of the emotional ties involved. Inevitably he and Beatriz fall in love with each other, although both, of course, are loath to admit it. Their attraction is made to seem normal and inevitable, but we can only deduce that it is intended to be seen as

[1] See Barbara Matulka, 'The feminist theme in the drama of the *Siglo de Oro*', *Comparative Literature Series, Publications of the Institute of French Studies Inc.*, Columbia University.

[2] Probably written in 1635. See Hannah E. Bergman *Luis Quiñones de Benavente y sus entremeses* (Madrid, 1965), 333–41.

[3] In writing this play Calderón obviously had in mind two plays by Lope: *Los melindres de Belisa* and *Los milagros del desprecio*. From the first he took the idea of the *melindrosa* heroine, while the delight which Leonor and Inés take in subjecting Beatriz to love and its accompanying emotions is strongly reminiscent of the relish taken by Leonor and Beatriz in Doña Juana's downfall (*Los milagros del desprecio*). In fact, Inés's words, '¡ Ay señores! que ya siente' (Act III, B.A.E. IX, 321c) are almost an exact replica of those gleefully uttered by her counterpart Leonor, '¡ Ay, señores, que lo siente!' (Act III, Acad.N. XIII,19a).

[4] Carlos in *El desdén con el desdén* only feigns *esquivez*. Amongst the true *esquivos* are: the King in Lope's (?) *Los contrarios de amor*, Don Juan in Lope's *De cosario a cosario*, Don Félix in Calderón's *Gúardate del agua mansa* and Don Félix in Juan Vélez de Guevara's *Encontráronse dos arroyuelos*. It is illuminating, however, that the men are motivated in their *esquivez* by specific disillusionment or specific doubts and fears, often related to an incident in their past. They never reject love and marriage on grounds of so-called principles which have their real roots in vanity or pride.

the *proper* outcome for their prejudices by considering the alternatives – promiscuity with lower-class girls for Alonso, conceited spinsterhood for Beatriz. For Calderón does not speak of love and marriage in the hushed, reverent tones which Lope tends to adopt. In fact, after making the couple fall in love, Calderón mischievously shifts position and uses them as a warning against love. Furthermore, the warning is issued by Moscatel and Inés, who throughout the play have played the part of love's champions,

> Moscatel En fin, el hombre más libre,
> de las burlas de amor sale
> herido, cojo, y casado,
> que es el mayor de sus males.
> Inés En fin, la mujer más loca,
> más vana y arrogante,
> de las burlas de amor,
> contra gusto suyo sale
> enamorada, y rendida,
> que es lo peor.
>
> (Act III, B.A.E. IX, 328c)

and finally, Alonso says of love,

> No se burle con él nadie,
> sino escarmentad en mí.
> todos del amor se guarden.
>
> (Act III, 328c)

The bulk of the evidence provided by the play, however – the plot itself and the remarks made by the characters during the course of the action – point to the conclusion that Calderón's views were the same as Lope's, and Calderón's other *mujeres esquivas* certainly confirm this. But, unlike Lope, Calderón was capable of speaking of love and marriage tongue in cheek, and of expressing the conventional horror and fear of them affected by those who seek to amuse and entertain.

The psychological precept behind the reform of the *mujer esquiva* who suffers from vanity, is as Narciso Alonso Cortés points out, the age-old *similia similibus curantur*.[1] Her *esquivez* itself is

---

[1] In the prologue to his edition of Moreto's *El desdén con el desdén*, Clásicos castellanos XXXII (Madrid, 1916), 23.

equally based on a psychological truism – that what is easily
obtainable has little desirability. Thus the heroine of Moreto's *El
poder de la amistad*,[1] Margarita, although she has no theoretical
objections to men or marriage and is neither haughty nor conceited,
will not accept her suitor,

> Por ver que me quiere mucho.
>
> (Act I, B.A.E. xxxix, 23b)

Only when Alejandro makes himself inaccessible does she become
conscious of his attractions. There are two plays which concentrate
in particular upon the theme of the counter-suggestibility of
human-nature in matters of love: *Hacer remedio el dolor* by Cáncer,
Moreto and questionably Matos,[2] and Rojas Zorrilla's *Lo que son
mujeres*.[3] In both of them the familiar formula is given its logical
conclusion – when the girl is reduced to wanting her suitor, her
suitor no longer wants her. She is hoist with her own petard.
Casandra in *Hacer remedio el dolor* is an orphan who, after
disdaining her suitors in order to remain faithful to her books,
naïvely admits her love for Carlos. At this point, the other plays
normally end. But Carlos is a restless, irrational young man who
finds Casandra's capitulation distasteful and so he betakes himself
to Naples to embark upon the conquest of another woman.
Casandra, however, is quick to realize that the only way to win
Carlos back again is to create the illusion that he is once more the
pursuer and she the pursued. This she does, and he is soon brought
to heel. Serafina in *Lo que son mujeres* is not so fortunate as Casandra.
For her *esquivez* she is humiliated to the point where after each of
her four former suitors has rejected her, she is reduced in her
desperation to proposing to the servants,

> A ti te he elegido
> Esteban.
>
> *Esteban*   Eso me agrada,

---

[1] Miss Kennedy ascribes the play to the year 1652, *The Dramatic Art of Moreto*, 21.
[2] Written in or before 1649. It is probable that the play was written by Cáncer and
Moreto alone. See Miss Kennedy's Appendix, 220. The play appeared in *Esc.* xi,
1659.
[3] Published in the *Segunda parte del autor*, 1645. See Cotarelo y Mori, *Don Francisco
de Rojas Zorrilla, noticias biográficas y bibliográficas* (Madrid, 1911), 175–6.

¿pues cuándo fue una dejada
alhaja de un presumido?
Serafina   Tú alcanzaste la victoria,
merecerás por constante.
Jacobo   Acordáraislo adelante,
para que tenga memoria.

(Act III, B.A.E. LIV, 211c)

She is not even compensated for her loss of dignity by love and a husband. The play is a savage one, lacking in the warmth and understanding with which Lope always treats his *mujeres esquivas*. The disdainful woman is normally humbled by her lover because he loves and wants her, but all that Serafina's suitors want is their revenge. The only sympathetic character in the play is the sister, Matea, and even she is frivolous and unstable. Rojas Zorrilla has modified the usual tale of feminine disdain in several ways: first, the *mujer esquiva* is off-set by a girl who has an indiscriminate fondness for all men; second, none of the suitors really loves Serafina; third, the change in her is not brought about by jealousy but by pique at seeing the less attractive sister favoured; fourth, she does not fall in love with any of the four men and fifth, neither of the girls finally marries. These changes are typical of the delight Rojas took in refusing to follow the conventions. Rojas's views about women and love, on the other hand, seem to have been entirely conventional, for like Lope he is convinced that woman's place is at man's side,

Ser inclinada a los hombres
ni es liviandad ni flaqueza;
éste es un bien natural,
y aunque algunos riesgos tenga
de pesarle a una mujer
que no la estimen ni quieran,
aunque pesa el desdén tanto,
vale el amor lo que pesa.

(Act I, 194a)

At the same time the picture he paints of the female character is not a pretty one. Women, he intimates, are fickle, shallow, unreliable, insincere and motivated by vanity and caprice. Admittedly, his portrayal of the male character is little less unattractive; the suitors are a ridiculous foursome, as cruel and capricious as Serafina herself. Obviously the play is not meant as a serious judgment upon human nature. It is a satire, a clever but rather unpleasant one, of the familiar dramatic situation of the disdainful woman and her admirers.

II

The undercurrent of harshness in *Lo que son mujeres* leads on naturally to a consideration of the second group of *mujer esquiva* plays – those in which the heroine's sin is a less venial one than vanity and in which the treatment of the theme is consequently sometimes more serious. The most important and the subtlest of these plays is Lope's *La moza de cántaro*.[1] It is devoted to an examination of this particular type of woman and might therefore be called the 'thesis' play on this subject. The heroine, Doña María, refuses to marry and despises all the suitors who present themselves, not only because she considers none of them worthy of her, but also because she will not subject herself to the authority of any man,

> si va a decir verdad,
> no quiere mi vanidad
> que cosa indigna le ofenda.
> Nací con esta arrogancia;
> no me puedo sujetar
> si es sujetar el casar.
>
> (Act I, Acad. N. XIII, 648a)

This arrogance of hers is doubly reprehensible in a woman because it smacks of masculinity. Doña María's streak of *varonilidad* is soon displayed in action when she takes upon herself the vengeance for her father's insult, a task which falls naturally and properly upon his son. Her arrogance has driven her not only to a defiance of Nature (by not marrying) but also to a defiance of Society (by

---

[1] According to Morley and Bruerton (p. 222) probably written before November 1627. Payment was made on 31 March 1627. See Shergold and Varey, 'Some Palace Performances . . .', 231.

usurping her brother's role). For this twofold rebellion she must be punished.

Society's revenge is immediate. The murder makes her a social outcast and in order to conceal her identity and to earn her living, she is reduced to the life of a maid. Her *esquivez* no longer has the protection and encouragement provided formerly by her elevated station. She is now exposed to the coarse realities of life and is forced to use all her positive masculine qualities to protect herself. At this point Nature takes *its* revenge. María refused marriage on the grounds that she could not submit to any man, even one she loved. Now she is at the beck and call of a foul-mouthed master who eventually tries to violate her. Hitherto she spurned the most worthy men; now she is forced into contact with the rough, the crude, the importunate. The lesson is severe but it is well learnt,

> El desprecio que tenía
> de cuantas cosas miraba,
> las galas que desechaba,
> los papeles que rompía;
>   el no haber de quien pensase
> que mi mano mereciese,
> por servicios que me hiciese,
> por años que me obligase.
>   Toda aquella bizarría
> que como sueño pasó,
> a tanta humildad llegó
> que por mí decir podía:
>   'Aprended, flores, de mí
> lo que va de ayer a hoy;
> que ayer maravilla fui
> y hoy sombra mía aun no soy'.
>
> (Act ii, 660b)

And once penance has been done, absolution is granted. Now that Nature has punished María, it proceeds to reward her by re-establishing within her its normal claims. With arrogance gone there is room for love, and María falls in love with Don Juan, her heart touched by the first courtesy and gentleness she has known since she fled from her home. To ensure that her love is properly motivated and not merely the result of gratitude, she is given a rival to cope with, but finally she achieves royal pardon and marriage with Don Juan.

The thesis of the play is clear – the desire for independence and the impulse to unnecessary (unnecessary because her father has a son to avenge him) self-assertion is improper in a woman. María's punishment is the transformation to a lowly status which brings the truth home to her. Once again, the seventeenth-century conviction that there could be no rationale behind a woman's *esquivez*, merely a moral fault, is strongly stated. With marriage, Maria accepts her position as a woman, so allowing the order of Nature to be restored and ensuring her own happiness.

The same grave view of female arrogance taken by Lope in *La moza de cántaro* is also taken by the unknown author of *De los contrarios de amor*[1] and by Tirso in his *El burlador de Sevilla*.[2] Neither of the women in question here, however, is the protagonist of the play and their *esquivez* is not the central theme. The Queen of Scotland in *De los contrarios de amor* is a proud and arrogant woman who refuses to subject herself to any man. Her hatred of men is matched by that felt by the King of England for women, but while his feelings are the result of some personal incident in the past which has embittered him, the Queen's are based on arrogance alone. They plunge their countries into war merely in order to defeat and humble each other, but since the Queen's fault is greater she is the one who must give way. Their ultimate change of heart is unconvincing, but the point being made is unmistakeable. The sub-plot is, in fact, the case for marriage. Marriage – that is the fulfilment of the laws of Nature – brings back harmony and prosperity to the two countries. In other words, it restores order on a *national* scale and heals the breach created by the Queen's wrongful self-assertion.

---

[1] Ascribed to Lope. But Rennert, in his review of the Academy's *Nueva Edición* of Lope's works, *MLR* XIII (1918), 115, and Morley and Bruerton, 268–9, do not consider that the play is Lope's.

[2] Published in 1630 in *Doce comedias nuevas de Lope de Vega y otros autores*. A theatrical lease of 1625 from the notarial archives of Naples mentions a play '*Il convitato di pietra*', which may be Tirso's *Burlador*. See J. G. Fucilla, '*El convivado de piedra* in Naples in 1625' *Bulletin of the 'Comediantes'*, x, University of Wisconsin (Spring 1958), 5–6.

The marriages at the end of Tirso's *El burlador de Sevilla* are also a symbol of the restoration of harmony, in this case of the social harmony which has been disrupted by the anarchy of Don Juan. Tisbea, the second of the four women Don Juan deceives and the most interesting of them, is another *mujer esquiva*. This sets her apart from her three co-heroines and makes her the only woman in the play in whom there takes place any dramatic conflict. Casalduero's statement that 'Tisbea . . . es una figura de égloga piscatoria y se comporta según todos los precedentes literarios'[1] is an oversimplification of Tisbea's character. The arrogant pride which leads her to reject love and disdain her suitors adds a new dimension to the Don Juan theme of pride and self-assertion. Tisbea delights in making men suffer as Don Juan does women,

> en tirano imperio
> vivo, de amor señora,
> que hallo gusto en sus penas
> y en sus infiernos gloria.
> (Act I, N.B.A.E. IX, 628b)

The immunity she claims to the laws of Nature is a parallel to his self-assured immunity to divine retribution. She is above love, he above all social convention. Both are arrogant, both self-assertive, both egoists, and both suffer from a sense of their own superiority. Tisbea's contribution to the Don Juan theme, however, is implicit not explicit, and it is not fully integrated into the play. Her rebellion against Nature is not brought properly into relation with Don Juan's rebellion against Society and, furthermore, Tirso misses the opportunity to develop the Tisbea theme in the other women.

In spite of this, Tirso's disapproval of Tisbea is obvious. She is shown to be the victim not of Don Juan but of her own character. Convinced of her superiority to her fellow fisherfolk, she regards the arrival of Don Juan as a heaven-sent opportunity to rise above her own status. Don Juan's handsome figure and flattering words do not attract her. Before he opens his mouth her *esquivez* has already disappeared, simply because Cataliñón has told her who his master is. In spite of her refrain of misgiving, '¡ plega a Dios que

---

[1] 'Contribución al estudio del tema de Don Juan en el teatro español', p. 4, *Smith College Studies in Modern Languages* XIX, 1937-8.

no mintáis!', her dreams of grandeur make her prefer to believe Don Juan's promise of marriage.[1] Her sensitivity about her humble state has already manifested itself before she meets him

> ¡Dichosa yo mil veces
> amor, pues me perdonas,
> si ya, por ser humilde,
> no desprecias mi choza!
>
> (Act I, 628a)

Because of her ambition Tisbea refuses love only to succumb to lust. Her pride is humbled, her ambitions shattered. It is absurd to see Tisbea as the hapless victim of Don Juan's charm. Tisbea, no less than the other three women, is an illustration of Tirso's premise that Don Juan's sexuality relies for its success on circumstances exterior to itself.

The motive of pride is the one most often used by seventeenth-century dramatists in their depiction of the *mujer esquiva*, mainly because so often it is the most appropriate. The *esquivez* motif appears frequently in plays with either a superwoman or a ruler for heroine, and in these cases the attribution of *esquivez* to the arrogant self-assertion which refuses to subject itself to man is entirely logical. Lucinda in *La fe rompida* (Lope),[2] Doña María in *La varona castellana* (Lope),[3] Queen Rodiana in *El soldado amante* (Lope)[4] and Madama Inés in *Mujer, llora y vencerás* (Calderón)[5] are all such women, and naturally they all eventually fall in love. The treatment here is more or less conventional and consequently not heavy-handed. There is no question of punishment; Nature simply takes its course and the *esquivez* of the heroines evaporates in the face of the stronger compulsion of their new-found love.

Two more interesting examples of the *mujer esquiva*, both rulers whose disdain is likewise based on arrogant pride, are Cristerna

---

[1] Cf. Esmeralda Gijón's statement 'Es conmovedora de sinceridad la descripción del proceso del rendimento espiritual de Tisbea a Don Juan' ('Concepto del honor y de la mujer en Tirso de Molina', *Tirso de Molina, ensayos sobre la biografía y la obra* (Madrid, 1949), 601).

[2] Written between 1599–1603. See Morley and Bruerton, 18 and 36.

[3] Written between 1597–1603. See Morley and Bruerton, 155.

[4] Written between 1590–1600, probably 1593–5. See Morley and Bruerton, 152–3.

[5] Printed in 1662 in *Esc.* XVII and written probably in 1660.

in Calderón's *Afectos de odio y amor*[1] and Laura in Lope's *La vengadora de las mujeres*.[2] Their interest lies in the fact that they are not merely *esquivas*, but also militant feminists. Cristerna propagates feminism by actually legislating in women's favour, abolishing the Salic law, admitting women to public positions and forbidding them to marry beneath themselves on pain of death. In support of this last, Cristerna explains,

> el amor
> no es disculpa para nada.
> Porque ¿qué es amor? ¿Es más
> que una ciega ilusión vana,
> que vence, porque yo quiero
> que venza?
>
> (Act I, B.A.E. IX, 102c)

and it is immediately obvious that for this arrogant assertion that love is a mere figment of the conscious imagination, Cristerna will be taught a lesson. Laura who, like the female bandit, is a self-appointed avenger of women, translates her hatred of men into rather different action. Her proposed vengeance on men for their cruelty and injustice to women takes three courses: she studies hard to equip herself for intellectual battle with men; she gives her ladies-in-waiting lessons in 'misandry'; and she refuses to submit to any man by marrying, as society and her royal position demand. She is a much less sympathetic character than Cristerna, who, in spite of her feminist pride, is a brave, wise and generous queen. Laura is not only extremely arrogant but also presumptuous, rude and exceedingly vain. Moreover she is neglecting her duty by refusing even to consider marriage. Both women, of course, gradually and reluctantly have to submit to the normal workings of Nature, their pride holding them back, their jealousy urging them forward. Laura, because of her greater arrogance, receives a severe, though temporary, blow to her pride by falling in love with someone who is apparently her social inferior. The plays are both fairly

---

[1] Written for performance on Shrove Tuesday (5 March), 1657.
[2] Written 1613–20, probably 1615–20. See Morley and Bruerton, 246. Performed between 5 October 1622 and 8 February 1623. See Shergold and Varey, 'Some Palace Performances . . .', 239–40.

light-hearted, however, and the lesson the heroines are taught is a mild one. The fact that Laura is won in the tournament frees her even from the necessity of admitting that she wants Lisardo. Cristerna's capitulation is more extreme, for she actually bears witness to her new faith, asserting that women are born to be men's vassals.

> Estése
> el mundo como se estaba,
> y sepan que las mujeres,
> *vasallas del hombre nacen*;
> pues en sus afectos, siempre
> que el odio y amor compiten
> es el amor el que vence.
>
> (Act III, 122c [my italics])

Neither of the plays is in any sense a 'thesis' play. Calderón is writing in a tradition established years before by Lope. While even in *La vengadora de las mujeres* the action is contrived largely to make possible a theoretical discussion of a subject – women – which allows of ingenious philosophizing and witty analogies, a verbal battle where the weapons of both attack and defence are quotations from Aristotle and Plato. Nevertheless, both tell the familiar story of the *mujer esquiva*'s reconciliation to love, and both betray the conviction that this reconciliation is right. The capitulation of Calderón's heroine is more extreme than that of any of Lope's. And Lope, of course, would not be Lope if he failed to take this opportunity of expressing his views on women, love and marriage. Every character at some time extols the wonders of love and marriage and affirms the inevitable dependence of woman on man. In fact, in both the play and its dedication, Lope describes in detail those views that can be deduced from most of his plays, views like,

> Arnaldo . . . al imperio del hombre
> se ha de rendir la mujer
>
> (Act I, Acad. N. XIII, 615a)

and

> Julio   ¿Qué os parece?
> Lisardo   Que es belleza
> sin igual, pero ofendida

161

          de aquel rigor, que *corrida*
          tiene a la naturaleza.
          Ser mujer y no querer
          contradice, aunque porfía
          la human filosofía.
Julio   Bien sabe que la mujer
          ha de apetecer el hombre
          cual la materia a la forma,
          y aunque en esto se conforma,
          es con diferente nombre,
          y tanta bachillería
          que no se deja entender.

(Act I, 623 [my italics])

The peculiar value of the play lies in these statements of faith rather than in the action itself, which is rather contrived, or in the character of Laura, which is not nearly as subtly drawn as that of María in *La moza de cántaro*.

III

There remains to be discussed a group of plays which fall outside the main body of the *mujer esquiva* plays in that the motives of their heroines cannot be strictly described as either vanity or pride. In three cases out of the five, the heroine's views are much more truly rational and considered than those of the usual *mujer esquiva*, whose attempt to rationalize them does not succeed in hiding their true origin. The fourth makes no attempt whatsoever to justify her disdain, for it is purely the result of whimsy. And the fifth, one of the most interesting characters in the whole of the Golden-Age theatre, is nothing less than a case of psychological narcissism.

    The attitude shared by Serafina, Duchess of Mantua, in Mira de Amescua's *Galán, valiente y discreto*,[1] and Celia, in Lope's *De cosario a cosario*,[2] is entirely reasonable. Their wariness is based on the very natural fear of committing themselves to the wrong man.

[1] Performed on 6 June 1632. See Shergold and Varey, 'Some Palace Performances . . .', 226.

[2] Dated by Morley and Bruerton, 185–6, as 1617–19.

Celia has no desire to give herself and her fortune to any of the worthless gallants about the court, and similarly, Serafina wants to be loved for herself, and not for her wealth and position. Her desire to preserve her independence is born of the dread of surrendering it unwisely. The manner in which love eventually overcomes their fears is different in the two plays, both extremely skilfully handled love-intrigues. Serafina proves the love of Don Fadrique by pretending to be her own maid, while Celia is attracted to a man as reluctant to marry as she, and of such uncompromising cynicism that she resolves to humble him. Jealousy, of course, does its work in both plays and the two women are reconciled to marriage with the 'right' man. Lope as usual cannot resist including some of his marriage and love propaganda,[1] but Mira indulges in no theorizing on these topics. He is merely producing an entertaining, graceful play in a popular tradition. When Serafina yields there is no question of subjection, just a dignified acceptance of a worthy man. Approval of love and marriage, however, is implicit.

The third more rational *esquiva* is *la belígera española* in Ricardo de Turia's play of that name,[2] one of the most pleasing of the more unusual women in the Spanish theatre. Her peculiar interest lies in the fact that while nearly all the other disdainful women have to learn to accept that love and subjection to man are one and the same thing, Doña Mencía de Nidos has to be convinced that the opposite is true. The very epitome of *varonilidad*, she leads the Spanish settlers against the resurgent *araucanos* in Chile and eventually becomes Governor of the city of Concepción. Unlike the usual Spanish virago, however, she is neither haughty nor cruel; she does not mock her suitor Don Pedro nor despise him, but explains calmly and rationally that while she likes and respects him she cannot love him. In other words she behaves like a mature, responsible person. None the less hers is a psychologically intricate approach. She has no quarrel with love and marriage for women in general, merely for herself, because, she reasons, the courage

[1] See Celia's speech beginning 'Quedó toda mujer, por ley divina/sujeta al hombre' on p. 644, Acad.N. XI (Act I).
[2] Published in *Norte de la poesía española*, Valencia, 1616.

and endurance demanded of a soldier are incompatible with emotional commitments:

> Publica un enamorado,
> que en su dama, en quien se encierra
> su gusto, está transformado,
> pues un hombre afeminado
> ¿qué vale para la guerra?

> (Act II, *P.D.V.* II, 536b)[1]

Now the interesting point about this objection is that Doña Menciá is so masculine in her character and tastes that she judges love, not by its effect on woman, but by the effect it has on *man*. Woman, she is convinced, 'para sujeto ha nacido' so how can man be at once strong and subject to an already subject being? In her desire to avoid becoming weak and effeminate, her identification with the opposite sex is complete. Even more interesting is the fact that Doña Menciá is not ultimately 'reduced' to femininity. Don Pedro's courage proves to her that love is not detrimental and that subjection to it does not imply inferiority; whereupon she yields to her growing love and accepts his hand. But there is no question of her 'giving herself' to him; she accepts him as an equal and not as lord and master. Her essential character has not changed, but whereas before she considered herself a man, she can now accept that she is a remarkable woman and that those qualities she recognizes in herself are not alien to femininity. The lesson she learns is that to accept one's womanhood is not to accept inferiority.

Turia's approach to the *mujer esquiva* is obviously very different from Lope's. Both believe that woman, like man, is subject to all-powerful love, but Turia is prepared to allow woman her pride and to confine himself to showing her that self-assertion is not incompatible with love and marriage. For Lope, woman's revolt against her sex is heresy, for Turia it is merely unnecessary, and while Lope sees the capitulation of the *mujer esquiva* as a humble, grateful submission to man, Turia, like Mira de Amescua in *Galán, valiente y discreto*, can conceive of it as a dignified acceptance. He wrote within the pattern established by Lope but brought to it a

---

[1] The edition used is E. Juliá Martínez's in *Poetas dramáticos valencianos*, II, Biblioteca selecta de clásicos españoles, Ser. 2 (Madrid, 1929).

personal dimension of liberalism and of imaginative psychological insight.

The severity of Lope's disapproval of the *mujer esquiva* is shown again in his treatment of the fourth heroine in this group. Belisa in *Los melindres de Belisa*[1] is a superb protrayal of the *melindrosa*, the spoilt child, and a much more complex character than the run-of-the-mill disdainful adult woman. The indulgence that her parents have shown her since the day of her birth has made her selfish, hysterical, violent and irresponsible. Her reasons for refusing her various suitors are the purely arbitrary ones of a mentality which delights in contrariness: one has lost an eye, another is too heavy, one is bald, one has large feet and dirty nails, another is merely French, while a sixth she turns down because of the 'lagarto' on the chest of his *hábito de Santiago*. The touchstone in her conversion is naturally love, but the method by which Lope chooses to bring about the transformation from spoilt child to responsible woman is here particularly suitable and particularly impressive, revealing the psychological finesse of which Lope was frequently capable, above all in his female characters. Lope's remedy is to subject Belisa's system to a series of shocks which rudely jolt her out of her dream world where everybody seeks to humour her and where everything is designed to please her. First, her infantile temperament is made to cope with an adult emotion, sexual love, and then almost simultaneously, her child's mentality has to grapple with the social problems posed by falling in love with her slave. The competition provided by Celia and the suspicion that the slave is not all he appears, confuse Belisa even further, and for the first time in her life she has lost command of the situation. The final blow is her discovery that her mother, who has formely gratified her every whim, is also in love with the slave and intends to marry him. This discovery shocks Belisa into a concern for the family honour, a development which denotes, at least in seventeenth-century terms, the growth of a certain sense of responsibility.[2]

---

[1] Written between 1606 and 1608, probably nearer 1608. See Morley and Bruerton, 220–1.

[2] She herself has already decided that her love for the slave is impossible – her order to have him branded is a subconscious attempt to kill love by making the object of it unsightly.

Such is the process by which Belisa the child achieves woman-hood. The full punishment for her *esquivez*, however, is yet to come, for Nature has avenged itself not only by making her conceive a passion for her inferior – this problem is resolved by the revelation of Felisardo's true identity – but also by making that man inaccessible. Felisardo loves Celia and a chastened and wiser Belisa has to be content with Eliso. She has missed the opportunity of choosing a husband for herself and as a result she has to accept the man chosen for her. Her reply to her brother's order that she marry Eliso, 'Eso es justo', echoes the submission to their female destinies of all Lope's women. In view of Lope's constant championing of woman's *libertad de amar*, the significance of this arranged match cannot be mistaken.

The desire to be a man is a common one amongst the more aggressive types of the *mujer varonil*, a desire obviously born of impatience with the limitations imposed upon them by their own sex. It is shared by the heroine of Tirso's *El vergonzoso en palacio*,[1] Serafina. Serafina, however, is *estrado*-bred and her motives are not nearly as straightforward. In the first act, Serafina is rather an unknown quantity. Much is said about her beauty but she appears only rarely. We gather from her father, however, that she is reluctant to marry, a reluctance which he attributes to her carefree youth. A hint that the reason offered by her father might not be the correct one, is given at the end of Act I where although willing to recognize that Mireno is a handsome man, she can summon up no great interest either in him or in her sister's affairs,

> Serafina   Yo confieso
> que a rogar por él me inclina
> su buen talle
> Magdalena   ¿Eso desea
> tu afición? ¿Ya es bueno el talle?
> Pues no tienes de liballe
> aunque lo intentes.
> Serafina   No sea.   (*Vanse*)
> (Act I, B.A.E. v, 211a)

[1] Cotarelo y Mori ascribes the play to the year 1610 (prologue, N.B.A.E. IX) but Américo Castio (prologue, Clásicos castellanos, Madrid 1932, II) thinks a date at the beginning of the century is more plausible.

In Act II, it appears that she ardently wishes she had been born a man, and she therefore delights in the opportunity to dress as one with which the performance of a play presents her. When Doña Juana expresses shocked amazement, she replies,

> Fiestas de carnestolendas
> todas paran en disfraces,
> deséome entretener
> deste modo; no te asombre
> que apetezca el traje de hombre,
> ya que no lo puedo ser.
>
> (Act II, 215b)

Another hint about Serafina's nature is given by Doña Juana's warning to Serafina when she looks at herself in the mirror,

> Si te miras
> en él, ten, señora, aviso
> no te enamoras de ti.
>
> Serafina   ¿Tan hermosa estoy ansí?
> Da. Juana   Temo que has de ser Narciso.
>
> (Act II, 215c)

Doña Juana is not merely anticipating an event; she unwittingly puts her finger on its cause. Serafina's desire to be a man is, soon afterwards, amply borne out by the verve with which she enters her part. She identifies herself so completely with the jealous lover she is portraying that she attacks Doña Juana as if she were the rival lover, embraces her as if she were the wife, then attacks the poor woman again as if she were bride, groom, priest and congregation all rolled into one. This absorption in her part is important because it contrasts so strongly with that indifference in her we have already noted. The final two stages in the development of her character follow on from there: first, with extraordinary indifference she ignores Doña Juana's warning that she is secretly being painted; then, as a result of this particular example of apathy, she falls in love with her own portrait. Indifference, the desire to be a man, the ability to identify herself with the jealous lover and the attraction to her own image, these are the keystones in Serafina's personality. They are related qualities carefully built up by the dramatist to form a coherent whole, a consistent image. Serafina is a narcissist.

Her indifference is the first pointer to this conclusion. She is incapable of reacting positively to anything outside herself and is utterly self-involved. Her play-acting she enters into with passion because it allows her to indulge her self-preoccupation. Further-more the part she chooses to play is entirely appropriate for who more self-involved than the jealous husband / lover highly conscious of his honour and his dignity? Her masculine role is advisedly chosen since in the drama of the Golden Age self-preoccupation is normally the prerogative of the male, and her desire for masculinity is based on a subconscious recognition of this, presupposing as it does that man's greater self-preoccupation goes hand-in-hand with an awareness of his greater importance. It is Serafina's self-preoccupation which makes her reject marriage and which leads her to fall in love with her own image. Her interests are so entirely directed towards herself that there is no room in her psychological make-up for a concern for anybody else. The portrait is a projection of herself; at the same time it purports to be a man, therefore she falls in love with it. What is this but a hetero-sexual manifestation of a narcissus complex? Doña Juana, the play's champion of love, thinks that this is heaven's way of punish-ing Serafina,

> Castigo ha sido
> del cielo, que a su retrato
> ame, quien a nadie amó.

(Act III, 222c)

and there certainly *is* a nice irony in it. Lope would have regarded it in the same light as Doña Juana, but Tirso depicts it as the logical outcome of Serafina's almost pathological love of self and the note of condemnation with regard to the *esquivez* is negligible. No-where else in the play is her attitude to love criticized. In Act II she justifies her attitude quite rationally, with what is substantially the same argument as one of those put forward by Cervantes' Marcela,[1]

---

[1] 'Yo conozco. . . que todo lo hermoso es amable; mas no alcanzo que, por razón de ser amado, esté obligado lo que es amado por hermoso a amar a quien le ama. Y

> ¿Puede ser
> el no tener voluntad
> a ninguno, crueldad? Di.
>
> Juana   ¿Pues no?
>
> Serafina   ¿Y será justo cosa
> por ser para otros piadosa
> ser yo cruel para mí?

The painter who overhears her remark acknowledges the logic of her view,

> par diez, que ella dice bien
>
> (Act II, 216a)

and there is no indication that Tirso does not do the same. If he is condemning anything, it is not so much her *esquivez* as the self-preoccupation which gives rise to it, and Serafina is punished for this self-preoccupation with her seduction by Don Antonio and her marriage to him. This punishment aspect, however, is entirely unemphasized. Tirso's interest lies essentially in the psychological curiosity of Serafina's character and not in the morality or propriety of her behaviour.

Notwithstanding this variety of treatment given to the *mujer esquiva* theme, all the plays in which she appears primarily as *esquiva* (and not, for example as bandit or Amazon) have a very strong family resemblance and their plots all tend to follow the same stereotyped pattern. (Unfortunately, in pointing out the resemblance and in tracing the pattern one is in danger of reducing the plays to mere schematized units. But of course many of the characters are fascinating individuals in their own right – María in *La moza de cántaro*, for example, is one of Lope's best female portraits and the development of character throughout is quite masterly; in such a study as this those features which make of the plays distinctive creations have all too often to be sacrificed to the exigencies of the analytical approach.) The pattern that has been traced was initially created by Lope as a vehicle for his strongly-

---

más, que podría acontecer que el amador de lo hermoso fuese feo, y siendo lo feo digno de ser aborrecido, cae muy mal el decir: "Quiérote por hermosa; hasme de amar aunque sea feo'." *Don Quijote*, Part I, Chap. XIV.

held views on women, love and marriage; his followers imitated him and later dramatists then wrote within what was a well-established convention. The *mujer esquiva* is, as a result, one of the most familiar theatrical types in seventeenth-century Spain. Inevitably her appearance is not always accompanied by interesting variations of treatment and interpretation. *La fe rompida* (Lope), *La varona castellana* (Lope), *El soldado amante* (Lope) and *Mujer, llora y vencerás* (Calderón), *Las bizarrías de Belisa* (Lope),[1] *La romera de Santiago* (Tirso?)[2] and *El conde don Sancho Niño* (Luis Vélez)[3] are entirely conventional and unremarkable in this respect.

So predictable did the career of the disdainful woman become, in fact, that Rojas Zorrilla, who loved poking fun at theatrical conventions, wrote a satire of it – *Sin honra no hay amistad*.[4] His heroine, Juana, who harbours an entirely unmotivated hatred of men, is converted to love in the usual manner. The difference here is that she does not fall in love with any particular man, but with love itself, and she is therefore confronted with the dilemma of which man to choose. This is an obvious take-off of the heroine's inevitable subjection to a man through jealousy, and Juana's predicament is clearly intended to be an amusing one,

> ¿A cuál de los dos adoro,
> y a cuál de los dos olvido?
>
> > (Act III, B.A.E. LIV, 313a)

No sooner does she realize that she is loved, not scorned, than she promptly falls out of love again. The satire, however, is not directed wholly towards Juana. The whole ethos of the *comedia* and its traditional preoccupation with love and honour is being gently mocked. Juana's marvellously amusing account of the antics of the

[1] Written in 1634.
[2] This play is attributed by F. E. Spencer and R. Schevill to Luis Vélez de Guevara. It was presented at the palace in 1622–3. See *The Dramatic Works of Luis Vélez de Guevara, Their Plots, Sources and Bibliography* (California, 1937), 110.
[3] Originally attributed to Calderón. See Cotarelo y Mori, 'Luis Vélez de Guevara y sus obras dramáticos', *BRAE* IV (1917), 279; also Spencer and Schevill, *The Dramatic Works of Luis Vélez de Guevera*, 167–70.
[4] Published in the *Segunda parte del autor 1644*. See Cotarelo y Mori, *Don Francisco de Rojas Zorrilla . . .* , 222.

courting male; the two heroes' polite division of the duties of courtship; their inability to decide who is to kill Bernardo even when he
is attacking them; the ease with which Melchor forgets his father's
death and with which Antonio obligingly renounces Juana; the
continual falling in and out of love and hate; all show that the
playwright had his tongue well in cheek as he wrote. Furthermore,
there is no hint of a moral, no note of condemnation anywhere in
the play. Juana's behaviour is always shown as laughable, never as
irresponsible or wrong-minded. Bernardo is not criticized for
killing Melchor's father, and only Antonio finds Bernardo's forci-
ble abduction of Antonio's sister at all reprehensible. Melchor is
allowed conveniently to forget his vow to avenge his father's
death. This lack of moral concern, this absence of any true emotion,
this disregard of personal feelings, this humorous treatment of serious matters like murder and rape, are all typical of the satirical
method. Here the satire is light-hearted both in method and purpose. Rojaz Zorrilla is mocking not some aspect of real life but
certain theatrical attitudes. His play is a satire on other plays and
is therefore twice removed from the plane of reality. There is no
place here for the psychological truths contained by many of the
plays which belong to the convention he is satirizing. His sole
concern is with a type of dramatic plot and the omission of everything that would make this stereotyped plot meaningful is therefore logical.

The popularity of the figure of the *mujer esquiva* is not hard to explain. The challenge to men represented by the woman who is
seemingly immune to them is an accepted one, and the eventual
submission of the *mujer esquiva* must have been equally pleasing to
dramatist and male audience alike. Her appeal is inextricably
linked with the dramatists' views on women in general. Two facts
emerge from a reading of the *mujer esquiva* plays: that the playwrights are not prepared to emancipate woman from the demands
imposed upon her by Nature; and that they are not prepared to
allow her any worthwhile motives for wishing to assert her independence. Not all of them may share Lope's rigid views on this
matter or continually have the same axe to grind. Mira and Turia

may allow their heroines to accept marriage rather than submit to it; Turia may even allow woman her self-assertion. Tirso may conceive of a more complex and interesting motivation for female *esquivez*. But all of them subscribe to these basic tenets, even Doña Ana Caro, whose *El conde Partinuplés*, published in the *Quarta parte de diferentes autores*, 1635, is the only play I have found in which a *woman* depicts a *mujer esquiva*.[1] The continual insistence that love is part of the natural order of the Universe[2] is obviously an aspect of the seventeenth century's neo-platonic inheritance. The interesting question is why much *more* stress is laid upon this theory in imaginative literature in the seventeenth century than in the secular love literature of the sixteenth century. It is certainly not a familiar precept in the pre-Lope drama. The answer seems to be that the Platonic belief in love (in its widest sense) as an integral feature of universal harmony possessed in practical application a particular appeal for the seventeenth-century mind, which conceived of the world as the reflection of divine purpose and which therefore regarded order and balance as essential to well-being. In other words the Golden-Age theatre, which looked for nourishment in the vitals of its own society, shows Platonic theory at work within a Christian social context. It is in the seventeenth century that the hierarchal order of society, with its delegation of authority from God through the king down to the head of each family, is particularly emphasized and it is in the seventeenth-century drama that marriage is used at the end of a play as a

---

[1] Though apparently very popular in its day (see Mesonero Romanos' 'Apuntes biográficos', B.A.E. XLIX, pp. x–xi), the play is extremely bad and is interesting only in that it reveals to what extent even women of literary pretensions like Doña Ana were conditioned by the general attitude of the age to love and women. Her heroine, Rosaura, is *esquiva* not out of vanity or pride – that would be capitulation indeed – but because of a prophecy that she will be deceived and eventually murdered by a man, a mere variation on the usual inability to conceive of female *esquivez*'s having any spontaneous origins. Of course Rosaura falls in love immediately when she meets the right man and after the conventional difficulties accepts his hand with delight. The prophecy, having played its part as the creator of motive, is conveniently forgotten.

[2] These lines of Tirso's are typical: '¿Esperas que la mujer/haga el oficio del hombre?/¿En qué especie de animales/no es la hembra festejada,/perseguida y paseada/con amorosos señales?/Que lo demás, es querer/el orden sabio romper/que puso naturaleza.' (*El vergonzoso en palacio*, Act III, B.A.E. v, 219b–c).

symbol of the restoration of the good order of society. The seemingly haphazard batch of marriages with which nearly every plot
is brought to an end is not merely an empty convention employed
as an easy solution to the action; it reflects a philosophy of life,
the belief that continuing security depends on order. Woman has
her place in this order as wife and mother. A refusal to accept this
place is a threat to the whole pattern of life. In all fairness, however,
let it not be forgotten that for the seventeenth-century playwrights
man was as subject to love and marriage as woman. None of the
few *hombres esquivos* escapes them. The greater incidence of *esquivez*
amongst heroines is largely due to their greater entertainment-
value; in reality, of course, seventeenth-century women had a great
deal more to gain from marriage than they had to lose.

The dramatists' inability or unwillingness to conceive of any
plausible rationale behind the *mujer esquiva*'s self-assertion is inevitable, and must not be taken as a profound or perceptive piece
of motivational psychology. Rather it is contingent upon their
sex. Being men they are naturally reluctant to free woman of her
traditional dependence upon and dominance by the man. Equally
naturally they cannot imagine that woman is really capable of
disliking man, even less of being indifferent to him. That this
conviction is not peculiar to the seventeenth-century Spanish
theatre is clear from the fact that while *misogyny* exists to convey
the hatred of women, *misogamy* to convey the hatred of marriage
and *misanthropy* to convey the hatred of mankind, no word exists
at all to convey the hatred of men; some such word as *misandry*
would have to be invented for this purpose; a small point, but
significant.

The *mujer esquiva* represents an invaluable contribution to
seventeenth-century feminism because the treatment accorded her
reveals exactly how far the dramatists were ready to go in their
defence of woman and their tolerance of feminist aims. At the same
time the picture she presents is necessarily incomplete, and it must
not be forgotten that in certain very vital instances, illustrated by
other variants of the same theme, these playwrights championed
women to a degree remarkable for men of their time.

6

The amazon, the leader, the warrior

I

In a theatre which cultivated the type of the *mujer varonil* it was inevitable that the legendary archetype of *varonilidad*, the Amazon, should herself become a source of dramatic inspiration. She represented after all, the synthesis of many of the popular variants of a popular theme. Like the *bella cazadora* she had been brought up to the robust freedom and self-sufficiency of life in the wilds. Like the *esquiva* she rejected love and marriage. Again like the *esquiva*, but also like many of the *bandoleras*, she hated men and waged war against them. Like the warrior she knew how to fight. And lastly, like the leader she was a mistress of military tactics and of civil administration. Indeed, if it seems predictable that a theatre interested in these various aspects of female self-assertion should have recourse to Amazonian plots, it seems equally logical in view of these similarities that, by the reverse process of inspirational procedure, the Amazon tradition was an influential factor in the very establishment and growth of the *mujer varonil* fashion. The potential influence of this tradition should not be underestimated simply because there are only a few plays with Amazon plots. While it would have been astonishing had *no* dramatist exploited the story of the female warriors of Scythia, the image of them drawn by tradition was too precise and indelible to permit a wide variety of interpretation.

The first of the Amazon plays, *Las Justas de Tebas y reina de las amazonas*, was written before 1596 by Lope.[1] Its plot tells how Abderite, the Amazon Queen, falls in love with the Prince of Troy. Some years later, Lope returned to the subject with *Las grandezas de*

[1] Morley and Bruerton, 146–7. In the first edition of the *Peregrino en su patria* (1604) the play was called *La Abderite*, after its heroine.

Alejandro,[1] in which three Amazons figure very briefly. Queen Rojane, in love with Alejandro's fame, has decided that he shall father her children. She fails to realize this ambition but joins forces with Alejandro in his battle against the Persians. Between 1613 and 1618 Lope wrote yet a third Amazon play, his most important – *Las mujeres sin hombres*.[2] Here the Queen, Antiopía, her rival for the throne Deyanira, and a third, Menalipe, all fall in love with Theseus, who has come with Hercules, Jason and the Greek army to pit his strength against the Amazons in battle.

The recurring fascination the Amazons held for Lope does not seem to have created responsive echoes in other playwrights and few followed his example – on the evidence of extant material, at least. Amazons do appear in a play of Tirso's, but the title, *Las Amazonas en las Indias*,[3] is a misleading one. The play is in fact part of a trilogy which deals with the Pizarros and is the story of the events leading up to the death of Gonzalo Pizarro in Peru.[4] The Amazonian Queen, Menalipe, and her sister Martesia are in love with Pizarro and his lieutenant Carvajal repectively, and warn them

[1] Between 1604 and 1612 and probably between 1604 and 1608. See Morley and Bruerton, 202.

[2] Menéndez Pelayo puts the play before 1604 since he assumes that it is the same play as *Las Amazonas*, mentioned in the first (1604) edition of the *Peregrino*. Cotarelo y Mori (Acad. N. I, vii–viii), however, thinks it is a *refundición* of the earlier play, and Morley and Bruerton (223) state that *Las mujeres sin hombres* cannot be before 1604, which would seem to support this. They suggest as date 1613–18.

[3] Ruth L. Kennedy gives it an *ab quo* of 1631. See 'On the Date of Five Plays by Tirso', *HR* x (1942), 209, n. 77.

[4] Otis H. Green in his article 'Notes on the Pizarro Trilogy of Tirso de Molina' (*HR* IV [1936], 201–25) points out that a legend of the existence of Amazons in the New World is one of long standing. 'It was originated by Francisco de Orellana, who broke away from Gonzalo Pizarro on the expedition into the land of the cinnamon trees (*jornada de la canela*), sailed down the Amazon instead of returning to his captain, reached the island of Trinidad and went from there to Spain, claiming for himself the territory he had discovered. To make his *relación* the more astounding, he stated that in those forests he found a race of women of great valour whose customs were essentially the same as those of the Amazons of classical literature. This tradition is reported briefly by the historian Zárate (B.A.E. XXVI, 494) and is scoffed at by Gómara (B.A.E. XXII, 210). Father Acuna says simply that 'time will discover the truth', and Garcilaso the Inca, 'I can neither believe nor affirm owing to the difficulty of discovering the truth' (208–9).

of the betrayal to come. The Amazons are not really necessary to the plot and are included to provide extra drama, a love interest and a vein of humour.[1] A much fuller treatment of the Amazons is to be found in Antonio de Solís's *Las Amazonas de Escitia*.[2] Here the authority of the Amazon Queen, again Menalipe, is challenged by her cousin Miquilene, who accuses Menalipe of effeminacy in yielding to love. Soon afterwards, however, Miquilene herself falls in love and the two finally marry their princes.

These brief plot summaries are given not so much to show what ingenuity can do with even the most stereotyped and rigidly delineated characters, but to show that the plays have one salient feature in common. The Amazon *persona* may differ peripherally from play to play – Tirso's is ferocious and actually eats male captives, while Lope's in *Las justas de Tebas* entertains no active hatred of men – but all the Amazons sooner or later revert to the feminine norm and fall in love.[3] The emphasis placed on the workings of Nature's irremediable self-fulfilment varies from play to play. Rojane (*Las grandezas de Alejandro*) falls in love with the Macedonian general before she meets him. She needs a partner in procreation and he alone meets the requirements of her pride. There is no emotional struggle here. The same is true of Tirso's *Las Amazonas en las Indias*; Tirso shows no concern with the idea of an exclusively female society. Solís's play and Lope's other two are a different matter. Even so, the latest, Solís's *Las Amazonas de Escitia*, is far less interesting than Lope's dramatizations of the theme because it is merely a reiteration of the accepted response that the Amazon phenomenon provoked. Queen Menalipe is already in love when the play opens, and Miquilene falls in love with Astolfo at first sight and without resistance. From this point

---

[1] Martesia has supernatural powers and the *gracioso*'s contact with these provides the play's comedy.

[2] Published in *Comedias de don Antonio de Solís y Rivadeneyra* (Madrid, 1681).

[3] Tradition itself, of course, attributes to one or two of the Amazon queens a relationship with some hero. Antiope (sometimes Menalipe) fell in love with Theseus (Apollodorus, *Epitome* i, 16), while Hippolyte is either said to have offered Heracles Ares's girdle as a love gift (Apollodorus, ii. 5. 9; Plutarch, *Greek Questions* 45) or to have been given to Theseus by Hercules after he had won the girdle by force (Diodorus Siculus *Bibliotheca historica* v. iv. 16).

on, the love intrigue follows the pattern of complications typical of the *comedia de capa y espada*. When the two pairs marry, Astolfo, conveniently the son of the last Queen, becomes King of Escitia, thereby ending Amazon rule, and Menalipe is demoted to the position of a prince's consort. The play, in other words, is a straight-forward glorification of love and marriage and ends with a vote of confidence in normal sexual relations: 'Vivan los hombres, las mujeres vivan'.

Las justas de Tebas is a more sensitive and thoughtful portrayal of the gradual but inevitable subjection to love of a woman who has been brought up from birth to consider herself fully independent and self-sufficient. The *mujer esquiva* in a heterosexual society defies the social conventions when she refuses to fall in love and marry, and conforms to them when she eventually yields to man. In the case of the Amazon the reverse is true and in her, Society and Nature, instead of working in unison, are in conflict with each other. However, as we have seen before, where social mores and natural instincts conflict in matters of love Lope upholds instinct, and the peculiar situation of the Amazon is no exception. Social standards change, but the laws of Nature are immutable. *Las mujeres sin hombres* is likewise the story of Love's victory over the Amazon tradition. It is also much more. The play, in which Lope returned to a serious consideration of the theme after the intervening and more conventional *Las grandezas de Alejandro*, is his analysis of the whole concept of the Amazons, of women who live by and for themselves, and of the questions to which the idea of an exclusively matriarchal society gives rise. Are women equipped for independence and self-sufficiency? Given that they are, is it right that they should exercise their independence and self-sufficiency? And finally, does the existence of such qualities in women affect their traditional relationship with man? Any incredulity as to the solemnity of Lope's concern with such problems will be allayed by a reminder that for the men of his age the existence of the Amazons was a historical fact. Lope was not playing with vague theories; he was trying satisfactorily to adapt a historical phenomenon to the realities of human life as he knew them to be. The first and the third plays not only illustrate the different ways in which Lope maximized the dramatic effect of an inherently dramatic situation, but they also show how he progressed towards an acute apprehension of the issues involved.

Compared with *Las mujeres sin hombres*, *Las justas de Tebas* is a crossbreed in that it owes much to the chivalresque and Byzantine-influenced plots that Lope favoured in the early years of his career. The barest detail establishes the resemblance. Abderite, the heroine, remains incognito throughout the play – the only Amazon in the Spanish theatre to do so. Dressed as a knight, she appears in Thebes in search of her brother, the Prince of Greece, whom she has naturally not seen since an early age. She is far from her kingdom and from her Queen's authority – in fact for the strict purposes of the plot she need not be an Amazon at all. Her story could be that of any of the *mujeres varoniles* who strode the Spanish stage around the end of the sixteenth century, and the plot's ingredients – the knightly disguise, the search for a man (in this case a brother not lover), the duels, the victory at the jousting and the winning of the princess's hand – are all familiar. Nevertheless it is clear that even at this early date Lope was attracted to the idea of the Amazon and aware of her peculiar dramatic possibilities. Abderite is by far the most carefully portrayed character in the play and her conversion to a new set of human values is convincingly done.

Lope lays the foundations of this conversion at the very outset by portraying Abderite's tender feelings for her brother. As a result of this sisterly affection Abderite harbours no hostility towards the opposite sex, and in a sense Lope is in this early play skirting the initial psychological and emotional conflict inherent in the Amazon's situation. Abderite responds gracefully and immediately to Ardenio's gallant appearance and generosity, and accepts willingly the realization that she has fallen in love with him. Her maid, Pirene, embodying the Amazonian conscience that Abderite lacks, sternly upbraids her mistress,

> ¡Ay, cómo veo en verte
> que eres mujer, al fin, cuando más fuerte!
> (Act II, Acad.N. I, 260a)

reminding her that to marry Ardenio would be to flout the very laws it is her duty as Queen to uphold. But Abderite is converted, and Christian morality and European romance shine through her answer,

> ¿No ves que se engañaron [los pasados]
> que por guardar su ley varón buscaron,
> sin fe de matrimonio, deshonrados?
> Más justo es mi deseo
> si le gano con Venus y Himineo.
>
> (Act II, 260b)

She is willing even to renounce her kingdom to follow Ardenio and expresses the hope that her brother will *allow* her to marry him: the triumph of love in effect is accompanied by an acceptance of the social machinery of contemporary Spain.

The element of conflict which Lope omitted from Abderite the victim of love, however, he now introduces into the new Abderite in the form of a struggle between new-found femininity and ingrained pride and aggressiveness. What conflict there is in Abderite's character, in other words, is temperamental and not ideological. She humbly asks Ardenio whether she does not deserve his love, then suddenly becomes painfully aware of her loss of royal dignity,

> ¿Estoy fuera de mí, que a un hombre ruego?
>
> (Act III, 273a)

This struggle, which is eventually resolved by marriage, is intended to convey the tremendous power wielded by love. Inexorably it takes control of the human heart, mind and body, and all things in its path – the influences of tradition and environment, inborn traits of personality, laws even – are trampled to the ground beneath its weight. And no one – not even the leader of a society created to function almost exclusively without male participation – is spared.

In *Las justas de Tebas* the Amazon theme is only one of several motifs. Eventually, however, Lope turned his full attention to the idea and in *Las mujeres sin hombres* devotes himself entirely to a consideration of the Amazon world. He carefully traces from its beginnings the Amazons' progression from independence and self-sufficiency to dependence and emotional commitment. Even so, the dramatic plausibility he evidently considered it necessary to lend to this progression is a plausibility that grows out of his own vision of the Amazon predicament – the female warriors' attitude towards men is from the first ambivalent. Although it is made clear, however, that while tradition and upbringing encourage them to hate the opposite sex, Nature gives the women sympathetic leanings towards it, Lope does not here rely on Nature alone to achieve the transition to desirable normality. The rather vague, elusive concept of a 'Nature' that works for its own fulfiment is bolstered up by something much more concrete and easily accept-able – curiosity, a touch both psychologically effective and amusing. Never having seen men, the Amazons are excited by the very idea of them.

When we meet the Amazons we come immediately face to face with the full force of Amazon tradition. Antiopía, the new Queen, is giving laws to her people which, among other things, forbid even the mention of the name of man. This very extremism, however, is at once shown as breeding the spirit of inquiry and dissension. Deyanira admits to finding the laws excessively severe, and no sooner has Antiopía given orders for the ensuing battle with the Greeks than even *her* feelings start to betray her. As she speaks we realize that her severity as a lawgiver was merely a response to the treacherous murmurings of her femininity evoked by the approach of the Greek enemy,

> Sean mil veces bien venidos;
> que ya confieso que son
> amados del corazón
> y en la lengua aborrecidos.
>   Entre esta gente nací
> que aquella opinión sustenta,
> y que puede ser que sienta
> lo mismo que siento en mí.
>   ¿Quién os puede aborrecer,
> perfección, gracia y belleza,
> que a nuestra naturaleza
> dio principio vuestro ser?

Alguna que no os merece,
perdió vuestra compañía;
si el Filósofo decía
que la mujer apetece
al hombre como a la forma
la materia . . . mas ¿qué digo?

(Act I, Acad. VI, 43b)

This speech reveals very succinctly most of Lope's thoughts on the Amazon phenomenon. His interpretation of their historical existence might be summarized as follows: since men and women belong irrevocably together, some personal incident, creator of sexual hatred and spite, must have initiated the unnatural segregation; the incident eventually forgotten, the hatred was artificially propagated and perpetuated from generation to generation, breeding Amazons who claimed ideas and feelings which were really at odds with their true inclinations. In his plays about them Lope is showing how he thought they could be, and probably in many cases were, cured of the hallucinations which stood between them and true happiness.

Lope's ponderings on the problem of the Amazons do not of course affect his lightness of touch in their dramatic recreation. The initial meetings with the men are done with great comic deftness. So compelling are the forces of Nature working in Queen Antiopía that she is inordinately impressed by the first man she has ever seen – the highly surprised and flattered *gracioso* Fineo. And since the lord must naturally be more attractive than his servant her curiosity about his leaders is boundless. The reaction of Hipólita, her maid, is even funnier. She is so delighted with Fineo that she cannot stop chattering. Information and observation come pouring out in a stream of pent-up feeling as she makes up for her former lack of masculine company, and she takes the opportunity to ask the astounded Fineo to be her partner when the mating time for this Amazon generation comes around.

The scene with Fineo is not only intrinsically comical. It has a second dramatic function in that it heightens anticipation, both in the Amazons themselves and in the audience. With Teseo's arrival on scene the audience is aware that the battle between

Nature and tradition is virtually over. All three Amazons, Antiopía, Deyanira and Menalipe, are irresistibly drawn to the handsome, silken-tongued hero. It is this common fascination, with its possibilities for jealousy, which causes the storm to break. Antiopía, as Queen, will brook no competition and orders Deyanira's arrest. The rift in the united front of militant feminism has appeared, and Deyanira, accepting what she now regards as her female destiny, flees to the Greeks. The play's *dénouement* is the only possible happy outcome of the conflict which now ensues. Teseo and Antiopía both have their duty to their own people. Antiopía asks Teseo to help her fight the Greeks; he asks her to surrender the city to them. Both ask in the name of love and each refuses to yield. Hércules appropriately provides the solution, marriage, and the three heroes, Teseo, Hércules and Jasón, pair off with the three Amazons. Peace and personal happiness are by this one stroke achieved.

Las mujeres sin hombres, it is clear, is another of Lope's thesis-plays on women, those plays in which the whole of the action is an explicit statement of Lope's views on this subject. Nowhere in the play does Lope question the Amazons' courage or their ability to fight and rule, though he strongly implies that women might be more suitably occupied with other matters,

Deyanira	Las batallas que han de hacer
	las mujeres, no son éstas.
Menalipe	Tu discreción manifiestas:
	trate de amor la mujer;

(Act II, 50b)

But on one point he is adamant. However *varoniles* the Amazons are, they cannot hope to evade their destiny as creatures of love dependent on men. The Amazon may try to cut herself off from life's realities, but Nature overcomes this by instilling in her an intuitive awareness of love and man,

Hipólita	Un hombre desconfiado
	y que no puede imitalle,
	lo que le falta de talle,
	pone de amor y cuidado.

Fineo	¿De qué lo sabéis, si aquí
	nunca con hombres hablaste?
Hipólita	De ser mujer.

(Act III, 61b)

And in the face of this natural destiny the fact that women may be physically and intellectually capable of leading a separate existence loses all importance. Of course, it must be remembered here again that Lope's conception of love as one of life's major forces was an all-embracing one. He cannot resist repeating the traditional platitudes:

> . . . no puede en mujer
> haber perfección ni ser.
> si no le viene del hombre.

(Act III, 66a)

and again:

> . . . faltando los hombres
> no hay ser perfecto,

(Act II, 52b)

but he is as usual careful to point out that men are as subject to love as women. The play's final words are a sincere declaration of belief on Lope's part:

> Dale la mano, y con ella
> fin *Las mujeres sin hombres*
> aunque no los hay sin ellas.

(Act III, 69b)

– as sincere as his conviction that women cannot live without men. We do not even have to rely on our interpretation of the play to know that for Lope this was a tenet of faith. *Las mujeres sin hombres* is one of the few plays on which we have Lope's own comments. Like that to *La vengadora de las mujeres*, the dedication of *Las mujeres sin hombres* reveals the sincerity with which Lope held those beliefs that emerge from the development of the plot:

No es disfavor del valor de las mujeres la *Historia de las Amazonas*, que, a serlo, no me atreviera a dirigirla a Vm; antes bien las honra y favorece, pues se conoce por ella que pudieran vivir solas en concertada república, ejercitar las armas, adquirir reinos, fundar ciudades y dar principio a una de las maravillas del mundo, que fue el templo de Diana en Efeso.

Hubo antiguamente muchas, y en diferentes partes; de las africanas hace memoria Beroso; de las scíticas Diodoro, que éstas fueron las que mataron a sus maridos, y que jamás fueran vencidas de Hércules si Antiopía, en Temiscira, no se enamorara de Teseo; claro estaba que el valor de mujeres determinadas sólo con la blandura del amor podía ser vencido . . .; y aun he oído decir que andan algunas entre nosotros, como son viudas mal acondicionadas, suegras terribles y doncellas incasables, que todas éstas infaliblemente son amazonas o vienen de ellas; Vm juzgará a su gusto de esta opinión, pues en todas las cosas la tiene tan excelente, advirtiendo que no le ofrezco su historia para que con su ejemplo desee serlo, antes bien para que conozca que la fuerza con que fueron vencidas tiene por disculpa la misma naturaleza.

The reason for the dedication, made to Marcia Leonarda, or Marta de Nevares, who was about to or had just become his mistress, is only too apparent. The Amazons' fate was meant either to encourage or excuse this illicit relationship between a priest and a married woman by showing that resistance to love was useless. The letter, with its careful combination of flattery and information, jocularity and didacticism, is a little masterpiece of innuendo. Whatever the propriety of its intentions, however, it is also a statement of faith. Lope believed in, had to believe in, the power of love, because he had felt its power and been unable to resist. He interpreted life accordingly and by availing himself of the superior resources and perfection of art succeeded in imposing conformity even upon that most recalcitrant piece of Nature's jigsaw puzzle, the apparently historical existence of the Amazons. *Las mujeres sin hombres* shows Lope face to face with feminism taken to its ultimate. It shows too his resolute rejection, in the name of forces superior to himself and his opinions, of the very concept of life embodied in its title.

II

If dramatic treatment of the Amazons was necessarily inhibited by the details of their pseudo-historical *persona*, the related but far less rigidly delineated figure of the woman leader in general proved a happy and fertile source of theatrical exploitation. She is indeed a recurring feature of the seventeenth-century dramatic scene, as popular as the *bandolera*, though not of course as hugely successful as that prodigious progeny of the *mujer varonil* spawned by the *mujer esquiva*. The term leader is used here in its widest sense and covers a fairly wide range of female position and personality, from Tucapela, an American *cacica*, to Charles the Fair of France; from Jezabel to Doña María de Molina. And inevitably the leader encroaches upon other categories of the *mujer varonil*, for she is sometimes *esquiva* and she is often by the nature of her position to be found in the forefront of battle. She might even be called a career woman. The Amazon Queens already discussed are of course also leaders, but the peculiar nature of their kingdom demanded that they be dealt with apart. The leaders that follow are in one way more remarkable, for they stand in authority over members of both sexes.

Like Juan de la Cueva and Cristóbal de Virués before them, the dramatists of the seventeenth century never really question woman's *ability* to lead. History, after all, has proved that certain women do possess the qualities necessary for leadership and the legends that still passed for history in the seventeenth century were even richer in examples. The propriety, the advisability and even the efficacy of female leadership are very different matters, and it is here that we must look for any meaningful view of female leadership on the part of the playwrights. Not all the plays approach these questions at all; even fewer in any serious, considered way. Many of the women leaders are stereotypes, certainly in so far as their leadership is concerned. Casilda in *Bernardo del Carpio*,[1] who leads her people against her heretical enemy, is such a ready-made character, and so too is Isabella in Lope's *El triunfo de la humildad y soberbia vencida*,[2] who declares war on the prince who has taken her father prisoner. Both are essentially normal feminine women who, because of the death and imprisonment of their respective fathers, are compelled to resort to action which is by custom the prerogative of the male. They eventually marry and become *consort* Queens. The attractions of such a pattern are clear. It exploits the idea of the spirited female without seriously

---

[1] Attributed to Lope but the present text is generally accepted as not his. See Cotarelo y Mori, Acad.N. III, xxviii, and Morley and Bruerton, 260.

[2] Written between 1612 and 1614 according to Morley and Bruerton, 207-8.

challenging that of the superiority of the male. Equally unexceptional are five of Calderón's leaders: Arminda and Mitilene in *Hado y divisa de Leonido y Marfisa*,[1] Clodomira in *La exaltación de la cruz*,[2] Cintia in *En la vida todo es verdad y todo mentira*[3] and Astrea in *Las armas de la hermosura*.[4] The first four in particular, whatever their contribution to other aspects of the plays, are, *qua* leaders, without interest here. The warrior queens of *Hado y divisa* are obviously inspired by Ariosto's Marfisa – the plot is in the chivalresque tradition and its heroine acually called Marfisa – and Clodomira's one sign of feminist sympathies:

> Hoy verá el mundo si saben
> las mujeres manejar
> acero y gobierno iguales.
>
> (Act III, B.A.E. IX, 372a)

is a commonplace amongst these militant females. Cintia, Queen of Tinacria, fights for her overlord against the invaders and is unwittingly brought in the process into conventional physical confrontation with the man she loves. Astrea, Queen of the Sabines, on the other hand, while not intrinsically more interesting, is extrinsically significant in that she completes the play's dual presentation of feminism: Veturia is the intellectual feminist, Astrea the militant. She is, in other words, feminism in action, the active projection of that weight of female temperament which thickens the very air of the play. Calderón indicates no disapproval of this militancy. At the same time it is well to remember that Astrea is happily married to a husband whose authority she never challenges. She combines leadership with a tacit acceptance of the bounds of Nature.

The woman who rises to leadership on occasion, and the straight-

[1] The last *comedia* written by Calderón. It was produced at the Retiro on 3 March 1680.

[2] The mention in Act I of Queen Mariana's entry into Madrid dates the play 1648. See Cotarelo y Mori, *Ensayo sobre la vida y obra de D. Pedro Calderón de la Barca* (Madrid, 1924), 280–1.

[3] Written by 15 February 1659. See D. W. Cruickshank's edition of the play in Colección Támesis (London, 1971), xxxiiiff.

[4] Hartzenbusch suggested the date 1652 but A. E. Sloman thinks his argument by no means conclusive. See *The Dramatic Craftsmanship of Calderón* (Oxford, 1958), 61.

forward warrior queens are common enough figures in the Spanish theatre. In their constant search for material, however, the playwrights were by no means reluctant to wander more exotic paths for variations on their theme. Alas, distinctiveness does not necessarily entail distinction, and the presentation of even these female leaders is ultimately usually banal and automatic. That of Tucapela, the Indian *cacica* in Luis Vélez's *Las palabras a los reyes y gloria de los Pizarros*,[1] who falls in love with Francisco and when spurned tries to shoot him, certainly is. So too is that of Charles the Fair of France in *El rey naciendo mujer*,[2] also by Luis Vélez. The King here is really a woman brought up as a man in order to secure the throne for a particular branch of the royal family. The idea for this was possibly taken from a similar plot of Mira de Amescua's, *Amor, ingenio y mujer*,[3] where a princess poses as a prince because her father lacks a male heir. Mira's play is equally lacking in any special significance. Matilde in *Los yerros de naturaleza y aciertos de la fortuna*,[4] by Calderón and Antonio Coello, is more interesting, if only in so far as she has much in common with Semíramis in *La hija del aire*. Like Semíramis Matilde has a 'masculine' temperament and her compulsion to rule is so strong that she arranges her brother's murder in order that she may rule in his stead. The fascination with individual and sexual identity latent in the former plays significantly becomes more marked in the work of the greater dramatist. And this fascination elbows out any concern with the very concept of female leadership; although Matilde's reign is tyrannical it elicits from the other characters no generalizations on either women or female rule.

[1] Dates of composition and publication are unknown. See F. E. Spencer and R. Schevill, *The Dramatic Works of Luis Vélez de Guevara*, 210–16. There is a *suelta* of the play in the British Museum, cat. no. 11735.b.18.

[2] The date is unknown. There are two *sueltas* in the Biblioteca Nacional, one published in Seville s.a. (T. 12784) and the other s.l. ni a. (T.19073).

[3] Published in *Parte XXXII de comedias de diferentes autores*, Zaragoza 1640, and probably in some earlier edition. See Cotarelo y Mori, 'Mira de Amescua y su teatro', *BRAE* XVII (1930), 615–18.

[4] The second act and part of the third are by Calderón. The play's production licence is dated 1634. It bears resemblances not only to *La hija del aire* but also to *La vida es sueño*. See Juliá Martínez's 'Observaciones preliminares' to his edition (Serie escogida de autores españoles, 7, Madrid, 1930).

Indeed as one reads more and more of these plays it becomes apparent that the problem of female government was not one with which most seventeenth-century dramatists were particularly concerned. Their preoccupations, where preoccupations there are, are more generous both in scope and in depth. Where the qualities of leadership are under review they are rather those of leadership in general, for with this thorny problem, with theories of kingship and tyranny, the thinkers of the time were profoundly concerned, as the works of Mariana, Saavedra Fajardo and Quevedo amongst others testify. Only an acceptance of this wider view can reconcile the sort of superficially contradictory evidence offered by two of Tirso's lesser known plays. The first of these, *La mujer que manda en casa*[1] portrays the Jezabel of the third book of Kings. Jezabel marries King Acab of Israel and they embark together on a joint reign of tyranny and oppression. The play contains three explicit warnings about the dangers of female rule. When Jezabel threatens vengeance on Elias, Jehu says;

> Esto y mucho más peligra
> reino en que manda mujer.
>
> (Act I, N.B.A.E. IV, 468b)

Abdías consoles Raquel on the death of her husband thus:

> Será, muerto, ejemplo vivo
> del mal que a los reinos viene
> por una mujer regidos.
>
> (Act III, 482b)

And finally, Jehu, summing up at the end of the play, advises:

> y escarmiente desde hoy más
> quien reinare; que no permita
> que su mujer le gobierne;
> pues destruye honras y vidas
> la mujer que manda en casa
> como este ejemplo lo afirma.
>
> (Act III, 488b)

But these disparaging remarks arise organically from the nature of the plot, conditioned as it is by the evil character traditionally

---

[1] Published in *Parte cuarta de las comedias del maestro Tirso de Molina, 1635.*

ascribed to Jezabel. In violent contrast to Jezabel is the Empress Irene in *La república al revés*,[1] who is presented as the very model of the wise and just monarch. Her role in the play as a lesser María de Molina is small but important, for against her nobility and spiritual vigour the ignominy of her son Constantine is sharply silhouetted. Rather than the dangers of female rule she represents the standard of excellence by which Constantine is measured and found wanting. It is therefore impossible to draw any broad conclusions on Tirso's attitude to female leadership from these plays.

In spite of a general tendency on the part of seventeenth-century playwrights to regard their female leaders as individual case histories in an examination of the general concept of kingship, there are a few plays which do approach their female leaders from an angle which is more decidedly sexual. This still need not imply, of course, a serious investigation of the advantages and disadvantages of petticoat rule. Cristerna's salient feature in *Afectos de odio y amor* is her *esquivez* and her situation that of the woman who succeeds to the throne before a suitable marriage has been arranged to secure the future of the kingdom. There is a definite hint here at ultimate inadequacy to rule, but the play is primarily concerned with the arrogant feminism which impels Cristerna to defy Nature and to abuse her authority by legislating against men. As we have already seen, her renunciation of feminism is at the end complete: 'Sepan que las mujeres/vasallos del hombre nacen'. That other *esquiva* leader, Doña Mencía in Turia's *La belígera española*, on the other hand, appears to have been envisaged almost purely as an extraordinary personality without any trace of thematic sententiousness. Her conventional mind identifies love with effeminacy and women with inferiority; it follows that she identifies leadership with masculinity. The plot traces the process of her coming to terms with the apparent contradictions she represents, as she learns to reconcile her temperament with her sex and to accept that femininity is compatible with authority. The play is an exercise in self-discovery with not the slightest suggestion that the fulfilled Mencía is lacking either as a woman or as a governor and leader.

[1] Published in the *Quinta parte de las comedias del maestro Tirso de Molina*, 1636.

Of course, if any dramatist were to be concerned with the question of female rule and to write a play explicitly dedicated to an exploration of the problems it creates, experience would unhesitatingly point to Lope. *La discordia en los casados*[1] is Lope's thesis play on the subject. Its approach is thoughtful and serious, its conclusions unequivocal. Elena has succeeded to the throne of her country; the land is threatened by war and Elena recognizes that her subjects want a king. Since she subscribes to the idea that the husband is the 'head' of the body of marriage[2] and must for this reason be able to command her respect, she accepts the hand of the King of Frisia. Already it has been made clear that Elena on her own is inadequate to rule, but the difficulties only really start three years later when, on the basis of a lying testimony, the King accuses her of infidelity. Elena's reaction is significant, when she overcomes her incredulity enough to condemn his behaviour:

> No es príncipe el que deshonra
> una mujer inocente
> tan desamparada y sola.
>
> (Act II, Acad.N. II, 139b)

Her words reveal her sense of insecurity – her marriage has reduced her emotionally to the state of the dependent woman. None the less, her subjects rally to her aid. The King may be a necessary consort to the Duchess in that as a man he can command obedience and respect and lead his troops to battle, but it is the Duchess who embodies the sovereignty of the state and therefore commands the loyalty of her people. Lope was shrewd enough to endow the situation with a certain constitutional complexity.

In order to avoid marrying again, Elena decides to try and replace the King herself. And after making the usual defiant claims of the woman leader of the seventeenth-century Spanish stage about her 'masculine' courage and prowess, she makes valiant efforts to live up to them. Eventually, in an attempt both to avoid

---

[1] Written in 1611.

[2] An idea common to pre-Christian and Christian philosophy. See Aristotle, *Ethics* VIII, xi, and St Thomas Aquinas, *Summa Theologica*, Part I, Q. 92, Art. II. And cf. St Paul, Ephesians V, 23: 'For the husband is the head of the wife, even as Christ is the head of the church.'

large-scale bloodshed and to prove herself worthy of leadership, she meets the King in single combat and defeats him. Lope, clearly, is prepared to concede woman the courage, the ability and the will to rule. Yet he thinks these not enough and in Elena he shows us why. For all her sovereign power, for all her doughtiness, Elena is unable to command the same obedience as a man. When years later the King puts a price upon her head, her courtiers, acting on their own initiative, issue a reciprocal decree. And Elena is fully aware that had their sovereign been a man they would never have dared take matters into their own hands:

> pues aunque sobre el poder,
> en no viendo espada al lado
> se afrentan de obedecer.
>
> (Act III, 158a)

Furthermore, in Lope's eyes they do right. For the weakness lies not only in Elena's femaleness, but in the inescapable effect her sex has upon her own actions. Her nobles react aggressively only because she has failed to do so. Elena as a woman impelled by natural female impulses has put her love for her husband before considerations of state. Woman's very nature, Lope is trying to show, ensures that female rule is fraught with difficulties.

Faced with the problem of her inadequate authority Elena is forced to send for the King himself, threatening her courtiers with his arrival in the exasperated manner in which a mother conjures up paternal authority to frighten a child,

> Yo haré venir
> al Rey, que os haga temer.
> Hoy le tengo de escribir
> que os enseñe a obedecer.
> Su hijo es vuestro señor;
> ponga gobierno en su estado.
>
> (Act III, 158b)

And sure enough, with the King's return Elena regains the authority she lacked when she tried to rule alone. The decisions and commands may still be hers, but their effectiveness, it is clear, will depend on the King. The play's fabric, of course, is of a much denser weave than these details indicate. Elena's strong, unfailing love for her husband is as much the focus of attention as her difficulties with her inherited authority. Nevertheless these separate strands are firmly bound together to create the one dramatic vision – that of the problems that arise when a woman succeeds to the throne of her country. To Lope's mind, being female she is twice vulnerable – as a woman and as a queen. The age-old prejudices against women, together with their natural disadvantages, of which these prejudices are in large part born, make marriage necessary. Yet marriage necessitates choice and the choice might breed envy and dissension; not least the marriage will bring with it all the ambiguities of the consort's position.

Why Lope, in 1611, was interested in the problem of female succession is not an easy question to solve. No sufficiently striking historical event – other than the death of Elizabeth of England eight years previously – occurred at this time which might have prompted his interest. Neither was it a time when woman leaders were thick on the theatrical ground. Interest in theories of kingship in general grew in Spain after the death of Philip II, but the views which Lope expresses in *La discordia en los casados* he had already hinted at some years earlier in *El soldado amante*.[1] Its protagonist, Queen Rodiana, tries continually to prove to herself and to the world that her sex does not inhibit her qualities of leadership:

> ¿Porqué me llamas señora?
> ¿No soy Scipión agora,
> Aníbal cartaginés?
>   Al que señora me llame,
> sino capitán famoso,
> ¡vive el cielo! que derrame
> con este bastón furioso
> su vida y su sangre infame.
>   Hombre soy; no soy mujer;
>   (Act II, Acad.N. IX, 565a)

She has placed herself in this equivocal position by refusing to marry, on the ground that none of her suitors is good enough,

---

[1] Written, according to Morley and Bruerton, 152–3, between 1590 and 1600 and probably between 1593 and 1595.

and Lope clearly implies that when she does marry a man who can relieve her of the responsibilities of leadership, the problem will be solved. Accordingly, when at the end she tells the King, her lover's father,

> Yo soy tu esclava.
> Entra en esta ciudad y reina en ella,
> que para ti tan bien guardada estaba.
>
> (Act III, 589b)

this is more than the conventional courtesy of a daughter-in-law. Rodiana had succeeded to the throne and become the leader and warrior she had to be, but once she has a consort the duties of government effectively pass out of her hands into those of her husband, the man, the natural leader. And without hesitation Rodiana recognizes the precedence that in practice her husband's authority takes over her own. She has gratefully renounced the strain of single rule.

Lope, then, seems to have been a convinced disbeliever in successful female government. His attitude is summed up briefly and explicitly in a passing remark of Fabio's in *La boba para los otros y discreta para sí*:

> Señora, aunque gobernaron
> mujeres reinos e imperios,
> fue con inmensos trabajos,
> trágicos fines, y medios
> sangrientos, que no dejaron
> ejemplo de imitación.
>
> (Act I, Acad.N. XI, 479b)

But his is the only voice raised specifically and at any length on this matter. Other dramatists appear to have been either concerned with broader issues or merely eager to exploit the superficial dramatic glamour of the woman leader. This is not surprising: there was no reason for the seventeenth-century Spaniard to concern himself with the peculiar problems of female rule Only to a man as passionately interested as Lope in all aspects of female existence would such a theme seem of interest. This is not to say, of course, that the famous woman leaders of history and legend had no impact upon the imagination of other seventeenth-century dramatists. On the contrary, they were recognized to constitute splendid dramatic material, even if they did not appeal as vehicles for an exploration of the validity of specifically female rule. Before considering those three plays in which the vogue for the woman leader reached heroic proportions, however, I should like to draw attention to two minor plays based on historical figures. They are illuminating examples of a first-rate dramatist's ability to maximize the interest contained in a little-known story and a minor dramatist's failure to exploit that contained in a world-famous one.

Lope's play, *La reina Juana de Nápoles*,[1] is based on the true history of the fourteenth-century Neapolitan queen, Joanna I, who married her cousin Prince Andrew of Hungary and, after his death in 1345, another cousin, Louis of Taranto.[2] There is no evidence that the queen herself was implicated in her first husband's death, but it is probable that her confidants were, in particular a lady-in-waiting, Felipa Catanea.[3] The action of a later play called *El monstruo de la fortuna*, by *tres ingenios* of whom one was Rojas,[4] is built around the lady-in-waiting but Lope strangely omits this more immediately sensational character and instead projects all dramatic interest upon the Queen herself. His choice of protagonist in a history where quite a different participant had hitherto claimed the major share of attention seems to indicate that Lope was for some reason interested in the subject of female rule around this time: the present play was published in 1615, *La discordia en los casados* was written in 1611. Although Lope is not here propounding the inadequacies of female government, he is examining some of its dangers. The play is, as it were, part of a survey of the prob-

---

[1] Published in 1615 in the *Sexta parte de la comedias de Lope de Vega*. The play is sometimes called *El marido bien ahorcado* in *sueltas*.

[2] See B. Croce, *Storia del Regno di Napoli* (Bari, 1925), Chaps 1 and 2.

[3] She died on the rack. Her story is told in Juan Boccaccio's *De casibus virorum illustrium*, cap. xvi, lib. ix, and in Juan Pablo Mártir Rizo's 1625 translation of a history by the French chronicler Pierre Mathieu, called *Historia de la prosperidad infeliz de Felipa Catanea, la lavandera de Nápoles*, See Menéndez y Pelayo's 'Observaciones preliminares' in Acad. vi, cxxvii–cxxxii.

[4] Published in 1666 in *Esc* xxiv. Menéndez Pelayo thinks the play must have been written by 1654 because in *Esc.* vii, *Lope's* play is included as being written by *tres ingenios*, pointing at confusion between the two (see Acad. vi, cxxvii–cxxxii).

lem and its possible convolutions. This part comes to no adverse conclusions because the Queen here, unlike Elena, is not inhibited by any tender feelings for her husband and is therefore free to react decisively to the threat he represents to her person and to the state. Lope's Juana openly has her husband murdered, first because he is plotting to have her poisoned, and second because he has ordered the death of a noblewoman under Juana's protection, after the girl Isabella has successfully resisted his violent advances.

Menéndez Pelayo denounced the play, substantially on the grounds that its violence, and Lope's implied approval of Juana's actions, offend against the canons of good taste. Admittedly its flavour is rather that of an Italian *novella* than that of a seventeenth-century Spanish play. But together with the few lyrical and highly dramatic passages whose worth Menéndez Pelayo recognizes, a very interesting portrayal of the Queen lifts the play out of the morass of Lope's inferior pot-boilers.

Juana's actions throughout are set by Lope in the context of her responsibilities as Queen. She marries Andrés, in the face of his only too evident brutality, under pressure from her nobles, who fear he will lay waste the kingdom if she does not do so. Hitherto she has resisted him, threatening him not only with her army but even with the physical opposition of herself and her ladies-in-waiting (this boast becomes highly significant in the light of what happens later). But when Andrés threatens to murder all her subjects, including Prince Ludovico whom she loves, she yields – Lope revealing again his sensitivity to the peculiar vulnerability of the female monarch. Andrés becomes King of Naples and the remainder of the play is devoted to the unfolding of the personal and constitutional dilemma thus created. When the King's excesses become known, Juana reminds him that he is king only by virtue of her sovereignty, threatening that if he does not mend his ways she will force him to do so. The very real ambiguity of her position now she is married, however, is neatly conveyed, and Andrés wastes no time in showing her how he regards her changed state:

> Después que tenéis marido,
> aunque reina, estáis sujeta.
>
> (Act III, 547a)

But Juana, sure of the rightness of her complaint, skilfully turns his own arguments against him:

> Mi nombre muestra
> que soy la Reina y señora
> de Nápoles, aunque agora
> soy menos porque soy vuestra;
>   lo que importa es vivir bien,
> basta habéroslo rogado,
> o quien el cetro os ha dado,
> os le quitará también.

Andrés   Acabemos, no haya más;
> mujeres, es lo mejor
> que traten de su labor
> sin meterse en lo demás.

Reina   Podrá ser, tratando de ella,
> que trate de castigaros.

(Act III, 547a)

The conflict between the two in this scene is nicely done – Juana dignified, firm and threatening, Andrés unworried but conscious that he must not go too far as yet.

Juana's realization that something has to be done gradually hardens with encouragement from her lady-in-waiting Margarita (the shadow of Felipa Catanea lingers momentarily here), and the information that Isabella is dead and that she herself is going to be poisoned finally decides her. After a scene of considerable dramatic effect in which Juana truthfully tells the unbelieving Andrés that the handiwork she is engaged on is a silken cord to hang him with, Andrés is lured offstage by Juana and there, discreetly beyond the audience's gaze, is garroted and hanged by herself and her maids. His henchman is then forced to drink the poison he intended for Juana.

Thematically this play is more involved than the other two of Lope's discussed because it is effectively concerned with two problems: that of the female monarch who marries – in this case a man who infringes the moral and legal code he is supposed to uphold and constitutes a danger to the sovereign – and that of tyranny in itself. It is easy to see why Juana's story interested Lope and also why he altered the facts to produce his own personal version. As a play about female rule it presents the dilemma of a reigning queen faced with tyranny in a consort to whom, as monarch, she is constitutionally superior, but to whom, as wife, by social and religious tradition she is subject. As a play about tyranny, it deals with the peculiar situation of a tyrant who is not quite head of state and is therefore in a position to be justly assassinated by a superior in rank; the qualms about the inviolability of the monarch usually provoked by tyrannicide do not, by a hair's breadth, apply here. There is not the slightest indication that Juana's action is other than laudable and justified. She herself is convinced that she has acted as an instrument of divine justice by executing a brutal tyrant. However, she is fully conscious too of her wifely duties – the play after all depicts the dilemma of a wife who is also a Queen – and proclaims that she will observe a year's mourning before remarrying. There is not a hint of irony here: Juana is a good and just Queen who has reconciled her public and private duties in so far as this was compatible with the interests of her state.

In *La reina Juana de Nápoles* we have a play which, for all its flaws, squeezes considerable interest out of a minimum of historical facts. It shows Lope manipulating history to comply with an apprehension of the variety of dilemmas latent in female rule. A much later play, *La poncella de Orleans* by Antonio de Zamora,[1] on the other hand, illustrates the adaptation of historical persons and events for ends which are totally trivial. It is, of course, the story of Joan of Arc, but a Joan of Arc who is neither easily recognizable nor meaningfully transformed. In his depiction of one of the most eccentric and intriguing women of all time Zamora allowed himself to be sucked into the remorseless current of conventional trivia that surrounded the *mujer varonil* theatrical tradition.

Juana in fact is no different from scores of *mujeres varoniles* of the more active sort in second and third rate plays. She fights, she is haughty, she is over-confident, and all strictly according to pattern. The play opens in an orthodox enough way. In a latter-day

---

[1] Written after 1661, for the Figueroa brothers' *La dama capitán*, written in that year, is mentioned. I consulted a Valencia *suelta* dated 1763 in the Cambridge University Library (Hisp. 5.76.3.).

annunciation-scene shepherdess Juana is told by an angel that she must leave for Orleans to fight the English. Hereafter the plot strays from the path of historical or even legendary accuracy, Juana's new-found, divinely-inspired *varonilidad* is displayed for the audience in a hand-to-hand struggle with a wolf, earning her the name of 'hermoso prodigio nuevo' from the royal messenger who has witnessed the fight. Immediately afterwards she is given the opportunity of testing her prowess against human beings when the French contingent sent to escort her to the king is attacked by a band of Englishmen. When she embarks upon her military victories as leader of the French troops, Zamora ensures that we appreciate the active part she plays in them by portraying her at regular intervals fighting in skirmishes with the enemy, by now of course *vestida de hombre*. The *gracioso*, her servant Patín, makes the requisite jibes about her being a *marimacha*, and an amazona, and for good measure likens her to *la dama capitan*.

So far Zamora's procedure, if extravagantly conventionalized, does not go *against* history or dramatic plausibility. But he cannot resist introducing a love intrigue and Juana's downfall is eventually brought about by a jealous rival – Inés, the King's English mistress. To give Inés's vindictiveness an element of plausibility, the relationship between Juana and the King is made slightly ambiguous; the king is certainly aware of Juana's beauty – he calls her 'bellísima pastora' – and his attachment to her grows with acquaintance. When Inés in a scene of heavy-handed symbolism gives the King a rose from a bouqet she carries, Juana rather coyly gives him an iris from a bouqet *she* happens to have at hand. The effect produced by these absurd additions is lamentable. The wolf episode, the *gracioso*'s jokes, the boastful talk, Juana's 'beauty' even, but the love intrigue above all else, constitute the levelling process by which a unique figure is reduced to the status of yet another dreary manifestation of a conventional type. Only Juana's name and ultimate fate are her own; where the rest of her story as it unfolded from the point of Zamora's pen is concerned, she could be any María, Leonarda or Isabel.

The variations offered by minor plays can be as interesting and as instructive as the character-types in justifiably better-known plays.

But when one thinks of the female leaders or rulers that people the Golden-Age theatre it is not characters like Juana or Zamora's Joan of Arc, or for that matter any of the women already discussed, that spring immediately to mind. The names that do are María de Molina, Semíramis, and perhaps Cenobia, all historical figures and all, within the context of the plays that bring them back to life, leaders of heroic proportions. *La hija del aire*[1] and *La prudencia en la mujer*[2] must count amongst the most remarkable plays to come out of seventeenth-century Spain; Calderón's earlier play, *La gran Cenobia*,[3] is a lesser achievement. But all have one thing in common besides the sex and rank of their protagonists. They are plays concerned, not with female leadership as are Lope's, but with leadership in general and/or with individuals, with human beings, who are called or who force their way to leadership. Of course in the dramatic projection of their heroines the two playwrights might allow some flicker of an attitude towards women as leaders to show through, but it would be a mistake to interpret their conception of their protagonists, whether favourable or adverse, as the signpost to a determined view. The focus in these plays, is much wider. In dealing with remarkable individuals, it embraces, not half the human race, but mankind as a whole.

Calderón remains faithful to the traditional character of Zenobia and to the broad outline of her history. There are, however, many minor alterations the most important of which are that Aurelian, a man of perfect virtue according to Boccaccio,[4] appears as a tyrant and that Zenobia, instead of living the normal life of a Roman matron after her defeat, as she is said to have done, is

---

[1] Performed on the 13 and 16 November 1653. See Shergold and Varey 'Some Early Calderonian Dates', *BHS* xxxviii (1961), 278. The two parts are here referred to as one play.

[2] A. H. Bushee and L. L. Stafford in the introduction to their critical edition of the play (Mexico, 1948) xix–xxii, conjecture that the play was written between 1619 and 1623. Ruth L. Kennedy in her article '*La prudencia en la mujer* and the Ambient that Brought It Forth', *PMLA* lxiii (1948), 1131–90, narrows the date down to between 8 April and mid-June 1622. She gives as outside dates 31 March 1621, and 13 March 1623.

[3] Performed 23 June 1625. See Shergold and Varey, 'Some Early Calderonian Dates', 278.

[4] *De claris mulieribus,* Chap. xcviii.

made Empress of the Roman Empire. The effect of these changes is to emphasize the Queen's greatness and, by the principle of poetic justice, to make her reward equal to her merits. The plot, as a result, revolves entirely around this magnified figure. Almost as important as these alterations are Calderón's omissions. For he leaves out of his portrayal of the Queen all reference to Zenobia's *bella cazadora* upbringing and to her *esquivez*, both of which are mentioned by Boccaccio. Such an omission of ready-made popular detail on Lope's part would be well nigh inconceivable, and it seems unlikely that Calderón had not at least read Boccaccio's version, even if he was not familiar with Boccaccio's historical sources – Flavius Vopiscus's *Divus Aurelianus* and Trebellus Pollio's *Tyranni Triginta*. He might have omitted these features in order to avoid banality, but it seems more likely that Calderón wished to concentrate on Zenobia in her capacity as monarch rather than in her capacity as woman. Certainly the play is an exploration of her responses to her public duties rather than to her private emotions.

Calderón's attitude to Cenobia is one of unequivocal admiration. In her he has created a model of all he thinks the perfect leader should be. She is brave, prudent and moderate; she is industrious, steadfast and honourable; she is intelligent, tolerant and entirely without arrogance. By day she fights, at night she writes her *Historia Oriental*: so even the traditional opposition between arms and letters is resolved. She has the welfare of her people so totally at heart that when she is finally captured she willingly offers her own life in return for her country's freedom. Around this gem of monarchical perfection, the other characters, all save the fictitious general Decio, are arrayed in a contrasting setting. Each with his faults and weaknesses offsets Cenobia's shining virtue – even her handmaid, Irene, is a murderess and traitress. Above all, Aureliano the tyrant illustrates the capacity of power to corrupt. In vivid contrast to the Queen he possesses all the undesirable qualities too often found in those who rule. The play, in other words, is a study in leadership in which Aureliano represents the negative side and Cenobia the positive. It is the contrast between the two that preoccupies Calderón.

As drama, the play is defective. The issues are too clear-cut, the contrasts too extreme, the protagonist too blandly perfect. As a piece of political philosophy, however, it is interesting. And its true significance only emerges when it is considered in the light of Tirso's *La prudencia en la mujer*. The two plays were probably written within a few years of each other, Tirso's in approximately 1622 while Calderón's was performed in mid-1625. Ruth L. Kennedy has shown how Tirso's plot has direct relevance not only to the political situation created in medieval Castile by the death of Sancho IV, but by that created in seventeenth-century Spain by the death in 1621 of Philip III. The accession of a sixteen-year-old boy to the throne of the world's largest empire at a time when the fate of that empire was seen by Spanish writers and intellectuals to be in the balance, naturally created an urgent concern with the concept of kingship. The close parallels between the two historical situations, so painstakingly explored by Miss Kennedy, do not exist in *La gran Cenobia*. But Calderón's play is no less a *de regimine principum* in dramatic form than Tirso's and it would appear to be the projection of concerns born of an increasing disquiet with the progress of the new regime.

The issues under discussion in these two plays, clearly, are at once wider and more immediately compelling than the at-that-time hypothetical problem of the advisability and practicality of female rule. The choice of a woman to illustrate the perfect leader was undoubtedly influenced by the theatre's predilection for the *mujer varonil*, for women of force and spirit, but it is not in itself evidence of approval for the idea of female government. In the case of *La prudencia en la mujer* the similarity of situation must have made the choice of plot obvious to a playwright with Tirso's aim in mind. And no one would deny that Tirso had a taste for the creation of female characters with remarkable resources of personality. No one would deny either that Tirso's portrayal glorifies María de Molina nor that it bespeaks an awareness of woman's capacity for sublime virtue and nobility. The Queen's tremendous temperamental weight, and the love and care with which Tirso draws her in her three-fold majesty as perfect wife, queen and mother, have been illustrated and expounded too often to need illustrating and expounding again. But we must not be misled by

Tirso's hymn of praise to this particular woman into making extravagant claims for his feminism. We cannot, on the basis of this play, make generalizations even about Tirso's tolerance of female rule, because the plot has built-in qualifications.

So far as the theme of the play is concerned, the queen's sex has no intrinsic importance. It does play an extrinsic role, however, in the theme's elaboration, for her enemies repeatedly use her sex as a means of attack and of self-justification:

> Don Juan   Que es mujer, y en ellas arde
> la ira, y con el poder
> del límite justo salen;
>
> (Act I, B.A.E. v, 292a)

> Don Alvaro   ¿Qué no hará, si es arrogante
> y ambiciosa, una mujer?
>
> (Act II, 297c)

> Don Nuño   ¡Gracias al cielo que ya
> salió el reino del poder
> y manos de una mujer!
>
> (Act III, 300c)

These remarks are born naturally of the circumstances of the plot. To accuse a woman of being a woman has always been man's favourite way of trying to dismiss the opposition she represents and the nobles' hostility is channelled instinctively in this direction. The effect of the remarks, of course, is the very reverse of what they intend them to be, and this is the other reason for their inclusion. From these jibes the Queen's triumph gathers intensity. By using her sex to denigrate her, her enemies succeed only in bringing into sharper relief the true stature of this woman living in an age and society dominated by men. María de Molina is not only a remarkable ruler, she is a remarkable ruler against the usual odds. The fact that hers *is* an age and society dominated by men is never questioned. On the death of her husband María de Molina finds herself in a situation where she has to act the man in order to protect her son's interests. For all her personal resources, however, her success depends on two things. First, she is reigning in her son's name, wielding his authority. Second, she has behind her powerful male support of her own. In addition to these conditions for success her regency, by its very nature, has other limitations. Hers is essentially an interim government – she reigns that her son may reign. And this is her sole intention. As soon as she is relieved of her responsibilities she retires gladly to her village and to the decent obscurity of widowhood; only her son's folly and weakness make necessary her further exposure, this time short-lived, to politics and government.

These qualifications do nothing to detract from the stature of an exceptional woman; indeed they have in themselves no dramatic existence other than a negative one. But they are qualifications which should be borne in mind by those eager to give instances of Tirso's celebrated feminism, to detect championship of women in every flash of a spirited female eye. Even Tirso's feminism had its limits. His admiration for María de Molina is unbounded, but there is nothing in *this* play to suggest that he did other than accept the conventional view of woman's natural role in life.

If María de Molina is the noblest female figure on the seventeenth-century Spanish stage, Calderón's Semíramis is surely the most dynamic. His heroine is a Semíramis very different from Virués's portrayal of the famous queen. Calderón omits her legendary eroticism and her incestuous love for her son, and, except for one superbly dramatic moment, plays down Semíramis's abilities and achievements as a military and civil leader. He neglects, in other words, the sensational features of her historical *persona* and replaces them with a beautifully constructed two-part study of the inner workings of an ambitious soul, of a personality whose gigantic energy is directed solely towards the projection of self, towards a total fulfilment of will. The result is a Semíramis who is curiously beyond normal considerations of good and evil; this has been reflected in much criticism of the play, as Valbuena Briones has pointed out:

Lo interesante es que la acción no ha sido vista principalmente como un ejemplo moral, aunque moralidades pudieran deducirse de ella, sino una tragedia poética en la que el protagonista femenino cumple el destino trágico impuesto por los astros.

[1] In his introduction to the play in Aguilar, I (Madrid, 1966), 713b–14a.

The tragic element in the play is not the straightforward one generated by the victimization of a superior human being by an immutable external force called Fate, as Valbuena seems to suggest, but there is no doubt that our attitude towards Semíramis remains equivocal. At the beginning of the second half of the play, some twenty years after the first, she has, it is true, wandered further from virtue and from our sympathy than was the case with the young Semíramis. But the two parts form a whole, and the early Semíramis forms an integral part of our vision of the character and inevitably colours our final judgment of her. We cannot denounce her as wicked. That would be a simple dismissal, and Calderón's conception of his heroine and of the tragedy that gathers around her is both rich and profound.

The play, of course, is many things. It is a study of ambition, a study of the fickle workings of fortune, a study in selfishness and a study in passion – themes which, after the manner of Calderón, ripple to the very edges of the action and embrace the most minor characters. But it is above all a study of a woman who becomes a great leader, though not in the way that *La gran Cenobia* and *La prudencia en la mujer* are such studies. On stage Semíramis has a two-fold palpable image – she appears before us as a woman of staggering beauty and as a great and wilful queen. The two are inseparable because the one was an essential precondition of the other. And they achieve perfect dramatic synthesis in that justifiably famous scene at the beginning of the second part where Semíramis, still beautiful at forty and with a host of civil and military triumphs to her name, combs her hair while the King of Lydia and his army gather for battle outside her walls. But Calderón is not ultimately interested in either quality, and the play throws only an oblique light on his views concerning government. He conceived of Semíramis not primarily as a woman or as a leader, though both are obviously important in his elaboration, but as a synthesis of warring tensions. What fascinated him in the Semíramis legend was not so much the heroic accomplishments and the ruthless misdeeds, but the prophecy and its fulfilment. Legend held that Semíramis's fate was prophesied and that that prophecy came to pass. If man has the free-will necessary for self-determination, why should this be so? This is the question the play tries to answer.

The symbolism of the prophecy presents Semíramis, conceived in violence and born in violence, as a pawn in the struggle between the two goddesses Venus and Diana, and ultimately as a victim of Diana, who makes use of the attributes of Venus in Semíramis to help bring about her downfall. But we know that man is not a helpless victim of the gods and Semíramis knows it too. She is aware of the fate prophesied for her, but she also knows that if man has free-will she can avoid this fate:

> pues sé
> aunque sé poco, que impío
> el cielo no avasalló
> la elección de nuestro juicio.
>
> (I, Act I, B.A.E. XII, 28c)

And she is confident that by the imposition of her will, by the application of her understanding, she will be able to do so:

> ¿Qué importa que mi ambición
> diga que ha de despeñarme
> del lugar más superior,
> si para vencerla a ella
> tengo entendimiento yo.
>
> (I, Act I, 24a)

The tragic irony of her situation is that the very dynamism that gives her this resolution, this confidence, also drives her relentlessly towards the fate she seeks to avoid. But why? With her capacity for self-determination and her mental energy (in the form of the desire to survive) to set against the fulfilment of the prophecy, how can her mental energy (in the form of a desire for greatness and glory) alone effect her downfall? The answer is that it does not. There is another factor here, the decisive one – upbringing. Semíramis's upbringing inevitably channels her energies in a particular direction. She is free to decide her own fate, but the circumstances of her past are such that she is not free to make the *right* choice. Brought up in almost total isolation from human contact, she has never learned to modify her desires and her passions in the way that is essential to personal integrity and social harmony. A person brought up as an animal cannot be expected to think, feel and act like a human being, still less like a virtuous one. Semíramis has had nothing; in compensation the world must now give her everything. Valbuena Briones sees Semíramis's choice in the first part as that between ambition and love. But Semíramis does not love Menón, she is the object of his love. The selfishness is Menón's in regarding her as his creature, who will repay him for freeing her from darkness by consenting to return to darkness with him. Semíramis's plea for light and life, when she is offered poverty and obscurity with a man for whom she feels only gratitude, cannot fail to move,

> Menón, aunque agradecida
> a tus finezas me siento,
> ningún agradecimiento
> obliga a dar perdida
> toda la edad de una vida;
> que el que da al que pobre está,
> y con rigor cobra, ya
> no piedad, crueldad le sobra;
> pues aflige cuando cobra
> más que alivia cuando da.
> Si ya tu suerte importuna,
> si ya tu severo hado
> pródigos han disfrutado
> lo mejor de tu fortuna,
> la mía, que hoy de la cuna
> sale a ver la luz del día,
> la luz quiere; que sería
> error que una a otra destruya;
> y si acabaste la tuya,
> déjame empezar la mía.
>
> (i, Act iii, 40b)

Tiresias, in his effort to avoid the fulfilment of the prophecy by shutting Semíramis up in a cave, only brings that prophecy about. As Semíramis warns in the first act:

> pues nada se vio cumplido

> más presto que lo que el hombre,
> que no fuese presto, quiso.   (I, Act I, 28c)

Semíramis is as much a victim of Tiresias's obedience to the oracle as is Segismundo to Basilio's interpretation of the stars in *La vida es sueño*. But unlike Segismundo, Semíramis is left to work out her destiny alone.

In *La hija del aire*, then, Calderón integrates the motif of the female leader into a still wider design. *La gran Cenobia* and *La prudencia en la mujer* shift the focus from mere superficial exploitation of the theme and from Lope's concern with the problems of female rule to a consideration of kingship in general. Calderón goes further with Semíramis. In using her as the battleground for the massive conflict between the forces which decide each man's destiny – between his free-will and that collection of terrestrial factors called Fate – Calderón is using her as a representative of mankind, as a human being in whom this tension is found as it is in every other. And it might be argued that to use the mind and spirit of a woman as typical of the mind and spirit of Man is surely to accord that mind and spirit an equal importance – just as it might be argued that to use Cenobia and María de Molina as models of leadership is implicitly to grant woman equality in that sphere with men. Certainly these circumstances indicate a favourable habitat for the flowering of feminism. But further than this one cannot conscientiously go. The admiration is there, but the attentions are elsewhere and the choice of protagonist is partly dictated by fashion. No dramatist was a greater admirer of female excellence or more willing to pay homage to it than Lope, yet in his explicit treatment of the theme of the female leader he rarely fails to express serious reservations. As for Cenobia, Semíramis and María de Molina, they are not used as representatives of their sex, and no generalizations can be drawn from the part about the whole.

III

Compared with the Amazon and the woman leader, the ordinary *mujer guerrera* of the seventeenth-century Spanish stage is an insignificant creature, and her appearance is on the whole as unremarkable as that of the commonest form of the *mujer vestida de hombre*, the female page. In fact she is often one with the female page. Consequently the use of the term warrior, or *guerrera*, for such a girl may often appear a little grandiose. But it is the only one that conveniently covers both the professional and the occasional soldier and also the woman who, although neither of these, can when necessary put an effective hand to her sword. The first two, for obvious reasons, usually wear masculine dress; the last is generally propelled into action without warning and therefore has no time to get rid of her skirts.

The most familiar figure of the three is the occasional soldier, and it is she who often comes into the category of the female page. The only difference is that in her wanderings around the country-side she becomes involved in military skirmishes, sometimes in-stead of, sometimes in addition to, the usual amorous intrigues occasioned by her ambiguous sex. The motivation behind this intermittent soldiering is nearly always love. Thus Diana in Lope's *La serrana de Tormes* becomes a soldier in a desperate attempt to avoid a forced marriage and to rejoin the man she loves. Estela in *Bernardo del Carpio*[1] fights, and is prepared to die, at Bernardo's side because she cannot bear to be parted from him. Juana in González de Bustos's *El mosquetero de Flandes*[2] accom-panies her husband to Flanders rather than stay at home without him; in Act III, as his ensign she helps him win a fort from the enemy. Another wife who cannot bear to be parted from her warrior husband is María Coronel in Luis Vélez's *Más pesa el rey que la sangre*,[3] who goes to Tarifa prepared to fight at his side throughout the siege. She is the brave, chaste, loving wife of noble character and lofty ideals so dear to Golden-Age dramatists. Her relationship with the figure of the vigorous Roman matron is clear. In Lope's *El alcaide de Madrid*[4] Celima's love for her father's

[1] The text as it stands is not entirely Lope's. See Cotarelo y Mori's introduction to the Acad.N. edition of the play, vol. III, xxvi–xxviii; and Morley and Bruerton, 260.
[2] Published in *Esc.* XXXVI in 1671.
[3] Dates of composition and publication are unknown.
[4] The play was performed in Toledo on 23 April 1599. Morley and Brueton (131) think it was written shortly before.

prisoner Fernando is so great that she sets him free, then accompanies him in his dangerous attempt to reach his own lines. When Fernando is attacked she fights so vigorously by his side in her disguise as a Moorish soldier that his opponents never doubt she is a man. And when an excuse for these actions so unbecoming to her sex and station is demanded of her by the man who loves her, her reply is that love is justification enough:

> Donde amor la culpa ha sido,
> ¿qué tienes que preguntar?
>
> (Act II, Acad.N. I, 567b)

– a reply that rang out constantly from the boards of Spanish theatres, particularly in those years when Lope dominated the scene. Very occasionally the girl in question is driven by love to fight against, not for, the man to whom she is emotionally committed. This is the case in La fe rompida where Lucinda, seduced under promise of marriage by the King of Arcadia whose life she has saved, gathers together an army of peasants and declares war on his country when ingenuity alone fails to win him.

On the whole these episodes of the occasional soldier are very minor ones, and the appearance of the woman actually under arms is often limited to a single scene, after the manner of Tárrega. In Act III of Lope's La infanta desesperada[1] for example, Felisarda, who has not figured at all in Acts I and II, suddenly appears fighting at the side of the Prince whom she loves. She is merely an added complication in the love-affair between Lavinia and the Prince and is totally forgotten at the end of the play. Rarely, in fact, is the soldier-through-necessity motif woven throughout the entire structure of the plot. Even when it is, it does not form the main action of the play. For example, La pérdida honrosa o los caballeros de San Juan[2] is primarily concerned with the capture of Rhodes from the Knights of St John by the Turks and the action is only padded out by the incidents involving Isabel, a Moorish general, and Ana, a Knight of St John. Both originally left home to follow the men they loved and chance made both soldiers. Isabel's success is

---

[1] Written between 1588 and 1595, possibly 1590-5. See Morley and Brueton, 33.
[2] The play, if Lope's, was written 1610–1615, probably c. 1651 (Morley and Bruerton, 325).

largely due to her being the adopted 'nephew' of the Grand Turk, Ana's to her military prowess; but neither of them has become attached to her way of life and neither reveals any desire to continue in it. When they achieve their aim – reunion with their lovers – they are content to return to their female state. Extravagant feminist fantasy, in other words, gives way predictably to normality. But not before a particularly interesting piece of ambiguous by-play has taken place. When Isabel in disguise meets Ana in disguise, each assuming the other is a man, Isabel falls momentarily in love with Ana and asks 'him' to marry her. Structurally the episode is a painfully awkward device to give the pair a reason for revealing their identities to each other, but of course it is also a suggestive piece of dramatic irony. The unusual double deception in one way makes the irony doubly suggestive, yet in another the various resonances of the situation diffuse the audience's apprehension of its potential. The dramatic irony is increased but the sexual implications are in part diverted. This, and Isabel's foreseeably unperturbed readjustment to the truth, create a strong impression that Lope, though certainly aware of its added attractions, introduced the incident primarily as a structural device.

The preceding plays are nearly all by Lope or attributed to him, and they are on the whole comparatively early. The heroine's resort to arms in pursuit of her womanly desires appears to have been a stock device of the theatre during these years, certainly one of Lope's stock devices in the earlier stages of his career. Later on, and possibly under Tirso's influence, Lope and other dramatists, including Calderón, seem to have eschewed this rather naïve solution to the heroine's problems in favour of a more sophisticated and complex pattern of civilian intrigue and adventure.[1] The lady of the high baroque has recourse more naturally to her ingenuity than to mere courage, to mental rather than physical agility.

[1] The brothers Figueroa y Córdoba, however, managed to combine civilian intrigue with military adventure in *La dama capitán* (performed on 20 September 1661; see Cotarelo y Mori, 'Drámaticos españoles del s.XVII. Los hermanos Figueroa y Córdoba', *BRAE* VI (1919), 171-2). Here Elvira flees from home to avoid entering a convent, joins the army and to keep up appearances – another example of a play with female homosexual overtones – courts the woman with whom her brother is in love.

As incidental as the occasional, or temporary, soldier is the appearance of the other two categories, the complete amateur galvanized into heroism by circumstances and the professional soldier. The story of the Great Turk's challenge to Charles V to meet him in single combat in Rojas Zorrilla's *El desafío de Carlos Quinto*[1] is enlivened by the escapades of Leonor, who escapes from the besieged city of Linz in order to enlist the aid of her lover and who offers brave resistance to the Turkish battalion that captures her. But her part in the play is extremely slight; by including Leonor at all Rojas is merely paying lip-service to convention. Once again, the third act seems to have been a favourite time for introducing these isolated displays of maidenly *varonilidad*. In the last act of Calderón's *Hado y divisa de Leonida y Marfisa* the long-lost royal daughter, Marfisa, enters the lists against her unrecognized brother in an effort to defend his name. Similarly, Lope's *El grao de Valencia*[2] ends dramatically with Crisela, the heroine, killing a renegade general who tries to rape her, then gaining control of not one but four Moorish galleys and freeing all the slaves. Naturally, the obviously effective trick of last-act excitement was adopted too by minor dramatists. In *La renegada de Valladolid*, by Belmonte Bermúdez, Antonio Moreto and Antonio Martínez de Meneses,[3] Isabel appears in the third act 'con bengala y espada ceñida' helping her fellow Christians escape.

Most of these 'soldiers of the moment' are of little interest. A notable exception, however, is Doña Blanca de Guevara nicknamed *la barbuda* in Luis Vélez's *Los hijos de la barbuda*.[4] The fact that at the end of the play – again the same technique – she rides to Paris dressed as a knight to enlist aid for Navarre, then helps Saint James and the Christian army defeat the Moors, is

[1] A play called *El desafío del emperador* was performed on 28 May 1634. See Shergold and Varey, 'Some palace performances . . . ', *BHS* XL (1963), 222.

[2] Written 1589–95, probably 1589–90. See Morley and Bruerton, 125.

[3] Published in *Esc.* I, 1652 as Belmonte's. For authorship see E. Juliá Martínez, La renegada de Valladolid', *BRAE* XVI (1929), 672–9. The source of the play was a *pliego suelto*; see E. M. Wilson 'Samuel Pepys' Spanish Chap-Books', Part II, item 23/163. *Transactions of the Cambridge Bibliographical Society*, II, 3 (1956), 237–9.

[4] First printed in the *Parte tercera de las comedias de Lope de Vega y otros auctores* (Barcelona, 1612).

relatively unimportant. Fortunately these conventional heroics do nothing to lessen the splendour of her personality. She is another of Spain's medieval heroines in the María de Molina tradition, with a vigour of spirit entirely in keeping with the savage, warlike age in which she lives. Her courage and independence, her unyielding sense of propriety, her fierce integrity and stalwart patriotism infuse every scene in which she makes an appearance, however shortlived. Luis Vélez has achieved here a minor masterpiece of characterization.

Unlike her amateur sisters, the professional woman soldier does not often appear on the seventeenth-century stage, unless she is an Amazon or a leader, in which case war tends to be an inevitable part of a way of life rather than a chosen profession. The reasons are obvious. The professional woman soldier did not exist in the Europe of the day and would therefore have made a far less credible *dramatis persona* than the woman who took to arms temporarily and usually in disguise. More important, perhaps, the woman who soldiers or fights because she is in love or distress or both, is not only a more attractive figure to dramatist and audience alike, but also one capable of greater dramatic variation and adaptability than the woman with a vocation for blood-shedding. It is significant, therefore, that the warriors who do appear are lent an aura of romance and at the same time a greater degree of verisimilitude by geographical and/or temporal remoteness. Thus Timocles in (?) Lope's *La mayor hazaña de Alejandro magno*[1] defends Thebes with the help of three hundred soldiers against an unusually prudish Alexander. Alba in Luis Vélez's *El alba y el sol*[2] is a warrior who helps the Goths against the Moors and then falls hopelessly in love with the Gothic leader (showing once again that *varonilidad* is no proof against passion). Marfisa, Argalía, Bradamante and Flor de Lis in Calderón's two-act play *El jardín de Falerina*[3] are all *guerreras* taken straight from the corresponding

---

[1] Its authenticity is doubtful; see Morley and Bruerton, 309.

[2] Dates of composition and publication are unknown. There are two MS copies in the Biblioteca Nacional, nos. 16831 and 16060.

[3] Written in 1648; see Cotarelo y Mori, *Ensayo sobre la vida y obra de D. Pedro Calderón de la Barca* (Madrid, 1924), 169. Another full-length play with this title by Rojas Zorrilla, Antonio Coello and Calderón was probably performed

episode in *Orlando furioso*, while Marfisa reappears in *Los desdichados dichosos*,[1] not under her own name but clearly identifiable. To one particular professional soldier, however, nearly everything that has been said about the female warrior fails to apply. She is that extraordinary trans-sexual figure Catalina de Erauso, heroine of Pérez de Montalbán's (?) *La monja alférez*[2] and one of the few real-life examples – and an extreme one at that – of the seventeenth-century *mujer varonil*, Far from being an incidental figure she is the play's protagonist; she was Spanish, she was contemporary with her audience and the reality of her existence made her a credible, if none the less amazing, creature. The paradox here is that, faced with the possibility of dramatizing the story of someone who must surely have been Spain's only true *mujer guerrera*, Montalbán ignored Catalina's military exploits, her eventful trip to Rome and her subsequent commercial life as a carrier in South America and, concentrating on one probably fictitious amorous episode, produced what is essentially a *comedia de capa y espada*. And as a result, Catalina's undoubted gift for war, well-proven in the course of over sixteen years spent fighting in South America, is reduced in the play to two street duels.

Montalbán's reasons for selecting Catalina's amatory exploits at the expense of her other, better-documented adventures are by no means as obvious as they might at first sight seem. The spurious autobiography of the woman dubbed by Américo Castro a 'caso de desagradable androginismo'[3] relates several such exploits. Pietro della Valle described her as follows:

on 13 January 1636. See Shergold and Varey, 'Some Early Calderonian Dates', *BHS* xxxviii (1961), 279.

[1] Printed as by Calderón in *Esc*. xii, but not his. La Barrerra (Catálogo . . . , 62 and 541) attributed it to Antonio Manuel del Campo.

[2] The play was thought by J. Fitzmaurice Kelly on internal evidence to have been written in 1626. See *The Nun Ensign* (London, 1908), 292, note. V. F. Dixon in his unpublished Cambridge Ph.D. Thesis, *The Life and Works of Juan Pérez de Montalbán* questions the play's authorship and suggests instead of Montalbán, Belmonte Bermúdez (pp. 323–5).

[3] The autobiography is *Historia de la monja alférez Doña Catalina de Erauso escrita por ella misma*, first published in Paris in 1829, edited by J. María de Ferrer. J. Fitzmaurice-Kelly's book, *The Nun Ensign*, is a translation of this. Castro's remark occurs in *Lengua, enseñanza y literatura* (*esbozos*) (Madrid, 1924), 267.

Ella è di statura grande, e grossa per donna, che non si può per quella conoscere che non sia huomo: no ha petto che da giouinetta, mi disse hauer fatto no sò che di rimedio per farselo seccare, e restar quasi piano . . . di viso non è ingrata, ma non bella, e si conosce essere strapazzata alquanto, & horamai d'età, e con i capelli negri, e corti da huomo con vn poco di zazzeretta, com' hoggi s'vsa; rappresenta in effetto più un Eunucho, che vna donna: Veste da huomo alla Spagnuola, porta la spada, e ben cinta, e così anche la vita; ma la testa bassetta alquanto; è com'vn poco aggobbatella, più tosto da soldato stentato, che da cortegiano che vada sù l'amorosa vita. Alla mano solo si può conoscere esser donna, che l'ha pienotta, e carnosa, se bene robusta, e forte e la muoue ancora donnescamente alquanto.[1]

That description and Pacheco's portrait do not indicate that her physical appearance would readily attract women, and suggest that these tales were probably untrue. It is possible none the less that such stories were current at the time and that Montalbán used one of them for his play. It is equally possible that the incident was his own invention and that the author of the 'autobiography' based his elaborations on Montalbán. There is, however, one documented incident in the life of Catalina de Erauso which might have served as stimulus to those interested in embroidering her story. On her return to Mexico in 1630 she was asked to escort a girl from Vera Cruz to Mexico. So attached did she become to this girl that she violently resented her subsequent marriage and challenged the husband to a duel. The meeting never took place owing to the intervention of friends. This event, though, is rather different, for it points to homosexual tendencies which, tenuous implications apart, are absent from the autobiography and the play, where Catalina embarks on her amorous adventures solely for gain. Of course, although the incident occurred four years after Montalbán is thought to have written his play, it is difficult to believe that before this a person like Catalina would not have been the object of rumours, suspicions and jokes about her sexual tastes and life, especially in the more educated and liberal circles in which the author of the play moved. But the matter would not

[1] In *De' Viaggi* . . . *Parte Terza, ciò è l'India, co' l ritorno alla Patria* (Roma, 1658-63), vol. IV. Quoted by Fitzmaurice Kelly, 293-4, n. 24.

have been a suitable subject for dramatic treatment, and Montalbán would have had good reason to draw a discreet veil over this
aspect of the Catalina story. Spanish theatre audiences were used
to their heroines masquerading as men and on occasion, and for
their own good purposes, pretending to court another woman,
and thus far in dramatic irony Montalbán could safely go. Anything more overtly suggestive in the case of a living person of
ambiguous sexuality, who could not embrace normality with her
lover at the end of the play, was out of the question. Real intima-
tions of homosexuality would have provoked not only a furore of
ecclesiastical censorship but the displeasure of shocked audiences as
well. This is often overlooked today but, as Jeanette Foster points
out in her study of literary Lesbianism, 'Action on the public stage
of course cannot go as far as in the printed volume; furthermore,
theatre audiences included lower-class spectators more apt to be
shocked by homosexual implication than educated readers with a
classical literary background.'[1]

Whatever Montalbán's motive for reducing a startlingly eccentric life story to a love intrigue of the tamest sort, the sheer banality
of the play is unmistakable. It combines with Montalbán's dramatization of the protagonist to produce a rather odd effect. For
while he succumbs to theatrical tradition by giving his hero the
exterior image of the usual dashing gallant, in character Guzmán
is vastly different from the *galán* of the normal *comedia de capa y
espada*. He is unscrupulous and unprincipled; he accepts money on
false pretences and returns for more when he has gambled it away.
He consorts with a strange variety of people from noblemen to
thugs; he is for ever at odds with the law and kills on the slightest
provocation. And of course he has a violent antipathy towards his
true sex. This last characteristic is the only one that relates Guzmán
to the real Catalina de Erauso, for, this apart, the protagonist could
be any unpleasant bully-boy and I have expressly used the masculine personal pronoun in referring to him, since by all normal
recognizable standards the character created by Montalbán is a
man. Admittedly the depiction of such an ambiguous being was a
tricky undertaking, and this abortive attempt to do so underlines

[1] *Sex Variant Women in Literature* (London, 1958), 39.

the essential femininity of most of those *mujeres varoniles* that leaped from their creators' imagination on to the boards of the Spanish theatre. Montalbán's solution was to create a man and artificially graft on to him an aversion to femaleness and, at the end of the play, a 'feminine' meekness that is no more than a jarring concession to the demands of plot. Our inability to conceive of Guzmán as anything but a male amply illustrates his failure. For the play's effectiveness before a live audience Montalbán obviously relied heavily upon the actress's sex to get the point across, too heavily for the dramatization to be intrinsically convincing.

In fairness to Montalbán it must be said it is now impossible to guess exactly how Catalina de Erauso struck the contemporaries who met her. If the impression she made was as unequivocally male as Montalbán's play suggests, then she was, in the light of this play, unrewarding dramatic material. Naturally at the time Montalbán's instinct must have been a good one. Madrid society must have been agog with curiosity about this remarkable figure who extracted permission from Rome to dress habitually as a man and Montalbán was virtually assured of packed audiences. Armed with the details that rumour supplied, they probably derived from the play a much greater satisfaction than it is in itself capable of providing, and Montalbán of course must have anticipated this. Hence the conventional plot. Jeanette Foster[1] has suggested that, like Middleton and Dekker's *Roaring Girl, La monja alférez* was probably written to whitewash the heroine's reputation. But this motive seems an unlikely one. There were good commercial reasons for writing the play, and there were equally good reasons for leaving out of it any insinuations about homoxexual tendencies. Furthermore it is difficult to imagine why Montalbán, or any other dramatist for that matter, should be interested in such a white-washing. The theatrical vogues for the *mujer varonil* and the *mujer vestida de hombre*, on the other hand, make the real-life nun ensign an obvious choice for dramatic exploitation. The precedents were there by the score and this story had all the added piquancy of contemporary scandal.

[1] *Ibid*, 41.

Catalina, of course, is very different from the other *mujeres guer-reras* of the Spanish theatre. While she is a real-life oddity, the others for the most part belong essentially to the fairy-tale world of chivalry, romance and adventure. Their slight, though attractive figures, never become the vehicle for any meaningful exploration of woman's, or Man's, position before the various forces that shape existence. Like the female page, the *mujer guerrera* prances the stage in an atmosphere of admiration and amused tolerance which only her unreality makes possible. She is attractive and feminine, and her aims are fully consonant with conventional attitudes to her whole sex. The leader and the Amazon are different, because in theory and in historical, or pseudo-historical, practice, they represent a more positive challenge to man. Their greater reality poses serious questions, and they provoke con-sidered responses. The Amazon commands respect and admira-tion as well as belief, but, although a superwoman, there is no question of her being allowed to escape the destiny inherited at birth by even the meanest member of her sex. The leader pro-vokes further-ranging inquiries, but female rule, if not always regretted or condemned as in Lope, is rarely depicted as anything other than an uneasy situation; and it may be significant that not one of the plays considered ends with its female protagonist still alive and reigning without a consort. On the stage, female mili-tancy was a dashing and exciting spectacle, and sometimes the source of powerful drama. But one wonders how long those spectators who had cheered Cenobia and María de Molina would have hesitated if asked to state a preference for male or female rule. And one cannot but suspect how these heroines' creators would have answered the same question. Spectators and dramatist alike, they would all have been horrified to learn that their own or their neighbour's daughter had followed her lover to war.

7

The scholar, the career woman

Two of the most vital issues in the history of female emancipation have been women's right to equal education and, connected with this, their right to earn their own living according to their wishes and their capabilities. In the twentieth century, female suffrage once achieved, the extent of a man's feminist sympathies were, and still are, largely determined by his attitude to these questions. It would of course be pointless to seek rigidly to apply the same criterion to the seventeenth century. All the same, since the question of female education had been much debated in Spain in the sixteenth century and was still, though less formally and far less frequently, commented on with interest in the seventeenth, it is obviously of prime importance to a study of feminism in the theatre to try to establish what its attitudes to the matter were. The drama is rich in passing references to literate women, clever women and so on, but the evidence here is based on those plays whose *dramatis personae* include such women as distinctive types; plays, in other words, in which culture and even careers for women have, or appear at first sight to have, some importance in the development of the plot. Such plays are arguably more truly indicative of convinced attitudes than casual remarks dropped from the lips of often unreliable characters such as the *gracioso*.

I

The learned, or at least the cultured, woman could not have been an unfamiliar figure to the Spanish dramatists. The aristocrats they met or heard of through their patrons at the court must have included the eccentric noblewoman who had some reputation as a scholar. 'Scholarship' here is a variable. In most cases, it would not have meant a great deal more than acquaintance with something beyond the normal run of fashionable feminine reading; beyond the chivalresque and pastoral novels, the Spanish and Italian courtly-love poetry. A working knowledge of the more famous classical myths and a smattering of philosophical or theological terminology appropriately used, and one would be well on the way to a reputation as a prodigy. In addition, there were the female writers, the poetesses, the dramatists and the novelists. With these the *littérateurs* must have mingled occasionally on more or less equal terms. Certainly these women seem outwardly to have aroused in their male counterparts nothing but respect and admiration. Luis Vélez de Guevara in *El diablo cojuelo* (Tranco 9°) calls Ana Caro Mallén de Soto the 'décima musa sevillana' while Lope in his *Laurel de Apolo* refers to María de Zayas as 'la inmortal'. To like and respect the cultured woman one knows, however, is not necessarily to approve of cultured women in theory or in general. Any real views will be better found in the plays themselves; for the theatre, above all the popular theatre, is the best medium for the apparent depersonalization of opinion – everything can be attributed to the exigencies of plot. The cultured woman here, it must be added, does not include the woman with mere pretensions, the *précieuse ridicule*, for she was mocked as relentlessly by the Spanish dramatists as she was by Molière – in Calderón's *No hay burlas con el amor*, and in Lope's *El desprecio agradecido*, amongst others. Their mockery was directed both at the worthlessness of *culteranismo* itself and at the vain snobbery of those taken in by it. They did not see the fashion for precious speech as what, in many cases, it was – a pathetic attempt to grasp at an instant culture. If women were more gullible than men – and given their educational disadvantages they most likely were – it only reveals in them a not unworthy, if foolishly-directed, aspiration towards, even a need for, a wider intellectual horizon.

Apart from those heroines whose learning is introduced as a justification for their *esquivez* and who are duly taught the error of their ways, there are few female scholars in the drama. The attractions are understandably fewer than those of other abnormal female types, particularly to a popular audience of which a proportion was barely literate. The number dealt with in this section is further limited since those learned women who are also in some respect career women are included in a second category, their occupying a career being in the seventeenth century even more remarkable than their scholarship. In spite of her limited attraction, however, the learned woman had appeal enough to warrant occasional inclusion, after the manner of most of the *mujer varonil* types, but as an unexplored, or barely explored, presence. In these cases the main interests of the dramatist are directed elsewhere.

Thus in Luis Vélez's *La rosa alejandrina*,[1] which dramatizes the legend of St Catherine of Alexandria, a teacher of philosophy of such repute that the fame of her lectures attracted to them the Queen of Ethiopia, the main focus of attention is Santa Catalina the martyr and not the philosopher. Luis Vélez allows Catalina to show off her intellectual gifts but, as Spencer and Schevill pointed out, 'Catalina's philosophical arguments are without substance and rather detract from than add to her fame as a philosopher.'[2] In such a play there is naturally no favourable or adverse comment on female learning. Catalina's knowledge is part of the wonder of the future saint, and saints, of course, transcend their sex. In *Bellaco sois, Gómez*[3] the subject is explicitly, if briefly, raised, the author presenting both sides of the argument without seeming at first sight to come down on either. Don Gregorio withdraws his consent to his arranged match with the unseen Doña Ana on the grounds that by her predilection for hunting and philosophical argument she has betrayed her sex. Doña Ana, however, who uses all the resources of her considerable ingenuity to coerce Gregorio into marriage, disguised as her brother justifies her way of life:

> . . . en Italia no es nuevo:
> las mujeres de alta sangre
> desmentir ocios molestos
> en la caza y en los libros
> porque de pocas sabemos,

---

[1] Published in *Esc.* II, 1652.

[2] See Spencer and Schevill, *The Dramatic Works of Luis Vélez de Guevara*, 291. The legend of St Catherine was immensely popular at the time in Spain.

[3] The play has been ascribed to Tirso. Cotarelo y Mori in his 'Catálogo razonado del teatro de Tirso', N.B.A.E. IX, vb–vib, supports this view. There exists a manuscript with a licence date of 1640. See La Barrera's 'Índice de títulos', 531.

> de las prendas de mi hermana,
> que no alcancen, cuando menos,
> a entender letras latinas
> y ejercer por pasatiempo
> ya el cañón, que imita al rayo,
> ya el venablo y ya el acero.
> No privó Dios a las tales
> los ejercicios honestos
> de las letras y las armas
> si discurrir por ejemplos
> sólo (entre las maldiciones
> que en el delicto primero
> echó a la primera madre)
> fue el sujetarle al imperio
> del varón, consorte suyo;
> y sé yo que este precepto
> nadie con vos le guardara
> cual mi hermana, a ser su dueño.
>
> (Act I, N.B.A.E. IX, 595a)

and after this the subject is not raised again. Her reasonable self-justification has about it an air of finality which gives the impression that it is intended, in this play at least, to be the last word. Certainly Ana is presented as an admirable person and we are presumably meant to regard what she stands for as equally admirable. Furthermore, Gregorio himself concedes victory. At the end of the play he eagerly accepts the marriage whose very idea formerly filled him with repugnance and he now praises in Ana the qualities he criticized before:

> Cuando no traigáis más dote
> que las sutilezas raras
> de ese ingenio, que eternicen
> plumas, buriles y estatuas
> merecen que yo os adore.
>
> (Act III, 619a)

This play seems to reveal the dramatist as an advocate of intellectual freedom for women. Together with the heroine's peculiar brand of mental resourcefulness, this might suggest that the author was indeed Tirso, for the views here have much in common with those expressed in Tirso's *El amor médico*, which will be considered later.

Surprisingly, Lope himself wrote nothing which can properly be called a thesis play on the subject of learned women. His views can probably be extracted from the extravagant mixture of dramatic motifs that constitutes *La doncella Teodor*,[1] whose basic plot comes via the *libros de cordel* from the *Arabian Nights*.[2] The plot follows the adventures of a professor's daughter who is captured by the Moors and eventually achieves her freedom by impressing the Great Turk with her display of knowledge. The value of the play lies both in what the characters have to say about educated women and in the personality of Teodor herself. The discussions are not concerned with the principle of female education but, as is Lope's way, with its practical consequences for the potential husband. The disadvantages of learning in a wife are pointed out to Félix, Teodor's lover, by his cousin, Leonelo:

> Mirando
> que el ingenio y la doctrina
> deben estimarse en tanto,
> justo es amar quien le tiene,
> pero entre doctos y sabios;
> mas que para casamiento,
> cosa que dura los años
> que un hombre tiene de vida,
> tengáis vos por acertado
> llevar a casa mujer
> que, con ingenio tan alto,
> os desprecie y tenga en poco,
> y quiera tener el mando
> que Dios ha puesto en el hombre,
> sin otros cosas que callo,
> ¿no es desatino y locura?

He goes on to give a description of what a wife should be:

[1] Written 1610–15, probably 1610–12. See Morley and Bruerton, 190.
[2] See Menéndez Pelayo, *Estudios de crítica literaria,* Quinta serie (Madrid, 1908), 129–89.

> En la calle señora,
> devota en el templo santo,
> dama en el estrado honesta,
> cabra ligera en el campo,
> cuidadosa en su familia,
> animosa en los trabajos,
> regocijada en la masa,
> muda en enojos y agravios,
> fregona en casa, en la cama . . .
> harto os he dicho, miraldo.
>
> (Act I, Acad. xiv, 137b–138a)

And although this disquisition on the conditions of woman is taken more or less straight from the *libro de cordel* text, the warning about educated wives rings with the authentic voice of Lope in serious mood. This attitude, as Ricardo del Arco y Garay has pointed out[1] is of long and respectable descent. Martial said that one of his ideals was to have a wife who was not too learned – 'sic non doctissima coniux', while Quevedo was unequivocal about his preference – 'si hubiese de ser entendida con resabios de catedrático, más la quiero necia'. It is significant that in response to Leonelo's attack, Félix does not praise or even defend Teodor's scholarly bent. He confines himself to a reminder that woman was after all made, not out of mud, but out of man's rib, and he relies on the traditionally desirable in Teodor, her beauty, to reconcile his cousin to the match. There is no question that women are capable of exploring and enjoying the life of the mind, but there is here, as in many other plays with learned heroines, a distinct sense that such women are dismissed as eccentrics. Where her scholarship is concerned, Teodor is presented rather as a *monstruo de la naturaleza* and we feel she escapes censure only because in every other way she conforms to Lope's feminine norm. When she in her turn describes the qualities desirable in a woman, the adjectives she chooses are *generosa, casta, vergonzosa, labriosa, recogida, callada, mansa, quieta*, as well as 'discreta y bien entendida/esto sin ser bachillera' (Act III, 175a). She does hold to this last, albeit

---

[1] *La sociedad española en la obras dramáticas de Lope de Vega* (Madrid, 1941), 319b, n. 117.

223

qualified assertion, however, for when Fenisa is prompted by it to remark,

> Mucho será, si es discreta,
> el dejar de ser terrible.

she replies,

> No será entonces perfeta.
>
> (Act III, 175a)

This is Lope's concession to Teodor's remarkable qualities, which stand her and the plot in such good stead. Intelligence is acceptable, perhaps even desirable, as long as it is not assertive and as long as it does not give a woman wrong ideas about her role in life. Since Teodor's reading and her scholarly bent have not deflected her woman's impulses from their natural course, she has earned the tolerance, even the admiration, of her creator. The potential danger she and her kind represent for the married state, however, is clearly in Lope's mind.

The play contains a separate brace of female scholars –

> Demetria es docta en todas facultades,
> Fenisa es rara en lenguas y en historias.
>
> (Act III, 172b)

obviously included for their curiosity value alone; their presence only serves to highlight the lack of serious concern with female education in a play which seems to invite some real discussion of the principle. Lope's reservations about educated women are expressed elsewhere, sometimes in the extreme reactionary terms demanded at that moment by character or plot. Julio for example, in *La boba para los otros y discreta para sí* declares

> Más quiero boba a Diana
> con aquel simple sentido
> que bachillera a Teodora;
> pues un filósofo dijo
> que las mujeres casadas
> eran el mayor castigo
> cuando, soberbias de ingenio,
> gobernaban sus maridos.

> Lo que han de saber es solo
> parir y criar sus hijos:
>
> (Act II, Acad.N. XI, 489a)

while it is not without malicious glee that Lope allows his *dama boba* to triumph, through the good offices of love, over her cleverer and widely-read sister.

The possibilities that the 'female scholar' motif could yield are illustrated by Calderón's *El Josef de las mujeres*,[1] where it is used to produce a variation on the *mágico prodigioso* theme: the theme of the pagan philosopher converted to Christianity.[2] The play opens rather charmingly with the learned Eugenia poring over her books. Her motives for studying are by her own confession the conventional ones of the *mujer esquiva*:

> ¡Oh nunca mi vanidad,
> viendo que los hombres son
> por armas y letras dueños
> del ingenio y del valor,
> me hubiera puesto en aquesta
> estudiosa obligación
> de darles a entender cuanto
> más capaz, más superior
> es una mujer el día
> que, entregada a la lección
> de los libros, mejor que ellos
> obran, discurre veloz.
>
> (Act I, B.A.E. XII, 357a)

She wishes to prove woman's superiority. The curious thing about this explanation is that the reason is in no way demanded by the plot. The play is not a play of female protest. The immediate purpose of the contrivance is clear. Eugenia's intellectual curiosity brings the New Testament into her hands and the concept of the one God into her consciousness. It initiates her conversion, and once the action is under way Eugenia the scholar is forgotten. She ceases to be the intellectual prodigy and becomes the pagan

---

[1] Date of composition is unknown. The play was first printed in *Esc.* XIII, 1660.
[2] Calderón's *Los dos amantes del cielo* is yet another variation of the theme.

groping her way towards the light.[1] The plot, of course, demands an intelligent protagonist – as a seeker after knowledge she has to be able to question what she reads and to distinguish between the Devil's arguments and those of the old Christian, Eleno – but her initial feminist tendencies are not so easily justified. Possibly they are more meaningful in terms of the play's theme than those of its plot. Apart from identifying Eugenia as a woman of strong conviction and force of character they are an indication of the limitations of her pagan self. Before the Christians' New Testament falls into her hands, her intellectual energies are rooted in feminine pride and her reading is a means to a self-consciously feminist end. Confronted with the all-important problem of God, these selfish motives fade away and her considerable intellect is directed towards worthier, transcendental concerns. Vanity-inspired feminism becomes a quest for spiritual truth. And the change of mood that accompanies this change of motive prepares the way for Eugenia's conversion and final triumph.

As for the reactions that Eugenia's scholarly fame initially provokes within the play, these seem again to be the admiring ones inspired by the prodigy. Once things start going awry and Eugenia appears to suffer from hallucinations, however, her studies get the blame. The *gracioso* mouths the usual comic platitudes about scholarly women:

> ¿Para qué
> es bueno que sea, señor,
> catedrática una dama?
> Cosiera ¡cuerpo de Dios!
> o hilara; que una mujer
> no ha menester (que es error)
> más filosofías que rueca,
> almohadilla o bastidor.
> Vengan libros, vuelvan libros . . .

[1] In her progress towards martyrdom Eugenia has to resort to masculine disguise. The scene in which she has to counter, by revealing her sex, an accusation of rape brought against her by the woman whose advances she has scorned is strongly reminiscent of a similar one in the anonymous sixteenth-century play *Los cautivos* and also of Lope's *Las batuecas del duque de Alba*.

> sin mirar que aun las que son
> bobas, saben más que el diablo.
>
> (Act I, 358c)

and Eugenia's brother holds his father responsible for allowing Eugenia to indulge her appetite for books. Subsequently Felipo himself orders his daughter to burn the Christian texts that are threatening the balance of her mind. But these touches do not add up to a condemnation on the author's part. Supposedly addled wits were often ascribed to an over-heated brain, while a *gracioso*'s judgment has less authority than that of most characters. Eugenia was traditionally a scholar and her scholarship was necessary for Calderón's purpose. The responses to it in the play are automatic and conventional, and beyond this point Calderón's attention is not engaged.

Moreto's interests in *No puede ser*,[1] on the other hand, are specifically engaged in various aspects of the female problem. The play contains by far the most impressive (by normal standards) of the learned women of the seventeenth-century theatre, Doña Ana; and the thesis is that nothing can prevent a woman doing exactly as she wishes – 'no puede ser guardar una mujer'. Its tacitly understood corollaries are first, that virtue in a woman is her best protection, and second, that to try to guard a woman from danger is the surest way of driving her to it. The play is, in other words, an exposition of the principles preached years before by Cervantes. It is a plea for the recognition of woman's personal dignity and integrity and of her capacity for self-determination.

The character who personifies these liberal ideas is the glorious Ana, a poet of culture and learning who presides over the *academia* which meets regularly at her home. She it is who decides to prove to her fiancé, Don Pedro, that he is wrong to insist that a woman, in this case his sister, can be guarded against her will. And if Pedro wants any proof of woman's capacity for responsible behaviour he need look no further than his intended wife. Ana is mature and authoritative; she behaves as she sees fit and goes where she pleases unaccompanied by any Argus-eyed *duena* or guardian. The

[1] Written in 1659.

extraordinary aspect of the situation is that the apparently not over-intelligent Pedro treats his wife as the dignified woman she is, yet frets and fusses over his sister like an indignant cockerel. Ana's established freedom puts him at a slight disadvantage, while his complete authority over his sister releases in him the reactions of convention; Pedro's comicness is portrayed with a fine irony. Ana's outlook is so completely that of the emancipated woman that she is determined not to marry Pedro until he is cured of his narrow-mindedness and ill-conceived opinions. This ability to recognize his failings, and to perceive that unless they are corrected the personalities of husband and wife will clash, is that of a mature adult quite different from the more familiar figures of the impetuous madcap, the determined man-hunter or the submissive love-sick maiden. Ana is ruthless in carrying out the cure, but her every action is dictated by firmness and commonsense, never by arrogance or self-assertion. She is the nearest thing to the modern, emancipated female, the woman who takes her freedom calmly for granted, that the Spanish theatre produced.

Moreto, of all the Spanish dramatists, might have been expected to produce her. His men and women possess a moderation and urbanity which set them curiously apart from the figures we more readily associate with the seventeenth-century Spanish stage. Pedro, for example, is never very threatening. He is foolish and pig-headed but he is not obsessed with his own ego and his narrow-mindedness does not assume frightening proportions. Félix, the sister's lover, is pleasant, agreeable and honourable. He never addresses an improper word to Inés and is not extravagant in her praise. Most unusual of all, he honours his promise not to be importunate when he hides in the house for eight days – a trial to which the patience of the normal *galán* would soon have succumbed. Inés, for her part, regards her brother with intelligent good humour and is neither very subject to him nor very much afraid of his authority. Such behaviour, of course, does not easily yield high drama. And while Moreto's plots are more credible than most in seventeenth-century Spain, as a result of this same process of theatrical emasculation they sometimes lack bite. The *serious* social and moral implications of an action like that of *No puede ser* are barely indicated. Moreto makes his point with a fine, delicate nib and in a neat, restrained hand.

II

The phrase 'career woman', with its twentieth-century overtones, has an incongruous ring in a seventeenth-century context. And of course the number of such women in any country at that time must have been very small. The rich did not think in terms of putting their education and culture to good financial use, nor the poor in terms of acquiring an education or training which would free them from rural or urban servitude. Had they so thought, they would have been powerless to act, through social pressure on the one hand and absence of opportunity on the other. As we saw, the female publishers, merchants and repertory-company managers who did exist were almost invariably widows who stepped into their late husbands' shoes and continued to do business in their husbands' names. This virtual absence of real-life career women naturally heightens the interest of their appearance on the contemporary stage and immediately suggests the inquiries, Why are they there and What are they there for? Are the playwrights advocating careers for women, or are they perhaps rejecting them? If the latter, what made them do so? A close look at the career-woman plays soon solves the puzzle.

Two extraordinary characters who must surely qualify as career women have already been dealt with in a different context. These are Montalbán's (?) Catalina de Erauso and Turia's Doña Mencía. Catalina, serving for over sixteen years as a soldier and then entering the mule train business, is exceptional because her story is largely fact, not fiction. For the dramatist, for the audience and for the reader she is a freakish oddity, nothing more. Doña Mencía, elected governor of Concepción, on the other hand, reveals her creator's ability to grasp the significance of a gifted and powerful adult female personality, together with his willingness to recognize that this personality has the right to self-expression. There is no mention of her relinquishing her post on marriage, and furthermore, she is the only career-woman in the Golden-

Age drama who acquires her position *as* a woman. The others, in order to pursue a career as doctor, magistrate or barber, have to pass themselves off as men. This is a reflection of the illogically ambiguous nature of woman's position throughout the ages – she could rule but not lecture, she could nurse but not diagnose, she could (if absolutely necessary) fight on the battle-field but not in the court-room.

Just as the motives the playwrights ascribe to their *mujeres esquivas* are a pointer to their conception of woman within her normal domestic environment, so the motives ascribed in the plays to their career-women are the best indication of their conception of woman outside that environment. At the lowest level the career-woman theme is merely a minor variation on the vastly popular *disfraz varonil* motif. Instead of dressing as a page or a gallant the heroine adopts the distinguishing dress of a particular profession. Thus in *Sin honra no hay valentía*,[1] an insipid play with a lamentably weak ending, the supposedly dead Eugenia inexplicably disguises herself as a *letrado* in order to present herself at court, reveal that she is alive, and announce that she has obtained an annulment of her marriage from the Pope. Miss Kennedy says that Eugenia has the reputation of being an exceedingly clever judge and is in her role reminiscent of Shakespeare's Portia, but the claim does Portia an injustice. Eugenia's only reputation is that claimed for her by her servant at her own orders; she has never practised as a judge before, and when she is brought in to arbitrate on the marital tangle at court she reveals her identity immediately. Her posing as a judge has no real justification in the plot. It is a dramatic device copied from earlier plays like *El alcalde mayor* and *La hermosura aborrecida*, where the theme is better integrated into the fabric of the play.

The same is true of *La ocasión hace al ladrón*, a plagiarism of Tirso's finer *La villana de Vallecas*, and attributed like *Sin honra no hay valentía* to Moreto.[2] Whereas Tirso's Violante follows her

---

[1] Attributed to Moreto but Ruth L. Kennedy (*The Dramatic Art of Moreto*, 149) finds no trace of Moreto in the play. She suggests as date 1642 (148–9).

[2] Luis Fernández-Guerra y Orbe (introduction, B.A.E. xxxix, xxxix) thinks that the play's interior evidence proves Moreto to have been the author, but Miss

lover to Madrid dressed as a peasant girl, Moreto's (?) hurries after hers in the guise (for the sake of variety one assumes) of a student[1], studentship qualifying for the career theme since it is nominally a training for a career or position of some sort. When it suits her plans she changes her student's disguise for the more orthodox one of a rich American lady. Both Eugenia and Violante, then, put on professional male disguise for no cause other than that of theatrical fashion. Exactly the same ends could have been achieved had they employed any other masculine disguise or probably had they even worn their skirts. Their motive for adopting a disguise at all is in each case connected with love and marriage.

Far more important than this incidental use of professional disguise are the plays in which the heroine, while still in disguise, actually pursues a career. These can be divided into two groups: those in which the heroine voluntarily embarks on this course out of her love of learning, and those in which she is to some extent driven to it by events outside her control. This latter group is predictably the larger, and its constituent plays all have one salient feature in common: the heroine eventually attains a position of authority and power which requires her to sit in judgment over her erstwhile lover, arrested, in the commonest form of the story, for the murder or abduction of the heroine herself. The plays, in other words, are closely inter-related. The tale is basically that of

Kennedy (*The Dramatic Art of Moreto* 136-8) and Narciso Alonso Cortés (Prólogo, Clasicos castellanos xxxii [Madrid, 1922], 18), like most critics, think the attribution is doubtful. Miss Kennedy thinks the play was written in 1666.

[1] The use of *disfraz varonil* is one of the factors which lead Miss Kennedy to conclude that the play is not Moreto's. I am not sure that this is a reliable pointer. By this token, if the infrequency with which masculine disguise occurs in Moreto indicates that this *mujer vestida de hombre* might not be his, then the frequency with which it does occur in Tirso could indicate that the *mujer vestida de mujer* in *La villana de Vallecas* might not be *his*. Playwrights, after all, sometimes break their own rules. Other evidence apart, Violante in *La ocasion hace al ladrón* could well be a creation of Moreto's. She has the restraint and the calm dignity typical of many of Moreto's heroines. In fact, for a woman scorned, let alone one who pursues her lover dressed up as a student, she is remarkably placid. And there is a pronounced dissonance between the personality she reveals in the course of the action and that she perforce shows by the manner of her initial reaction to her abandonment, suggesting that the playwright was not entirely at ease with the sort of character he had chosen to reproduce.

María de Zayas's short story *El juez de su causa*[1] but for its source we have to look back to the middle of the sixteenth century and beyond.[2]

Lope produced two variations on the story, both during the same period of his career. *El alcalde mayor* stands slightly apart from the other plays in the group because its heroine Rosarda is the victim of circumstances rather than of her lover. When Dinardo, after arranging to elope with her, is on his way to meet her, he is attacked by and kills a rival and is arrested. On hearing the news Rosarda, not able to return home, has to flee alone and after a brilliant student career at Salamanca, where no one succeeds in penetrating her disguise, she becomes *alcalde mayor* of Toledo. This position she fills with great success, compensating for her youth and effeminate appearance with a stern diligence. The solution she adopts to her problems has been prepared for. We learn early on that Rosarda is interested in astrology and has acquired the reputation of being a lover of learning, deriving encouragement in her pursuits from the histories of famous women like Semíramis and Aenadnes. But the idea of a career has certainly never before entered her head and she decides to go to Salamanca because she is forced to go somewhere and because, given her scholarly bent, it seems the obvious place to go. She does not, however, become wedded either to success or independence. When she sees Dinardo once more, her love is reawakened and she resolves to bring about a reconciliation. To this end she schemes to prevent his marrying anybody else and to this end she arrests him for escaping prison and sentences him to death. And after a complicated intrigue has effected his pardon, she reveals her identity to him and renounces her career in favour of marriage. She reverts, in other words, to the conventional female role.

Inevitably the character of Rosarda has been said[3] to be probably based on the Feliciana mentioned by Lope in his *Laurel de Apolo*[4] and identified by La Barrera with Doña Feliciana Enríquez

---

[1] Published in the first part of her collection of stories *Novelas amorosas y ejemplares* in 1637.
[2] See Chap. x.
[3] See Justo García Soriano's prologue to the Acad.N. edition (vol. xi).
[4] *Silva tercera.*

de Guzmán.[1] The play does have details in common with the Feliciana tradition – the girl studying in disguise at Salamanca, the interest in astrology, though in the play this is little more than a passing remark on Rosarda's part – which it does not share with the other plays in the group. And Lope conceivably did have Doña Feliciana in mind when he introduced these details – he remembered her much later, after all, when he came to compose the *Laurel* – although one cannot help but wonder whether the chronology of supposed fact and dramatic fiction do not constitute a rather tight fit: Doña Feliciana was born, if La Barrera was right, at the end of the sixteenth century and Lope wrote his play somewhere between 1604 and 1612. Nevertheless, whatever their origin, these are mere details grafted on to the intrigue proper and the central source of the play is an earlier, literary one. To say that Rosarda is based on Feliciana, therefore, is misleading in that it detracts attention from the literary tradition to which Lope's play, in spite of its variations, firmly belongs.

Soon before or soon after *El alcalde mayor* (the difference in interpretation of the similar theme does not help in indicating which) Lope wrote *La hermosura aborrecida*,[2] which introduced the female judge theme into the *comedia nueva* in its traditional and subsequently common form, by merging with it a recurring motif of his – that of the offended woman. That he should have been drawn to the orthodox version of the tale is not surprising during the period of his interest in the *bandolera*. In Act III of the play, Doña Juana, who has been thrown out of her home by her husband, the Viceroy of Navarre, becomes a village barber-surgeon – in disguise, of course.[3] As a reward for curing the King of a serious wound she asks to be sent as judge to the court of Navarre whence have come strong accusations of the Viceroy's intemperate life. She vindicates her undeserving husband and he promises henceforth to love her as he ought. A somewhat more sensational variation is provided by Zabaleta and Villaviciosa's *La dama*

---

[1] Catálogo . . . , 142.
[2] Written 1604–10. See Morley and Bruerton, 203.
[3] Here again the disguise leads to amorous confusion. A peasant girl, Costanza, falls in love with the 'handsome surgeon'.

corregidor,[1] where the heroine is left by her suspicious husband on a desert island in the hope that she will be devoured by wild beasts. Safely off the island, she becomes first a Duke's secretary and then his *corregidor*. Zabaleta and Villaviciosa are even more faithful to tradition than Lope,[2] for Casandra really does judge her own cause – she has to preside over the suit her father brings against her husband Mauricio for the suspected murder of his wife. And that Zabaleta and Villaviciosa had María de Zayas's *novela* in mind is obvious from the closing lines of the play:

> y aquí la comedia acaba
> *La dama corregidor*
> y *juez de su misma causa.*

Casandra, of course, is unaffected by feminism or ambition. Her sole aim is to prove her own innocence and win back her husband. In the process of doing so, thanks to her reserves of courage and intelligence, she shows herself a shrewd and conscientious judge (so conscientious that the Duke finds difficulty in pursuing his own love affair on account of Casandra's efficient night patrol), but she never ceases to be the gentle, loving wife.

The ease with which these untrained women procure top legal posts and the skill with which they carry them out, evidently struck another playwright, Francisco de Leiva, as incongruous. In *his* version of the story, *La dama presidente*,[3] the heroine is well versed in law long before she is called upon to judge her own cause, and has even practised it unofficially as her father's assistant. For all her intelligence, she allows herself to be deceived with alarming alacrity under promise of marriage and then races after her lover vowing vengeance. She loses track of the culprit and becomes instead an adviser to the Duke of Florence and subsequently president of his council. Unlike Casandra she does not preside at her lover's trial when he is arrested for engineering her disappearance, for her emotions overcome her once again and she confesses her

---

[1] Published in 1658 in *Esc.* xII.
[2] See Chap. x.
[3] Dates of composition and publication are unknown. The play is to be found in B.A.E. xLvII.

identity to him while he is still in prison. Rather than have him put to death she somewhat irrationally begs that he kill her. He repents, and they are reunited. Angela in a sense belongs to both this and the following group of plays in that while she is driven to be first counsellor then president, she practised law under her father's auspices with no outside compulsion. Even so there is a strong suggestion that she has devoted herself to her studies partly as an attempt to rationalize an aversion to love and marriage which the playwright unequivocally attributes to the theatre's conventional motives of vanity and pride.

The *juez de su causa* story, then, inspired in seventeenth-century Spain at least four theatrical works and a *novela*. Its appeal for María de Zayas was somewhat special in that it eloquently illustrated her thesis that women had always been harshly treated by men. For Lope the theme of the offended woman must also have played its part, but the obvious attraction of the tale for the stage must have been its heavy dependence on dramatic irony. At the same time one should not overlook the pleasurable satisfaction offered to the seventeenth-century mind (and the phrase is used with a due awareness of its serious limitations) by the tale's element of metaphysical irony – by its connection with the *mundo al revés* topos. The plays seem to say that such are the vagaries of fortune and such is human nature that woman, to protect her rights, is forced to pass as a man and even occupy a man's position. Strength becomes subject to weakness and the offended sits in judgment upon the offender. Angela may manage to half-follow a profession while still sexually uncommitted; but once she has shown herself to be indeed a woman, masculine ability cannot help her and she has to adopt a masculine identity. It is an irrational, topsy-turvy world and the seventeenth-century was committed to aesthetic and moral exploration of the fact.

It is clear by now that none of these women who appear and/or act as professional women is a true career woman at all and that the titles *La dama corregidor* and *La dama presidente* are misleading. The heroines' motives are in every case orthodox feminine ones connected, like those of the women whose tenuous claim to a career is limited to professional disguise, with love and marriage.

And the plays contain no hint of awareness of the potential implications of the situations they create. The legal profession was closed to women, and the adventures that unfold are only exemplary fantasy. Apart from the special cases of Catalina de Erauso and Doña Mencía de Nidos, there are probably only two women in the theatre to whom the term 'career woman' can properly apply. These are Jerónima in Tirso's *El amor médico*[1] and Juana in Rojas Zorrilla's *Lo que quería ver el Marqués de Villena*.[2]

Jerónima is a self-willed woman interested at the start of the play only in her studies. Relations between herself and her brother Gonzalo are strained because she will not be persuaded to entertain the idea of marriage. This attitude she defends to her maid by stating that in studying she is only imitating her Queen – Isabel *la católica*. Her mind shrewdly points out that the Queen manages to combine learning with marriage, which stings Jerónima into retorting:

> Dam tú un rey don Fernando
> que, a Castilla gobernando,
> me deje estudiar, que yo
> haré mis dichas iguales.

> (Act I, B.A.E. v, 381c)

Jerónima is evidently a rational feminist. She objects to the limitations of woman's life, regarding her studies as an escape from the boredom to which women are condemned, and is unwilling to jeopardize the independence these studies give her by marrying. Jerónima's attitude would have been presented by Lope as the outcome of pride, but Tirso – who did not use the *mujer esquiva* theme in its conventional, Lope-inspired form – seems readier to accept it as both rational and sincere. If Jerónima is scholarly by nature, why should she not study? Her reluctance to marry, he implies, is reasonable enough if marriage entails intellectual stagnation. Her aim, after all, is irreproachable: to study medicine and become a good doctor.

[1] Cotarelo y Mori (introduction to N.B.A.E. IX iii a–b) gives the date as 1625 or slightly before, but Doña Blanca de los Ríos (introduction to the Aguilar edition II (Madrid, 1952) xxviii–xxix) thinks 1618–19 more likely.

[2] Published in the *Segunda parte del autor* 1644. See Cotarelo y Mori, *Don Francisco de Rojas Zorrilla, noticias biográficas y bibliográficas*, 174.

Consequently, when Jerónima falls in love Tirso handles the situation quite differently from Lope. There is no gradual, reluctant submission, no self-deception, no retreat into an appearance of indifference, no proud refusal to retract. Tirso does not philosophize on the power of love, or moralize on woman's proper role in life. Jerónima is accepted as a feminist and as a scholar with no suggestion that she is therefore incapable of love. When she follows Gaspar to Portugal it is not because she has claims upon him but because, like so many of Tirso's heroines, she translates her desires into immediate action. And when she obtains a post as a doctor,[1] is elected to a University chair and finally becomes Court physician, she does it, not to further her aims, but out of sheer professional ambition. The end of the play (whose kaleidoscopic brilliance is hardly hinted at by these few details) is equally removed from the Lope tradition, with no new-found meekness, no tender recognition of masculine authority, no glorification of love and marriage, no question of a lesson learnt. There is no suggestion that Jerónima will continue with her career or that she should be allowed to do so – in a society where the medical profession too, apart from low-level nursing and midwifery, was reserved exclusively for men, this element was as much a fantasy as the female-judge theme was seen to be. Jerónima succeeded as a man and she has now revealed herself as a woman. But neither is there any indication that Jerónima will give up her books. The couple are in love, they marry, but Jerónima's character has undergone no metamorphosis.

Unbelievably, Jerónima too has been thought to be based on Doña Feliciana Enríquez de Guzmán – by Cotarelo y Mori,[2] and Doña Blanca de los Ríos accepts this supposition.[3] As A. Zamora Vicente and María Josefa Canellada de Zamora[4] have pointed out, however, even if Doña Feliciana did study at Salamanca dressed as a man this is not 'suficiente para explicar esta doña Jerónima de

---

[1] Her employer's daughter Estefanía complicates thing by falling in love with the doctor 'Barbosa',

[2] See his prologue to Tirso's plays in N.B.A.E. IX, iii, and also *Tirso de Molina: Investigaciones bio-bibliográficas* (Madrid, 1893), 162–4.

[3] 'Las mujeres de Tirso' in *Del siglo de Oro, estudios literarios* (Madrid, 1910), 229ff.

[4] In their prologue to Clásicos castellanos CXXXI (Madrid, 1947), x-xi.

la comedìa; son demasiado abundantes las mujeres transformadas en hombres que andan por el teatro de Tirso. En último término puede ser una probable coincidencia, pero nunca un "modelo vivo"'. Tirso did not have to look outside the theatre for a woman scholar or even a woman masquerading as a professional man on whom to base his Jerónima.

Juana in *Lo que quería ver el Marqués de Villena* is, if anything, even more career-minded than Jerónima and the position she occupies is in no way precipitated, let alone motivated, by love. She is a learned doctor at Salamanca and when the play opens is competing with another learned doctor for a chair. She has studied there in disguise for six years. Since infancy she has been dedicated to her books and when, at the age of twelve, she refused to marry, her understanding father bowed to her wishes and employed a tutor to instruct her in both the arts and the sciences. When the death of her father left her a penniless orphan she set out for Salamanca to compete with men on their own ground. Driven on by her feminist instinct and by scholarly enthusiasm she has more than held her own in a highly competitive market. She has no objections to love, marriage or men, but she has been too busy to think of them. And when at last she finds herself in love, she makes no attempt to resist her feelings; she is merely taken aback at this sudden proof that for all her masculine way of life she is still a woman. The change in Juana, however, is accompanied by all the familiar signs missing in the case of Jerónima. She now sighs and weeps, experiences jealousy and suspicion; for love has revealed her 'femininity'. It is illuminating how in the conversion to love of the *mujeres varoniles*, tears, sighs, jealousy and suspicion are almost invariably regarded as symptoms of a hitherto concealed femininity rather than of a highly emotional state which is asexual. But while Juana is not allowed to forget the conditions of her sex, she is allowed to prove her point, which she expounds in a reported monologue beginning:

> ¿De los hombres el ingenio
> el espíritu, el valor,
> acaso es mayor que el nuestro?
> A los hombres ¿quién les dió

este común privilegio
en las lides y en las ciencias
de ser árbitros a un tiempo?

(Act II, B.A.E. LIV, 337a)

She contends that men are endowed with no monopoly of intelligence or courage; that women are different because they have been brought up to be so; and that even if men are physically stronger, they have no mental advantage over women. And her reasoning goes unchallenged.

A close look at the career-women plays soon makes it obvious that the dramatists are not seriously contemplating the possibility of careers for women at all. The possibility was as remote from their imaginations as it was from their experience of reality. This is not to say that they necessarily believed women to be incapable of following professions, though on the evidence of his attitude to female rule Lope probably had serious doubts. But we cannot know, for the success with which the dramatic heroines acquit themselves is by the nature of the plays an exigency of plot. The presence of this handful of career women in the Spanish drama is the outcome of the progressive development of a literary tradition. Lope, Zabaleta and Leiva side with the aggrieved heroines in their plays, but the woman-judge is for them essentially a fairy-tale figure, a magic-wand substitute which enables the good to triumph. Tirso's physician and Rojas's academic are imaginative extensions of this career-woman theme. The essential abnormality of the stage career-woman is emphasized by the fact that even Jerónima and Juana, who are predisposed towards a professional life, have initially to be precipitated into an active decision – Jerónima by losing her lover, Juana by the death of her father. They embark upon careers out of ambition, not in pursuit of love, but even so a crisis of some sort is needed, for verisimilitude's sake, to lever them out into the world.

There seem to me, however, to be two separate issues involved here. One is the career question, which has proved to be unreal. Careers were not possible for women at the time and therefore not easily envisaged. On the stage, verisimilitude of the most tenuous sort could be achieved only by the depiction of women who masquerade as men. The other is the underlying implication of the career-woman plays, which links them to those works where the heroine has pretensions to learning but is content to follow them at home. This is the more significant, because more realistic, matter of a life of the mind for women. Women of intellectual pretensions did exist in the sixteenth and seventeenth centuries and, being a small and generally wealthy minority, could be seen to do so without any uncomfortable inquiries about the ultimate and logical outcome of education for women necessarily rising to the conscious mind. I said earlier that the motives ascribed to the career-women of the Spanish stage are the best indication of their creator's approach to the concept. And this remains true even when the basic unreality of the career motif becomes evident. In five out of seven cases the motive involved is love and love alone – the fact that it is sometimes offended love makes no difference. In other words, the impulse behind the action in each case falls well within the limits of orthodox feminine behaviour. In Lope's case this insistence on normality harmonizes with his reservations about educated women expressed in La doncella Teodor. His obviously strong conviction that education for women could mar both the woman and her relationship with man seems to flavour perceptibly the presentation of his 'career women'. We never feel that Rosarda's love of learning, like Angela's legal training in Levia, is anything more than an expository necessity in preparation for what follows.

On the other hand, just as Tirso (?) in Bellaco sois, Gómez and Moreto in No puede ser with their Doña Anas convey a definite sense of awareness of the attractions of an intelligent, mature and informed woman, so Tirso in El amor médico and Rojas in Lo que quería ver el Marqués de Villena are capable of envisaging women whose intellectual curiosity and ambition at least do not entail other abnormalities, women with aspirations after something beyond the normal female routine who yet are ready to experience the important events in the more conventional woman's life – love and marriage. Tirso in particular creates a plot and a heroine which take the combination of intellectual and emotional life entirely for granted. These attitudes seem to reveal in certain dramatists an appreciable glimmer of feminism in respect of female education. In comparison, Lope's fear of learning in women is conservative, even reactionary. Exalting the twin ideals of love and marriage as the supreme state of normality for women, he disapproved of anything that might threaten them. Conceivably he was led to think that intellectualism represented such a threat by the intellectually 'emancipated' women he came across. If this were so, he failed to see beyond the shock tactics of feminism's front-line. Tirso and Moreto, amongst a few others, less passionately involved in the concept of female normality, seem to have done so. Where Calderón is concerned, the evidence provided by one play is ambiguous. One might accuse him of inability to attribute to woman intellectual curiosity for its own sake, but this accusation would imply that the feminism in *El Josef de las mujeres* is irrelevant. And irrelevance was a sin which Calderón rarely committed. I am more inclined to think that Eugenia's initial feminism has a thematic importance that entirely vindicates its inclusion and that it sheds no light on his views on the learned woman.

8

The *bella cazadora*

There are numerous Golden-Age plays in which the heroine is
initially characterized as a beautiful huntress whose keen eye,
fleetness of foot, horsemanship, courage and strength, are the
admiration of adoring suitors and awestruck villagers. These
modern Dianas have so much in common with the latter-day
Amazons of the seventeenth-century theatre that the term 'bella
cazadora' can be used as a generic one for all those women who
have been allowed a physical freedom not normally associated
with female upbringing and who have consequently developed a
temperament which by conventional standards is not wholly
'feminine', together with skills which are decidedly masculine.

To hunt and freely roam the countryside is often in the drama a
feminist gesture on the part of the strong-minded woman. The
favourite pastime of the man-hating Infanta of Navarre in Luis
Vélez's *El conde don Sancho Niño*[1] is the chase. Don Gregorio in
Tirso's *Bellaco sois, Gómez*, refuses the hand of the scholarly and
independent Doña Ana partly because she prefers shooting game
to sewing. A love of the outdoor life, in fact, is almost a sure sign
of female unorthodoxy and is often used by the dramatists as a
short-hand method of indicating that something of the kind is to
come. It becomes, in other words, a technique of instant characterization. The heroine presented as a *bella cazadora* can normally
be expected to reveal other signs of *varonilidad*, most usually
esquivez. And the *varonilidad* need not necessarily involve a
dramatic development of the theme or even a continuation of the
chase motif – even Jezabel in Tirso's *La mujer que manda en casa*
makes her first appearance on stage 'en hábito de caza'. In due
course the *bella cazadora* became in her turn a theatrical conven-

---

[1] A rare *suelta*, copies of which are to be found in the Bib. Nat. in Paris and in the
Bib. Palat. in Parma.

tion, and the visual appeal of the female dressed in hunting garb, wielding bow or blunderbuss, ensured her appearance in plays not otherwise concerned with female unorthodoxy. In Calderón's *En la vida todo es verdad y todo mentira*, Libia's love of hunting – which earns her the following descriptions from the *graciosos*:

Sabañón	Marimacha destas selvas.
Luquete	Saltamonte destos campos.

(Act I, B.A.E. IX, 53c)

brings about her first precipitous appearance on stage[1] and Focas's initial confrontation with his past. But she subsequently betrays no other signs of unorthodox activity.

A popular version of the *bella cazadora* figure is the girl who has been brought up in the wilds – like the long-lost Princess Marfisa in Calderón's *Hado y divisa de Leonido y Marfisa*, whose farouche-ness is emphasized by the skins she wears, and who eventually enters the lists against her unrecognized brother in order to defend his name. Or another princess, Nereida in Lope's (?) *El satisfacer callando y princesa de los montes*,[2] who has lived all her life in the wilds near her parents, one of whom is imprisoned in a tower, the other in a cave. Nereida is an intrepid fighter and so wayward that her parents often miss her for days on end. The only comment on this eccentric behaviour is a reprimand from her father:

> Nereida, ¿no echas de ver
> que hacen, tras ser novedades,
> tus rústicas libertades
> liviano tu proceder?

(Act II, Acad.N. IX, 279b)

(His concern is justified, for this time Nereida has been seduced by the heir to the crown of Naples.) But more usually the *bella*

---

[1] A fall, or a runaway, fallen or falling horse, was repeatedly used as a method of introducing the heroine either into the play itself, or into a particularly dramatic scene within the play – sometimes on, sometimes off stage. It happens in *La vida es sueño* and twice to Joan of Arc in Zamora's *La poncella de Orleans*.

[2] The play is possibly one of Lope's recast; as it stands, attribution to Lope is doubtful. See Morley and Bruerton, 339–40. It was published as Lope's in *Parte sexta de comedias escogidas de los mejores ingenios de España* (Zaragoza, 1653) and as Moreto's in *Esc.* XXXVI, 1671.

cazadora is a peasant girl. Lucinda in Lope's *La fe rompida* and Dominga in Luis Vélez's *El amor en vizcaíno, los celos en francés y torneos de Navarra*[1] are two energetic women renowned for their beauty and their hunting skill. They are both seduced under promise of marriage (seduction seems to be one of the *bella cazadora*'s occupational hazards – an indication perhaps of masculine cynicism[2]) and both set out to avenge their honour. The seduction in these cases is used as a device to shatter the girls' self-sufficiency and make them aware of their femaleness. Lucinda in particular has tempted Nature by refusing marriage and love; Dominga too is being taken down a peg or two, in this resembling another of Luis Vélez's superwomen, Gila in *La serrana de la Vera*.

Related to these by reason of her courage and energy is Tirso's Mari-Hernández.[3] When we first meet her she is about to strike a blow for the Faith by dropping a large stone on top of the sleeping Don Álvaro, whom she takes for a Jew. Being unaccustomed to courtly manners, she falls in love immediately with the polished Álvaro when he wakes, and then, in her forthright practical way, sets to thinking in terms of marriage and a job for him. Consistent throughout with Tirso's vision of her, Mari-Hernández, once committed to Álvaro, has no intention of giving him up. When attacked by a rival with a dagger she retaliates with her sling. Later, in an effort to win him back, she becomes a spy for the Portuguese, first cannily extracting two promises from the Portuguese King – Álvaro's hand, and a title. Her love and her courage are eventually rewarded with both. Mari-Hernández, it will be obvious, is a *bella cazadora* with brains. In this she represents the successful fusion of two distinct theatrical types: the formidable country wench and the quick-witted little miss who for the sake of love poses as a dashing gallant (a particular favourite of Tirso's). Hers is a double image. The stone-dropping hoyden looks into the mirror, but it is the Gallician aristocrat who delights everybody with 'his' charming ways that gazes back. The result is uncanny

---

[1] Written before 1637 according to Spencer and Schevill, *The Dramatic Works of Luis Vélez de Guevara*, 150.

[2] See p.302.

[3] *La gallega Mari-Hernández* was performed on 24 April 1625. See Shergold and Varey, 'Some Palace Performances . . . ', *BHS* XL (1963), 226.

but the identification is complete. But for Mari-Hernández the combination would seem implausible, and it is difficult to think of any dramatist but Tirso who, by skilful manipulation of the *personae* of the two types, by endowing the country wench with just a little finesse and the gallant with a proportionate leavening of ferocity, could have carried it off.

Rojas Zorrilla, as we have already seen, took an especial delight in irreverent send-ups of dramatic conventions, and the *bella cazadora* was one of his victims. The parody is complete. He demotes the *bella cazadora* to the level of *graciosa* and then turns her inside out by a reattribution of motive. The result is brilliantly funny. Mari Bernardo in *El desafío de Carlos Quinto* has led an extraordinarily free and adventurous life, not because of any feminist desire for independence but because of her devotion to her man, Buscaruidos, a devotion which drives her to imitate his every action with excessive energy and boldness. Generalized sexual envy has become in her case the flattery of personal imitation; identification with the opposite sex has become identification with one man. The 'normality' of love taken thus to extremes ends with Mari Bernardo's very sex being called into question. Buscaruidos, understandably weary of Mari Bernardo's mimicry, is convinced that she is a hermaphrodite, being,

> muy mujer en porfiar
> y muy hombre en la experiencia.
> (Act I, B.A.E. LIV, 409b)

He finally decides that the only way to rid himself of his shadow is to marry her. The comic appeal of this character, whose ambiguity is unambiguously conveyed by her bi-sexual name and the stage direction that she be 'vestido de hombre y mujer', is strong even now and it seems surprising that the *mujer varonil* was not used more often for purely comic effect.

What commended the *bella cazadora* motif most to playwrights was probably its adaptability. If a play was felt to need a little female spice and vigour its author had only to put a gun, a bow or a sling in his heroine's hand. This adaptability was a function of the type itself as it was conceived, developed and exploited. For the *bella cazadora* in herself has no thematic significance. Her exploits may be integrated into the action, they may even constitute a large part of it, but they have no deeper meaning. Her *selvatiquez* is more often an embellishment to the dramatic pattern than an indispensable component. It sometimes provokes the dramatist into an indirect comment on female independence and its eventual outcome sometimes reveals something of his general attitude to the matter, but it never really forms the 'point' of the play. The *bella cazadora*'s particular brand of unorthodoxy is a comparatively venial one for all its panache, and it lends itself more naturally to action and to supplementary characterization than to theme. Thus of the six outstanding women in this group, two being bandits immediately fall into a much more significant category and the other four (of whom three have only secondary importance) occur in plays of the legendary-historical type.

These are the women who equal, even surpass, the prowess of the legendary Amazons. Their strength is Herculean: when they hunt, weapons are superfluous, for they can kill with their bare hands. Those who turn to a life of crime we have already met. One of them, Leonarda in Lope's *La serrana de la Vera,* is probably the first of the theatre's *mujeres hombrunas* (the term *varoniles* is here inadequate). The other is Luis Vélez's Gila. Both dramatists, as we saw, condemn their heroine's aggressive masculinity, Luis Vélez particularly strongly. These, however, are necessarily special cases, having psychological and thematic ramifications of a serious nature. The girls' masculinity is closely related to a high degree of arrogance which under the pressure of outside events eventually drives them out of society.

The first of the more law-abiding superwomen is also an early creation of Lope's: the María of *La varona castellana*,[1] who according to legend defeated Alfonso I of Aragon in single combat and made him prisoner, so earning both for her descendents and for the field of battle the name of Barahona.[2] María is a true *varona*.

---

[1] Written 1597–1603. See Morley and Bruerton, 155.
[2] *La varona* is alluded to in two other works by Lope: *La Filomena,* Part two, and *La Jerusalén Conquistada*, Book xix. See also Menéndez Pelayo, Acad. viii, 'Observaciones preliminares', p. xxxviii ff.

Because of a prophecy that she was born to conquer men, her brothers have brought her up in strict seclusion. She knows nothing of love and her only pastimes have been hunting and riding:

> Luján　　　En toda España
> no hay tan grande cazador;
> cuerpo a cuerpo, le acontece
> matar un oso.
>
> (Act I, Acad. VIII, 208a)

Even towards the beginning of the play, however, Lope cannot resist a little sententious sign-posting. María's basic femininity is hinted at by her reaction to her first sight of a man. In a reflective sonnet she muses that the snow-capped mountains, the forests and the fountains

> muy buenos sois para gozar un día;
> mas para la mujer, fuera del hombre,
> no ha hecho el cielo alegre compañía.
>
> (Act I, 211a)

The second stage in the wakening of María's femininity is also marked by a sonnet.[1] But the conversion is as yet far off, and first Lope has to maximize the dramatic effect of María's *varonilidad*. Weary of country life, María greets with excitement her brothers' suggestion that she accompany them, disguised, into battle. At court and subsequently in war, María maintains her reputation for ferocity and strength. She dispatches two men in a duel; she challenges three Moorish kings to fight her; she tames a lion – 'conociste el valor de aquestos brazos' she boasts (Act II, 232a); she kills the enemy of the man with whom she is fast falling in love; she takes on three soldiers whom she hears doubting their Queen's chances of victory; then to cap the lot, she fights throughout the night like a female Caupolicán with the disguised King himself. The play, in other words, provides a veritable feast of aggressive *varonilidad*, epitomized perhaps by that lovely moment when María discovers the servant Ordoño trying to escape the battle and drags him off threatening,

[1] Act II, 230b.

> que a mi lado
> te quiero hacer hombre.
>
> (Act III, 245b)

Not surprisingly Maria goes through a stage of regretting that her sex does not match her temperament,

> ¡Oh gran perfección del ser
> de ser hombre! ¡Oh gran nobleza!
> ¿Cuál agravio pudo hacer
> mayor la naturaleza
> que a un alma el ser de mujer?
>
> (Act II, 222a)

and finds the disparity between the two rather confusing. Her situation becomes even more complicated when, for the sake of her masculine image at court, she has to embark upon the courtship of one of the court ladies. For all her conviction that she is incapable of love and that manhood is the perfect state, however, María is naturally destined to fall in love and to learn to accept her womanhood. The formula of disdain and jealousy that Lope adopted for his own and then passed on to other dramatists proves infallible here too, and Maria becomes a loving, if rather fearsome, wife.

María's role in the play is a comparatively small one, despite the title. The struggle between Castile and Aragon occupies both the centre of the stage and the forefront of Lope's thoughts. Perhaps for this reason María is a somewhat cardboard figure. Menéndez Pelayo is right when he points out that she never degenerates into a *marimacho* or caricature – and this in the circumstances is a not inconsiderable achievement – but exaggerates her 'cierto encanto juvenil, cierto desenfado de buena ley, cierta indefinible gracia poética'.[1] This so-called second Bradamante[2] is a fairly pedestrian character. Her development is shaped by those views that

[1] In his 'Observaciones preliminares', p. xliv.
[2] By Adolf von Schack: 'Seine Varona Castellana fürht das Schwort wie eine Zweite Bradamante' (*Geschichte der dramatischen Literatur und Kunst in Spanien*, II (Frankfurt, 1854,) 248) and repeated by Ricardo del Arco y Garay: 'Esgrime la espada como una segunda Bradamante' (*La sociedad española en las obras dramáticas de Lope de Vega*, 298a).

crystallized early on in Lope: she represents the triumph of love and Nature over upbringing. There is no suggestion here that strength and daring are reprehensible in a woman, and María is not tamed. But her strength and ferocity are in any case grotesquely unreal, and too far removed from any normal apprehension of the probable or even possible to elicit a response from a Lope, whose principal attentions are engaged elsewhere. Apart from that, María does not have to withstand the full force of Lope's disapproval, since her subjection to love is not presented as the defeat of an unnatural denial of female instincts on her part.

Two more Marías are amongst these six, both based on the same quasi-historical person. Lope's *El valiente Céspedes*[1] and Luis Vélez's *El Hércules de Ocaña*[2] dramatize the adventures of Captain Alonso de Céspedes, one of the most famous soldiers of sixteenth-century Spain, whose physical strength became a legend. He is thought to have played a large and heroic part in the battle of Mühlberg, the decisive battle in Charles V's campaign against the Smalkaldic League and the German protestants (1546–7). Céspedes had two sisters, Doña María and Doña Catalina, and according to Méndez Silva in his *Compendio de las más señaladas hazañas que obró el capitán Alonso de Céspedes Alcides Castellano* (1647), Catalina (not María) was renowned for being as strong and as bellicose as her brother. Doubtless the two *comedias* played no small part in the embellishment of the legend, but that Céspedes was supposed to have had a remarkable sister is obvious from Lope's 'Advertencia al lector', though Lope disagreed with Méndez Silva as to the identity of the sisters:

Adviértase que en esta comedia los amores de D. Diego son fabulosos y sólo para adornarla, como se ve el ejemplo en tantos poetas de la antigüedad; porque la Sra Dª María de Céspedes fue tan insigne por su

---

[1] Written 1612–15 according to Morley and Bruerton, 244, though it is not included in the second list (1618) of *El peregrino*.

[2] The date is unknown. Spencer and Schevill (*The Dramatic Works of Luis Vélez de Guevara*, 178) point out that if the *comedia* is an imitation of Lope's play and of his *El Soldado Píndaro* the date would be after 1626. But Schaeffer in his *Ocho comedias desconocidas*, I (Leipzig, 1887), pp. ix–x, gives the date as before 1612. The play might well of course, postdate *El valiente Céspedes* and predate *El soldado Píndaro*.

virtud como por su sangre y valentía, y celebrada entre las mujeres ilustres de aquel tiempo, sin reconocer ventaja a las más valerosas del pasado, e igual a Camila, Zenobia, Lesbia y Isicratea . . .

This eagerness to distinguish fantasy from reality emphasizes Lope's belief in the authenticity of the sister's reputation.

With his María de Céspedes, described rather charmingly by her lover as 'un gigante de alabastro y rosas' (Act I, Acad. XII, 193a), Lope pushed even further the tomboy image he had experimented with in *La varona castella*. For this María's trials of strength are not limited to the hunt: like Gila in Luis Vélez's *La serrana de la Vera*, she spends much of her time wrestling and putting a seventeenth-century version of the shot with local villagers and passing muleteers, and it may indeed be significant that the plays were probably written within a few years of each other. María's brother obviously disapproves of such games, for at his approach she pushes her partners out of sight saying,

> Mete estos hombres allá;
> que si los ve, me dirá
> lo que suele, y razón tiene.
>
> (Act I, Acad. XII, 195b)

And Lope's reassurances about the authentic Doña María reveal that the fictitious María's behaviour throughout the play was not for him entirely compatible with female virtue. As well as being *hombruna* – although strangely she is never called this, or even *varonil* – María is, or was before the start of the play, *esquiva*. This former *esquivez* is evidently introduced as a stock trait of the type, for it does not figure in the action at all. Once smitten, María yields immediately to love. Of course, since Lope is grafting the love affair on to a historical person, this rapidly conceived affection is not accompanied by any real change of character. The only thing of which love rids María is her self-confessed but unapparent *esquivez*. Soon afterwards she throws out a bailiff by force, and fights off the *corregidor* and all his men, Then, dressed as a man, she follows her brother to Germany and kills two soldiers she hears belittling him. She escapes from prison, and with Teodora, who loves her brother, she follows Céspedes into battle. In seeking to remain true to the historical *persona* of his heroine, therefore, Lope paints a love which is entirely convincing because it blends with María's character instead of altering it. María loves with the gusto she puts into her trials of strength, yet this love is unusual in the Golden-Age theatre in that it transcends pride and honour. When Diego leaves her, she feels angry and humiliated but she has no thought of vengeance. When she next sees him, lying wounded, not a word of reproach escapes her. And none of this is out of character. Lope has created a genial giantess who was never at any stage a hoyden, never boorish, haughty or ungenerous. She has a proper respect for her brother as head of the family, though she disobeys him behind his back, and unless strongly provoked is reasonable and equable.

Because of the distinctiveness that he manages here to inject into the boisterous wench of the Spanish stage, Lope succeeds with María de Céspedes where he fails with *la varona*. Like the gods, María shares in the pastimes of her inferiors without loss of dignity, and far from being ridiculous or antipathetic, she is a creature of charm, an endearing mixture of strength and sweetness, of bravado and sincerity. Apart from a few hints that her behaviour is not all a lady's should be, María evokes no critical response from her creator. This is partly because she does not denounce her sex and so incurs no moralizing on this score, but mainly because she is portrayed not as a representative, even a remarkable representative, of her sex, but as one half of an intersibling phenomenon – always subject of course, like her brother, to the normal laws of love and gallantry upheld by the *comedia*.

María in Luis Vélez's play has a smaller role than in Lope's. The splendid opening scene of *El valiente Céspedes* showing María wrestling with the muleteers becomes a reported incident in *El Hércules de Ocaña*. Omitted too is the trial of strength between María and her noble suitor disguised as a labourer. The character, however, is substantially the same: one María is as beautiful, courageous, quick-tempered and *bizarra* as the other, though Luis Vélez's has more pride in her make-up and is discernibly the less boisterous of the two. Were it not for Gila in *La serrana de la Vera*, in fact, one might think that Luis Vélez balked at the idea of trying to depict successfully on stage such extremes of unfeminine behaviour, for he relies heavily on narrative in the building up of María's personality. Thus the audience has to be content with a mere description of how María publicly shoots the Governor, who has been wearying her with his attentions. This reluctance to show María's deeds of strength and daring suggests at once an attempt to avoid a too obvious similarity with Lope's play, and a reliance on popular familiarity with this work to fill in the gaps – which indicates that Luis Vélez's play was written after Lope's[1] but within memory's reach. Other changes are introduced, too, one of which is the conventional courtship with which Don Rodrigo has been wooing María long before the action of the play begins. María has no objection to Don Rodrigo himself or to marriage; she merely resents what she considers the insolence of a man who instead of asking formally for her hand, thinks he can win her (and the implication is, into bed, rather than into marriage) by serenades and gallantries. Unfortunately, in his efforts either to take short cuts in the depiction of María's character or to produce something different, Luis Vélez only succeeds in creating a character of less psychological variety and less charm, and one which is finally inconsistent as well, for María's eventual acceptance of the Governor's hand is a betrayal of all she stands for.

For all Lope's success in his depiction of María de Céspedes, the crown in this gargantuan beauty contest must go, not to her, but to Tirso's Antona García. Antona too has a historical basis. She was a woman of Toro who in July 1476 conspired with two fellow citizens to oust the Portuguese from the city. The plot was uncovered and all three put to death.[2] But as Margaret Wilson points out, Tirso's version derives less from history than from popular tradition. I would add that he obviously relied too on the popular

[1] Menéndez y Pelayo thinks Luis Vélez's play is later than Lope's because Lope is more faithful to the true biography of Céspedes, 'Observaciones preliminares', Acad. XII, lxxxix-xc.

[2] See Margaret Wilson's introduction to her edition of the play (Manchester University Press 1957), xi. Also Cesáreo Fernández Duro, *Colección bibliográfico-biográfica de noticias referentes a la provincia de Zamora*, parte quinta, Número 80. Ruth L. Kennedy believes the play was written around 1622-3. See 'On the Date of Five Plays by Tirso de Molina', HR x (1942), 198-208. But Margaret Wilson, pp. ix-x, thinks the play was revised as late as 1625.

traditions that had grown up round two other famous Spanish heroines – *la varona castellana* and Doña María de Céspedes – and particularly on the theatrical tradition to which these and others had given rise. For Antona's characterization has a great deal in common with that of the three Marías and with that of other *bellas cazadoras*; it cannot be a coincidence that Gila and María de Céspedes, as well as Antona García, delight in pitting their strength against the locals.

This oversight has led to misunderstanding: for example, I. L. McClelland, in her otherwise excellent study of Antona García,[1] criticizes Antona on the grounds that her masculine strength and adventurousness are overdrawn, citing in particular what she calls 'the indelicate scene at the inn on the road of Medina del Campo' and the grudging revelation of maternal love which, she argues, is Tirso's way of making amends. She then adds 'Whether loyal to a historical tradition, or to a not very artistic vision of his own, he obstinately recalls her at every turn to a strong-man exhibition by which even he is only half-convinced.'[2] But of course Tirso was being loyal not to historical tradition or to a personal vision, but to the Golden-Age dramatic tradition of the *mujer varonil*, in particular the *bella cazadora*, a tradition which he himself helped foster. Once we accept this, Antona's almost laughable physical strength and stamina, which for Miss McClelland serve only to disfigure her, can be regarded as another of the conventional devices of the seventeenth-century theatre, and hence need not detract from Tirso's portrayal of her character, whose true greatness lies underneath her uncouthness. As Miss McClelland herself says, 'Remove the exaggeration from her horse-play, her herculean strength, her desperado prison-breaking and the other abnormalities and there remains an idealistic peasant woman with a dominating personality strong as a man, sometimes both mentally and physically so; a woman with insight and something of a sense of humour.' The exaggeration is merely Tirso's comic irony, pushing the tomboy figure to the limits of credibility to see how much he can persuade his audiences to swallow.

---

[1] 'Antona García and the Mob', *Tirso de Molina, Studies in Dramatic Realism*, Part II (Liverpool, 1948), 67ff.   [2] *Ibid.* 69.

Miss McClelland's doubts about Antona García go further than the incongruity of her abnormal behaviour: 'The disconcerting fact about Antona is that sometimes she has a man's might and a woman's mind, and sometimes a man's might and a man's mind too.'[1] And she thinks that this lack of integration and this failure to produce a composite character have just prevented Tirso from completing a potential masterpiece. Her conclusion is right, but her reasoning is wrong. A personality like Antona García's cannot be broken down into two well-defined components – masculine might and feminine personality. Tirso is attempting to portray a much more complex being than that would imply. And this very complexity, which Tirso has apprehended and which he has managed, albeit somewhat crudely, to convey, is what makes Antona García a potential masterpiece. Tirso, whether he realized it or not, has hit upon the truth that the dividing line between masculinity and femininity is impossible to draw. Antona García is not a disintegrated character. It is not by the variance of her characteristics that Tirso fails to make her a masterpiece but by his failure to portray that variance convincingly. And he fails because, with history as well as character laying claim to his attention, he has not time to succeed. Antona García is a victim of the division of interests typical of Golden-Age drama.

For Tirso, Antona García is what María de Céspedes is for Lope – first and foremost an extraordinary human being and only secondly a woman. By attaining the realms of legend both have in a way transcended sex. There are, however, two interesting passages in *Antona García*; first the advice given to Antona by Queen Isabel,

> Antona, ya estáis casada;
> vuestro esposo es la cabeza;
> id con la naturaleza
> en sus efectos templada.
> No hagáis de hazañas alarde,
> porque el mismo inconveniente
> hallo en la mujer valiente
> que en el marido cobarde.

[1] *Ibid.* 69–70.

Olvidad el ser bizarra,
viviréis en paz los dos;
aliñad la casa vos,
mientras él tira la barra.
No os preciéis de pelear,
que el honor de la mujer
consiste en obedecer
como en el hombre el mandar.

(Act I, N.B.A.E. IV, 619a–b)

the second is the opinion expressed by the four Portuguese travellers about the famous Antona García,

Por 2º   El poco seso
de mujer, que se ha metido
en lo que no va ni viene.
Por 3º   Hile y barra.
Por 4º   No la tiene
sino el mandria del marido.
Si ella fuera mi mujer
un roble descortezara
cuando en aquello tratara,
en sus costillas.
Por 1º   Querer
usurpar lo que le toca
al hombre, es mundo al revés,
y hacer cabeza a los pies.
Por 3º   Ella debe ser gran loca.

(Act III, 635b)

The Portuguese merely speak as enemies, expressing their disgruntlement at the Castilian successes in terms of the sex-war. The description by Antona's enemy, the vicious María Sarmiento,

vituperando
su misma naturaleza,
en el acero templado
trueca galas mujeriles.

(Act I, 616a–b)

255

is also provoked by enmity.[1] But how should we take the Queen's words about wifely duties? Are they seriously meant, or only theatrical platitudes? The answer is 'both'. By tradition and theatrical convention the situation demands a little moralizing of this sort. At the same time, the fact that the words are put into the mouth of a queen who enjoyed the reputation of a perfect wife, and who was for all her prudish modesty no laggard in displaying physical courage and energy beyond the call of duty, lends them authority as well as a delicate irony. Tirso probably *would* support everything Isabel says; after all, it is little more than a condemnation of female rowdyism. But he is not really interested here in the propriety of Antona's behaviour and he is certainly not condemning her. Had she obeyed the Queen, after all, Toro would never have been won. What is interesting about Tirso's portrayal of Antona García, however, is that he does not hesitate to attribute to her a willingness to marry and remarry. Lope found it difficult to envisage a woman refusing to conform to the usual pattern of feminine behaviour yet at the same time accepting with equanimity the idea of love and marriage. Tirso never doubted that the two were entirely reconcilable.

The *bella cazadora*, then, covers a fairly wide variety of women, from the noblewoman who escapes from the boredom of her *estrado* to go hunting, to the girl indulging in displays of immoderate strength. But whether of gentle or peasant birth, and whatever their degree of *varonilidad*, they have one thing in common – they have all rebelled against the restrictions of their sex and achieved at least their physical freedom. And given always that their extravagant behaviour has an element of fantasy in it, this freedom is something their creators seem prepared to allow. Of course, there is no threat to man or to man's society in the sort of physical freedom which has on stage – and perhaps in life too – the appeal of incongruity. In physical freedom itself no revolt against Nature is involved, no serious principle is at issue, so the

---

[1] Of the historical María we know only that she occupied the Alcázar of Toro after her husband's death and held out there for a month after the rest of the city had surrendered.

dramatists can afford to be indulgent. Overtly masculine behaviour
– fist crushing, ox-lifting and so on – understandably provoke a
sceptical grin or a frown of disapproval, depending on the dramatist's stance in the particular play, but the high spirits of youth and
the natural expression of pent-up energy are on the whole ignored.
Allied forms of rebellion, like *esquivez*, receive the treatment that
they normally do. Naturally one is not to assume from this that
the playwrights are giving woman *carte blanche* to go anywhere and
do anything she please. Woman in seventeenth-century Spain did
occasionally go hunting – accompanied of course – so that in a way
this stage behaviour was a dramatic extension of real-life activities;
but this is very different from gadding about alone in a crowded
town. (Traditionally Nature has been regarded as a substitute
chaperone, lending protection and imparting respectability, though
even this hallowed tradition became at the time the object of
scurrilous levity on the part of the less credulous.[1]) And of course
tacit acquiescence on the stage by no means necessarily implies
approval in practice. Often no obections are raised, but then normally the problem is not at issue. We can assume the dramatists
recognized the rational justification for a moderate physical freedom for women only because their depiction of the *bella cazadora*
nowhere incorporates an argument against it. The dramatist who
did make his views explicit and considered the problem in a
practical light was predictably Lope, and to some extent he presumably represented realistic opinion. In his dramatized chronicle
La campana de Aragón,[2] Doña Elvira, for reasons which are not
made immediately clear, has been brought up as a boy and has
grown to love the freedom which this entails. Although an entirely
unnecessary complication to the plot, Elvira has considerable interest here, for having known what it is like to live the life of a
man and observing what it is like to live that of a woman, she
gives an impassioned denunciation of the disparity between the
two. And all the emphasis in this speech is on freedom. The

[1] See p. 302.
[2] The play belongs to the same period, 1596–1603 (probably 1598–1600, see
Morley and Bruerton 140) as *La varona castellana*. Here again the disguised
heroine becomes the object of the amorous attentions of another woman.

conversation with one of her father's retainers, Porcelo, of which the speech is a part, is remarkable in that it is a crystal-clear reflection of Lope's comprehensive view. He can sympathize with Elvira and see the unfairness of woman's position but at the same time he believes that this state of affairs represents a social and natural order which cannot be overturned. Everything has its own being and its own natural element outside of which it is not complete; therefore Elvira cannot refuse to accept her rightful state, with all the disadvantages that this may involve. The conversation is worth quoting for what it reveals of the dichotomy inherent in Lope's position:

> *Elvira*   Mi padre . . .
> volverá, por justa ley,
> a aquel su primer estado.
>   Pero yo, mudando el traje,
> mudaré de libertad,
> perdiendo mi voluntad
> lo que gana mi linaje . . .
>   Traíame desta suerte
> desde que pequeña fui
> donde a ser hombre aprendí
> robusto, gallardo y fuerte.
>   Y como mudar costumbre,
> que es otra naturaleza,
> ofende y causa tristeza,
> dame mortal pesadumbre.
>   No sé como he de sufrir
> dejar tal hábito agora.
> *Porcelo*   Con el contento, señora,
> de verte en quietud vivir;
>   con volver a ser mujer
> en vida honesta y segura;
> que cuanto hoy vive, procura
> estar en su mismo ser.
>   Que es la pretensión del fuego
> subir siempre a su lugar,
> la de la tierra, bajar,
> buscando su centro luego . . .

	Todo, en fin, está en su ser
	mejor que en ajeno está;
	tú también descansas ya
	si hoy vuelves a ser mujer.
Elvira	No me digas más, Porcelo;
	que aunque el ser hombre es fingido,
	muestra en la mujer que ha sido
	un bien perfecto del cielo.
	Aquella gran libertad
	de andar, hacer y decir;
	aquel gallardo seguir
	la luz de su voluntad.
	Aquel gozar su albedrío
	sin seguir dueño tirano;
	aquel estar en su mano
	su condición, gusto y brío.
	No puede dejar de ser
	imperfección el faltar,
	ni dejarle de envidiar
	la más honesta mujer.
	Verás mil hombres perdidos
	buscando varias mujeres
	con diferentes placeres
	alma y cuerpo divertidos,
	darse al juego o a otros daños
	de su salud o su nombre;
	y con ser vicio en el hombre
	durar con honra mil años.
	Desdichada la mujer
	que hiciera un yerro!
Porcelo	Es ansí.

(Act I, Acad. VIII, 259a–b)

The *bandolera* has shown how sensitive Lope and his colleagues were to the hypocrisy of the moral double standard, but his 'Es ansí' has a note of resignation missing from those plays where he confronted the problem more boldly. Yet Porcelo's admission of the justice of Elvira's arguments follows his previous consolatory philosophizing. Of course Elvira has to take up her rightful sex again, but no-one is going to be allowed to forget what she loses in so doing. This, of course, was Lope's difficulty. Always fiercely committed to abused or offended womanhood, he had somehow to reconcile this championship of the underdog with his and his society's convictions about woman's appointed role. His outlook was not that of the ardent feminist of his day or ours. The woman who rejected her role and thereby trespassed on his sexual philosophy had to be made to conform, and with conformity to accept injustice as long as this did not become abuse or offence. In Elvira Lope leaves us with the view that while freedom for women was intellectually justifiable, it was not a realistic goal.

9

The avenger

A study of the *mujer varonil* of the Golden-Age theatre would be incomplete if one small but significant group of women were overlooked. These are the women who refuse to accept with Griselda-like passivity the wrongs perpetrated against them and theirs, and themselves seek positive satisfaction for the crime committed. Woman's capacity for revenge is by no means a discovery of seventeenth-century Spanish dramatists, but in the context of seventeenth-century Spanish society female vengeance acquires the peculiar importance it must have in any society which recognizes revenge as a social weapon and at the same time accords woman no social responsibilities other than those based on her sex. The social conventions which made honour the patrimony of the male made vengeance a masculine duty. Honour was his, and his the revenge when honour was lost. Strictly speaking, woman's role in this social structure was an instrumental one. She had no honour of her own that was distinguishable from virtue, but upon her virtue depended the honour of her male relations. In the light of these conventions (which were probably accepted in theory if not adhered to in practice by the majority of Spaniards), the significance of a *female* avenger becomes immediately obvious. By taking the revenge upon herself, she not merely usurps the role played by the male in the maintenance of social order, but more important, reveals herself to be as sensible of honour as man himself, thereby presenting a direct challenge to the superiority of the male. The woman with a sense of honour is conscious of her worth and dignity as a person. To allow her that sense of honour, with the duties it entails, is to proclaim her a repository of law and order with social responsibilities which transcend sex. In other words, in terms of the honour code supposedly in force at the time, based on the conception that society lived by the good name of each of its members, the woman with honour should be well on the road towards equality.

But a full survey of woman's position before the honour code lies outside the scope of this work. The female avenger, and of course the female bandit, have an important contribution to make to this theme and serve to link it to that of the *mujer varonil*, but many of the heroines who would enter a full treatment of the subject have not even the most tenuous claim to *varonilidad*. The avenger is *varonil* because by taking such positive action she is ousting the male.

The circumstances of the revenge naturally vary from play to play, and with them the tone of the action, the importance of the female-avenger theme and the attitude of the dramatist. The commonest and most straightforward situation is that of the girl who vows vengeance on the man who has abandoned her. It is closely related to that of the girl-page who goes in search of her lover, the main difference being that the avenger has usually given herself to the man in question under promise of marriage and is consequently motivated by rather more complex emotions than love. Rosaura in *La vida es sueño* in these circumstances desires Astolfo's death, though finally she settles for marriage. Even so, these complex emotions do not invariably give rise to a desire for vengeance: Violante in Tirso's *La villana de Vallecas*, for example, sets out after her faithless lover to oblige him to marry her and restore her honour. The theme is even more closely related, of course, to the dishonoured woman turned bandit. The girl's feelings of anger, shame and wounded pride are expressed in animosity towards the particular culprit instead of towards society in general, but the protest is basically the same. And it is obvious from the plays that this form of protest has the whole-hearted approval of the playwrights. The offended girls always achieve their aims, albeit usually in a somewhat mellowed form. Lucinda in Lope's *La fe rompida*, having failed to get Felisardo to honour his promise, gathers an army of peasants and declares war on his country. The King is so impressed that he marries her. Nereida in *El satisfacer callando y princesa de los montes*, also by Lope, follows her faithless lover back to Naples, delays his coronation and projected marriage, then sails against him with the Sicilian fleet. She in her turn is rewarded with marriage. Mari-Hernández in Tirso's *La gallega Mari-Hernández*, on the other hand, while she too sets out to punish, is more strongly motivated by love than by pride (possibly because she has never actually yielded to Don Álvaro) and at one point she even saves his life. Her main aim is marriage, and to this end she is prepared to betray Monterey to the Portuguese and coerce Don Álvaro into wedlock. For her pains she gets a husband *and* a title.

These plays show woman in rebellion against their cavalier treatment by men and standing up for their rights. They are offered, and they accept, marriage as satisfaction for this treatment because for them marriage is the only real satisfaction. In the seventeenth century the jilted woman was an unmarketable commodity. Marriage in these circumstances almost invariably means marriage to the guilty man. It is with surprise, therefore that one reads Luis Vélez's *El amor en vizcaíno, los celos en francés y torneos de Navarra*, where Dominga is compensated for her seduction by the Dauphin of France with marriage to no less a person than the King of Navarre. Not for a moment does Dominga entertain the idea of marriage to the Dauphin himself. In the best chivalresque tradition she swears with controlled fury that she will live a life of abstinence and deprivation until she has restored her honour, and she fulfils this vehement vow. She is satisfied only when she kills the Dauphin, whose arrogant assumption of immunity to any normal morality justifies the extreme nature of his punishment. Her action earns her nothing but respect and admiration from the other characters, and she is finally rewarded for her zeal with a crown:

> que a valor tan alto
> le viene un imperio estrecho.[1]

Dominga's reaction to her predicament, then, is totally different from that of the other three. She does not want the patched-up respectability that marriage to her offender would bring her. She even forgets the love she once felt for him. Her only thought is to restore her integrity in her own eyes and in the eyes of the world. That she is allowed to do this, despite the moral and social pressures

[1] Act III, *Esc.* XVIII (1662), f2ob.

usually brought to bear upon her sex, seems to reveal a sizeable chink in the armour of seventeenth-century male prejudice.

Mira de Amescua appears to go even further than Luis Vélez in granting woman equality before the honour code, at least so far as revenge is concerned. Dominga's grudge is essentially a feminine one. She has been enjoyed and discarded. Within the rigid orthodoxy of sexual morality there is nothing one could do to a man which would induce quite the same degree of humiliation and degradation. Furthermore, since she has to live by her reputation, she is justified in trying to restore it. Arminda in Mira's *No hay burlas con las mujeres o casarse y vengarse*,[1] however, has suffered no such degradation and her reputation is intact. Her lover's offence is a comparatively light one – his suspicions about her fidelity have driven him to slap her face. But Arminda reacts to the blow like the typical *pundonoroso* male, demanding satisfaction. Up to this point, it is easy to believe that the play is a straightforward defence of female integrity, of woman's right to discard her traditional passive role and to react to events according to the accepted standards of behaviour of her age. But now the situation becomes more complicated. For Arminda does not rest until she has killed her former lover; and she does not do this by challenging him openly in the usual manner, but by murdering him in mysterious circumstances.[2] Obviously Mira cannot seriously be recommending that a woman slapped by her lover should resort to an inversion of the wife-murder method of revenge. It cannot even be his way of stating that sauce for the gander must be sauce for the goose. No Golden-Age husband commits wife-murder because his wife has dared to hit him. Mira certainly *is* upholding woman's right to vengeance in a society which condones vengeance. Of this the end of the play, where Arminda marries another of her suitors, is sufficient proof. And this is the main point of interest in the present context.

[1] Written after March 1621 (internal evidence). See Cotarelo y Mori, 'Mira de Amescua y su teatro', *BRAE* xviii (1931), 41–4.

[2] This *desenlace* shocked Cotarelo y Mori's sensibilities (*ibid*, 44): 'es brutal e improprio de una dama fina como era Arminda'. He suggests that a duel between Don Diego, the man who actually marries Arminda, and Don Lope, the man who hit her, would have been more fitting. Obviously he missed the significance of the play.

But it is as well to point out that Mira is not advocating equality at the cost of sanity. By making the disparity between the revenge and the motive for revenge so ludicrously great, he is surely condemning the concept of revenge itself. He shows, in fact, how the honour code taken to its logical and just conclusion must degenerate into a senseless and bloody free-for-all.

Mira realized that his *pundonorosa* heroine was a new departure in the theatre. The play's closing words show this

> Y que en tan nueva invención
> de caso tan encubierto
> halle aplausos el acierto
> y el desacierto perdón.

But to say, as Valbuena Prat does,[1] that by depicting 'la mujer que vuelve por su honor' Mira was attempting something original and strange, is clearly wrong. The woman who reacts positively to dishonour, whether by turning criminal, by punishing her offender or by simply seeking marriage, is a familiar figure not only in the seventeenth-century theatre but in the pre-Lope drama as well.

Valbuena Prat makes this claim for Mira in response to the usual claim that Rojas Zorrilla was the creator of *la mujer vengadora de su honor*. While it is untrue that Rojas was the creator of the theme of female vengeance, it is certainly true that he produced some of the profoundest plays on this subject. Two of these – *Progne y Filomena* and *Cada cual lo que le toca* – I shall leave until last, as being the most significant plays on the woman-avenger theme. The other two – both excellent plays – are interesting in that they deal with theatrically unorthodox forms of revenge. Lucrecia in Rojas's *Lucrecia y Tarquino*[2] avenges her dishonour by committing suicide. Rojas's hands were tied here by history, which led him away from the theme of aggressive female vengeance, but the story gave him the opportunity to explore, as he does in *Casarse por vengarse*, the various facets of woman's revenge. The stark contrast of *Cada cual* and *Progne y Filomena* reveal Lucrecia's

---

[1] In his prologue to Clásicos castellanos LXX (Madrid, 1926), 45.

[2] Closest likely dating is 1635-40. See Raymond R. MacCurdy's introduction to his edition of the play (Albuquerque, 1963), 4.

suicide as a tacit admission that woman is a possession which once enjoyed by someone other than its master is worthless. At the same time it is a betrayal of her sex, for by equating technical chastity with virtue, dignity and integrity – all the qualities of which she was formerly so proud – she forgets that she is a human being, remembering only that she is a woman. In short, her psychological reactions to the rape, and the action she subsequently takes, are from the feminist point of view retrogressive. Few of the heroines of the Golden-Age theatre capitulate so easily to sexual victimization as Lucrecia. Blanca in *Casarse por vengarse*[1] is a more tragic figure. Abandoned by Enrique because of the conditions of his succession to the throne, she impulsively takes what is probably in real life the commonest form of revenge. In desperation she marries someone else. This spirited yet pathetic attempt to strike back at the injustices of life, by punishing not only Enrique who still loves her but herself for allowing herself to get hurt, rebounds upon her with tragic intensity. She forgets that the Condestable her husband also has feelings, she forgets that he loves her and that, hurt in his turn, he too might want to strike back just as she struck back at Enrique. She forgets all this when on her wedding night she breaks down and cannot bring herself to receive her husband's embraces. Above all she forgets that, unlike her, her husband, being a man, will be influenced more by the thought of his sullied honour than by feelings of disappointed love. She is as much the victim of her own revenge as Lucrecia herself, and when she sees the folly of the course her grief has driven her to it is already too late:

> ¡cuánto yerra
> la que por vengar su enojo
> contra su gusto se casa
> habiendo querido a otro!
> Pues darse entonces la muerte
> era una desdicha sólo;
> pero casarse a disgusto
> vienen a ser dos ahogos:
> uno, no poder jamás

[1] Published in *Parte veinte y nueve de comedias de diferentes autores,* Valencia 1636, where it is attributed to Calderón.

> desechar el amor propio,
> que es natural, el primero;
> y es el otro tener odio
> por los impulsos de amante
> a los afectos de esposo.
>
> (Act II, B.A.E. LIV, 113b)

The avenging woman of the Golden-Age theatre, however, is not invariably motivated by personal dishonour. Sometimes, as in the case of Elvira in Cristóbal de Morales' *El caballero de Olmedo*,[1] she kills to avenge her murdered lover. Elvira, however, is not a figure of a kind that appears often, because few lovers in the drama meet with such a sad end. In any case, although Elvira is probably the first female perpetrator of secret vengeance (she pretends ignorance and the murderer remains undiscovered), the situation is not a particularly significant one, since Don Alonso has no one else to avenge him and Elvira is put in a situation where vengeance and self-protection become indistinguishable. (Admittedly she also revenges herself rather gruesomely on the porter who admits her enemy to her bedroom, by sewing him to the corpse before she orders him to fling the body from the balcony.) More significant is the situation where the girl seeks to avenge her family honour; where a member of her family, usually her father, has suffered an insult, and where she, identifying herself with his dishonour, feels called upon to wipe it out as if she were his nearest male relation. The propriety of her vengeance depends upon the family circumstances. If the father is incapable of avenging himself and if he has no son to do it for him, then his daughter is justified in undertaking his vengeance herself. She is not, however, compelled to do so. This is the situation in Moreto's (?) *La negra por el honor*.[2] When Leonor's old and senile father learns that she has challenged his offender to a duel, he is impressed and proud. Lope, however, makes it quite clear in *La moza de cántaro* that if the daughter's

---

[1] Written 1606. See Juliá Martínez's introduction to his edition (Madrid, 1944).
[2] First published 1668 in *Esc.* xxx. Ruth L. Kennedy (*The Dramatic Art of Moreto*, 148) lists the play as apocryphal. The play is a ragbag of dramatic motifs thrown untidily together, with, however, some interesting characterization certainly reminiscent of Moreto.

action is uncalled for it must be condemned. Here Doña María avenges her father although he has a son upon whom the duty properly falls. Her action is therefore a wilful and presumptuous rebellion, born of arrogance, against the laws of society, and the play tells how she pays for this rebellion by learning the hard way to accept the limits of her sex. Lope, it must be said, is the only dramatist to criticize an act of female vengeance. But this may be simply because he is the only dramatist to deal with a case of *unnecessary* female vengeance. The two important factors here are first that María has a brother and second that she is not the injured party.

Lope uses María to explore once again the exact position of woman within his own society. Rojas Zorrilla in *Cada cual lo que le toca*[1] poses a much more urgent problem. What is a wife to do if the conjugal honour is threatened and her husband refuses to act? In the play, Isabel suddenly finds herself in the most dangerous position. Several years before, she had a disastrous affair with Don Fernando, then reluctantly married Don Luis. Don Fernando now turns up again and presses his attentions upon her. Don Luis cannot discover the identity of the interloper he surprises one night in his house and he cannot bring himself to kill his wife. Isabel, therefore, realizing that unless something is done Fernando will violate her, lures him into her room and stabs him to death. The play, not surprisingly, was booed by the Madrid audience when it was first produced. Isabel, entering marriage after having been enjoyed and discarded by another man, and subsequently being pardoned by her husband, was an affront to their belief in the 'double standard';[2] even worse perhaps, Don Luis by vacillating in the pursuit of his duty both offended their sense of propriety and robbed them of their pound of flesh. Américo Castro has pointed out that the really significant detail in the plot is that here we have a *married* woman avenging not only her past humiliation

---

[1] The date is unknown. Earliest mention occurs in 1661; see A. Castro's introduction to his edition of the play, Teatro antiguo español II (Madrid, 1917). 176.

[2] For a fascinating account of the double standard in England and its consequences, see Keith Thomas's 'The Double Standard', *Journal of the History of Ideas* XX (1959), 195–216.

but the present threat to her own and her husband's honour.[1] And he is justified in saying that Isabel represents an extraordinary exaltation of the female personality. The implications of the situation cannot be overlooked. By usurping her husband's role as the protector and avenger of their conjugal honour, Isabel reveals herself to be as conscious of that honour as he and even more capable than he of defending it (partly because she knows the identity of her would-be seducer). In other words, she adopts a position of equality in honour and hence in marriage itself. The dagger that kills Fernando is her husband's; the hand that drives it in is hers. That is, they are one in the pursuit of honour.

This position is strengthened by her husband's attitude. Critics, including Américo Castro, have been too ready to dismiss Don Luis as weak and irresolute. Admittedly, Isabel emotionally and temperamentally dominates the play and Luis's is neither a strong nor a particularly admirable character. He married Isabel out of love in spite of her warning that the match was inadvisable:

> no conviene . . .
> ni a mi casarme con vos
> ni a vos casaros conmigo.
> (Act I, Teatro Antigua Español II, 16, 391–4)

and then, Isabel seems to suggest, he permitted something of this shadow from the past to come between them:

> en dos años
> que en unión y en lazo fijo
> eres tu mi digno amor
> y yo tu desdén indigno.
> (Act I, 18, 427–30)

He has allowed his wife's mysterious advice to gnaw away at the vitals of his affection for her. When the shadow begins to acquire substance, he prevaricates, eaten up with suspicion yet disconcerted by what he knows of her virtue, His urge to talk over with Isabel his predicament and its logical solution – her death – is distasteful,

[1] In his Introduction, 183–97.

but it is the urge of a man who cannot reconcile himself to the idea of simply erasing another human being, whom he loves. His decision to give her a day's grace is a means of gaining time for himself. But surely a husband's inability resolutely to murder his wife is not evidence of a lack of moral fibre. What the seventeenth century found theatrically contemptuous and improper we now consider natural. Don Luis's anguished uncertainty is far more convincing than the conventional mouthings about the harshness of the honour code uttered by vengeful husbands. His reluctance betrays not only his own irresoluteness but also an awareness that Isabel is something more than an expendable threat to his honour. The play, therefore, represents a direct challenge to the normal interpretation of conjugal honour by presenting a situation which is a direct contradiction of the normal wife-murder situation. The woman is allowed an active, responsible role instead of her usual one of sacrificial lamb; the man is allowed to prove incapable of playing the butcher. Don Luis's '¿Luego perdonarte debo?' is more than a reluctant admission of error. It marks an acceptance of Isabel in spite of her past, and a recognition of her true status within their marriage. The temporary reversal of roles has revealed what the true balance of those roles should be.

The humane and liberal views expressed by Rojas Zorrilla in this play could not have been the result of dramatic convenience. He must have known his audience too well not to suspect that they might take it amiss. In any case Rojas was not a playwright who cared overmuch about the conventions of the stage for which he wrote. Conclusive proof that these were views he did seriously consider with an open mind is provided by another revenge tragedy, *Progne y Filomena*,[1] his second important review of female honour. Guillén de Castro before him had dramatized the story from Ovid's *Metamorphoses,* revelling in its Senecan horrors. But all the emphasis in Rojas's adaptation points to the conclusion that he did not only see in the tale, as Raymond MacCurdy suggests, another opportunity for pursuing his favourite theme – revenge

[1] A play by this name was performed on 10 January 1636. Whether this play was Rojas's or Castro's is not known. See Shergold and Varey 'Some Palace Performances . . . ', *BHS* XL (1963), 235.

– by dressing it up to please his public in the conventional trappings of the honour code:

> Rojas did not compose *Cada Cual* and *Progne* simply to demonstrate his attitude towards women's position under the honour code (and I grant for the moment that the code was more than a dramatic device). In *Cada Cual*, as in his dramatization of the classical story of the two sisters' revenge, Rojas was pursuing his favourite theme. He was writing revenge tragedies in which the revengers happened to be women. . . . Rojas grafted upon the revenge tragedy the terminology of the honour play because it was the language, the 'motivational jargon' which he and his audience were accustomed to and understood.[1]

He also found it an opportunity for exploring the implications of the idea of female revenge in relation to the conventions of his time. To attribute the choice of this particular myth for dramatization to mere chance in itself seems high-handed. Rojas does not merely make honour, as distinct from revenge without sanction of reason, the sisters' motive; he takes considerable pains to analyse their attitude to honour, following carefully the mental processes of each sister. Filomena, violated and injured,[2] has spent two years in the wilds, brooding over what happened, feeding her hate, nursing her shame and plotting vengeance. When she meets her father and her lover, she has the opportunity, and indeed the right, to leave vengeance to them. In terms of the code, they have been dishonoured through her by Tereo, and the revenge should properly be theirs. But Filomena does not ask for aid, and the part played by the appropriate male characters in this dramatization of the honour/vengeance format is minimized to lend emphasis to that played by the women. In Filomena's eyes her dishonour is greater than theirs; at the same time she is the cause of *their* dishonour. The onus of seeking satisfaction for both insults – the direct and the indirect – therefore falls upon her. Her use of Hipólito's dagger is a symbol of this double satisfaction: the instrument of death will be his, the guiding hand her own.[3] Progne's reasoning

---

[1] *Francisco de Rojas Zorrilla and the Tragedy* (Albuquerque, 1958), 36.
[2] Rojas's Tereo pierces her tongue but does not cut it out.
[3] Cf. Isabel's use of her husband's knife in *Cada cual*.

is a little more involved. She considers the affront she has suffered to be even greater than her sister's, because it has affected her honour both as sister and wife. This self-identification with her sister's dishonour is important, because it was normally the prerogative of the male members of a girl's family. Even more important is her evident conviction that either partner in marriage is dishonoured by the adultery of the other, signifying as it does a belief in marital equality. Her two-fold argument is expressed by her analogy between her own situation and that of the husband with the adulterous wife,

> Di, ¿cuando hace un adulterio
> una mujer, no merece
> la muerte?
>
> *Filomena*   Ya lo confieso.
> *Progne* ¿Por qué?
> *Filomena*   Porque va el honor
> de su esposo.
>
> *Progne*   Luego es cierto,
> que si a mí me va el honor
> tuyo, siendo mi honor mesmo,
> con adulterio y agravio
> incurro en el mismo duelo.
>
> (Act III, B.A.E. LIV, 59c–60a)

Both Progne and Filomena, therefore, feel that theirs is the right and the duty to punish Tereo.[1] Together they exemplify woman's equality in honour. Of the two, Progne's is the more revolutionary case. Filomena has, after all, been grievously harmed, while as an unmarried woman she is not subjected quite so rigidly to the honour code as her sister. Progne's reaction is that of the seventeenth-century male. Like any brother she shares in her sister's dishonour and avenges it, and like any husband she is dishonoured by Tereo's adultery and avenges that. Each acts partly out of provocation (Filomena is raped and injured, Progne naturally reacts violently to her sister's treatment) and partly on principle (Filomena feeling she must avenge her lover and father as well as

---

[1] Américo Castro (*Cada cual lo que le toca*, 191–3) makes this point about Progne but it is equally true of Filomena.

herself, Progne feeling she must avenge her conjugal honour).
With Progne, however, the provocation is less and the motive of
principle considerably more alien to the seventeenth-century mind.
Husbands, unlike wives, were allowed their infidelities. Had
Tereo's crime been less serious, *Progne y Filomena* might also have
been booed by its audience. But this time Rojas avoided outrage by
explicitly marrying off Filomena to Hipólito at the end of the
action.

The small body of revenge plays discussed above is of immense
importance on two counts. First, it reveals an almost unanimous
belief in woman's equality in honour and its protection. Rojas
Zorrilla even supports equality in conjugal honour. Lope alone
voices reservations (María is not equal in family honour with her
brother). Secondly, it contains an extraordinary attack – in Luis
Vélez's *El amor en vizcaíno* and in Rojas's *Cada cual* – on the
double standard of sexual morality. Lucrecia upholds this double
standard, true, but here Rojas is bound by tradition. This is the
furthest any of the seventeenth-century dramatists go in their
emancipation of woman. Even by modern standards it is a long
way. It is essential in considering the theme of the avenging
woman to bear in mind that one is talking in terms of a code of
behaviour which, to a degree that is difficult to establish, was
probably an artificial one. Was the honour code a realistic arbiter
of human actions off the stage,[1] or was it merely a dramatic convention? Did the theatre in this respect reflect public opinion at the
time or did it help create it? The only certainty is that the honour-
vengeance concept must have appealed to the seventeenth-century
Spanish mentality, or it would not have survived in a theatre
which depended for its existence upon public approval. To say
therefore that the girl who improperly avenges her father and
the wife who avenges her conjugal honour contravene the laws
of their society, is to refer to unwritten laws which were not

---

[1] Husbands of course occasionally murdered their wives (see Pellicer, *Avisos*, 28
de julio de 1645, for example) but it is dangerous to assume that their motives for
doing so were determined by the honour code. Furthermore the fact that public
sympathy seems generally to have been for the wife is an indication that the
honour code was not considered an adequate excuse.

necessarily put into practice but which most would readily have upheld in theory. Rojas Zorrilla would not have felt his points about honour worth making had there not been considerable prejudice working against it. However artificial the framework of the honour code into which the theme of female vengeance fits, the views and prejudices about women that it reveals and the protests it provokes on the part of the dramatists are as valid as if the code really were a working part of the social machinery.

Certainly María de Zayas, writing contemporaneously with most of the playwrights we have been looking at, regarded female honour and the related concept of female vengeance as a vital aspect of the feminist question. In at least two of her stories she portrays women who refuse categorically to compromise with dishonour or to contemplate a marriage based on a false footing. In *Al fin se paga todo* Hipólita kills with her husband's knife the brother-in-law who has taken her husband's place in her bed, then refuses to return to her all-forgiving husband because of an unconsummated affair with another man, Gaspar:

diciendo que honor con sospecha no podía criar perfeto amor ni conformes casados, no por la traición de Don Luis que esa, vengada por sus manos, estaba bien satisfecha, sino por la voluntad de don Gaspar, de quien su marido entre el sí y el no había de vivir receloso.[1]

And in *La burlada Aminta*, although her new admirer and husband-to-be begs her to let him deal with the matter, Aminta insists on avenging herself upon her seducer and betrayer, arguing,

Yo soy la que siendo fácil la perdí [i.e. her honour], y así he de ser la que con su sangre la he de cobrar. Ya sabéis que las mujeres en aprendiendo una cosa, tarde se arrepienten; pues siendo esto así, como lo es, dejadme que os merezca por mí mísma, que si vos por vuestras manos vengáis mi afrenta, poco tendréis que agradecerme.[2]

To these two cases María de Zayas brought a woman's sensibility and consciousness, and a conception of what dignified and responsible independence in a woman *could* be which is very different

[1] *Novelas amorosas y ejemplares*, ed. A. G. de Amezúa y Mayo (Madrid, 1948), 326.
[2] *Ibid.* 109–10.

from the external intellectual approach of the male dramatists. But the interest, the preoccupation are in both cases the same. These writers all used the traditional theme of the vengeful female to explore the idea of sexual equality within the terms of the reigning personal and social code of their day. A concern with the equality in honour of *all* human beings was, after all, a natural progression from that belief in the equality in honour of all men so strenuously upheld in the drama of the period.

10

Sources and influences

In Chapter 1 I suggested that the dramatists of the Golden Age could not have looked only to the Spain of their own day for material for their plays about female *varonilidad*. The isolated examples of female heroics recorded by commentators cannot have been in themselves the source of the procession of *mujeres varoniles* who trod the Spanish stage throughout the course of almost a hundred years. The storehouse of inspiration which enabled the playwrights first to create their heroines and then to keep them alive over such a period of time, was necessarily much vaster than contemporary life; vaster in range, kind and time. The *mujer varonil* of the Golden-Age drama represents a fusion, in time and place, of nearly all the manifestations of the extraordinary woman which history, mythology and literature, from the days of classical antiquity down to the seventeenth century itself, can offer. For the most part these sources remained constant, although naturally the process of influence varied; Lope might take a heroine straight from a ballad or a chronicle, and a later dramatist might then take that heroine from him. But, as the seventeenth century advanced, to these continuing sources there was sometimes added a new one – a contemporary Queen like Christina of Sweden or a contemporary 'personality' like Catalina de Erauso. These were adopted for dramatic purposes in response to the vogue for the *mujer varonil*; at the same time they infused the vogue with new life and thus helped to maintain its popularity and continued growth. This chapter considers those factors which obviously influenced the playwrights in their depiction of the *mujer varonil* and those which conceivably might have done so.

The 'bandolera'

The female bandit, as first portrayed in Lope's *La serrana de la Vera*, is, as the name of the play suggests, a descendant of the medieval *serranas.* Lope's direct source in this instance, however, was not the *serranillas* of Juan Ruiz or the Marqués de Santillana but a traditional ballad specifically called the *Romance de la serrana de la Vera,*

Allá en Garganta la Olla, – en la Vera de Plasencia,
salteóme una serrana, – blanca, rubia, ojimorena.
Trae el cabello trenzado – debajo de una montera,
y porque no la estorbara – muy corta la faldamenta.
Entre los montes andaba – de una y otra ribera,
con una honda en sus manos – y en sus hombros una flecha.
Tomárame por la mano – y me llevara a su cueva:
por el camino que iba – tantas de las cruces viera.
Atrevíme y preguntéle – qué cruces eran aquellas,
y me respondió diciendo – que de hombres que muerto hubiera.
Esto me responde y dice – como entre medio risueña:
– 'Y así haré de ti, cuitado, – cuando mi voluntad sea.'
Diome yesca y pedernal – para que lumbre encendiera,
Y mientras que la encendía – aliña una grande cena.
De perdices y conejos – su pretina saca llena,
y después de haber cenado – me dice: 'Cierra la puerta.'
Hago como que la cierro, – y la dejé entreabierta:
desnudóse y desnudéme – y me hace acostar con ella.
Cansada de sus deleites – muy bien dormida se queda,
Y en sintiéndola dormida – sálgome la puerta afuera.
Los zapatos en la mano – llevo porque no me sienta,
y poco a poco me salgo – y camino a la ligera.
Más de una legua había andado – sin revolver la cabeza,
y cuando mal me pensé – yo la cabeza volviera.
Y en esto la vi venir – bramando como una fiera,
saltando de canto en canto, – brincando de peña en peña.
– 'Aguarda (me dice), aguarda, – espera, mancebo, espera,
me llevarás una carta – escrita para mi tierra.
Toma, llévala a mi padre, – dirásle que quedo buena.'
– 'Enviadla vos con otro – o sed vos la mensajera.'[1]

The popularity of the ballad can be judged from the fact that Menéndez Pidal and María Goyri collected twenty-one different

[1] Printed in *Amenidades, florestas y recreos de la provincia de la Vera Alta y Baja en la Extremadura . . . compuesto por D. Gabriel Azedo de la Berrueza* (Madrid, 1677). Reprinted in Menéndez Pelayo's appendix to Wolf and Hofman's *Primavara y flor de romances,* tomo II, 209, in the series *Antología de poetas líricos castellanos,* IX.

versions of it. That both Lope and Luis Vélez had the ballad in mind is clear, not only from their titles, but because they actually quote extracts from it in the body of the texts. Both alter the words somewhat, perhaps in accordance with some other version of the tale, but if anything Luis Vélez sticks more closely to the *extremeña* version reproduced above:

Lope		Luis	
	Salteóme la serrana	Vélez	Allá en Garganta la Olla
	junto al pie de la cabaña.		en la Vera de Plasencia,
	ojigarza rubia y branca,		salteóme una serrana
	que un robre a brazos arranca,		blanca, rubia, ojimorena.
	tan hermosa como fiera.		Botín argentado calza,
	Viniendo de Talavera		media pajiza de seda,
	me salteó en la montaña		alta basquiña de grana,
	junto al pie de la cabaña.		que descubre media pierna.
	(Act III, Acad. XII, 36b)		(Act III, T.A.E. I, 98)

Valdivielso, too, includes a version of the ballad in his auto *La serrana de Plasencia*, of which the first three lines are identical with those of the *romance*; his title, though different, is likewise taken from the ballad.

Menéndez Pidal and María Goyri pointed out that while the plays of Lope and Luis Vélez have much in common, Luis Vélez's owes more to the original *romance* than does Lope's[1]; and in so far as Gila is much fiercer than Leonarda and is of peasant origin, they are right. Since Luis Vélez's play is definitely later than Lope's they concluded that both dramatists independently made use of a third play earlier than Lope's. But there is no need to look for this mysterious third play. The redating of Lope's *Las dos bandoleras* shows where Luis Vélez could have obtained those details not present in Lope's *La serrana de la Vera*. Inés and Teresa provide an adequate precedent for the abandoned woman who reacts to her shame with an excess of ferocity. That Luis Vélez's play is closer to the *romance* in itself means nothing. It is quite conceivable that, wanting to write a play after the manner of Lope, he referred back to the original ballad in order to refresh his memory of the traditional tale. The search to establish literary sources too often leads

---

[1] 'Observaciones y Notas', *Teatro antiguo español* I (Madrid, 1916), 136ff.

the zealous scholar to invent a more logical process of borrowing than really existed. There is, therefore, no good reason for accepting any dramatist other than Lope as the adaptor of the *Romance de la serrana de la Vera* and the creator of the female bandit of the theatre. This process of adaptation and creation must not be underestimated. Lope took a highwaywoman with a thirst for blood and sex and made of her a human being of some complexity. None of the *serrana* ballads throws any light upon the serrana's background; the emphasis in them all is placed upon her sexual appetites, and we only guess that she kills in order to prevent the victims of her lust reporting her. For a ballad this is enough; the plot of a play, of course, demands much more. Lope provided dramatic detail by supplying convincing motivation and he used the traditional *serrana* to explore the theme of the aggrieved woman.[1]

Whether the *Romance de la serrana de la Vera* was partly based on a historical happening is impossible now to say. By the seventeenth century most traditional ballads had become an almost indivisible amalgam of fact and literary embellishment. And in many cases the incident which initially inspired the original ballad had receded into the forgotten past. But if there did once exist a woman who earned the title of the *serrana de la Vera*, Lope's direct source was, none the less, the literary one. The same is probably true of the highwaywoman in his *auto, La venta de la zarzuela*. The original *romance* has not survived but its former existence is indicated by the glosses *a lo divino* to which it gave rise.[2] Some basis of historical fact seems likely to have inspired the ballad, but, as with all ballads, a few years would have made the imaginative, literary reality the only living one.

So far as the rebel who does not resort to banditry is concerend, there is no need to look for a concrete source. The theme of the

[1] The female bandit of the stage subsequently entered the world of popular balladry. Durán in his *Romancero general* II, under 'Romances vulgares que tratan de valentías, guapezas y desafueros' prints two such ballads – 'Espinela' (B.A.E. XVI, no. 1330. pp. 365–7) and 'Doña Victoria Acevedo' (No. 1327, pp. 359–61).

[2] One of these is included in Juan López de Ubeda's *Cancionero y vergel de plantas* (Alcalá de Henares, 1588). See Menéndez Pelayo, *Estudios sober el teatro de Lope de Vega*, I (*Edición nacional de las obras completas de Menéndez Pelayo*, XXIX, 1949), 119–22.

persecuted maiden is, as Mario Praz remarks,[1] as old as the world. And in a society where arranged marriages were still the rule, what more likely context for such persecution than the forced match? The other two principles behind the girl who rebels against her parents' choice of a husband are equally old: that of the unevenness of the course of true love and that of the ruthlessness of the woman in love. The second was, for love's great theoretician, Ovid, the essential difference between woman's love and man's. As far as the persecuted maiden is concerned, Marta *la piadosa* is the Golden-Age version of Samuel Richardson's Clarissa; at least Marta is a potential Clarissa. Their fates are different because they belong, not only to different literary genres but, more important, to different worlds of artistic sensibility. Marta's sly intriguing is a product of that part of the Italian *novella* tradition which Spain's less bawdy standards allowed it to accept; the flight from home of her more forthright sisters is an alternative resort which occurred naturally to minds accustomed to the atmosphere of feminine mobility conjured up in the chivalresque and Byzantine novels. Clarissa, on the other hand, is the heroine of the new romantic sensibility of the eighteenth century, whose duty it was to sigh and suffer and who was to invade almost every realm of the arts from the Gothic novel to the opera and Victorian melodrama. However, if Richardson and the Spanish dramatists resolved their plots in different ways, their theme and their message were the same. All condemned the forced marriage and that concept of woman as a marketable commodity on which the forced marriage was based.[2]

While it is probable that the persecuted maiden theme needed no direct source, there were precedents which might have influenced the dramatists in that they made the theme to some extent fashionable. In the case of Lope's *La discreta enamorada* the influence

---

[1] 'The shadow of the divine Marquis', *The Romantic Agony*, Chap. III, trans. A. Davidson (London, 1951), 95 and *passim*.

[2] For a discussion of the theme of property marriage in *Clarissa Harlowe*, see Christopher Hill's excellent re-assessment of the novel in his aricle 'Clarissa Harlowe and her times', included in his *Puritanism and Revolution* (London, 1958), 367–94.

of one of Boccaccio's stories is easily discernible,[1] although Lope has refashioned the tale quite considerably, transforming the heroine, a woman married against her will to a man of humbler birth and determined to take a lover who is her social equal, into a young girl who avoids such a catastrophe by scheming to marry the man she loves. The story of a maiden who flees from home to escape marriage is found in Molza,[2] while the influence of Bandello's tale of Romeo and Juliet[3] was probably greater than the two extant Spanish stage adaptations (Lope's *Castelvines y Monteses* and Rojas's *Los bandos de Verona*) would indicate. Lastly, of course, there was Cervantes's brilliant *novela ejamplar, El celoso estremeño*, published a year or two before Tirso wrote his *Marta la piadosa*, which illustrates so eloquently the folly of parents who dispose of their daughters without thought for the girls' happiness. Whatever the influences upon the theatre, however, it was the theatre itself which popularized the theme in Spain, and in its turn it entered the body of popular ballads.[4]

The 'mujer esquiva'

The relationship of the woman who shuns love and marriage to the feminist debates of medieval and Renaissance literature has been pointed out by Barbara Matulka.[5] The theme of female morality first appeared in the Spanish drama early on in Juan del Encina's *Égloga de tres pastores*, where Fileno attacks women with the traditional arguments of the misogynist and Cardonio replies in their defence. It re-occurs in Sánchez de Badajoz's *Farsa del matrimonio*, in Álvarez de Ayllón's *Comedia Tibalda* and in Gil Vicente's *Auto de la Sibila Casandra*. These plays echoed the enormous interest aroused by the subject in Spain in the fifteenth century,

---

[1] Day III.3. See C. B. Bourland, 'Boccaccio and the Decameron in Castillian and Catalan literature', *RHi* XII (1905), 91–4.
[2] The circumstances here are rather specialized since the prospective husband is the girl's father.
[3] *Novelle* II, 9.
[4] See Durán *Romancero general* II, no 1327 B.A.E. XVI, 359–61, and nos. 1287 and 1288, pp. 293–7.
[5] 'The Feminist theme in the drama of the *Siglo de Oro*', *Comparative Literature Series*, Columbia University.

inspired largely by Boccaccio's *Corbaccio*, which gave rise to similar works of condemnation, like the Arcipreste de Talavera's *El corbacho* and, in greater number, to works in defence of women such as Alonso de Cartagena's *Libro de las mujeres ilustres*, Rodríguez de la Cámara's *Triunfo de las donas*, Diego de Valera's *Defensa de virtuosas mugeres* and Álvaro de Luna's *Libro de las virtuosas e claras mugeres*. Miss Matulka traces the use made of the debate in a handful of *esquiva* plays and shows how the champions of women on the Spanish stage are protagonists in the surviving controversy concerning the specific merits and defects of the sexes. So far as her article goes it can be accepted, with certain reservations. Her argument, however, rests on a false premise, for she states that 'this feminist theme usually takes up the age-old controversy of the superiority of men or women by presenting as the leading character a lady who is a *Siglo de Oro* version of the 'Belle dame sans mercy' who has read of the deceptions of men and the evils which women have suffered through love, and has vowed never to fall a victim to passion but instead sets out to avenge women of their male betrayers'.[1] The *mujer esquiva*, in other words, was created to allow the Spanish dramatists to carry the feminist theme on to the stage. But in the majority of the *esquiva* plays the heroine's disdain is not provoked by desire for vengeance on men, nor is it the result of her studies. Furthermore the feminist debate itself is, in most cases, never mentioned nor even echoed, while the woman who demands 'equal rights for her sisters' is the odd exception, not the rule. Miss Matulka's argument certainly applies to plays like Lope's *La vengadora de las mujeres*, Calderón's *Afectos de odio y amor*, Zorrilla's *Sin honra no hay amistad* and Juan Vélez de Guevara's *Encontráronse dos arroyuelos*. It does not apply to the female bandits who are *esquivas before* they are dishonoured; it does not apply to Lope's *Los milagros del desprecio*, *El valiente Céspedes* or *La moza de cántaro;* nor does it apply to a host of other plays including Turia's *La belígera española*, Tirso's *El burlador de Sevilla*, nor even Moreto's *El desdén con el desdén*. In the plays the origin of the heroines' *esquivez* varies widely within the spectrum of vanity and pride. Some resent the idea of subjecting themselves to a man, others are so mannish that

[1] *Ibid.* 2.

the very notion of love and marriage is anathema to them. Some think no man worthy of them, while for others to fall in love is folly for men and women alike. Occasionally (Serafina and Belisa, for example), the motive is [peculiarly eccentric. I do not wish to deny the importance of the feminist controversy in the formation of the *esquiva* plays; merely to suggest that the figure of the *mujer esquiva* is not just a vehicle for the dramatization of a particular literary theme and that Miss Matulka, by trying to apply her thesis too strictly, has given an incomplete and rather oversimplified view of a complex phenomenon. Her article leaves the crucial question unanswered and at the same time fails to take into consideration several important points. The question is this: why, after centuries of discussion about the merits and demerits of women, does the feminist theme suddenly burgeon into a female revolt against love and marriage? Why does it not remain a theoretical discussion as in the early theatre? In other words, where did the *esquiva* come from, and why did she become a popular dramatic type?

The *esquiva* was not new to Spain with the theatre of the late 1590s. The two great influences on Spanish secular literature of the sixteenth century were the culture of the Italian Renaissance and the medieval concept of courtly love (by now modified first by Petrarch and then the Neo-platonists). The latter was built around the image of the unattainable, unresponsive mistress; indeed it depended on her, for the suffering necessary to perfect love rested on the supposition that that love was unrequited or at least unfulfilled. The *dueño* of the *cancioneros*, of the sentimental novel, of the poetry of Garcilaso and Herrera, had to seem immune to her lover's pleas, and she is addressed in terms of snow, ice, rock and marble which refuse to be melted by the ardour of his passion. The reason for her *esquivez* is rarely given because it is unimportant, a necessary pose; motives, however, the theatre could readily supply. For more specific examples of *esquivez* we have to look no further than the classical literature revived with the Renaissance, Ovid's *Metamorphoses* offers many of them. First, Diana, the virgin goddess, goddess of the moon, who when asked at the age of three by her father Zeus what gift she would like, requested eternal virginity. Then Athena/Minerva, who repelled the advances of all who wished to marry her. Daphne, says Ovid, replied to her father's request for grandchildren with these words: 'da mihi perpetua, genitor carissime . . . , virginitate frui, while Proserpina too hoped to remain a virgin. The crow who warned the raven against informing on Coronis of Larissa was once a disdainful beauty whom Diana saved from rape by turning her into a bird. Procris, disillusioned by her husband Cephalus's deceitfulness, conceived a loathing for all men, while Atalanta tried to rid herself of insistent suitors by imposing harsh terms upon them. Venus, according to Ovid, had no power over the wood nymph Pomona whose only passion was her garden, and the tale of Anaxarete who for hardheartedness was turned into stone did not succeed in moving her. Arethusa, who thought it wicked to please men's eyes, invoked Dictynna (another version of Diana, the moon goddess) when chased by Alpheus and was transformed into a stream. Finally of course there were the Amazons who rebelled *en masse* against love and marriage and enjoyed the freedom of an all-female society.[1] The evidence that the dramatists were familiar with these classical myths and had them in mind as they wrote, is overwhelming. The Amazon plays themselves reveal the attraction this widespread legend held, while it would be impossible to to count and tedious to relate how many times the disdainful heroines invoke the memory of Penthesilea, Menalipe and other famous Amazon queens, and above all, the goddess of chastity, Diana. Descriptions like that of Calderon's Cristerna are a theatrical commonplace,

> no sólo pues de Diana
> en la venatoria escuela
> discípula creció; pero
> aun en la altivez severa,
> con que de Venus y Amor
> el blando yugo desprecia.
>
> (Act I, B.A.E. IX, 100b)

Not neglected either are those women less commonly associated

---

[1] Their story was told by a host of historians and writers, amongst them Apollodorus, Diodorus Siculus, Justin and Herodotus.

with *esquivez*. Diana in *El desdén con el desdén* has surrounded herself with pictures of Daphne fleeing from Apollo and also of

> Anaxarte convertida
> en piedra por no querer;
> Aretusa en fuentecilla,
> que el tierno llanto de Alfeo
> paga en lágrimas esquivas.
>
> (Act I, B.A.E., xxxix, 2a)[1]

while Casandra in *Hacer remedio el dolor*, also Moreto's in part, was formerly called the Minerva of Milan, as she admits at the beginning of the play:[2]

> Comúnmente de Milán
> me llamaban la Minerva.

In the courtly love tradition, therefore, and in classical literature, the theatre had a ready-made *esquiva* figure – a figure who does not belong to the traditional medieval controversy of the sexes. The Amazons and Diana and her disciples were feminists, but they were not part of the feminist theme in its narrow literary sense. Add to these the most famous contemporary example of the woman who shuns marriage and is equivocal even about love – Elizabeth the virgin queen of England – and there would seem to be inspiration enough for the creation of the type of the *mujer esquiva* as portrayed in the Golden-Age drama. But this does not explain why she was created at this particular point and why in *Spanish* literature. The courtly-love tradition was centuries old; even the vogue for Greco-Roman culture was well-established by the end of the sixteenth century. Both influences were as strongly felt in other countries. The circumstances were admittedly propitious: the continuing hold of the courtly-love theme upon the imagination and the enthusiasm for classical revivals; the medieval feminist debate which had taken on new life with the Renaissance; the new atmosphere of comparative tolerance towards women which resulted from the teachings of Erasmus; all these contributed. But something was needed to act as precipitator, and that something was

---

[1] Diego Hurtado de Mendoza has a poem on the myth of Anaxarte, *Carta en redondillas*. It is mentioned also by Garcilaso, *Canción* v.

[2] To be found in *Esc.* xi.

Lope de Vega. The *mujer esquiva* was his creation; she is one of the few manifestations of the *mujer varonil* who do not appear in the pre-Lope theatre. Gil Vicente's Casandra is the only possible antecedent, and the historical gap is too wide and the circumstances too different for the *Auto* to have been more than an extremely tenuous influence. Lope, as his treatment of the *mujer varonil* in all her forms indicates, was interested to an extraordinary degree in the subject of woman, and her position *vis-á-vis* love, marriage and society. Furthermore, he had passionately-held views on these matters. He sermonizes about them in a way no other dramatist does. His vehemence and sincerity are so great that one cannot but think that something spurred him into action. No one protests so much unless there is something to protest about. And I cannot be persuaded that his indignation was provoked by a handful of literary heroines or by a distant recalcitrant Queen. The clue, I think, lies in his dedication of *La vengadora de las mujeres* to Señora Fenisa Camila,[1] who was obviously, from what he says, a real-life *esquiva* who expressed a dislike of men and refused to marry. It seems she even thought of herself as the avenger of woman's wrongs, 'previene dirigirla a v.m., como a persona a quien más justamente tocaba el título'. Lope had evidently talked to her and she had been prepared to argue her case: 'Mas responderá v.m. que Dios, habiéndole creado lo halló solo y que le dio la mujer por compañía'. Fenisa Camila was not the only woman with such views. Lope's words to Señora Marcia Leonarda (the poetic pseudonym of Doña Maria de Nevares y Santoyo) in the dedication of *Las mujeres sin hombres*: ' . . . no le ofrezco su historia para que con su ejemplo desee serlo, antes bien para que conozca que la fuerza con que fueron vencidas tiene por disculpa la misma naturaleza', apart from being a piece of persuasive personal propaganda, indicate that he thought the message of his play needed to be brought home. That the arguments of the feminist heroines of the theatre were used by women in real life is obvious from Maria de Zayas's preface to the first part of her novels, and they are, on the whole, arguments which are not used by women's male champions:

---

[1] Quoted in full at the beginning of Chap. v.

. . . si esta materia de que nos componemos los hombres y las mujeres
. . . no tiene más nobleza en ellos que en nosotras . . . ¿qué razón hay
para que ellos sean sabios y presuman que nosotras no podemos serlo?
Esto no tiene a mi parecer más respuesta que su impiedad o tiranía en
encerrarnos, y no darnos maestros; y asi la verdadera causa de no ser
las mujeres doctas no es defecto del caudal, sino falta de la aplicación,
porque si en nuestra crianza como nos ponen el cambray en las almo-
hadillas y los dibuxos en el bastidor, nos dieran libros y preceptores,
fuéramos tan aptas, para los puestos y para las cátedras como los
hombres.

The evidence therefore suggests that Fenisa Camila was one of a
number of women in Spain at the time who, as a result of their
reading, decided that their sex had been hard done by. A very small
minority, certainly, but a minority with the intellectual curiosity
that led them to think, read and inquire in the first place, the intelligence which allowed them to assess what they read, the mental
stamina which enabled them to cling to their views, and the
eloquence which meant they could express them. That their
feminism should have taken the form of a revolt against love and
marriage is psychologically consistent. Their need to assert themselves would have been translated quite naturally into a gesture of
defiance against the institutions which curtailed their independence most effectively. We know that women sometimes parti-
cipated in the *academias*, even ran some of them. The position of
woman, the feminist theme in other words, must have been one
of the favourite topics of discussion.

The feminist debate, therefore, *is* behind the *mujer esquiva* plays
but not in quite the way Miss Matulka indicated. The *mujer
esquiva* of the drama, I suggest, is not so much the extension of the
literary theme of feminism but more the reaction against a contemporary aspect of feminism which was, within a restricted
circle, very much alive. Against the background of the traditional
debate and of Erasmian influence, Lope reacted to the feminism of
his female contemporaries (a feminism born of that debate and that
influence) by depicting their *esquivez* on the stage, giving it the
motives (vanity and pride) he thought were the true ones and
finally making it submit to the laws of Nature. The literary

esquivas of old were but grist to his mill; he drew on them for plots and situations, and for arguments to put into his heroine's mouth. When he wanted his characters themselves to argue his theme, he had the formalized feminist debate to refer to. His heroine became a convention, adopted by other dramatists. Both he and they used her in a variety of ways, employing her *esquivez* now as their main theme, now as an insignificant incident. As a result the plots in which she appears cover a much wider range of subject, treatment and psychological motivation than Miss Matulka allowed. The plays are held together as a group not by the controversy of the sexes but by the constantly recurring figure of the *mujer esquiva*. This is why the *esquiva* herself is the real key to the phenomenon of the *mujer esquiva* plays.

The Amazon, the leader, the warrior

In their depiction of the Amazons the Golden-Age dramatists were borrowing from the legends of classical mythology. There was a whole host of sources they could apply to for details and information. Fray Baltasar de Vitoria in his *Teatro de los dioses de la gentilidad*[1] refers his readers to Virgil, Plato, who affirmed that shortly before the age in which he lived the Amazons flourished, Hipocrates, Justin and Diodorus Siculus amongst others. Whether the playwrights went straight to the original sources is a moot point. But it is likely that for convenience and speed they consulted digests of classical knowledge such as the *Teatro de los dioses* of Fray Baltasar himself, the *Filosofía secreta* of Pérez de Moya (1585), or the *Silva de varia lección* of Pedro Mejía (1540). Mejía's book, which enjoyed tremendous popularity and renown both in Spain and abroad in the sixteenth and a large part of the seventeenth centuries,[2] includes most of the information the dramatists would have needed. As well as mentioning the classical authorities on the historical truth of the Amazons, Mejía recounts their origins and conquests, their power and fame, their meetings with Hercules,

[1] Part II, VIII (Madrid, 1673), 101ff. The work was published in 1620 with an *aprobación* by Lope.
[2] See Justo García Soriano's introduction to the edition published in Madrid 1933 by the Sociedad de bibliófilos españoles.

Theseus and Alexander, and finally their decline. He precedes his account with a passage eulogizing women in general, and declaring them superior to men in every respect, except in military prowess.[1] This is because war entails cruelty and fierceness, for which women were not made, and even to this rule there are exceptions, amongst whom the most famous are the Amazons. Further proof of the impact made upon the sixteenth-century imagination by the Amazons is the tale invented by Franciso de Orellana that there were Amazons in the New World,[2] and also the *Romance de la Reina de las Amazonas* which was published in the *Tercera parte* of the *Silva* of Zaragoza 1550;

> Por los montes de Carasco – que están en el medio día,
> vi asomar una bandera – de incomparable valía,
> de raso verde y morado – trenada de argentería,
> con unas franjas de oro – también la cordonería,
> el asta era de marfil – a donde puesta venía
> con un mote rodeada – que desta suerte decía:
> 'Donde falta la ventura – no aprovecha la valentía.'
> Trecientas damas de guarda – esta bandera traía
> con sus flechas y carcaxes – tocadas de gallardía,
> con unas escofias de oro – a guisa de Lombardía,
> las sayas de tela eran – poco más de la rodilla,
> en trecientos unicornios – cabalgando a la su guisa,
> tras estas vienen sus damas –siguiendo aquesta devisa
> de altibajo ataviadas, – ansí como convenía
> encima de dromedarios – con muy grande flechería,
> y en mitad de las mil damas – Pantasilea venía,
> reina de las Amazonas, – la cual iba en la conquista
> de los griegos y troyanos, – la cual a Héctor seguía
> con un arco y un escudo, – más que el sol cuando salía
> y una guirnalda de aljófar – trenzada con pedrería;
> la cual como llegó a Troya – Troya con mucha alegría,
> a ella y a todas sus damas – con Paris la rescebía,
> la cual hizo tantas cosas – que apenas las contaría

---

[1] Part I, x and xi. It is interesting to learn in the introduction that Mejía was influenced by the ideas of Erasmus and Luis Vives.

[2] Hence the appearance in the drama of American Amazons. Otis H. Green's article on the Pizarro trilogy of Tirso is referred to in Chap. vi, p. 175, n. 4.

aquel gran poeta Homero – que desta guerra escrebía,
aunque nada aprovechara – su ardid y valentía,
pues do la fortuna falta – el esfuerzo fallescía.[1]

W. J. Entwistle thought that the Amazon ballad began its career
in France and spread from there to Spain and Northern Italy.[2] It
eventually reached Czechoslovakia, Yugoslavia, Greece, Rumania
and the Ukraine. A slightly later ballad was *Nabucadnosor y las
Amazonas*, in which the Queen of the Amazons, Sofonisba, suggests to Nebuchadnezzar that they produce a child to be either
King of Babylon or Queen of the Amazons.[3] This is a *romance
artístico* and is attributed by Durán to the last thirty years of the
sixteenth century.

The Amazons did not merely inspire plays specifically about
their own legendary adventures. They lurk in the background of
all those plays which depict a valiant female leader or warrior. So
also do other heroines of classical antiquity. Isabella in Lope's
Triunfo de la humildad names Penthesilea, Hippolyta, Sicratea, Amala-
funta and Camilla to prove that women too can fight.[4] When
Estela in Lope's *Bernardo del Carpio* claims she will be 'otra Semíramis nueva', Bernardo proclaims her a 'valiente amazona'.[5] Irene
in Tirso's *La república al revés* bewails the fact that instead of a
'Penélope tejedora' she has had to be a 'Semíramis guerrera'.[6] The
heroines of Dionisa in Cubillo's *Añasco el de Talavera* are Zenobia,
Artemis, Penthesilea and Tomires. *La Baltasara* in the play of that
name by Luis Vélez, Coello and Rojas, is called by the Saladin a
'Palas en guerra'; she calls herself 'otra Pallas [sic]' and 'Ebadnes
nueva'.[7] In the same play the Devil calls Leonor Pallas and she also
uses the name herself.[8] Gila in Luis Vélez's *La serrana de la Vera* is
'otra Semíramis, / otra Evadnes y Palas española'.[9] In Luis Vélez's

---

[1] Reprinted by Menéndez Pelayo in his Appendix to Wolf and Hofmann's *Primavera y flor de romances* II, 214.
[2] *European Balladry* (Oxford, 1951), 274.
[3] Reprinted by Durán from the *Primavera y flor de romances, Romancero general* I, No.
448, B.A.E. x, 297.
[4] Act II, Acad.N. x, 87b.   [5] Act III, Acad.N. III, 669a.
[6] Act I, N.B.A.E. IX, 84a.   [7] Act I, *Esc.*, I, ff5v and 6r.
[8] Act III, *ibid*, f.11 verso.   [9] Act II, *Teatro antiguo español*, I (Madrid, 1916), 60.

Más pesa el rey que la sangre María Coronel is called a 'nueva Evadnes'.[1] Both Isabel and Antona in Tirso's *Antona García* are called Semíramis.[2] The list is almost endless. Of the semi-historical figures, Zenobia Queen of Palmyra was a great favourite, though only one major dramatist – Calderón – wrote a play entirely about her.[3] She was dealt with by Boccaccio in his *De claris mulieribus*,[4] the Renaissance text-book on famous women, which was translated into Spanish in the fifteenth century as *Las mujeres ilustres*, printed in 1494 in Zaragoza and again in 1528 in Seville.[5] Together with Boccaccio's *De casibus, De claris mulieribus* was 'referred to as authoritative and [was] quoted side by side with Genesis and the works of St Augustine'.[6] Amongst others it includes the stories of Semiramis, Minerva, Orithya and Antiope, Procris, Penthesilea, Camilla, Sappho, Venturia, Irene, and Pope Joan, all of whom would qualify as *varoniles*. Most popular of all the ancient leader/warriors, however, was Semiramis. As Professor Ashcom has pointed out[7] she was not newly discovered by Spaniards with the Renaissance, but had long been a favourite of Spanish writers including the chroniclers. She is mentioned in the *General Estoria*, in Lucas de Tuy's *Crónica de España* and in the *Sumas de Historia Troyana*. (The detail that seems to have impressed the chroniclers most was that, according to tradition, it was she who first invented trousers.) Not only were several plays written about her in the Golden Age (Virués's *La gran Semíramis*, Vélez's *La corte del demonio*[8] and Calderón's *La hija del aire*), but few *mujeres varoniles*

---

[1] Act II, B.A.E. XLV, 102b.

[2] Act II, N.B.A.E. IV, 628b and 632b.

[3] La Barrera ('Índice de títulos', 535) mention two other Zenobia plays, one an eighteenth century translation by Ameno, the other an anonymous and unpublished sixteenth-century work.

[4] Chap. XCVIII.

[5] See Caroline B. Bourland, 'Boccaccio and the Decameron in Castilian and Catalan Literature', 12. The translator is unknown.

[6] *Ibid.* 18.

[7] In an article à propos of Carmen Bravo-Villasante's *La mujer vestida de hombre en el teatro español*. (*Siglos XVI–XVII*), called 'Concerning "La mujer en hábito de hombre in the *comedia*"', *HR* XXVIII(1960), 43–62. The article is an attack on the inaccuracies of Señor Bravo-Villasante's work and an assessment of her conclusions concerning the origins of what she calls 'la mujer heroica-guerrera'.

[8] An extraordinary play which concentrates entirely upon the love affair between

survive three acts without either referring to or being compared to 'la gran Semíramis'.

For the female leader and warrior, of course, there was a multiplicity of prototypes. Boiardo's *Orlando innamorato* and Ariosto's *Orlando furioso* offered 'la vergine Marfisa'[1] and Bradamante; Marfisa wields her sword for pleasure, Bradamante because she is compelled to protect herself in her long search for her lover Ruggero; both types appear in the Spanish drama under other names. Sometimes they even appear under their own names, in plays of the epic-chivalresque kind, like Cervantes's *La casa de los celos* (Marfisa) and Calderón's *El jardín de Falerina* (Marfisa and Bradamante). Neither Marfisa nor Bradamante themselves appear to have been adopted by the early Spanish ballad-makers, though Bradamante is the subject of a *romance erudito* by Lucas Rodríguez called *Bradamante mata al moro Urgel*.[2] The two women reappear in Italy as Clorinda and Herminia in Tasso's *Gerusalemme liberata* and Lope in his turn reproduced the Marfisa – Clorinda figure in his *La Jerusalén conquistada*.[3] Ismenia, Princess of Limeria, is less of a virago than the other two and is subjected to the normal Lopesque treatment: she falls in love. These stanzas from Ismenia's monologue sum up Lope's view of womanhood.

> Como me ha de querer, quien oy me ha visto
> Teñida en sangre despejar vn muro
> De Turca gente, y que el furor resisto
> Con varonil furor aspero y duro;
> Si en vez de seda, y oro, azero visto,
> Y tal ferozidad mostrar procuro,
> Aunque diga que soy mi propio nombre,
> Alfonso no querra muger tan hombre.

Semiramis and her son, while in the background Lucifer and Jonah (whale and all) battle for Nineveh. Semiramis's *varonilidad*, her prowess as leader and warrior are hardly mentiond.

[1] Ariosto, Canto XVIII, Stanza XCIX.
[2] It appeared in the sixteenth-century *Romancero historiado*; it was reprinted in Durán's *Romancero general* I, B.A.E. X, 276 (no. 422). Durán assigns it to the last thirty years of the century and thinks it unlikely that the *romance* had any popular currency.
[3] Published 1609.

Pero no digo bien, que quando diga
Como muger mi pena, y como amante,
Yo tendrè la blandura à que me obliga,
Que buelve e[n] cera amor qualquier diama[n]te:
Yo mostrarè que soy piadosa amiga,
No con la voz sonora y arrogante,
Sino quebrada, enferma, dulce y tierna
Tal que se duela de mi pena eterna.[1]

And here Lope had to respect the demands of neither plot nor *vulgo*. In addition to these chivalresque heroines there was Virgil's Camilla,[2] called by Menéndez Pelayo 'una amazona itálica que a su vez sirvió de tipo a las Bradamantes, Marfisas, Clorindas y demás mujeres belicosas que con tanta frecuencia aparecen en los poemas caballerescos'.[3] There were also the female warriors of Bohemia described by Pope Pius II in his history of Bohemia, and the Gothic female warriors who appear in the life of the Emperor Claudius II and who were believed to be descended from the Amazons.[4] All these women were well known to the Spanish dramatists. Professor Ashcom thinks the possibility of the influence of medieval French literature should not be under-estimated: Aye d'Avignon in Nanteuil's *Tristan* fought under the name of Gaudion; Ide in *Huon de Bordeaux* fought in the army of the Holy Roman Emperor. But I have found no evidence that these women had been heard of in Spain and Professor Ashcom offers none.[5] One French warrior whose story was certainly familiar was Joan of Arc. She is mentioned by Mejía and was the subject of several plays, such as Zamora's *La poncella de Orleans* and *La poncella de Francia*[6] (attributed to Lope).

Of course, as far as woman leaders were concerned, the Spanish playwrights did not have to look further than their country's

---

[1] *Libro undécimo*, Ed. J. de Entrambasaguas (Madrid, 1950–54), II, 22, lines 1–16.
[2] *Aeneid* XI.
[3] Introduction to *Las mujeres sin hombres*, Acad VI, xxxi.
[4] Mentioned by Pedro Mejía, *Silva de varia lección*, XI.
[5] Cf. Rudolf Schevill, 'Although Lope may have known something of the French language, I find practically no evidence of any acquaintance with contemporary French literature'. *The Dramatic Art of Lope de Vega* (New York, 1964), 71.
[6] Performed between 15 December 1635 and 10 January 1636. See Shergold and Varey, 'Some palace performances . . . ', *BHS* XL, (1963), 234.

history for inspiration. Doña Jimena who ruled Valencia for four years after the Cid's death;[1] Doña Urraca who governed Zamora; Doña María de Molina, regent during the infancy of her son; and, of course, Isabel herself, all proved woman's capacity for leadership. Isabel, indeed, enjoys in the plays the status of a modern Semiramis or Penthesilea. Nor did the playwrights have to look beyond their own age. Philip II made a woman, his sister Margarita, regent of the Netherlands; Isabel Clara Eugenia governed Flanders upon the death of her husband; Margaret of Savoy became governor and vice-reine of Portugal in 1633; Catherine de Medici became regent of France on the death of her husband, Henry II, in 1559 and achieved a notoriety which spread throughout Europe. Even Ricardo de Turia's Doña Mencía de Nidos had a historical existence, though much elaborated in his play. She was a 'matrona respectable' who urged the Governor of Concepción, Francisco de Villagrá, to resist the rebellious *araucanos*.[2] England's Queen Elizabeth, as daughter of Ana Bolena, as a potential wife for Philip II, as the staunch defender of Anglicanism, as one of Spain's strongest rivals and as the Virgin Queen who resisted all persuasion to marry, surely made a profound impression on popular imagination in Spain. It is unfortunate that Cervantes in the favourable picture he paints of Elizabeth in his *novela ejemplar, La española inglesa*, gives such inadequate information about how the Queen really appeared to Spanish eyes. Her 'I know I have the body of a weak and feeble woman but I have the heart and stomach of a king' speech to the troops at Tilbury in 1588 might have served as the text for half a dozen variations on the *mujer varonil* theme. Neither Catherine de Medici nor Elizabeth, as far as I can discover, figure in the Golden-Age drama.

The most extraordinary woman leader of the time, however, is the protagonist of Calderon's *Afectos de odio y amor* and his auto *La protestación de la fe* – Queen Christina of Sweden. Christina might have been born to prove that the *mujer varonil* of the Spanish

---

[1] None of the ballads about Jimena, however, mentions this part of her story. We are told only that Rodrigo left all his lands and possessions to her. See Durán, *Romancero general* I, nos. 897 and 898, B.A.E. x, 568 and 569.

[2] See C. Fernández Duro, *La mujer española en Indias*, 23.

drama was not merely an imaginary creation. Her father, who died when she was only six years old, left instructions that she should be given the physical and intellectual education of a Renaissance prince. The product of this education was an extremely mannish woman, half blue-stocking, half tomboy, who wore her hair cropped short and was rarely to be seen in a skirt. Juan Pimental de Prado, the nephew of Spain's ambassador to the Swedish court in the 1650s, wrote of her,

. . . no tiene nada de mujer, sino el sexo. Su voz parece de hombre, como también el gesto; venla cada día a caballo, y aunque como las mujeres suelen, sin embargo, se está de modo que a no verla muy de cerca se dijera ser caballero muy plático,[1]

while Barrionuevo said of her, 'Dícese hace mal a un caballo, como si fuera un hombre.'[2] According to Carlos Clavería,[3] although some news of Christina had filtered through to Spain before, she did not really excite the interest of Spaniards until her abdication in 1654 and her conversion. This interest was very largely due to the conviction that Philip IV and his ambassador had played an important part in her renunciation of Lutheranism. Calderón's *auto* was written to celebrate the event, and for presentation in Madrid on Corpus Christi 1656. In the *comedia* (written for performance in 1657) Calderón dealt with Christina with considerable dramatic licence. The Queen, while averse to marriage, was by no means averse to men and by no means a champion of her own sex. Rather, she was notoriously unchaste and much preferred the society of men to that of women. García de Illán, who accompanied the Queen to Hamburg, wrote in a letter to Lorenzo Ramírez de Prado on 3 September 1654, that she was 'poco aficionada a las mujeres'.[4] And, of course, Cristerna's ultimate subjection in the play is entirely fictitious. Calderón in other words

[1] M. Lasso de la Vega, 'Don Antonio Pimental de Prado, embajador a Cristina de Suecia', *Hispania* I, 3 (1941), 61.

[2] *Avisos* I, ed. A. Paz y Melia (B.A.E. CCXXI, Madrid, 1968), 58a.

[3] 'Gustavo Adolfo y Cristina de Suecia, vistos por los españoles de su tiempo', II, Clavileño 18 (1952), 17–27.

[4] Quoted by Clavería, *ibid.*, 19. This is not of course necessarily incompatible with the Lesbianism she was suspected of.

took a contemporary newsworthy figure and superimposed upon it the conventional framework of *esquivez*, love and marriage.[1]

The possibility of Cleopatras is as old as monarchy itself or at least as old as the recognition of female sovereignty, but all these forceful women of Spanish history and of sixteenth and seventeenth-century European politics helped create, and contributed to, a living tradition of female leadership. Filling as they did the normal masculine role, they were the *mujeres varoniles* of real life, exceptions to the norm understandably found more often within royal families or the ranks of the aristocracy, where powerful personalities have always had greater opportunities to blossom into influence and eccentricity by the very fact of their wealth and power. It is impossible to assess accurately the extent of their influence on the *mujer varonil* of the theatre, but this influence cannot be ignored. For as famous exceptions to the norm, they could have had a disproportionate effect on the attitudes of both playwrights and audience. Spain also, of course, had her historical or semi-historical *guerreras*; women like *la varona castellana* who defeated Alfonso I of Aragon in single combat, Doña Catalina de Céspedes, *la Barbuda*, Antona García and María Coronel. That the concept of the warrior maiden was a familiar one in the Peninsula is shown by the spread of the romance of *La doncella que va a la guerra* of which Menéndez Pelayo lists ten versions.[2] The Castillian version, called *Don Martinos*, goes as follows,

> Estaba un día un buen viejo – sentado en un campo al sol.
> – Pregonadas son las guerras – de Francia con Aragón . . .
> ¿Cómo las haré yo, triste – viejo, cano y pecador? –
> De allí fue para su casa – echando una maldición.

---

[1] The discrepancy between the play and the historical reality has worried some critics, including Clavería, to the point where in order to explain it, they have concluded it must have been written years before it was performed, when very little was known about Christina (see Clavería, *ibid.* 22–3). I do not follow their logic. Calderon could have been taking deliberate liberties with his material.

[2] In his *Suplemento* to Wolf and Hofmann's *Primavera y flor de romances* (Madrid, 1923), III, 121–2. See Américo Castro's essay 'La mujer que fue a la guerra' in *Lengua, enseñanza y literatura (esbozos)*, (Madrid, 1924). Castro sings the praises of the *Romancero's* more energetic heroines, but makes the following proviso: 'Lejos de mi ánimo estaría buscar en el Romancero precedentes al femenismo moderno' , 266.

– ¡Reventares tú, María, – por medio del corazón;
que pariste siete hijas – y entre ellas ningun varón! –
La más chiquita de ellas – salió con buena razón.
– No la maldigáis, mi padre, – no la maldigades, non;
que yo iré a servir al Rey – en hábitos de varón.
Compraráisme vos, mi padre, – calcetas y buen jubón;
daréisme las vuestras armas, – vuestro caballo trotón.
– Conoceránte en los ojos, – hija, que muy bellos son,
– Yo los bajaré a la tierra – cuando pase algun varón.
– Conoceránte en los pechos – que asoman por el jubón.
– Esconderélos, mi padre; – al par de mi corazón.
– Conceránte en los pies, – que muy menudinos son.
– Pondréme las vuestras botas – bien rellenas de algodón.
¿Cómo me he de llamar, padre, – cómo me he de llamar yo?
– Don Martinos, hija mía, – que así me llamaba yo. –
Y era en palacio del Rey, – y nadie la conoció,
sino es el hijo del Rey – que della se namoró.
– Tal caballero, mi madre, – doncella me pareció.
– ¿En qué lo conoceis, hijo; – en qué lo conoceis vos?
– En poner el su sombrero – y en abrochar el jubón,
y en poner de las calcetas, – mi Dios, como ella las pon!
– Brindaréisla vos, mi hijo, – para en las tiendas mercar,
si el caballero era hembra – corales querrá llevar. –
El caballero es discreto – y un puñal tomó en la man.
– Los ojos de Don Martinos – roban el alma al mirar.
– Brindaréisla vos, mi hijo, – al par de vos acostar,
si el caballero era hembra, – tal convite non quedrá. –
El caballero es discreto – y echóse sin desnudar.
– Los ojos de Don Martinos – roban el alma al mirar.
– Brindaréisla vos, mi hijo, – a dir con vos a la mar.
Si el caballero era hembra, – él se habrá de acobardar. –
El caballero es discreto, – luego empezara a llorar.
– ¿Tú qué tienes, Don Martinos, – que te pones a llorar?
– Que se me ha muerto mi padre, – y mi madre en eso va;
si me dieran la licencia – fuérala yo a visitar.
– Esa licencia, Martinos, – de tuyo la tienes ya.
Ensilla un caballo blanco, – y en él luego ve a montar. –
Por unas vegas arriba – corre como un gavilán,
por otras vegas abajo – corre sin le divisar.
– Adiós, adiós, el buen Rey, – y su palacio real;

que siete años le serví – doncella de Portugal,
y otros siete le sirviera – si non fuese el desnudar. –
Oyólo el hijo del Rey – de altas torres donde está;
reventó siete caballos – para poderla alcanzar.
Allegando ella a su casa, – todos la van abrazar.
Pidió la rueca a su madre – a ver si sabía filar.
– Deja la rueca, Martinos, – non te pongas a filar;
que si de la guerra vienes, – a la guerra has de tornar.
Ya están aquí tus amores, – los que te quieren llevar.[1]

This ballad, which is found all over Europe, originated, according to Entwistle,[2] in France, and is probably not older than the fifteenth century. There is nothing quite like it in the drama but the *romance* is obviously a significant precedent.

The scholar, the career woman

The learned woman of the drama also had a classical prototype; Minerva was the name of Pallas Athene in her aspect of goddess of wisdom, and stage heroines are often likened to her,

> me di al estudio
> de las naturales letras
> Historia, Filosofía
> y Humanidad; de manera
> que creciendo mi hermosura
> con la opinión de discreta,
> comúnmente de Milán
> me llamaban la Minerva,[3]

Of course, female learning becomes a convention in those plays where the nature of the heroine's *esquivez* makes it a dramatic necessity. In such cases the heroine's disdain of love and marriage or her hatred of men is a cerebral *esquivez* born of her studies. At the same time, I have suggested that it is possible that the figure of the *mujer esquiva* was at the start based on a few real-life examples. For while Minerva could be always used as a neat basis for com-

---

[1] *Suplemento*, III, no. 46, 119–21.
[2] *European Balladry*, 79–80. A very similar ballad is known in China.
[3] Cáncer, Matos y Moreto's *Hacer remedio el dolor*, beginning of Act I.

parison, it is unlikely that the woman scholars of the Golden-Age drama were created in her likeness, and highly likely that they were created in that of a female minority in existence at the time. The very fact that such women would have been an exception means that they would have attracted attention. The use of figures like *la doncella Teodor*, Santa Catalina and Zenobia, certainly the references made to their intellectual gifts – even where these do not figure prominently in the plot – reflect the wave of interest in female education which the Renaissance had set in motion. The fame of Doña Feliciana Enríquez de Guzmán bears witness to the curiosity which such singular women evoked. And, of course, the seventeenth century could not have forgotten Francisca de Nebrija who taught philosophy and rhetoric at Alcala when it was founded. The tale of Isabel *la católica*'s Latin lessons was certainly still current,

> La reina Doña Isabel,
> que a tanta hazaña dio fin
> empieza a estudiar latín,
> y es su preceptora en él
> otra, que por peregrina,
> no hay ingenio que no asombre,
> tanto que olvidan su nombre
> y la llaman *la Latina*.[1]

As for the career women of the theatre, while women like Doña Feliciana and Antonia de Nebrija, in particular the former, are possible sources, it is not necessary to call upon them to explain the incidence of *letradas* and *estudiantes* on the stage. Many of these are merely a variation on the popular *disfraz varonil* motif. The source of the woman who sits in judgment upon her lover or husband is very definitely literary. The origin of the tale in its seventeenth-century dramatic form is a short story by Juan de Timoneda[2] which is in turn an adaptation of one of Boccaccio's.[3] In Timoneda's *patraña*, the offended wife Finea becomes a *regente de caballería* and presides at the law-suit brought against her husband Casiodoro by her father Herodiano. Casiodoro is tortured

---

[1] Tirso's *El amor médico*, Act I, B.A.E. v, 381c.
[2] *El Patrañuelo* (published 1597), no. 15.
[3] *Decameron*, Day II, 9. Lope de Rueda's *Comedia llamada Eufemia* and *Cymbeline* are, much more loosely, based on the same *novella*.

and he confesses the truth about his wife. Finea then begs the King to give Casiodoro the office she holds and this he does on condition that Casiodoro hears all his cases in her presence. In Boccaccio's *novella*, Ginevra does not actually judge the case herself (although she is the superintendent of merchants) but instead persuades the Sultan to compel Ambrogiuolo to admit he lied about Ginevra, and her husband Bernabio to reveal what he did with her. Zabaleta's *La dama corregidor* is the nearest play to the sources, since he dramatizes the whole story of the merchant's wager and the false testimony made against the wife's virtue. Even he is closer to Timoneda than to Boccaccio, however, for he takes from him the details of the desert island, of Casandra's rescue and of the subsequent shipwreck.[1]

As for Jerónima in Tirso's *El amor médico* and Juana in Rojas Zorrilla's *Lo que quería ver el Marqués de Villena*, they seem to me the outcome of a logical progression from the separate themes of professional disguise and female scholarship to the theme of the dedicated professional woman. Sercambi has a story of a girl disguised as a doctor who exposes the queen's paramour masquerading in turn as a woman,[2] but there is no evidence that this had any influence in Spain. Francisca de Nebrija and Feliciana Enríquez de Guzmán probably lent an air of authenticity to the two plays, but there is no reason to believe that the dramatists would not have arrived at the professional woman had these real-life cases never existed.

The 'bella cazadora'

The sources of and influence upon the type of the *bella cazadora* are to a very large extent identical with those which apply to the

---

[1] Caroline B. Bourland points out Timoneda's debt to Boccaccio in 'Boccaccio and the Decameron in Castilian and Catalan literaturé', 84–91, but she does not mention the plays or María de Zayas's *El juez de su causa*.

[2] *Novelle*, no. 4. Durán prints a *romance* by Juan Miguel del Fuego called *La peregrina doctora*, in which the heroine after being abandoned by her husband is given a magic ointment by the Virgin Mary with which she acquires a reputation as a healer. (*Romancero general*, II, nos. 1269 and 1270, B.A.E. XVI, 260–4.) The romance is an adaptation of Zayas's *La perseguida triunfante*. Zayas's *El juez de su causa* also served as the basis for a *romance*, *Don Pedro Juan de la Rosa*. See E. M. Wilson, 'Tradition and change in some late Spanish verse chapbooks', HR XXV (1957), 212–13.

leader and warrior. First however comes the goddess of the hunt herself, Diana. The combination of chastity and the chase as epitomized in her is one that recurs frequently in the drama. So also does the combination of a hatred of men and the chase associated with the Amazons. But Diana and the Amazons were not the only classical *esquivas* who roamed the woods. According to Ovid's *Metamorphoses*, when Procris had been deceived by her husband she fled from home and devoted herself to the pursuits of Diana. Atalanta lived alone in the woodlands after hearing the god's oracle; she had grown to womanhood among a clan of hunters and drawn first blood in the Calydonian boar-hunt. Arethusa's favourite pastime was hunting in the forest, while even Venus, when she fell in love with Adonis, devoted all her attention to the chase with her skirts tucked up as high as her knees. The tradition of the beautiful huntress is so long-established and widespread[1] that it would be pointless to try and trace the process of influence, although it is probably safe to assume that in Europe it begins with Diana herself. The tradition reflects one of the more common psychological reactions of women to their envy of men's greater freedom, and as such it is scarcely surprising that it is as endemic in literature as it is common in life. The popularity of the figure, appearing as she does in contexts as varied as the classical legends and the world of chivalry and medieval romance, Malory's *Morte d'Arthur*,[2] Georges Sand's *Mauprat* and the twentieth-century cinema western, is obviously due to the attractive combination of female beauty and masculine energy. In the Golden-Age drama it was simply excellent theatre, providing the playwright with off-the-peg panache and at the same time the opportunity to put his heroine into masculine clothes without necessarily affecting the plot. It must be remembered too that the huntress was not merely

---

[1] Cf. Boccaccio's description of Zenobia's girlhood: 'They tell us that from childhood she scorned all womanly exercises, and when she had grown up somewhat and become strong she dwelt for the most part in forests and woods and, girding on the quiver, pursued and slew goats and stags with her arrows. Then when she had become stronger, she dared to come to grips with boars and pursued or lay in wait for leopards and lions, killing or capturing them.' *De claris mulieribus*, trans. Guido A. Guarino (New Jersey, 1963), p. 226.

[2] XVIII, 21.

a literary convention. For centuries riding and hunting were the only outdoor sports open to energetic women and often their only means of legitimately escaping the confines of their home. The incentive to achieve momentarily the freedom of men by aping a male sport was very great. However, in the sixteenth century at least, riding and hunting do not seem to have been such a common form of female amusement in Spain as in England. Andrés Muñoz in a letter from Richmond on 16 August 1554 wrote,

El que inventó y compuso los libros de Amadís y otros libros de caballerías desta manera fingiendo aquellos floridos campos, casas de placer y encantamientos, ántes que los descubriese debió sin dubda de ver primero los usos y tan extrañas costumbres que en este reino se costumbran. Porque ¿quien nunca jamas vió en otro reino andar las mugeres cabalgando y solas en sus caballos y palafrenes, y aún á las veces correrlos diestramente y tan seguras como un hombre muy ejercitado en ello?[1]

If Diego Hurtado de Mendoza's cynicism about Diana was shared by men in general in sixteenth-century Spain, there was considerable disincentive to follow her example:

> Señora, la del arco y las saetas
> que anda simpre cazando en despoblado,
> digame por su vida: ¿no ha topado
> quien la meta las manos en las tetas?
> Andando entre las selvas más secretas,
> corriendo trás algún corzo ó venado:
> ¿no ha habido algún pastor desvergonzado
> que le enseñase el son de las gambetas?
> Hará unos milagrones y asquecillos,
> diciendo que a una diosa consegrada
> nadie se atreverá, siendo tan casta;
> allá para sus Ninfas eso basta;
> mas acá para el vulgo, por Dios, nada,
> que quien quiera se pasa dos gritillos.[2]

---

[1] *Viaje de Felipe segundo a Inglaterra*, ed. Pascual de Gayangos, Sociedad de Bibliófilos Españoles, xv (Madrid, 1877), 113.
[2] *Posías satíricas y burlescas*, III (Madrid, 1876), 6-7.

From the woman who rides to the woman who wrestles there is, on stage, but a step. The female roughneck of the theatre is the *bella cazadora* emancipated from all the restrictions of her sex. This logical progression apart, there was a modern-Amazon tradition in Spain. The medieval *serranas* often combined physical strength and toughness of character with beauty, while four of the female Hercules of the drama are based on women who are supposed to have existed – *la varona castellana*, Doña Catalina de Céspedes and Antona García. These three in themselves were sufficient archetypes for the *mujer hombruna* of a theatre eager both for national inspiration and for variations on the theme of the *mujer varonil*, and Catalina de Erauso can have served only to strengthen the convention of female strength and *brío* that they had helped create.[1]

The avenger

Female vengeance is as old as time. The fury of the scorned woman is an accepted psychological generalization to which the Spanish female bandit plays bear witness. Woman's revenge in the Golden-Age drama can be considered masculine because of the nature of the honour-vengeance syndrome of the time but in life and literature vengeance is not more characteristic of man than of woman. In a theatre where the themes of honour and vengeance were extremely popular and where the bold and resolute woman was almost a stock character, the conjunction of woman and revenge was inevitable. The prevailing ideas about woman and honour, together with the playwrights' interest in these ideas, guaranteed the use of the theme and also its popularity. Here again classical literature offered precedents. Lucretia was a favourite with the champions of female virtue and there existed in Spain at least two anonymous ballads about her, one a straightforward narrative,[2] the other a satire,

Dándose estaba Lucrecia
de las hastas con Tarquino

[1] Zenobia too, according to Boccaccio, surpassed the young men of her age in wrestling and all other contests.

[2] Reprinted by Durán from the *Cancionero de romances* in *Romancero general* I, no. 519, B.A.E. X, 353.

Potente rey de romanos,
Mal vencedor de sí mismo.
Decíale la matrona:
– Pasito, señor Tarquino,
Que de mi honor la cerraja
Tiene muy recio el pestillo:
No me sobaje su Alteza,
Conquiste con amor liso,
Y no con fuerza brutesca
Los muros de mi castillo.
Por eso al hijo de Vénus
Le pintan desnudo y niño,
Porque los niños no saben
Pedir sino con gemido.
¡Quién fuera el castor agora,
Aquel animal bendito
Que perseguido se corta
La causa de su peligro!
¿Cómo miran las deidades
Desde su teatro altivo
Este tuerto enderezado
A profanar mi albedrío?
¿Para tal fuego no hay agua?
¿No hay rayos para tal brio?
¿Tal pujamiento de sangre
No degüellen sus cuchillos? –
El rey, más duro que marmol,
Apenas oyó su grito;
Que la razón alterada
Obedece al apetito.
El suyo ha cumplido el Rey:
La matrona no ha cumplido
Con el himeneo santo,
Porque manchó sus armiños;
Que la voluntad forzada
Es voluntad en juicio,
Y en Lucrecia aun vive y reina
La de más cortantes filos.
Y dando satisfacción
De su honor, ¡gentil castigo!,

A su violado pecho
Aplicó un puñal buido.
Al fin murió, dando ejemplo
A los venideros siglos,
Pues la ofensa ha de lavarse
Con sangre del que la hizo.[1]

This ballad is patently a *romance artístico*. The story of Procne and Philomela on the other hand gave rise to a ballad which became traditional in many parts of Spain. Although it keeps fairly closely to the original tale, it has been noticeably naturalized. The following version called *Blanca Flor y Filomena* is Asturian,

Por las orillas del rio – Doña Urraca se pasea
con dos hijas de la mano – Blanca Flor y Filomena.
El Rey moro que lo supo – del camino se volviera;
de palabras se trabaron, – y de amores la requiebra.
Pidiérale la mayor – para casarse con ella:
si le pidió la mayor, – le diera la más pequeña;
y por no ser descortés – tomara la que le dieran.
– Non sea cuento, rey Turquillo, – que mala vida le hicieras . . .
– Non tenga pena, señora; – por ella non tenga pena.
Del vino que yo bebiese, – también ha de beber ella;
y del pan que yo comiese, – también ha de comer ella.
Se casaron, se velaron, – se fueron para su tierra;
nueve meses estuvieron – sin venir a ver la suegra.
Al cabo de nueve meses, – Rey Turquillo vino a verla.
– Bien venido, Rey Turquillo. – Bien hallada sea mi suegra.
– Lo que más quiero saber – si Blanca Flor queda buena.
Blanca Flor buena quedaba; – en días de parir queda,
y vengo muy encargado – que vaya alla Filomena;
para gobernar la casa – mientras Blanca Flor pariera.
– Filomena es muy chiquita – para salir de la tierra;
pero por ver a su hermana – vaya, vaya en hora buena.
Llévela por siete días; – que a los ocho acá me vuelva;
que una mujer en cabellos – no está bien en tierra agena. –
Montó en una yegua torda, – y ella en una yegua negra:
siete leguas anduvieron – sin palabra hablar en ellas.

[1] Printed in the *Romancero general* of 1600. Reprinted in Durán's *Romancero general* II, no. 1717, B.A.E. XVI, 564.

De las siete pa las ocho, – Rey Turquillo se chancea;
y en el medio del camino, – de amores la requiriera.
– Mira, qué haces, Rey Turquillo, – mira que el diablo las tienta;
que tú eres mi cuñado, – tu mujer hermana nuestra.
Sin escuchar más razonas – ya del caballo se apea:
atóla de pies y manos – hizo lo que quiso della;
la cabeza le cortara, – ye le arrancara la lengua,
y tiróla en un zarzal – donde cristiano non entra.
Pasó por allí un pastor, – de mano de Dios viniera.
Por la gracia de Dios padre – a hablar comenzó la lengua.
– Por Dios te pido, pastor, que me escribas una letra:
una para la mi madre, – nunca ella me pariera!
y otra para la mi hermana, – nunca yo la conociera!
– Non tengo papel ni pluma, – aunque serviros quisiera . . .
– De pluma te servirá – un pelo de mis guedejas;
si tu non tuvieres tinta, – con la sangre de mis venas:
y si papel non trujeres, – un casco de mi cabeza. –
Si mucho corrió la carta, – mucho más corrió la nueva.
Blanca Flor, desque lo supo, – con el dolor malpariera;
y el hijo que malparió, guisólo en una cazuela
para dar al Rey Turquillo, – a la noche cuando venga,
– ¿Qué me diste Blanca Flor, – que me diste para cena?
De lo que hay estamos juntos – nunca tan bien me supiera.

– Sangre fué de tus entrañas – gusto de tu carne mesma . . .;
pero mejor te sabrían – besos de mi Filomena!!
– ¿Quién te lo dijo, traidora; – quién te lo fué a decir, perra?
¡Con esta espada que traigo – te he de cortar la cabeza!
Madres las que tienen hijas, – que las casen en su tierra;
que yo, para dos que tuve, – la Fortuna lo quisiera,
una murió maneada – y otra de amores muriera.[1]

The appeal which the female vengeance theme held for the
vulgo is further shown by a romance called *Venganza de honor*, four
versions of which are known in Asturias,

Por aquellos campos verdes – ¡qué galana iba la niña!
Llevaba saya de grana, – jubón broslado traía;
el zapato pica en verde, – la calzas de lana fina;

---

[1] Printed by Menéndez Pelayo in his *Suplemento* to Wolf and Hofmann's *Primavera
y flor de romances* III, no. 21, pp. 68–70.

con los sus morenos ojos – amiraba a quien la mira.
Mirábala un caballero, – traidor, que la pretendía
que diba, paso tras paso, – por ver si la alcanzaría.
Señera la fue alcanzar – al pie d'una fuente fría.
– ¿Adónde por estos prados – camina sola la niña?
– A bodas de una mi hermana, – d'una hermana que tenía. –
Los dos del agua bebieron, – y se van en compañía.
El trata quitarle el honra – y la dice con falsía:
– Más abajo do bebiemos, – quedóme la espada mía.
– Mientes, mientes, caballero; qu'ende la traes tendida. –
Dieron vuelta sobre vuelta; – derribarla non podía.
A la postrera que daban, – una espada le caía.
Trabóla con las sus manos – temblando toda la niña;
metiósela por el pecho, – y a la espalda le salía.
Con las ansias de la muerte, – el caballero decía:
– Por donde quiera que vayas – non t'alabes, prenda mía,
que mataste un caballero – con las armas que traía.
– Con los mis ojos morenos – la tu muerte lloraría;
con la mi camisa blanca – la mortaja te faría;
a la iglesia de San Juan – yo a enterrar te llevaría;
con la tu espada dorada – la fosa te cavaría;
cada domingo del mos – un responso te echaría.[1]

There is also the *Romance de Rico Franco*, where the captive damsel asks her kidnapper to lend her his knife, with which she then kills him:

Cortaré fitas al manto–que no son para traer.
Rico Franco de cortese, – por las cachas lo fue tender;
la doncella que era artera, – por los pechos se lo fue a meter: –
así vengó padre y madre, – y aun hermanos todos tres.[2]

The dramatists adapted such stories to the honour code by which their society in theory lived, not merely in order to make them more comprehensible or more suitable but that they might reflect in some way upon that code.[3]

---

[1] *Ibid.* no. 34, 100.
[2] Printed by Durán, *Romancero general* I, no. 296, 160a, from the *Cancionero de romances*.
[3] Durán prints an eighteenth-century ballad by Pedro de Fuentes, called *Doña Josefa Ramírez* which is very obviously inspired by the female vengeance and

Professor Ashcom's disagreement with Carmen Bravo-Villasante over the source of the *mujer varonil* – by which both mean primarily the *mujer heroica-guerrera* – makes an assessment of the overall importance of the preceding sources and influences very necessary. Señora Bravo-Villasante believes that the type of the *heroica-guerrera* of the Spanish stage comes from Boiardo, Ariosto and Tasso,[1] while Professor Ashcom holds that classical antiquity played a much greater part in the formation of these women than Italian literature. Professor Ashcom is right; and he is right to a far greater degree than even he realized. For the influence of classical antiquity upon the *mujer varonil*, in the wide sense in which the term has here been used, is much greater than that of any other source. Classical literature and mythology provided inspiration not only for the Amazon, the leader and the warrior, but also for the *esquiva*, the *bella cazadora* and the avenger. The references to Bradamante and Marfisa are far outnumbered by those to Penthesilea, Semiramis and Diana. The *mujer varonil's* heroine is almost invariably a classical figure. When the *mujer varonil* began to appear on the stage and to increase in popularity, Spain was still intoxicated with the classical learning of the Renaissance. Cueva and Virués, who introduced the *mujer varonil* into the theatre in most of her aspects, were greatly indebted to this learning for their plots and themes. Translations, popularized versions and compilations of classical learning abounded; the gods and goddesses, heroes and heroines, became virtually household names; sometimes they even entered the *Romancero*. It would have been surprising had they not influenced a theatre which sought inspiration anywhere and everywhere. Italy's major contribution to the *mujer varonil* theme was the detail of masculine dress. The 'female page' was almost certainly of Italian origin[2] and the growing popularity

banditry tradition of the Golden-Age theatre and also by those plays where the heroine disguised as a man is captured by Turks and then has to ward off the advances of Turkish wives. *Romancero general* II, nos. 1328–9, B.A.E. XVI, 361–5.

[1] *La mujer vestida de hombre en el teatro español*, 33ff. and 61ff.

[2] See Carmen Bravo-Villasante, *La mujer vestida de hombre en el teatro español*, 33ff.; and B. B. Ashcom, 'Concerning "La mujer en hábito de hombre . . . "', 44–5. See also Victor O. Freeburg, *Disguise Plots in Elizabethan Drama* (New York, 1915), passim.

of this figure must have helped put the *mujer varonil* proper into armour or breeches and hose. Except in the case of Semiramis, the garments of the classical heroines are never described by Latin and Greek writers as particularly unfeminine. Even so, the Italian influence here is limited because masculine dress is only an embellishment of the *mujer varonil*. Often – as in the case of the *esquiva* or avenger – she does not wear masculine dress at all; and often, particularly in the later theatre, even the more aggressive types wear women's clothes.

The influence of Italian literature was, in short, surprisingly small. Marfisa, Bradamante and Clorinda were supporting players to the classical heroines from whom they had themselves initially derived. The *novelle* offered little; even the woman who sits in judgment on her husband owed much more to Timoneda than to Boccaccio. In fact, Spain's own history, legends and literature must probably be considered the major source of inspiration for the *mujer varonil* after the classics. By far the most important single *form* of influence was that of literary tradition, whether classical, Italian or Spanish, cultured or popular. History, as opposed to literary knowledge of history, counts for remarkably little. The only category of the *mujer varonil* to have received its initial impetus from contemporary Spanish life was, if I am right, the *esquiva*.

The *mujer varonil* of the Spanish theatre was to a very large extent the product of Europe's awareness of the extraordinary woman. The goddesses and heroines of antiquity were familiar figures. The existence of the Amazons was an accepted fact; so was that of Pope Joan.[1] The feminist debate had caused all women of any ability or virtue to be extricated from the books and legends in which they were buried, and to be held aloft as shining examples of female worth. Any contemporary woman of great energy or ability received the attention she deserved in a world where both qualities were still considered the prerogatives of men.[2] Even

---

[1] Durán prints a sixteenth-century ballad called *Romance de la papisa Juana, Romancero general* II, no. 1248, B.A.E. XVI, 223, She is included in Boccaccio's *De claris mulieribus*.

[2] During the fifteenth century pictures of men and women famous in history and story often decorated the face cards in a player's pack. Lope mentions such a

churchmen could not deny the heroism of biblical characters such as Esther, Jael and above all Judith, a favourite of Spanish writers.[1] These conditions, however, existed in many countries. The factor which decided that the *comedia nueva* would adopt the extraordinary woman and make it one of its most popular types was the one which figured in the dramatization of the *esquiva* – Lope himself. Lope realized that the *mujer varonil* was a dramatic type of great theatrical impact, capable of endless variations and possessing enormous popular appeal. So he made her one of his stock characters, using her in a variety of ways and for a variety of purposes; and since where Lope led all others followed, the *mujer varonil* then became a stock character of the Golden-Age drama as a whole. Lope did not create the *mujer varonil*, any more than he created the Spanish theatre, but he made her what she became – one of the most consistently rewarding dramatic types that the *comedia* has to offer.

picture of Laurencia, a Griselda figure, in his *El exemplo de las casadas*: 'Házense retratos della / por sus soberanas partes / en toda Francia y Castilla / con excelencia y honras tales. / De los quales este es vno / que le puse en este naype / que es Reyna aunque en este juego / la fortuna le descarte.' See Caroline B. Bourland, 'Boccaccio and the Decameron in Castilian and Catalan literature', 25. Such cards might well have contributed considerably to the public's familiarity with, for example, classical heroines.

[1] Heroines often refer to her e.g. Elvira in Morales' *El caballero de Olmedo*: 'qual Judith, he triunfado / deste Holofernes cruel' (Act III ed. Juliá Martínez (Madrid, 1944), 155, lines 2540–1. Lope wrote a sonnet about her, *A la hermosa Judit*. Plays include Godínez's *Judit y Holofernes*, Vera Tassis's *El triunfo de Judit y muerte de Holofernes*, and an anonymous *comedia La judit española*. [See Shergold and Varey, 'Some Palace Performances . . .' 228.] Judith also entered the *Romancero*; Menéndez Pelayo (Appendix to Wolf and Hofmann's *Primavera y flor*, II, no. 57, p. 257) reprints 'Otro romance viejo ó historia de Judich, cuando siendo viuda degolló á Holofernes' from Valderrábano's *Silva de sirenas*, published in 1547. Durán includes six ballads about Judith in his *Romancero general* (I, B.A.E. x, 291–7, nos. 442–7), which are listed in his *Catálogo* of sixteenth century *pliegos sueltos*. He also includes a romance called *Judith y Holofernes* by Lorenzo de Sepúlveda (no. 44, 290).

11

Conclusion

To understand the importance of the *mujer varonil* in the Golden-Age drama, some idea of her general distribution is necessary. The inadequacy of our detailed information about theatrical production makes precise figures impossible, but even an approximation yields illuminating results. As far as can be judged from the dates of composition and publication available, every year from about 1590 to 1660 witnessed the appearance of at least one new play featuring a *mujer varonil*, with some periods, of course, producing concentrated clusters. This estimate does not take into consideration those plays which deal with the related theme of the straightforward *disfraz varonil*, which add up to many more, and being based only on extant plays the estimate must be regarded as a conservative one. Though the *mujer varonil* remained a constant favourite of the Spanish theatre throughout the greater part of its heyday, a certain pattern of popularity is discernible. Lope established the *mujer varonil* as a stock character early on, and during the 1590s and early 1600s himself turned out at least one new *mujer varonil* every year. His pace then seems to have slackened, but he still had the field almost to himself for some years until other dramatists began to awaken to the possibilities of the *mujer varonil* theme. By 1612 Mira de Amescua had written *El esclavo del demonio*; by 1612 too, Luis Vélez de Guevara had written *Los hijos de la barbuda*; Tirso by 1613 had produced *La condesa bandolera o la ninfa del cielo*, and Ricardo de Turia by 1616 *La belígera española*. Nevertheless, Lope was to remain the *mujer varonil*'s greatest exponent: in one form or another she appears in the cast of more than fifty of his plays – over a tenth of his surviving dramatic output. In complete accord with this, J. Homero Arjona has shown that, contrary to established belief, Lope and not Tirso was also

311

the most habitual exploiter of the *disfraz varonil* device.[1] After Lope's death in 1635 there was naturally a fall in the numbers of *mujeres varoniles*, but every year that passed still produced another version. In the 1660s several plays still introduced the figure, but her appearance in new works then became intermittent. Doubtless the late *refundiciones*, now lost, of earlier plays ensured that she remained a familiar figure to Spanish audiences. The only dramatist of any note who, apart from his barely discernible 'bandolera' in *El tejedor de Sevilla*, II, ignored the *mujer varonil*, was Alarcón, who was never really happy with female characters and who in any case studiously avoided the extreme and the bizarre.

As for the popularity of the various categories of *mujer varonil*, the recurrence of a particular type is obviously the best indicator of its rating among theatre audiences. By this gauge, and unless a disproportionate number of plays containing other categories of abnormal women has been lost, which is statistically unlikely, the *esquiva* was by far the most popular. The bandit and the leader came second, with the warrior a close third (this not counting the *mujer vestida de hombre* who occasionally brandishes a sword, for otherwise the *guerrera* would come higher up the scale). Then followed the *bella cazadora*, the scholar and the career woman, the avenger and the Amazon, in roughly descending order of preference.

It can be safely said that Lope popularized all these types, although dramatic precedents existed for all of them except the Amazon, the scholar and the career woman. He can even be recognized as the virtual creator in the theatre of two others – the *esquiva* and the *bandolera*, for Gil Vicente's Casandra and Virués's Felina are far removed from the characteristic dramatization of these types in the seventeenth-century theatre, the first in time and both in treatment. So that, while the *mujer varonil* was a prominent feature of the pre-Lope theatre, it was Lope who

[1] The device appears in one hundred and thirteen of Lope's plays as compared with twenty-one of Tirso's. See Homero Arjona's 'El disfraz varonil en Lope de Vega', *BHi* XXXIX (1937), 120–45. S. W. Brown reduces the estimate even further and says that out of the fifty-nine plays which are certainly Tirso's, masculine disguise occurs only in nine. See his introduction to his edition of *La villana de Vallecas* (Boston, 1948), xix, n. 2.

recognized her real potential, both as a box-office draw and as a fertile source for serious investigation of social responses to one of the subjects that fascinated him most – women. It was he who knew what aspects of the *mujer varonil* to isolate and emphasize and he, therefore, for the most part who fashioned the unusual, assertive woman of the existing theatre into distinctive dramatic types. Most of these he started using in the 1590s. He introduced the career woman into the theatre slightly later, producing two (*El alcalde mayor* and *La hermosura aborrecida*) between 1604 and 1612.

Once these figures were absorbed into the inspirational storehouse of the theatre in general, their patterns of popularity varied. Existing information shows that the *esquiva* was a constant favourite until 1660, but barely survived that date in new productions. The *bandolera* made appearances throughout the whole period, with a concentrated patch of popularity before 1613, possibly because this was the period when Spain's bandit problem was at its most serious. The leader seems to have grown in popularity in the second and third decades – a historical explanation also seems plausible for this – then virtually disappeared after the early 1650s. The *guerrera*, the scholar and the career woman all enjoyed a wide spread, although with differences in density, with a concentration of popularity towards the early years. The *bella cazadora*, after an initial flourish, settled into a routine of regular appearances until about 1640, after which date she almost faded from sight. The avenger was fairly slow to gather popularity, prospered in the second, third and fourth decades, perhaps the period of maximum interest in the honour-vengeance theme, then fell out of favour. Lastly, the Amazon made her few appearances at widening intervals throughout the century.

The changing distribution of these female types was naturally accompanied by fluctuations in the quality of the dramatic treatment, but unlike Señora Carmen Bravo-Villasante, I do not find that the late manifestations of the *mujer varonil*, such as Elvira in *La dama capitán* or Juana in *El mosquetero de Flandes,* are morally degenerate. This seems to me an excessively ponderous judgment. They are merely the creations of inferior imaginations and lesser minds, and as such are not conceived with the same intuition nor drawn with the same skill as the creations of Spain's major dramatists. They are symptomatic of the decline of the theatre in general, nothing more. The late *mujeres varoniles* are certainly not more *hombrunas*, as Señora Bravo-Villasante suggests.[1] None of them is as bloodthirsty as Gila, Inés or Teresa, nor as hoydenish as the three Doña Marías or Antona García. And they succumb just as inevitably as these to love and marriage. If they are less attractive characters, if their swashbuckling bravado has a cardboard masculinity, it is because their creators were unable to cope successfully with the complex dramatic types they were seeking to imitate.

When, in her discussion of these later plays, Señora Bravo-Villasante comes to talk of Cubillo de Aragón's *Añasco el de Talavera*,[2] her indignation knows no bounds. And certainly this is a remarkable play, the only one of the whole lot which might be called degenerate – if lesbianism qualifies as degeneracy, that is. The situation where one female character in a play unwittingly falls in love with another whom she takes to be a man is a common feature of the *disfraz varonil* motif. But I know of no play other than *Añasco el de Talavera* where a woman claims to be in love with someone she knows to be also a woman. By presenting the *varonil* Dionisa as being in love with Leonor her cousin, Cubillo was obviously treading a path which was potentially dangerous. Certainly the provocative overtones seem clear today. His motive in taking the concept of the *mujer varonil* to its logical conclusion was patently to try and squeeze as much novelty as possible out of a theme which had long ago been sucked dry of all conventional originality and worn threadbare for third-rate playwrights by repetition. But in the event he funked the issue. In order, we presume, to avoid the inevitable censure of the authorities and obtain his *licencia*, but not inconceivably because the situation's full implications did not appeal or even completely strike home, he made Dionisa's love in her own words a platonic one;

¿No es amor correspondencia?
¿No es platónica opinión
que amor es confrontación

---

[1] *La mujer vestida de hombre en el teatro español,* 153–78.   [2] *Ibid.* 155–8.

de estrellas y de ascendencia?
Pues si ésta concibiré en mí
y es confrontación de estrellas,
¿cómo para obedecella
dejaré de amarte a ti?

(Act 1)[1]

He reinforced the ambiguity of the situation by making the infatu-
ation short-lived and by putting in the mouths of the other
characters a condemnation of this 'amor imperfecto'. It is interesting that Dionisa's family and Leonor are not scandalized; they
just refuse to take Dionisa seriously, and one wonders whether
contemporary audiences did not react in the same way. In any
case, normality is soon restored. Although Dionisa in the usual
way of physically aggressive *mujeres varoniles* wishes she were a
man, not once does she express a desire for manhood in order to
make her love either orthodox or possible – any real issue of
sexuality is avoided. And as soon as she leaves home she forgets
her former feelings, eventually marrying Don Juan without the
slightest sign of reluctance.

There is no point, I think, in trying to explain Dionisa's declaration of love or her subsequent conversion, since they are not
susceptible of explanation within the character's psychological
make-up as conceived and portrayed by Cubillo. Until the end of
the play Dionisa is a sexless ruffian, and the homosexuality appears
to be merely an arbitrary attempt at novelty. I suppose one might
now see the episode as an illustration of the normal emotional
homosexuality of adolescence, but I think it would be foolishly
speculative to ascribe any such awareness or motive to the author
himself. *Añasco el de Talavera* represents the decadence of the *mujer
varonil* theme, not because it approaches the theme of lesbianism,
but because in it Cubillo de Aragón substituted sensation for
inspiration.

This is an opportune moment for raising the inevitable question
of lesbianism with regard to the theme of the *mujer varonil* as a

---

[1] An undated, unlocated copy of the play exists in the Biblioteca Nacional, Ref.
14781[5]. The above quotation is from a 1750 edition of the play in the British
Museum, 11728.c.16, A3ᵛ.

whole. The very phrase *mujer varonil* or masculine woman has, in the twentieth century, sexual overtones of a potentially deviant nature. And the expected comments have been forthcoming. Professor Ashcom in his consideration of Señora Bravo-Villasante's book,[1] states 'The Lesbian motif is implicit in most of the plots involving masculine women.' At the considered risk of appearing naïve, I should like to disagree with, or at least seriously qualify, this assertion. The motif might be seen to be implicit by the modern observer, increasingly familiar as he is becoming in his reading and in his viewing with human sexuality in all its aspects. But whether it was intended by the dramatists to be implicit and whether it was seen to be implicit by contemporary audiences is a different matter, and the two issues must not be confused. It would be both foolish and arrogant automatically to ascribe our own sexual awareness to other societies as if such awareness were a universally static factor; this is particularly true in the case of female homosexuality which throughout the greater part of European society until the present day has been very much, through ignorance and sublimation, a subterranean phenomenon.

To begin with, it is essential always to bear in mind that while the phrase masculine woman in English has strong derogatory overtones, *varonil* in the Golden Age was invariably a term of praise and admiration, as much when it was used of women as of men. It was indeed the highest accolade bestowed by man on female behaviour. More important, none of the *mujeres varoniles* of the theatre except Dionisa shows any evidence of a fondness for her own sex. Many indeed despise their own sex, and prefer the company of men. That such feelings are often the first psychological manifestations of lesbian tendencies does not mean that they lead inevitably to lesbianism. And in the manufactured world of the Golden-Age drama they certainly do not. Those who argue that they do are confusing feminist statements with deviant tastes – an understandable lapse of judgment on the part of the layman but perhaps less forgivable in those in tune with the ethos of the seventeenth-century theatre. Careful distinctions must be made if

[1] 'Concerning "La mujer en hábito de hombre" in the *comedia*', *HR* XXVIII (1960), 59.

hasty amateur psychology is not to lead one to misunderstand the whole nature of the *mujer varonil*'s revolt. That revolt is against Society and convention, and woman's inferior position in them, not against her sexual role *via-à-vis* man. The *esquiva*'s revolt against Nature is prompted, not by homosexual impulses, but by the way the concept of Nature is invoked by men to justify their delegation of women to an inactive and inferior role in life. The age-old tradition of the physically aggressive woman is a reflection not so much of lesbian tendencies (if at all), as of one of the more basic forms of female envy. The *guerrera* and particularly the *bella cazadora* are an expression of woman's envy of man's freedom, resentment of his self-claimed superiority and jealousy of his unrestricted access to pleasures forbidden to her.[1] The *bandolera* is driven to her life of crime and the avenger to revenge by powerful emotional and psychological factors that have nothing to do with homosexuality. While by no stretch of the imagination can the ability to govern or the desire for intellectual equality and possibly a career be called unnatural in the 'variant' sense. The Amazons are the nearest approximation to female homosexuality apart from Dionisa, and even they are presented as sexually normal, if intellectually wrong-minded.

The attraction of one woman towards another dressed as a man is, as has been pointed out throughout the course of this work, a common situation in disguise plots. Common too are declarations of love from woman to disguised woman and even from disguised woman to woman; the first are misplaced and shortlived, not surviving the revelation of true identity, the second are invariably pieces of calculated acting. Sometimes the situation leads to a *rendez-vous* and occasionally to consummation, the *disfrazada*'s place being taken at the last moment by a man. These situations were obviously introduced deliberately by the dramatists and doubtless provoked a great deal of pleasurable excitement

[1] Cf. C. J. S. Thompson talking of transvestites: 'the chief causes of their action among women, apart from the physiological [i.e. hermaphrodites], appear to have been a spirit of adventure, ambition, a physiological desire for domination and to play the man, or a criminal desire to obtain money or property'. *Mysteries of Sex. Women who posed as Men and Men who impersonated Women* (London, 1938), II, 18.

amongst theatre audiences. I strongly suspect, however, that their appeal lay not in their lesbian insinuations but in their dramatic irony. I suspect too that one should not underestimate the visual impact of such a situation. This, after all, was one of normality, of woman and gallant, and less obviously suggestive, therefore, than the visual impact created by a situation in which man is attracted to girl dressed as man. The very fact that the former situation was exploited quite frequently and the latter very rarely, and then in the most tenuous way, does suggest that the mistaken attraction of female for female dressed as male was doubly innocuous compared with any suggestion of male homosexuality. In other words, implications of male homosexuality would be detected where those of female homosexuality would be overlooked. And hence the all-female ambiguity created by the disguise plot could be exploited without fear of censure on grounds of immorality.

Such a position would certainly accord with the relative ignorance about lesbianism, as compared with male homosexuality, that has apparently reigned until modern times. In the past, all evidence appears to indicate, the two belonged to widely separated levels of sexual consciousness. It is certainly hard to believe that a predominantly middle and lower-class and largely male audience would have responded favourably to such sophisticated implications as lesbianism, had they been aware of their presence in the play. It could of course be argued that the playwrights' more sophisticated implications were for their own amusement and for the more aware minority in their audiences, but such arguments, although not inherently implausible, are purely speculative. There is certainly no evidence to support them. And it is interesting that even when the dramatists dealt with historical women of suspected lesbian tendencies – Catalina de Erauso, Christiana of Sweden – they omitted all such sophisticated innuendo. It is interesting, too, that Calderón, writing as court dramatist for an audience less likely to be shocked by homosexual undertones, used the masculine disguise plot in this particular way hardly at all, possibly because of ecclesiastical disapproval of women in revealing masculine costume, but more likely because of disenchantment with a hackneyed device. When he wished to create a disguise intrigue his normal procedure was to provide his heroine only with a veil, which ruled out the possibility of misplaced passion. Furthermore, if seventeenth-century moralists and critics of the theatre never used the so-called lesbian motif as ammunition in their denunciations of the theatre as a corrupting influence, this must have been because it simply did not occur to them to regard the *mujer vestida de hombre*, and the complications she sometimes gave rise to, in this light. And if it did not occur to over-vigilant moralists, one wonders whether it occurred to any-one. In all probability audiences and censors alike reacted to the romantic confusion created by the use of *masculine disguise* in exactly the same way. The contrast between the *mujer varonil* of the Spanish theatre and the true sex variant seems glaringly apparent and certainly supports J. Foster's conclusions about the absence of the sex variant in the literature of this period:

. . . the whole field of fiction was largely fallow during the seventeenth and eighteenth centuries . . . The drama, too, yields a thin harvest during these centuries. In romantic plays sex disguise was fairly common but it produced no variant situations comparable to those cited from romance and pastoral.[1]

The reactions and behaviour of women like the *esquiva,* the *guerrera,* the *bella cazadora* and others, may sometimes sound like a classic description of the psychological background of the sexually variant woman, but there is no evidence that this particular form of female revolt was consciously exploited by seventeenth-century dramatists, other perhaps than Cubillo de Aragón. On the contrary, the evidence points firmly the other way.

We certainly do not need to explain the *mujer varonil*'s lasting popular appeal in lesbian terms. Lope realized, and other dramatists soon learned, that she would draw the crowds for a complex variety of less sophisticated reasons. The basic attraction is obvious: she had all the charm of unreality, the unreality of a woman rivalling, even surpassing, man in a man's world. The *mujer varonil* was not a person normally met with in the course of everyday life. People heard perhaps of Elizabeth, Catherine and Catalina

[1] *Sex Variant Women in Literature,* 39.

de Erauso, they probably referred fondly to their *gran* Isabel, they were familiar with the legends of the maid who went to war and Antona García, but to see such figures walk the stage before their very eyes was to watch fairy tales come true. Professor Ashcom may offer a list of historical or semi-historical cases of women who were transvestites and passed as men or acted like men,[1] but they amount to a mere handful over a period of many centuries. They provided the drama with real-life precedents but at the same time they show how limited transvestism and overt *varonilidad* really were until the last hundred years.[2] The number of women chasing their lovers across the countryside, robbing and killing in the mountains, posing as men so successfully that they attracted amorous female attention, and fighting manfully in battle, must obviously have been minimal. Commonsense, as well as the available evidence, points to this. Even the scholars and *esquivas* were a select minority. Audiences flocked to see them all on stage because they were rare and remarkable figures.

For the women theatre-goers the *mujer varonil* provided the pleasure of vicarious freedom and adventure. Through her, for an hour or two, they became brave, daring, resourceful; they met men on their own ground, competed as equals, and often beat them at their own game. They could, under the guise of masculinity, extort the admiration and respect of men, then with a flourish reveal their sex and earn even greater respect and admiration. In a society in which woman was restricted and under-privileged, her jealousy and envy of man, though perhaps buried deep in her subconscious mind, would inevitably lead her to identify herself with the spirited woman she was watching on stage, and this alone would be sufficient to explain the fascination the *mujer varonil* held for the woman in the audience. She represented a form of female catharsis.

For male onlookers the *mujer varonil* had an even more basic attraction. For if the warrior queen or the *bella cazadora* provoked feminine fantasies of freedom vicariously enjoyed and of power vicariously wielded, she must have provoked very different

[1] 'Concerning "La mujer en hábito de hombre" . . . ' 59–62.
[2] Cf. Foster, *Sex Variant Women in Literature*, *passim*.

masculine reactions. If she strutted the stage in masculine dress her appeal was blatantly sexual. Nowhere but in the theatre could a man publicly enjoy the sight of the female leg clearly outlined from ankle to thigh. This was enough to prompt churchmen and moralists to agitate for laws forbidding the use of male clothing by actresses, and enough to persuade legislators to pass them. Cotarelo y Mori quotes the following excerpt from Francisco Ortiz's description of theatre-going in his *Apología en defensa de las comedias que se representan in España* 1614, which is unequivocal about the nature of the *mujer varonil*'s appeal:

. . . pues ha de ser más que de hielo el hombre que no se abrase de lujuria viendo una mujer desenfadada y desenvuelta, y algunas veces, para este efecto, vestido como hombre, haciendo cosas que movieran a un muerto.[1]

Even without masculine dress, as Lope said,

con acciones de hombres
no agradan mal las mujeres.[2]

As a result of the popularity of the *mujer varonil* and the *mujer vestida de hombre* some actresses specialized in these parts and playwrights then produced plots with particular actresses in mind. Lope in the dedication of *La mocedad de Roldán* says he wrote the play, 'a devoción del gallardo talle, en hábito de hombre, de la única representante, Jusepa Vaca'.[3] Luis Vélez dedicated *La serrana de la Vera* likewise to Jusepa Vaca. Luis Vélez, Coello and Rojas even wrote a play *about* another actress who took these roles, *La Baltasara*, while Bárbara Coronel, later an *autora* in her own right, became so type-cast that she took to wearing male clothing and riding a horse almost habitually.[4] The *mujer varonil* role was a marvellous opportunity for actresses to indulge any desires – subconsciously lesbian or not – they themselves might have had to act the tomboy or the dominant woman. And doubtless the

[1] Quoted in *Contraversias sobre la licitud del teatro en España* (Madrid, 1904), 494a.
[2] In *Dios hace reyes*, Act III, Acad.N. IV, 606b.
[3] Acad. XIII, 205.
[4] See Casiano Pellicer, *Tratado histórico sobre el origen y progresos de la comedia y del histrionismo en España. Parte II* (Madrid, 1804), 28.

enthusiastic attention they provoked ensured they were much sought after. According to Narciso Díaz de Escobar and Francisco de P. Lasso de la Vega the appearance on scene of Ana Muñoz dressed as an Amazon and on horseback, caused so much excitement that the horse took fright, causing the premature birth of the actress's son.[1]

If the *mujer varonil* appealed to male spectators through her incongruous actions and tight hose, these were not the whole secret of her attraction. One must not underestimate the effect of her challenge to masculine pride and the male conquering instinct. The popularity of the *esquiva*, a type as often given to verbal as to physical aggressiveness, can only be explained in this way. Watching the inevitable subjection of female to male was a marvellous opportunity for self-congratulatory male esteem. Each man in the audience could happily identify himself with the hero who, by deceit, by psychological warfare or by his essential nobility, gradually thawed out and won over the disdainful heroine. There must have been more than a little of this in the *esquiva's* attraction for the dramatists themselves. Furthermore, contradictory as it may seem, the *esquiva's* progress from indifference to warmth and concern probably had a strong hidden appeal for the spectators in the *cazuela*. What, after all, is the *esquiva* but a more sophisticated version of Sleeping Beauty? Both are waiting to be awakened to love and life. The prince is a stylization of the man who wins the unattainable woman. And the 'prince' is probably the most common form of female wish-fulfilment. The woman of great strength or ability, one imagines, similarly appealed to the conqueror in man, if in a slightly different way. Every man was the hero who transformed the masterful or powerful woman into an adoring consort, who made the scholar forget her books, and the career woman abandon her career, and who made the intrepid warrior dissolve into tears and start at the sight of a mouse. To the basic instinct of sexual conquest is added the instinct of sexual rivalry. Each man has not only conquered his mate but has won for himself a better mate than his fellows have.

Although the *mujer varonil* was an inexhaustible source of sexual fantasy, her appeal was not exclusively sexual. At the same

[1] See their *Historia del teatro español*, I (Barcelona, 1924), 144.

time she was a product of, and was directed at, the Baroque mentality. She shared the appeal that the complex, the unusual and the contradictory possessed for the seventeenth century. She was part of the outcome of the seventeenth-century fondness for extremes of personality – the saint, the bandit, the *pícaro*, Don Quijote, the husband jealous to the point of murder – a fondness which began in the theatre towards the end of the sixteenth century under the influence of Seneca. *Il cortegiano* had no place in the Golden-Age theatre, apart from that corner of it occupied by Moreto. The *mujer varonil* is as much a product of her age as Ribera's *La barbuda*; certainly the portrait could not, in the circumstances, have been painted at any more appropriate time. The theme of the *mujer varonil* even contains the requisite Baroque tension: the tension between the reality of woman's position and her illusions, emotional needs and desires. In the *mujer varonil* herself the theatre provided a temporary appeasement. It is not too fanciful, perhaps, to imagine that the mind that is attracted by the literary conceit will be attracted by a living conceit, whether in the form of a woman dressed as a man or the woman who behaves in a manner not normally associated with her sex. Appearances deceive: the *mujer varonil* is not what she seems to be nor what she is expected to be. Either her sex hides her masculine characteristics or her masculine characteristics (clothes, actions) hide her sex. In other words, the reality she seems to present is an illusion, and this is the essence of the conceit.

All this lay behind the popularity of the *mujer varonil*, and it was for this range of interests that the dramatists were catering when they built their plots around her. That they regarded her as a good commercial proposition, and that they were governed by theatrical conventions and considerations of plot, does not mean that they did not infuse into their presentation their own ideas and views concerning women in general. They did. Explicitly or implicitly, by direct comment through some character who can be considered the author's mouthpiece,[1] or by the development of the plot, they conveyed fairly clearly, though obviously not with

[1] Very rarely the *gracioso*; his protestations of horror and alarm at the sight of

treatise-like lucidity, where they stood in the battle between the defenders and denigrators of womanhood. For a comparable preoccupation in the theatre with the subject of women and their rights we have to look to late Victorian England where, after the first English performance of Ibsen's *A Doll's House* in 1869, most of the important plays in the following years dealt with that crucial issue the Marriage Question, the very question broached by Rojas Zorrilla, though from the point of view of a society that knew no divorce. The Edwardian analogy is by no means a complete one. Samuel Hynes, in his work on Edwardian England, points out that though many plays written in the 1890s might at first glance create the impression that 'advanced thought had seized the Victorian theatre', most playwrights were simply using the Marriage Question as another way of writing melodramas about adultery, and their attitudes were ultimately conservative.[1] If the dramatists sometimes protested at the complacent conservatism of their audiences, they also to some extent shared it. Now there is no doubt that in comparison with modern standards the feminism of the Spanish dramatists was in some respects also decidedly conservative. But it seems to me that there is a basic difference here which works to the credit of the Spaniards. The Victorian playwrights were exploiting for dramatic purposes subjects of fierce current debate – divorce, the Marriage Question, the legal and constitutional rights of women. This was not true of the Golden-Age dramatists. There is in their work the strong element of exploitation natural in a popular and prolific theatre, but the feminist preoccupations were largely their own, with Lope giving his intensely concerned, if somewhat prejudiced, lead. Female independence might have been a subject of interest to a small minority of aware women, but it was far from being a controversial issue in society at large, even among intellectuals. Education for women was no longer the subject of reformers' concern that it had been, and while the concept of honour was of considerable philosophical and moralist interest, Lope and his fellow

varonilidad and his denunciation of the heroine as being a *marimacho* (a term rarely used by any other character) were conventional comedy.

[1] *The Edwardian Turn of Mind*, 174ff.

dramatists were the ones who looked at the matter from a specifically female angle. The Spaniards, in other words, treated with a real and sensitive concern and occasional marked independence of thought, issues that they amongst few others saw to be inherent in the society in which they lived, while the Victorian playwrights were cashing in on a bitter controversy which even involved the heir to the throne.

The most important aspect of the Spanish theatre's exploration of woman's position is that it was, within the dramatists' own terms, a realistic one. Their acute apprehension of woman as a being distinct from man is the outcome of this. Cueva and Virués approached and presented their female characters with the same indifference to sex with which they approached and presented their male characters. And this, in absolute terms, is true feminism. Within the context of their society, however, it was not enough. Cueva and Virués behaved as if the battle for equality were over and as if they could take for granted the general recognition of sexual equality. Their successors, on the other hand, realized that the battle had barely begun, that woman had not yet been conceded certain basic human rights, let alone equality. And these basic rights they were prepared to stand up for by pouring out propaganda in their plays. So that while they do not appear the unmitigated feminists that Cueva and Virués seem to have been, their contribution to the progress of the feminist cause was potentially much greater. They actively and consciously drew attention to the equivocal nature of woman's position and the injustices under which she lived. And thus the answer to Américo Castro's indirect question:

. . . cómo pudo ser que la literatura española, la literatura de un país donde se dice la situación de la mujer era más precaria que en otros países europeos, influyese en que Molière desarrollara una concepción amplia y moderna de la personalidad femenina . . .[1]

lies in the liberal, realistic and above all questioning views of the Spanish dramatists of the seventeenth century. Castro is correct when he stated 'En el siglo XVI deberán, pues, buscarse los

---

[1] *Teatro antiguo español*, II (Madrid, 1917), 246–7.

gérmenes de la concepción de la mujer que desenvuelven el teatro y la novela'[1] – Erasmian literature and Erasmian ideals had created a new atmosphere of inquiry and tolerance with regard to women. But it was the dramatists almost alone who kept this atmosphere alive in the following century and no-one before them had really explored woman's position in relation to the society in which she lived. Woman, her actions and reactions, and their emotional and psychological motivation, needed to be shown in a variety of relevant situations and circumstances. This need the drama supplied, even if its interpretation was sometimes the conventional one, by its very emphasis on woman's sex managing to show how alike man and woman are in their common humanity. The rather vague and unformed sympathy and enthusiasm for woman widespread in the sixteenth century was formulated and defined, and reconciled, and inevitably partly sacrificed, to the realities of seventeenth-century life as the playwrights saw them.

To a large extent this more realistic approach to women was part of the general tendency towards realism in Spanish literature towards the end of the sixteenth century, a realism quickly verging on pessimism which was the outcome of the religious and philosophical upheaval that held captive a Europe fast forgetting its Renaissance dream of human perfection. The drama of the Golden Age is the supreme example of the remarkable fusion of the religious and the secular in literature which this upheaval, under the name of the Counter-Reformation, produced in Spain; and it is not surprising, that the move towards a more realistic appraisal of woman and her role appears fairly early in the drama with the young Lope and his contemporaries. Ironically, the realistic liberalism of the theatre does not seem to have been accompanied by any practical improvement in women's conditions. On the contrary, the lively interest in the upbringing and education of women that was so marked a feature of sixteenth-century thought was stifled in the seventeenth century, possibly because of its suspect associations. In Great Britain, on the other hand, the upheaval had an effective emancipating influence of a specific and narrow sort upon attitudes to women. The Renaissance is always

[1] *Ibid.* 246.

regarded as the high-water mark of female emancipation in Europe before the twentieth century, but between the two there appears to have been a short-lived and isolated pocket of emancipation of a peculiar kind.[1] Puritanism with its Calvinistic emphasis upon the equality of all souls before God produced a new conception of woman as man's help-meet and spiritual partner in life that had for a time tangible consequences. In certain religious sects women were accorded a remarkable degree of religious and social equality. The first Quaker preachers in London, Dublin, Oxford and Cambridge and even in the American colonies, were all women, while women often played a leading part in the formation of small independent congregations and joined with enthusiasm in the outbreak of lay preaching. Seventeenth-century Spain, needless to say, saw no such eccentric flowerings of female activity.

Of course the term 'realistic', applied to the attitudes of the Spanish dramatists, must be understood as meaning realistic as far as the seventeenth century was concerned, and not realistic by our standards today. Western society may still be stiff with hidden prejudice against women, but even so the reality of their existence has undergone monumental changes. The playwrights' approach was a practical one which, although in many ways laudably broadminded, was for the most part ultimately circumscribed by the attitudes of their age and their society. Their views, in other words, were liberal without, apart from one instance, being revolutionary. The problem, as dramatists from Lope onwards saw and presented it, was this: woman was an area of conflict between Nature and Society. This conflict was a complex one. Nature had predestined woman for love and marriage. At the same time it had endowed her with intelligence, pride, dignity and ability. Nature had also predestined *man* for love and marriage, but while Society allowed him to reconcile this destiny with *his* intelligence, pride, dignity and abilities, it denied this reconciliation to woman. In addition, Society often tried to dictate to woman even in matters of love and marriage. As a result, woman in an effort to assert her natural feelings, either revolted completely

[1] See Keith Thomas, 'Women and the Civil War Sects', *Past and Present*, XIII (1958), 42–62.

327

against Society (the bandit, the girl who flees her home) or at least behaved in a socially unacceptable manner (the avenger); while in the attempt to fulfil her intellectual and/or physical gifts, she only succeeded in risking the disapproval of Society (the *bella cazadora*, the warrior, the leader, the scholar and the career-woman). Furthermore, seeing Society try to force upon her her natural destiny – love and marriage – she was driven to rebel against Nature itself (the *esquiva*). These are the dramatic hypotheses used by the playwrights in their presentation of the conflict. And their sympathies can be broadly summarized thus: they were generally prepared to uphold woman against Society but never against Nature. Within this generalization, of course, they have their personal differences of opinion.

One thing they believed in unanimously was woman's *libertad de amar*. Woman should be allowed to follow her natural inclinations in the choice of a husband, and parents who try to force their daughter to embark on marriage against her will must accept responsibility for the consequences. Perhaps the most moving defence of woman's right to decide her future for herself is given by Julia in Calderón's *La devoción de la cruz*. She says to Curcio,

> Solo tiene libertad
>   un hijo para escoger
> estado; que el hado impío
> no fuerza el libre albedrío.
> Déjame pensar y ver
>   de espacio eso; y no te espante
> ver que término te pida;
> que el estado de una vida
> no se toma en un instante. . . .
> La libertad te defiendo,
> Señor, pero no la vida.
>   Acaba su curso triste,
> y acabará tu pesar;
> que mal te puedo negar
> la vida que tú me diste:
>   la libertad que me dió
> el cielo es la que te niego.
>
> (Act I, B.A.E. VII, 57b)

This belief that woman should marry where she chose was based on the dramatists' belief in love itself. Love for them was all-powerful, a living force which drove man on in the face of society's disapproval and prejudices, in the face of all obstacles, in the face of reason itself. Thus Finea in Tirso's *La mujer por fuerza*, after falling in love with a man she has never seen, is allowed to achieve her aims by trampling ruthlessly on the feelings of nearly all the other characters in the play. In Lope's *La dama boba*, another Finea's stupidity is cured by love; in Calderón's *De una causa dos efectos*, Fadrique is cured of his frivolity and irresponsibility, again by love. As the title of another of Calderón's plays puts it, *Fieras afemina amor*. It was this conception of love, of course, which led to their disapproval of the *esquiva*. Who was she, after all, to try to deny this tremendous life-force which was present in every-body, high or low, man or woman? Her claimed indifference to man could only be the outcome of some moral fault such as vanity or overweening pride.[1] And eventually every *esquiva* had to recognize and submit to this life-force within herself. Because woman *must* succumb to love and marriage, everything not compatible with these two must give way. Hence, the Amazons renounce their independence; hence the woman leaders become consorts and either rule jointly with their husbands or transfer authority to them. Hence the career-women, not taken seriously anyway, renounce their professions. This is an argument which inevitably puts relations between the sexes unequivocally on a level of sexuality. And it might be seen as a divinely sanctioned relegation of woman to an inactive and inferior role in life. The Spanish playwrights' attitude, however, was on the whole more of an active compromise. The scholar, as long as she keeps them in perspective, may retain her books. Woman's place is by man's

---

[1] This sort of interpretation was not confined to the Spanish theatre. Cf. S. Hyne talking of Pinero's *The Notorious Mrs Ebbsmith*: 'Pinero's assumption that the desire for rights and freedom in a woman is a neurotic symptom is one that continued through the two decades that followed, and not only among writers of Pinero's conservative slant', *The Edwardian Turn of Mind*, 179. What Lope considered a moral fault, the English dramatists of the turn of the twentieth century interpreted as psychological inadequacy.

side, but as long as she remains there she can be allowed her female integrity, her dignity and her honour.

Although Lope was, intellectually and emotionally, more intensely concerned with the question of woman's life and rights than any other dramatist, he was at the same time woman's sternest judge in these matters. No one who reads *Fuenteovejuna*, *Peribáñez y el comendador de Ocaña*, *La estrella de Sevilla* (if indeed this is by Lope) and a host of other plays by him, could doubt that he had an enormous admiration and respect for womanhood and the highest opinion of woman's capacity for moral courage, devotion, steadfastness and nobility. No one who reads *La moza de cántaro* could doubt that he had a warm and perceptive understanding of the female heart and mind. But he deplored any attempt on woman's part to deny her essential femininity. He, above all the dramatists, saw her as a sexual being. The *esquivas* were stray sheep who needed to be firmly, and not always gently, brought back to the fold. Like the other dramatists, perhaps more than most, he was prepared to fight for a saner social attitude towards woman, for a recognition of her personal worth and of female honour in the active sense; but, again like them, only more emphatically, he was not prepared to emancipate her from her dependence upon the male. Turis's vision of marriage as an equal partnership was not a common one.

Lope's views on women followed rigid lines. Tirso, however, had a broadness of outlook which Lope lacked. While he had the same views on woman's essential nature, he could, for example, envisage a woman who, although not conforming to accepted standards of femininity, had no objection to love and marriage (*Antona García*). Again, like Rojas he could at least envisage – if only for the purposes of his plot – a woman wishing to embark on a career simply for the sake of it (*El amor médico, Lo que quería ver el marqués de Villena*). His understanding of female psychology was subtler than Lope's and his tolerance of female independence and of female eccentricity greater. His greatest service to woman was, perhaps, to allow them to a high degree a quality which other dramatists tended to pass over or at least underrate. Lope's women have warmth, great spirit, courage and determination. Tirso's have, in addition, intelligence. If Lope's women rise to the occasion, Tirso's create it. Their intelligence, furthermore, is almost invariably greater than that of their men. The *mujer varonil* very often causes the play's hero to pale in comparison with her moral energy but in Tirso the discrepancy is particularly great. Calderón at times seems to have been potentially as much a feminist as Tirso, though his conception of woman was more orthodox. His tendency, in plays like *La devoción de la cruz* and *La hija del aire,* to transcend sex altogether in his investigation of profoundly human themes, indicates, as well as a preoccupation with broader issues than the feminist one, a true belief in woman's spiritual equality. Woman for Calderón was as much a sinner as man, and more often sinned against. His compassion included them both equally. In terms of this world, however, he too considered that woman's destiny was love and marriage, although he fiercely upheld her right to self-determination within these limits.

The lesser dramatists on the whole shared the same basic pattern of views as Lope, Tirso and Calderón. Rojas Zorrilla, however, held certain views which came very near to being revolutionary in the seventeenth century. The statements he makes in *Cada cual lo que le toca* and *Progne y Filomena* on female honour within the bonds of matrimony, his implied attack on the double standard of morality, are a demand for equality in the region where female inferiority was most strongly marked – the honour code itself. No other dramatist went as far in this particular direction. Less radical but almost as interesting is Moreto's *No puede ser.* While seeming everywhere else to share his fellow-dramatists' views on women, here he produced a remarkable portrait of a mature, independent woman who is totally different in her approach to love, marriage and life in general, from the other Golden-Age heroines. She is the only glimpse of the truly emancipated woman which the Golden-Age theatre produced.

To talk about the equality of the sexes is not as straightforward a process as it might seem. There are many kinds of equality – physical, intellectual, social, spiritual, and professional equality, and equality of opportunity. Equality to one century will not mean the same as to another. And, of course, absolute equality is perhaps impossible given woman's more demanding biological role in the reproductive process. In a society where woman, as a result of social or financial pressures, is child-raiser as well as child-bearer, equality of opportunity also is out of the question. To use terms like equality and feminism when one is talking of sixteenth- and seventeenth-century Spain is, as I have stressed continually, a dangerous procedure unless one constantly bears in mind, not only the period, but also the particular society with which one is dealing. The modern observer would probably denounce the feminism of the Golden-Age dramatists as very limited indeed. And the dramatists in their turn would have been horrified had they known how far the equality of the sexes was to go. Nevertheless, for men of their day they were feminists. For all their qualifications, they were interested in and concerned with the issues that affected women's life, and they made an honest attempt to reconcile the anomalies they detected with their convictions about the nature of human existence. They would not emancipate woman from man but neither would they emancipate man from woman. Love for them was the greatest equalizer of all. The workings of Nature were God-ordained – as Beatriz remarks in *Los milagros del desprecio*, 'Dios obra en el casamiento' – and they were therefore immutable, good and right. The workings of Society, while an integral part of God's universe, were dependent on man and therefore susceptible to human weakness. Woman was in many ways a victim of this human weakness. The wrongs perpetrated against her by Society could and should be put right. The role appointed her by God for her own greatest happiness and that of mankind was one to be gratefully undertaken.

Such ideas were inevitably conditioned by the social idiom and moral vocabulary of their time. The dramatics explored, even when they explored in order to denounce, what seemed to them to be possibilities. And what was socially possible for women in the Spain of the sixteenth and seventeenth centuries was, for all the inaccuracy of the wife-murder myth, severely restricted by the standards of present-day societies. The fact that the Spanish dramatists were little concerned with educational and career emancipation for women, and not even remotely interested in political emancipation for women – the two major concerns of twentieth-century Western feminists – merely underlines the social parameters within which they thought, lived and wrote. Female emancipation in political terms would have been an absurd anachronism in seventeenth-century Europe and, as the beneficient shadow of Erasmus faded from the Spanish consciousness, so the early flowering of concern for female education faded with it. The dramatists' cavalier attitude towards the question of female education, and particularly towards careers for women, cannot, therefore be realistically used as ammunition against them. The sixteenth century in Europe may have seen massive progress in literacy and education, and in Spain both schools and universities had gained financially, but seventeenth-century Europe was educationally much less favoured, and 'in Spain the general level of education was adversely affected by the political and economic collapse'.[1] The high hopes of the Italian humanists of the early Renaissance for more widespread education were now far from realization,[2] and the more active concern for general education stimulated by the Counter Reformation was also fast fading.[3] In these circumstances it is no indictment of the feminist sympathies of the Spanish dramatists that they should have allowed this particular aspect of feminism a relatively limited role in their plays.

Dramatists' attitudes to underprivileged groups inevitably fluctuate with the fortunes and potential for progress of such a group. One can trace the altering attitudes of society towards Jews, blacks and homosexuals, and indeed towards women, the largest underprivileged group of all, in the literature of Western Europe; and the greatest literary response almost invariably mirrors the periods of most heightened interest. For whatever conjunction of reasons – whether the aspirations of the humanists, or the new realism of the Catholic Reformation, whether imitation of famous female contemporaries or the predilection of Lope's

---

[1] Carlo M. Cipolla, *Literacy and Development in the West* (London, 1960), 53. See also L. Stone, 'The Educational Revolution in England, 1560–1640', *Past and Present* 28 (1964), 41ff; and J. H. Hexter, 'Renaissance Education' in *Reappraisals in History* (Evanston, 1961), 45–70.

[2] E. Garin, *L'educazione in Europa* (Bari, 1957), 74ff.

[3] Cipolla, *Literacy and Development in the West*, 51.

genius, whether the Baroque pleasure in the conceit or the reactions excited by women in male costume, whether for reasons profound or essentially trivial – Spain in the Golden Age was such a period of heightened interest. And so for the purposes of propaganda, didacticism, moral teaching, righteous indignation and occasionally whole-hearted approval, woman's potentialities and possibilities were explored. But explored within the limits of what was socially conceivable. Just as the black had to conform to the changing prejudices of his literary audience – from *Uncle Tom's Cabin* to *Go Tell It on the Mountain*; just as the homosexual has progressed from the literary suicide almost inevitable when the subject was still daring and the audience demanded death or conformity; so the *mujer varonil* in the Golden Age was still a woman being explored at the very early stages of emancipation and was therefore habitually compelled to conform to the social norm, however exciting her temporary departures from it had been.

Consequently it is by such behavioural norms that the *mujer varonil* must be assessed. She, and the attitudes of her creators towards her, must be judged in terms of her own society, its language and expectations. Within these limits the possibilities experienced, examined and explored on the Spanish stage were both varied and advanced. By the standards of their day the Spanish dramatists of the Golden Age were enlightened and sympathetic men in their attitude to women. One cannot ask for more. One cannot expect miracles even of the great.

Index

(Guides to works used and to further reading are provided in the footnotes of each chapter.)